AA

Essent

expl

FLORIDA

AA Publishing

Essential

Written by Emma Stanford
Additional writing and research by Carolee Boyles-Sprenkel
Series Adviser: Ingrid Morgan
Series Editor: Nia Williams
Copy Editor: Audrey Horne
Designer: Tony Truscott Designs

Edited, designed, produced and distributed by AA Publishing, Fanum House, Basingstoke, Hampshire RG21 2EA.
© The Automobile Association 1993.
Maps © The Automobile Association 1993.

A catalogue record for this book is available from the British Library.

ISBN 0 7495 0562 1

This book was produced using QuarkXPress™, Aldus Freehand ™ and Microsoft Word ™ on Apple Macintosh ™ computers.

Colour origination by Fotographics Ltd
Printed and bound in Italy by Printer Trento S.r.l.

The contents of this publication are believed correct at the time of printing. Nevertheless, the publishers cannot accept responsibility for errors or omissions, or for changes in details given. Assessments of attractions, hotels, restaurants and so forth are based upon the author's own experience and, therefore, descriptions given in this guide necessarily contain an element of subjective opinion which may not reflect the Publisher's opinion or dictate a reader's own experience on another occasion. The views expressed in this book are not necessarily those of the Publisher. Every effort has been made to ensure accuracy in this guide. However, things do change and we would welcome any information to help keep the book up to date.

Published by AA Publishing.

Emma Stanford has written, edited and contributed to books in the *All-in-one* series of travel guides published by Macmillan US/AAA. She has also contributed to guides published by the BTA, American Express and Fodor, and is author and project director of the AVIS *Personally Yours* series of guides to driving routes.

Key Islamorada marina

St Pete's beach on the Gulf coast

About this book
This book is divided into three principal sections.

The first part of the book discusses aspects of life today and in the past. Places to visit are then covered region by region, along with Focus on... and Close-up features, which highlight areas and subjects in more detail. Drives and walks are also suggested in this section of the book. Finally, day-to-day practical information for the visitor is given in the Travel Facts chapter, along with a selected Directory of hotels and restaurants.

Some of the places described in this book have been given a special rating:

 Do not miss

 Highly recommended

 See if you can

General Contents

Walks

7

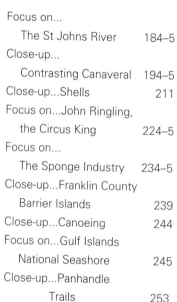

Drives

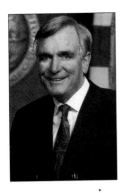

My Florida
by Governor Lawton Chiles

It is a pleasure to announce this edition of **Explorer Florida**. This new guide will help you to discover the many and extraordinarily varied facets of the Sunshine State just waiting for your next visit.

Sugar white sand beaches, clear blue waters and Florida's famous sunshine will greet you. Attractions, both natural and man-made, will entertain and dazzle you with excitement. Kick back and relax in one of the luxury resorts, pampered with a multitude of amenities; or take life at your own pace surrounded by family and friends in self-catering accommodation. The choice is always yours.

From sporting events to shopping sprees, there is something for everyone. Golf and tennis are at their finest in Florida. There are watersports of every description, from boating, waterskiing and jetskiing on our sparkling bays to scuba diving and snorkelling around natural coral reefs and intriguing artificial sites. Baseball, the all-American sport, can be seen at any of Florida's several spring training grounds. It's a chance to watch the major league in action at a great low price. Shopping is a ball in Florida. World-famous department stores present a scintillating array of goods, and there are discount malls which will turn your holiday spree into great savings.

If you love the outdoor life, Florida's definitely for you. Over 100 state parks offer unrivalled opportunities for outdoor pursuits from hiking and fishing to canoeing and horseback riding. You'll be amazed by our wildlife, and Florida's spectacular aquatic parks can bring you face to face with the beauties of the deep.

No matter what path you choose to explore, Florida has it all, from coast to coast to coast. We look forward to seeing you soon.

Daytona beach

My Florida
by Charlie Weeks

I was born and bred in Coconut, a little community just north of Bonita Springs on the Gulf of Mexico. So I can say I'm a native Floridian, and there aren't many of us around. Coconut hasn't changed much in the 45 years I've lived here, and I like it that way. There are 15 families in Coconut, and of them 10 are Weekses.

My mother arrived from Georgia in a covered wagon during the 1920s, and she and father, who was a fisherman, founded Coconut's marina. I was the eighth of nine children, and I got my first boat when I was six. The back bay islands were my playground – and they kept our larder well stocked too, with rabbits and wild turkeys. There were manatees (they're protected now) and black mullet, snook, flounder and Spanish mackerel in the bay. All us boys had to work the garden, but we could also exchange fish for vegetables grown in Bonita's market gardens. We didn't have a lot of money, but we never went to bed hungry. The weekly trip to Fort Myers for provisions used to take three to four hours each way in the old days; the road was often awash, so us boys could catch fish and turtles along the way. One of the few improvements down in modern-day Coconut is that you can shop near home now.

Two of the things that bug me about Florida today are overdevelopment along the coast and sewage pollution. Still, people are waking up to the need to look after the Florida coast's natural habitat, and that's improving the situation.

I used to work in the air-conditioning business, but now I'm back full time in the boating life since my father died. I helped run the marina for a while, and did a spot of commercial fishing, but it's wildlife that attracts the tourists today. We run Weeks' Fish Camp here in Coconut. It isn't big business and we like it that way – any developer thinking of muscling in had just better think again. Now I guide visitors – some come back more than once – around the back bay islands. I know them like the back of my hand – where to find manatees, see ospreys, ibis and pelican rookeries. Sometimes we go out on the bay at sunset and see the bottle-nosed dolphins. This is my home. I guess I'm a lucky man.

Charlie Weeks is a native Floridian and has lived in Bonita Springs for 45 years. He is an expert on the wildlife of Estero Bay such as dolphin, manatee and birds, as well as being knowledgeable about the extinct Calusa Indians.

FLORIDA

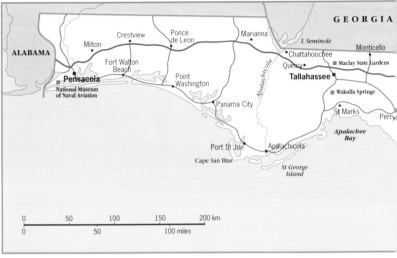

A one man band in
Miami

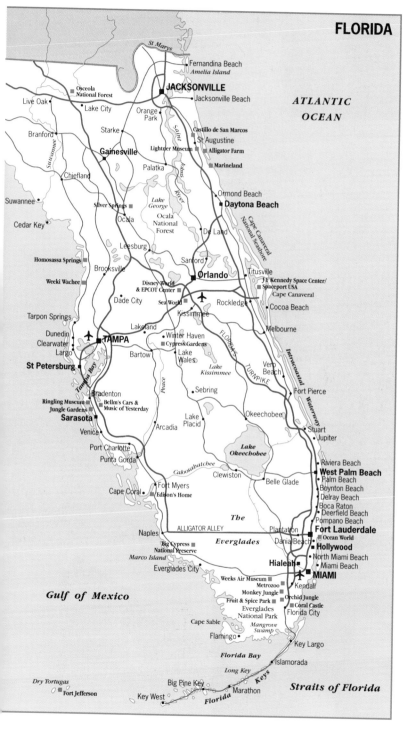

FLORIDA

St Marys

Fernandina Beach
Amelia Island

Osceola
National Forest

JACKSONVILLE

Jacksonville Beach

Live Oak

Lake City

Orange
Park

ATLANTIC

OCEAN

Branford

Starke

Castillo de San Marcos

St Augustine

Lightner Museum
Alligator Farm

Gainesville

Palatka

Saint

Johns

Marineland

Chiefland

Suwannee

River

Suwannee

Silver Springs

Lake
George

Ormond Beach

Daytona Beach

Cedar Key

Ocala

Ocala
National
Forest

De Land

Cape Canaveral
National Seashore

Homosassa Springs

Leesburg

Sanford

Brooksville

Disney World
& EPCOT Center

Orlando

Titusville

J F Kennedy Space Center/
Spaceport USA

Weeki Wachee

Dade City

Sea World

Rockledge

Cape Canaveral

Cocoa Beach

Tarpon Springs

Lakeland

Kissimmee

Dunedin

TAMPA

Winter Haven

Melbourne

Clearwater

Cypress Gardens

Largo

Bartow

Lake
Wales

FLORIDAS

Vero
Beach

St Petersburg

Tampa Bay

Lake
Kissimmee

TURNPIKE

Intracoastal

Bradenton

Bellm's Cars &
Music of Yesterday

Peace

Sebring

Fort Pierce

Ringling Museum
Jungle Gardens

Sarasota

River

Arcadia

Lake
Placid

Stuart

Jupiter

Venice

Okeechobee

Port Charlotte

Caloosahatchee

Riviera Beach

Punta Gorda

Clewiston

West Palm Beach

Belle Glade

Palm Beach

Cape Coral

Fort Myers
Edison's Home

Lake
Okeechobee

Boynton Beach

Delray Beach

Boca Raton

Deerfield Beach

Pompano Beach

The

ALLIGATOR ALLEY

Plantation

Fort Lauderdale

Naples

Everglades

Dania Beach

Ocean World

Hollywood

Big Cypress
National Reserve

Hialeah

North Miami Beach

Miami Beach

Marco Island

Weeks Air Museum

MIAMI

Everglades City

Metrozoo

Kendall

Monkey Jungle

Orchid Jungle

Fruit & Spice Park

Coral Castle

Everglades
National Park

Florida City

Cape Sable

Mangrove
Swamp

Flamingo

Key Largo

Florida Bay

Islamorada

Long Key

Dry Tortugas

Fort Jefferson

Big Pine Key

Keys

Marathon

Straits of Florida

Key West

Florida

Gulf of Mexico

Orange Blossoms

■ **From Atlantic surf to the Gulf of Mexico, tropical Key West to Old South Tallahassee, Florida is many worlds. The Everglades shelter rare and endangered species; the beaches are beautiful; the theme parks are legendary; and the famous Florida sunshine produces exotic fruits …..■**

Florida and orange juice are synonymous. As far as statistics go, the state is the world's largest citrus-growing region, and its groves produce around 25 per cent of the orange juice and 50 per cent of the grapefruit juice on the world market. Count Odet Philippe planted the first grapefruit in America near Tampa Bay in 1825. By this time, wild orange trees could be found all over the state, probably spread by Native Americans. With the improvement of water and rail transport in the 1880s, citrus growers multiplied in the Central Florida region. Their glossy-leaved groves spread south to Indian River, around Fort Pierce, then down to Miami after the frosts of 1894-5. The marvellously fragrant white orange blossom was adopted as Florida's official State Flower in 1909 – orange juice became the State Beverage in 1967.

An infinite variety Florida's citrus fruits come in all shapes and sizes – hefty Duncan white and rosy-pink grapefruits, oranges, tangerines, tangelos (tangerine-grapefruit), Temple oranges (tangerine-orange), lemons, limes and the nut-sized kumquat. Marmalade, preserves, candies, orange blossom honey,

A Florida citrus grove

even citrus wine are a tribute to the ingenuity of local residents.

Most citrus fruits require at least 300 days of sunshine and take 12 months to mature. The citrus harvest begins with grapefruits in October and ends with oranges in July. Ripe fruits can be stored on the tree for several months, so it is not unusual to see last year's crop surrounded by the new season's blossom. A mature grapefruit tree can produce around 1,000 fruits each season.

Key lime pie The Key lime is a Florida speciality, a small, round, yellowish-coloured fruit which is an essential ingredient for Key lime pie. This delicious tangy dessert is said to have been invented by a cook named Sarah at the Curry Mansion in Key West. However, the exact construction of the Key lime pie – the consistency of the pie crust, and the choice between meringue or whipped cream topping – remains a contentious issue in kitchens across the state (suggested recipe below).

Key Lime Pie Filling

4 eggs
14oz can condensed milk
8tbs sugar
half cup Key lime juice
1tsp lemon essence
Separate eggs. Beat together yolks, condensed milk and juice. Add one pinch salt. Beat whites to soft peaks; add lemon essence, beat in sugar. Fold one-third of egg white mixture into lime filling and place in pie shell. Top with remaining egg white. Bake at 180°C /350°F/gas 4 for 20–25 minutes. Chill before serving.

Taste them fresh! Roadside stalls piled high with fresh fruit and vegetables are a familiar sight throughout Florida. Beyond the Greater Miami city limits, Dade County is one of the Top 100 producing counties in the US. The winter 'market basket' of Homestead is laden with avocados (once known as alligator pears), cucumbers, canteloupe and water-melons, limes, strawberries and tomatoes. Buy them fresh from the farmers' markets or roadside stalls for a real taste experience.

In the central region, look out for glossy purple aubergines (egg plant), squashes and okra. There are apples, pears and pecan nuts in the north.

Black gold The fertile drained Everglades region around Lake Okeechobee is another prime winter fruit and vegetable producer. It is also the land of black gold: not oil, in this case, but sugar cane makes Clewiston the sugar capital of the state. Half the nation's raw sugar consumption (around 1.5 million pounds) is hand-harvested here by

Trucking the oranges

Jamaican labourers wielding machetes. Clewiston's other claim to fame is its cabbage palm business, which supplies the fresh hearts of palm dished up in smart Florida restaurants.

The southern corner of the state boasts an abundance of exotic tropical fruits. Home-grown bananas, carambolas (star fruit), figs, guavas and papayas can be found in local supermarkets. The origins of the mango crop can be traced back to a shipment of 35 mango trees delivered from Calcutta in 1888.

<< Florida will use any excuse for a festival. For two fruit-inspired extravaganzas, check out the annual Plant City Strawberry Festival in February; while June's Monticello Watermelon Festival features an unusual trial of skill: the hotly contested melon seed spittin' competition. >>

■ **Anchored to the North American continent by Georgia and Alabama, the Florida peninsula is bordered on every side by salt water. The 58,665-square-mile state can claim a tidal shoreline extending over 8,000 miles via hundreds of sandy beaches, wide bays, estuaries, lagoons and a host of offshore islands .....■**

Around the coast The East Coast is protected from the Atlantic by a string of barrier islands. These taper off like stepping stones into the gentle curve of the Florida Keys, to Key West, just 90 miles from Cuba. The rounded southern tip of the peninsula holds the Everglades, a vast swampland region stretching over 10 million acres which crumbles into the labyrinthine waterways of the Ten Thousand Islands region nestled in the lee of the lower West Coast. A smattering of sandbars and islands line the West Coast and Gulf of Mexico; while the northern Gulfshore, bordering the Panhandle, offers some of the finest barrier island beaches of all, blinding white quartz sand washed down from the Appalachian Mountains over thousands of years. Areas of these magnificent coastal dunes are protected as part of the **Gulf National Seashore**.

Flowing water Inland northern Florida is a land of rolling hills and pine forests, freshwater springs and swift tannin-stained rivers like the Apalachicola, Blackwater and Suwannee. Below Florida's thin covering of soil, deep fissures in the limestone foundations release freshwater springs fed by subterranean watercourses. **Wakulla Springs**, south of Tallahassee, claims to be one of the world's deepest springs, pouring forth 600,000 gallons of water per minute. At **Florida Caverns State Park** there is an opportunity to look below the earth's surface. This is the only place in the state where the water table drops sufficiently to reveal spectacular stalagmites and stalactites in limestone caverns.

Still waters A low ridge extends from the north into the lakeland region of Central Florida. Forests give way to prairie, and an estimated 30,000-plus lakes and ponds varying in depth from a few inches to around 30 feet. **Lake Okeechobee** is the second largest body of fresh water wholly within the US, some 750 square miles in total area, but only 14 feet deep at its lowest point. This freshwater reservoir is the starting point of the Everglades, the primary source of a 50-mile-wide 'river of grass' which extends across the state to the Gulf of Mexico. The 1.4-million acre **Everglades National Park** covers only one-seventh of the true Everglades region, but acts as a showcase for its diverse flora and fauna.

The Everglades Marooned amid the waving sea of grass, patches of brilliant green denote the presence of hardwood 'hammocks', the local name for stands of trees which have found a slightly elevated limestone outcrop on which to take root. Just a few feet or several acres in size, they are a refuge for bobcats, deer, hawks, owls and other wildlife. Pinelands and areas of cypress swamp (one of the finest for sightseeing purposes is **Corkscrew Swamp**) also provide useful animal habitats. Coastal mangrove forests flourish where the Everglades meet the Gulf. The nutrient-rich brackish water trapped in the mangroves' complex root system creates an ideal habitat for numerous native animals and birds.

Bays and islands The mangrove-lined back bays of the West Coast are a fascinating unofficial wildlife

Florida's watery wildernesses provide refuge for many creatures

refuge teeming with fish and wading birds. This is a favourite haunt of manatees, too. These 3,000lb sea cows enjoy a plentiful supply of river weed and water hyacinths in the warmer waters. On the Gulf, the islands of **Sanibel** and **Captiva** are renowned for their seashell beaches, as is **Cayo Costa State Park**, where sea turtles lay their eggs. **Pine Island Sound** is a favourite playground of the friendly bottle-nosed dolphin.

> **<<** The Gulf Stream flows north around the Florida Keys and southern tip of the peninsula, warming the reef-strewn seas. This is a diver's paradise with aquatic parks like the John Pennekamp Coral Reef State Park off Key Largo, and the vast Biscayne National Park, south of Miami. The Atlantic waters are still warm enough to provide interesting diving as far north as the Gold Coast. **>>**

The Florida Keys are a 150-mile chain of fossilised coral rock islands, short on beaches but fringed by reefs. Vegetation is sparse with pockets of tropical hardwoods, slash pine, mangroves and prickly pears. Midway up the East Coast, naturalists should not miss two exceptional protected areas: the **Canaveral National Seashore** and **Merritt Island National Wildlife Refuge**. The latter harbours 22 endangered species in its freshwater lagoons, saltwater marshes and hammocks – all within plain view of the Kennedy Space Center. In winter the population is swelled by a magnificent roll-call of migrating birds.

Dolphins haunt West Coast bays

Trees and Plants

■ **Florida could be described as 'floribundant'. The subtropical climate, with its four distinct growing seasons, is augmented by extraordinarily diverse natural habitats to support a wealth of native and imported plant life. Brilliant hibiscus, oleander, azaleas, scented gardenias and clouds of bougainvillea gladden the eye; palms, seagrapes and magnificent live oaks cast welcome shadows in the heat .....■**

Everglades flora Botanists from around the world have marvelled at the sheer variety of plant life that flourishes in Florida. Temperate and tropical plants grow side by side – no less than 2,000 different species in the Everglades alone. The predominant vista here is **sawgrass**, nearly 8 million acres of it. Sawgrass is part of the sedge family, one of the oldest plant species in the world, sharp enough to discourage explorers and tough enough to endure the months of burning sunshine.

Willows, pines and tropical hardwoods such as **mahogany** and **live oak** find purchase on outcrops of limestone to create shady hammocks. The **gumbo limbo** is also found here, affectionately known as the 'tourist tree' for its peeling red bark. An unwelcome addition is the parasitic **strangler fig**. Its seed, carried on the wind or by birds, lodges in the host tree; as the strangler fig grows, it drops a tangled mass of aerial roots to the ground while wrapping itself around the host trunk depriving it of light, water and nutrients. Hammock woods are also festooned with airplants (epiphytes) such as **orchids** and **bromeliads**. Although attached to a host tree, these plants are non-parasitic, gathering water and nutrients as they run down the bark. **Spanish moss**, which tumbles from the live oaks and cypresses, is another epiphyte. In addition to lovely orchids like the creamy vanilla orchid, mule-ears and fragant night-blooming epidendrum, Everglades flowers include colourful pink gerardia, morning glory, spider lilies, purple pickerel weed and Glades lobelia, yellow carpets of splatterdock, and waterlilies.

<< For a gentle familiarisation course in what plants to look out for, visitors to Miami should head for the peaceful surroundings of Fairchild Tropical Gardens, which are at Coral Gables.
Other glorious gardens around the state include AB Maclay State Gardens, Tallahassee; Cypress Gardens, Winter Haven; Leu Botanical Gardens, Orlando; Marie Selby Botanical Gardens, Sarasota; and Washington Oaks State Park, Anastasia Island. The prize for the biggest banyan tree is captured by the Edison Home in Fort Myers. **>>**

An exotic hibiscus bloom

Trees of the swamplands Cypress trees can grow in water where most trees would drown. It is thought their curious cone-like 'knees' help them to breathe. Dwarf **pond cypress** is the most common variety; few lofty **bald cypresses** survived the 1930s lumber era. However, several of these formidable 600- to 700-year-old giants can be found in Big Cypress Swamp and Corkscrew Swamp, north of the Everglades National Park.

Pines and palms On higher ground, **saw palmetto** and **slash pine** forests survive on next to no soil, finding purchase in hollows and potholes filled with a rich residue of peat and marl. The feathery **Australian pine**, prevalent throughout Florida, is considered a pest. This non-native tree is fast encroaching on native species, and in several woodland areas attempts are being made to eradicate it. Palms are an essential ingredient of the Florida skyline. Of the hundreds of palms to be seen, 11 species are native to the state. **Cabbage palms**, **coconut palms**, **queen palms** and the elegant **royal palm** appear in hammocks and along the roadside, as do the tall, thin **Washingtonia**

Native Keys palms

palm and the fan-tailed **traveller's palm**; while the squat **jelly palm** is common in northern parts of the state. In the Panhandle, glossy **magnolia** forests make a change from the endless march of pine, and the live oaks in this neck of the woods are truly awe-inspiring.

Plants of the coast Mangroves form probably the single most important plant system in Florida. They stabilise the shoreline, reduce storm damage, filter run-off, feed and harbour a multitude of land, sea and air creatures. Their ability to obtain fresh water from salt water is unique. **Red mangroves** grow closest to the water's edge, supported on arched prop roots. **Black mangroves** push up hundreds of pencil-thin root tips (pneumatophores) to help them breathe; while **white** and **buttonwood mangroves** are found higher up the shore. Coastal hammocks are **seagrape** territory, with their round, leathery leaves and bunches of fruit used to make jellies. Clumps of **sea oats** anchor the coastal dunes and are protected by law.

For the Birds

■ **Birdwatching in Florida is as simple as getting out of bed. An early morning stroll along the beach will almost certainly be accompanied by brown pelicans, gulls galore, terns, scurrying sanderlings and maybe a cormorant or two .....**■

Early records Florida's native bird life has fascinated and enchanted visitors from the early days. One of the first records, Catesby's *Natural History of Carolina, Florida and the Bahama Islands,* was published in London in 1731. A century later, renowned American ornithologist John James Audubon ventured down through Florida as far as Key West making studies for his epic *Birds of America.* Audubon's enthusiastic descriptions of the rare roseate spoonbill, pristine white snowy egret and flocks of flamingos 'arrayed in more brilliant apparel than I have seen before' were translated into beautiful etchings (the Audubon House in Key West has several copies). Fifty years on these same birds were on the verge of extinction, slaughtered for their gorgeous plumage, a popular period fashion accessory. Nowadays, the only flamingos in Florida are domestic creatures. Their distinctive pink colouring may owe more to modern chemicals than the seafood-rich diet which produces the effect naturally.

Birds of the wetlands The Everglades National Park is one of the most remarkable natural preserves in the world. Together with its northern neighbours, Big Cypress and Corkscrew Swamps, these southern wetlands support an extraordinary treasury of birdlife. As well as providing sanctuary, this is a prime breeding and feeding ground for myriad species of wading birds. The **roseate spoonbill** has survived here, though it is still on the endangered list. A Florida native with rose-coloured plumage, red eyes and a bald head, it has a distinctive spatulate beak which it sweeps from side to side in order to trap food.

<< One of the strangest birds is the anhinga, or 'snakebird', which swims through the water with only its thin, flexible neck above the surface. Anhingas dive to skewer fish on their pointed beaks, surface, flip their catch in the air, retrieve and swallow it with practised aplomb. Despite its aquatic life-style, the anhinga's feathers are not waterproofed, so it is common to see these birds drying their wings by the water's edge. >>

The endangered **wood stork** nests in swampland cypress hammocks. Largely white, it has black-tipped wings with a span of over five feet; it feeds for fish using its sensitive beak to feel beneath the water surface. White clusters of apple snail eggs cling to Everglades trees and plants from May to September. The adult snails are the sole diet of the few hundred remaining **Everglades kites** with their purpose-built curved bills for extracting the snails' bodies. The eggs are also an important food source for the jerky-legged **limkin**, an ibis-like wading bird.

Herons and egrets The **great blue heron** and dainty **little blue heron** can be seen throughout the state, while the Keys are the best place to spot a **great white heron** (the white race of the great blue). They can be distinguished by their yellow-green legs from the **great egret** which stalks tall on spindly black legs. The smaller **snowy egret** only just survived the plume hunters. Its beak and legs are black, but the outsize feet are clad in 'golden slippers'. **Cattle egrets** arrived from Africa in the 1950s. They feed off insects

disturbed by cattle, and can often be spotted perched comfortably on a cow's back.

Raptors Birds of prey are a dramatic addition to Florida's wide blue skies. The handsome **red-shouldered hawk**, with its black and white back feathers and reddish breast, lives off frogs, lizards and snakes. It can often be seen perched on telegraph poles or fence posts near the road. There are graceful **swallow-tailed kites**, **black** and **turkey vultures** and, most exciting of all, the **Southern bald eagle**, another endangered species. Rangers in the Everglades and at Merritt Island, on the East Coast, will point out their enormous nests.

Purple gallinule

Perched high in the trees, some can be more than 10 feet thick and 6 feet across.

Birds of the woodlands In the woods, woodpeckers can be heard if not seen, drilling into dead wood for beetles and ants. The **pileated woodpecker** has a distinctive red crest contrasting with its all-black back plumage. Another woodland resident, the **barred owl** is named for the distinctive brown bars on its breast. Look out also for minute **gnatcatchers** zipping around the bushes, or the crimson flash of a jaunty red **cardinal**.

Alligator Alley

■ **The alligator is to Florida what the kangaroo is to Australia – part of the exotic scenery and a favourite tourist attraction. The world's first alligator attraction, the St Augustine Alligator Farm on Anastasia Island, was founded in 1893, leading the way for a host of imitators .....■**

The American alligator An adult male of this species can grow up to 16 feet or more, though most are around 12 feet, and females are usually 8 to 9 feet in length. Cold-blooded reptiles, alligators need to bask in the sun to warm up enough to function. During the winter dry season, they earn the soubriquet 'Keeper of the Everglades', as they fulfil an important role by digging sizeable 'gator holes' in the ground. These fill with water and provide life-sustaining oases for plants, birds, fish and other animals. Alligators mate in the spring, and the female lays 20-60 leathery eggs around June. If the temperature rises above 90°F the hatchlings will all be male, below 87°F they will be female. Baby alligators feed themselves from the start, hunting crayfish, frogs, insects and snakes. Alligators will eat anything when hungry. They may appear slow and awkward, but can move at frightening speed, and their powerful jaws can snap shut with a force of 1,200 pounds per square inch. Do not feed them, for if an alligator loses its fear of humans, the next person it sees could be lunch.

The American crocodile This shy reptile is a much rarer sight, found only in the saltwater Florida Bay area. A lighter greenish-grey colour, crocodiles have narrow tapering snouts, and the teeth of their upper and lower jaws are visible in profile (an alligator's lower set fits inside the upper jaw).

On the 'endangered' list Another endangered Everglades inhabitant is the beautiful tawny **Florida panther**. The 30–50 remaining beasts are the last panthers in the US, seriously threatened by the destruction of their natural habitat. Female panthers can give birth to two or four kittens every other year, while an adult male will range over 500 square miles hunting for deer, racoons, wild pigs and other prey. Efforts to track the 6-foot-long, 60–130-pound cats by tagging with radio collars have enraged some animal rights activists, who believe the collars are dangerous. They fear a collar on a growing animal could become too

Young alligators are on their own as soon as they leave the egg

Gently smiling jaws

tight, or get caught. In one case, they claim, a panther tranquillised by researchers fell out of a tree and broke its neck.

The dainty **Key deer** is also living on borrowed time as development eats away its limited habitat on Big Pine Key and the surrounding islands. The smallest sub-species of the white-tailed deer, Key deer grow to only around 24–28 inches in height. Around 70 of a population numbering 250–300 deer are killed by motorists every year, despite a speed limit on Big Pine Key.

Other mammals Racoons and opossums share an often fatal attraction for crossing highways. **Racoons** that make it across can be seen along the water's edge searching for food, while **opossums** rootle about in the woodlands with **squirrels** and **wild turkeys**, all keeping a wary eye out for hungry short-tailed **bobcats**. **Armadillos** arrived from Central America in the 19th century. They dig and burrow into timber for insects and funghi, snuffle up overripe fruit, and rely on their speed for protection. The armadillo's shell is made of tough plates covered and joined by leathery skin. Females give birth to four offspring all of the same sex in the spring.

Cotton rats, marsh rabbits, otters and **spotted skunks** inhabit marshland regions throughout the state.

Lizards, snakes and amphibians
Native **green lizards** and **skinks** are a regular feature of the woodland scene, while **Cuban lizards** (the male has a puff-sack on his throat) can be spotted in urban areas. The largest and most poisonous Floridian snake is the **cottonmouth**, a relative of the rattle snake; **pygmy rattlesnakes, black rat snakes, indigo** and **king snakes** may also put in an appearance. **Walking catfish** have got to be one of the strangest sights in the state; and look out for pea-green **tree frogs**.

<< Turtle-watching is a fascinating Floridian pastime. Leatherback turtles, which can grow up to 6 feet long and weigh a ton (literally), loggerhead, green, rare hawksbill and Kemp's Ridley turtles all swim in Floridian waters, and must leave the relative security of the ocean to lay their eggs on the beach during the May to August nesting season. Federal laws have been introduced to protect the remaining nesting areas, and state laws prohibit bright lights on the beach at certain times as these might confuse hatchlings heading for the ocean. >>

Ranch Dressing

■ **Cowboy chronicler and artist Frederic Remington was not best impressed by the Cracker cow-hunters he encountered on a trip to Florida in 1895. 'There was none of the bilious fierceness and rearing plunge which I had associated with my friends out West', he complained, though his artistic nature allowed 'they are picturesque in their unkempt, almost unearthly wildness'. One of his subjects was folk hero Bone Mizell, who listed branding cattle with his teeth among his accomplishments .....■**

Life on the prairie The Spanish introduced cattle and horses to Florida in the 16th century. Livestock thrived in the rolling green central prairie region south of Gainesville, now known as Paynes Prairie, but described by William Bartram in the 18th century as the 'great Alachua Savannah'. Despite offering cattle and crop bounties to prospective settlers, the Spanish found few takers, so the missions taught the local native people to herd cattle. Later, white settlers in the 19th century were supposedly named 'Crackers' for the long cracking whips they carried. Remington noted

Western gear off the shelf

the Florida Cracker's use of cur dogs to round up the herd, saving the precious horses, and the practice of building strong log corrals approximately a day's march apart all through the woods of the vast ranch lands.

During the 1930s, Brahma cattle were introduced and cross-bred with native species. Herds of these humped-backed beasts are a familiar sight in fields along the roadside, often providing a comfortable perch for white cattle egrets. Senepol cattle can be seen at the 90,000-acre **Babcock Crescent B Ranch** outside Fort Myers. They also breed quarter horses here, named for the quarter-mile races these strong animals specialise in; and the ranch boasts a herd of bison. An adventurous swamp-buggy ride winds up at the 70-year-old commissary, once the company stores, with saddles hung over the verandas and a good chance of spotting a swaggering cowman.

Cattle towns Arcadia is a sleepy cattle town 20 miles north of the Babcock ranch. High noon in the restored main street looks like a scene from a Western movie. Though present-day cowmen are more likely to roll into town in a battered pick-up than on horse-back, the twice-yearly rodeo is as traditional as they come, and local Western outfitters do a roaring trade in pearl-buttoned shirts, string ties and cowboy boots. **Kissimmee**, just outside Orlando, is a curious combination of cattle town with a modern theme park dormitory

attached. Cattle auctions are held here every Wednesday. However, the strangest cattle town of all must be **Davie**. Almost a suburb of Fort Lauderdale, Davie is just waiting for John Wayne and the wagon train to head on through. It has hitching posts galore, cacti, swinging saloon doors on the Town Hall, even a 'ride-thru' service at the local McDonalds. The weekly Jackpot Rodeo features authentic bronco-riding, calf-roping and steer-wrestling.

Where champions are born Ocala is the crucible of Florida's thoroughbred horse country. Over 29,000 Floridians are employed in the state's billion-dollar equine industry; 400 of its 600 farms and training centres are located right here in Marion County. Florida runs the other major US equine centres, California and Kentucky, to a close contest. The Sunshine State enjoys similar advantages to Kentucky with its famous 'blue grass'. Florida has its own limestone-enriched pastureland which translates into the strong, light bones of dynamic Kentucky Derby winners such as the great Needles and, more recently, Unbridled. Drive US301, or better

Don't miss Davie's rodeo

still minor roads like SR200, for a beguiling vista of rolling green meadows, miles of pristine white fencing and burnished thoroughbred horseflesh gambolling about the lush paddocks. Many of the farms are open to the public. For details, call the **Florida Thoroughbred Breeders' Association** (tel: (904) 629 2160), or see the panel on page 112 for individual farms.

<< To get a real close look at Florida's ranch culture, nothing beats a top rodeo. Fans from all over the state and beyond roll up for Arcadia's All Florida Championship Rodeo (March and July, tel: (813) 494 3773); Davie's Florida State Championship Rodeo (November/ December, tel: (305) 581 0790); and Kissimmee's Silver Spurs Rodeo (February, tel: (407) 628 2280). Davie's Thursday night rodeos take place at the Davie Rodeo Arena, 6591 SW 45th Street, starting at 20.00hrs. >>

■ **Florida is not the proverbial melting pot, rather a colourful array of different cultures maintaining strong identities within the community. There are Arabs in Jacksonville, Haitians in Miami, long-haired Hassidic Jews in Miami Beach, but the Hispanic influence is the most immediately noticeable .....■**

Fly into Miami Airport and the air is thick with Latin American accents, Spanish announcements, raucous welcomes and histrionic departures. The cab into town could belong to a Brazilian, a Puerto Rican, a Dominican or a Nicaraguan (Miami has the second largest Nicaraguan urban population outside Managua). The *Miami Herald* publishes a Spanish-language edition, and the local Hispanic community accounts for almost half Miami's total population of 1.9 million.

The Cuban factor Cubans represent by far the largest immigrant group – around 75 per cent of Greater Miami's Hispanic population. The first wave of Cuban immigrants arrived in 1959, fleeing the Castro

Florida is a diverse community

regime in the same manner that revolutionary hero José Marti fled here from Spanish-occupied Cuba in the late 19th century. Marti's name is everywhere in Cuban districts from Miami to Tampa. He managed to drum up support for the Spanish-American War which finally dislodged the Spanish from his homeland. Similar attempts by present-day would-be mercenaries find little favour, though some sympathy, with the authorities. So near and yet so far from home, the Cubans buckled down to make a success of their new situation. Run-down suburbs have been transformed into bustling commercial centres, friendly restaurants, bakeries and traditional shops abound. Miami has had a Cuban mayor; Cuban doctors, lawyers and financial power brokers all play a significant role in shaping Miami in the 1990s.

Black Florida The down side of the Cuban success story is the resentment it has caused, not so much among sour-grapes Anglo-Saxons, but among the urban African-American population where distrust and anger simmer. Just as Florida was beginning to emerge from the injustices of segregation during the 1960s Civil Rights movement, the Cubans began to arrive in force – 260,000 Cubans migrated to the state within six years. Prepared to work at any price, Cuban immigrants undercut the job market, and their strong sense of community left the Blacks feeling cheated and alienated. Though the profile of Florida's Black community was lifted in the 1970s by several government appointments, ethnic

Alligator wrestling: a tourist attraction, but hardly authentic

violence erupted in the 1980s. Riots in the Black Liberty City and Overtown neighbourhoods of Miami were exaggerated by distrust of the police force which is 46 per cent Hispanic.

The outlook for Florida's Black community is improving. Students at the predominantly Black Florida A & M University in Tallahassee just need to look up the hill to the Capitol for notable role models in government circles. Floridian musician Ray Charles is pretty inspirational stuff as well.

<< Cracker is a native Floridian. Preferably one who can trace his roots back to the early white settlers, eats grits for breakfast and addresses one or a group of people as 'y'all'. The rural Panhandle is Cracker country, with hogs in the backyard and slow southern speech, light years from the brash, modern face of Florida. The origins of the name are doubtful. Some say it was 17th-century English for a story-teller; others that it came from cracking corn for grits. Or maybe it goes back to the long, cracking whips wielded by cattle-men in the 19th century. >>

Native Americans Hollywood, near Fort Lauderdale, is the headquarters of Florida's native Americans. There are two main groups of Seminoles, most of whom speak Miccosukee. A few have Muskogee, or Creek, as their native tongue. Tribal customs differ as well. The larger Seminole group runs a successful cattle operation at the Brighton Seminole Reservation on the northwest shores of Lake Okeechobee; they also control the Big Cypress Reservation west of Miami. Across Alligator Alley from Big Cypress, the smaller Miccosukee Reservation has a tourist village open to the public. Traditional *chickee* huts, demonstrations of tribal crafts such as sewing, and the less traditional alligator-wrestling, give some idea of life as it was. Today's reality is a continuing battle with the legislators negotiating reparations for long-lost land and protecting special hunting rights. High-stakes bingo games, which can operate outside state and federal legislation within the reservations, airboat concessions and the tourist village generate additional revenue. Increased efforts are being made to maintain Seminole cultural heritage: Miccosukee children are taught in their native language as well as in English, and traditional ceremonies like the Green Corn Dance provide a vital link between the modern Seminoles and their past.

For Sports Lovers

■ **Florida is a magnet for sports lovers. Everything from golf to greyhound racing, croquet to speedway has found a band of loyal supporters in this sports-crazy state, and millions of holidaymakers a year enjoy the excellent facilities .....■**

In Palm Beach County alone, there are 142 golf courses, 1,100 tennis courts, 47 miles of oceanfront beaches offering scuba-diving, surfing, sailing and other watersports, plus sportfishing. Baseball, croquet, greyhound racing, jai-alai and three polo fields just about complete the sporting picture in this one small area.

Courses and courts Florida's golf courses are glorious. The 'Sunshine State' has developed into a top golfing destination well-supplied with challenging designer courses by the likes of Pete Dye and Tom Fazio, plus a tremendous choice of excellent public courses. This is the birthplace of Jack Nicklaus, after all. Naples, on the West Coast, claims to be the 'Golfing Capital of the World'. Although golf is played year round, winter is the busiest season.
Tennis resorts and training schools

Tennis aces can have a ball

are another intrinsic feature of the Florida sporting scene, with famous Floridian and top women's champion, Chris Evert, providing inspiration for a new generation of racquet fans. In recent years, sporting resorts have become a popular alternative to straightforward hotel accommodation, while most hotels can assist sporting guests to track down their particular pastime.

Head for the water and a whole new vista of sporting opportunities opens out. As the first rays of sun glimmer across the Atlantic Ocean or the Gulf of Mexico, **surfers** can be seen crouching over their boards waiting to catch the first wave of the day. **Waterskiers** and **jetskis** carve trails through the water; twin-hulled hobie cats zip to and fro; and there is **para-sailing** for the adventurous, or **pedalboats** for the less flighty. Marinas are packed with charter boats offering **sportfishing** excursions for marlin, pompano, sailfish and shark. Islamorada in the Florida Keys claims to be the 'Sportfishing Capital of the World' – Pompano on the Gold Coast, and Destin in the Panhandle might beg to differ. Meanwhile, **scuba divers** and **snorkellers** flock to the Gold Coast and Keys to explore the dazzling coral reefs and artificial dive sites warmed by the Gulf Stream. A sporting way of exploring Florida's inland water courses is a **canoe** trip. The Blackwater and Suwannee rivers in the Panhandle, the Myakka and Peace rivers near Arcadia, the southern tip of the Everglades, and the Keys are just a few of the prime locations. Freshwater fishermen on the rivers and back bays should ensure they have a licence, readily available from tackle shops (nominal fee).

AINESVILLE RACEWAY

Sport is big in Gainesville

A watching brief Spectator sports such as basketball and football collect enthusiastic crowds for home games; in spring baseball is the big one. February signals the arrival of major league baseball teams for the start of the six-week spring training programme. Central Florida welcomes the Boston Red Sox to Winter Haven, Detroit Tigers to Lakeland, and Minnesota Twins to Orlando; on the West Coast, the Mets are in St Petersburg, Chicago's White Sox in Sarasota, and Canada's Toronto Blue Jays in Dunedin; over on the East Coast the New York Yankees train at Fort Lauderdale and the Atlanta Braves head for West Palm Beach, while the LA Dodgers claim Vero Beach. Fans can turn up for the 10.00hrs practice sessions. There is the Grapefruit League, which attracts a million-plus fans each year. Attending these small-scale games can be just as exciting as the regular league play-offs.

<< Similar to the totalisator system, pari-mutuel betting was legalised in Florida in 1931. It opened the doors to a flood of sporting activities, including the widely popular greyhound racing, horse racing (on four courses in Miami alone), and the fast and furious ball game of jai-alai, which is something of a Florida speciality. >>

No self-respecting auto-enthusiast should leave Florida without a visit to Daytona, 'The Birthplace of Speed', and home of 'the other 24-hour race'. US stockcar racing was virtually born here at the Daytona Speedway, and February's Race Weeks culminate in the world-famous Daytona 500. There are stockcar race tracks around the state from West Palm Beach to Tampa and Pensacola; Sebring's 12-hour endurance race is another classic; while Downtown Miami hosts an annual springtime Grand Prix.

■ Mickey Mouse hit Florida in 1971, when Walt Disney World's Magic Kingdom opened its doors outside Orlando. However, the state's love affair with theme parks was already well-established .....■

Cypress Gardens near Winter Haven, Florida's first and longest continuously-operated theme park, has been packing them in since the mid-1930s. Exotic animals and birds have come to roost in a wide variety of specially created 'natural habitats' like the African plains of Tampa's Busch Gardens or Orlando's Sea World. Family fun is on tap at any number of water parks, and there are fairground attractions by the dozen.

Walt Disney World WDW continues to draw the crowds, as the world's number one tourist destination. Fairytale **Magic Kingdom**, with its cast of Disney characters from Cinderella to Dumbo, and **EPCOT** Center's medley of Future World pavilions dedicated to communications, energy, imagination, the land and transportation, plus the World Showcase cultural experience, have recently been joined by Disney-**MGM Studios Theme Park**. The latter opens the can on movie production, animation and special effects with backstage tours, stunt shows and rides. The WDW complex also includes two great water parks, **Typhoon Lagoon** and **River Country**, plus the Discovery Island zoo park, and the nightclubs and restaurants of **Pleasure Island**.

More at Orlando Just down the road there is hot competition for MGM-Studios in the form of **Universal Studios**. E T, *Back To The Future*'s Doc Brown, Ghostbusters and King Kong (among others), feature in rides cute, stomach-churning and hair-raising respectively. Plus there are animal actors, television studios and a guitar-shaped Hard Rock Café. Orlando's **Sea World** opened in 1973, is another favourite. Florida's

most popular marine park boasts an all-star cast of whales, dolphins, sea lions and otters topped by the entire Shamu family of performing killer whales. Also a jolly **Penguin Encounter**; a toothsome collection of eels, venomous fish and sharks in **Terrors of the Deep;** plus a nightly Polynesian dinner show.

In addition to the two WDW water parks, Orlando's **Wet'n Wild** lives up to its name. Human torpedoes shoot Der Stuke, the world's fastest and highest speed slide, plunge down six-storey-high Blue Niagara or take it easy on Lazy River. Children's versions of the big slides prove popular, and there are less dampening pursuits, such as mini-golf and sunbathing areas.

Flowers plus Within easy striking distance of Orlando, **Cypress Gardens** combine spectacular botanical gardens with waterskiing extravaganzas Capt Robin's old-time Flying Circus complete with acrobats, high wire and trapeze artistes, an elaborate model railroad, and – the park's trademark – crinolined Southern belles.Some 8,000 plant varieties from 75 countries provide dazzling year-round colour; there are electric boat rides around landscaped canals; and panoramic views from a revolving observation tower.

Tampa adventures Theme park addicts in Central Florida can drive across to Tampa in 90 minutes. **Busch Gardens: The Dark Continent** is the top attraction here. Spreading out from the Serengeti Plain with its array of African wildlife, themed districts recreate corners of the 'dark continent' from a Moroccan souk to craftsmen in Stanleyville. A dolphin theatre, ice skating show, fun fair rides and children's play

areas add to the all-round family entertainment value. Back to back with Busch Gardens, **Adventure Island** makes a splash with its Tampa Typhoon waterslide, a leisurely ride through a simulated rainforest and more.

Panhandle duo Another great theme park duo is the pride and joy of Panama City Beach on the Panhandle's 'Redneck Riviera'. During the day, head for **Shipwreck Island Water Park** for six landscaped acres of pools and slides, sundecks and snack bars. At night, **Miracle Strip Amusement Park** flings open its doors to a gigantic fairground packed with traditional rides like the giant Ferris wheel, a 2,000-foot roller coaster, swinging gondolas and a host of contests and sideshows.

Main Street USA with Cinderella's Castle, centrepiece of Walt Disney World's Magic Kingdom

<< Best of the rest
Miami: Atlantis, the Water Kingdom; Miami Seaquarium
Keys & Everglades: Theater of the Sea, Islamorada
Central: Wild Waters at Silver Springs Ocala
Gold Coast: Ocean World, Fort Lauderdale; Lion Country Safari, West Palm Beach
East Coast: Marineland, near Anastasia Island
West Coast: Buccaneer Bay at Weeki Wachee Spring
Panhandle: Gulfarium, Fort Walton Beach **>>**

■ **Strange, but true, French science fiction writer Jules Verne predicted Florida's space age future in his novel *From Earth to the Moon*, published in 1863. Verne described 'Florida...shaken to its very depths' by the lift-off of a rocket named *Columbiad*. Could there have been a well-read boffin with a sense of humour at work on the 1980s Columbia space shuttle programme? .....■**

Into the space race The first scientific studies exploring the use of rocketry for space flight were published in the early 20th century. During the 1930s, German scientists made dramatic leaps forward in the development of rocket technology, culminating with the V-2 guided missile. Later many of these scientists continued their work in peacetime for the US and USSR. By the late 1950s the space race was on.

In October 1957, the Soviets launched *Sputnik I* into earth orbit, followed in January 1958 by the Americans' *Explorer I*. When the

<< The centrepiece of NASA'S space programme for the 1990s is a truly international affair. Space Station Freedom will be an orbiting scientific research facility and launch point for further trips to the moon. The component parts will be transported into orbit by a series of Space Shuttle flights, where they can be assembled by astronauts. Designs for the main structure, a 508-foot horizontal boom, incorporate docking facilities for the Space Shuttle and four special purpose modules – two US, one Japanese and one European – which will provide accommodation and work space for up to eight people. Canada is contributing a maintenance depot ,as well as a mobile service unit. >>

National Aeronautics and Space Administration (NASA) was set up later that year, it selected the missile testing range at Cape Canaveral Air Force Station, Florida, as its test base, modified the existing launch pads and rockets to launch satellites, and inaugurated the *Mercury* programme. Both Americans and Soviets launched a range of unmanned spacecraft over the next few years, including communications and meteorological satellites, but again the Soviets stole a march on the Americans with Yuri Gagarin's first manned space flight in *Vostok I* on 12 April 1961. Less than a month later, on 5 May, Alan Shepard became the first American in space, with a 15-minute sub-orbital flight in a *Mercury* capsule.

Gemini and Apollo Work on NASA'S giant Launch Complex 39 began in 1962 across the Banana River from Cape Canaveral. NASA'S operations moved across the water to Merritt Island in 1964, the first year of the two-man *Gemini* missions. This programme of 12 flights was designed to test astronauts' ability to function in space and develop orbital rendezvous and docking techniques which would be put to use in the *Apollo* programme. The *Gemini 4* mission of June 1965 saw astronaut Edward H White operating outside the spacecraft for 20 minutes. After several unmanned launches, the first manned *Apollo* flight was accomplished in October 1968, with a three-man crew. Neil Armstrong and Edwin 'Buzz' Aldrin Jr's

moonwalk from *Apollo II* made them the first men on the moon on 20 July 1969. Only 12 astronauts, all American, have actually walked on the moon, the last during the final *Apollo* flight in 1972.

The Space Shuttle NASA'S next target was to develop a reusable manned spacecraft, the Space Transportation System (STS), better known as the Space Shuttle. Three basic elements comprise the Space Shuttle system: a 212-foot Orbiter, shaped like an airplane; two solid-fuel booster rockets; and an external tank containing liquid hydrogen (fuel) and liquid oxygen (an oxidiser). These elements produce a degree of flexibility which permits the Orbiter to take off like a rocket, orbit like a spacecraft and return to earth, landing on a runway like a glider or airplane. At lift-off the combined Space Shuttle system stands 184 feet high, and weighs in at 4,400,000 pounds. Spent after lift-off, the

JFK Space Center, Rocket Garden

boosters are jettisoned after about two minutes and parachute to earth where they are retrieved and reused. The 15-foot by 60-foot cargo bay can transport bulky cargoes such as communications and scientific research satellites weighing up to 65,000 pounds into earth orbit. Disabled spacecraft and hardware can be recovered and repaired in the bay, and loads weighing as much as 32,000 pounds can be brought back to earth.

The Space Shuttle's maiden voyage on 12 April 1981, marked the real beginning of space travel. These reuseable craft are designed for years of service, allowing routine space flights which will service the major programme of the 1990s: Space Station Freedom. Florida is the heart of America's pioneering space programme, and there is no better place to see the story unfold than at the Kennedy Space Center.

Cypress swamp, primeval-looking Florida Landscape

■ **Tacked on to the bottom right-hand coner of the North American continent, much of the Florida peninsula is just about as flat as a pancake. Its highest point is a mere 345 feet above sea-level near the boder with Georgia. Thus, the story of its origins is something of a suprise .....■**

Fire and water About 200 million years ago, when the ancient continent of Pangaea began to break up, a chain of island volcanoes rose from the sea, curving south from the mainland towards Cuba and the Bahamas. As sea-levels rose and fell during the period of the Pleistocene Ice Ages, the volcanoes were gradually eroded, and the deep sea-filled trenches gathered sediment to create massive limestone deposits which can reach 18,000 feet deep in places. Fossilised remains found in the north indicate that Florida was still under water while dinosaurs roamed the rest of the continent, its warm waters home to the prehistoric forerunners of turtles, sharks, whales and manatees (sea cows).

Emergence of dry land Somewhere around 20–30 million years ago, Florida finally appeared, a flat, swampy plateau cemented to the mainland by millions of years of collected sediment, coated with a rich phosphorous residue from the waves. As the last Great Ice Age advanced from the north, its gigantic glaciers devoured the sea and Florida doubled in size as the waters receded. No glaciers reached as far south, so Florida became a safe haven for all manner of creatures from mammoths and sabre-toothed tigers to tiny deer, wolves, bears and swamp-dwelling alligators. Their fossilised remains are frequently uncovered by phosphate mining operations.

From island to peninsula After the Ice Ages came the rains. They flooded through the porous limestone creating underground freshwater reservoirs, transformed sinkholes into springs, filled numerous rivers and thousands of lakes. The outline of the peninsula was still being shaped by changing sea-levels, as can be seen from the graduated terraces sloping away from the central area into the Gulf of Mexico, but around 6,000 years ago the Florida of today was recognisable. Its 1,350-mile seashore, fringed with islands and coral reefs, enclosed a land rich in plant life, animal life and fresh water – a land ripe for human habitation.

Fairchild Tropical Gardens, Miami

■ **Christopher Columbus discovered the Americas blocking his passage westward in 1492. Convinced that India was just around the corner, he christened the off-shore islands the West Indies and dubbed all the native inhabitants 'Indians' .....■**

The first-comers In fact, the first Americans probably migrated from Asia across the Bering Straits after the last Ice Age, some 20,000 years ago. This extraordinary population movement may have lasted for up to 10,000 years, as different groups of migrants gradually spread out over the whole American continent. There is no trace of any large native primate from which man could have evolved here, so it is possible that all 'Americans', from the Inuit (Eskimos) of Alaska and Canada to the Araucanian people of Chile, are descended from the first Mongoloid migrants. However, there is a growing argument which supports the theory that certain South American groups developed separately and are quite unrelated. Archaeologists believe the first Floridians arrived in the northern Panhandle region about 10–12,000 years ago. The traditional view

Native American totem pole

maintains that they arrived as part of the general migration south, but similarities between early Floridian culture and the cultures of some of the tribes of Central and South America could indicate a remigration north.

The early arrivals were hunters let loose in a 'promised land' of sunny skies and rich hunting, surrounded by a bountiful ocean. Armed with simple flint-tipped spears, they roamed the peninsula and feasted off mammoth, bison, boar and deer, fish and shellfish, quail, duck and goose.

<< The people who inhabited the North American continent before the arrival of white men continued to be referred to as 'Indians' until recent times. The remnants of these proud people now prefer to be known as 'native Americans'. >>

Early settlement By 5000BC, groups of aboriginal peole had settled in villages along the St Johns River. These semi-permanent communities required the orderly disposal of rubbish, and their refuse dumps, known as middens, have provided archaeologists with precise clues to the habits and culture of the original settlers. Mounds of discarded shells indicate a healthy seafood diet; broken arrowheads and weapons chart the development from crude spears to more sophisticated hunting methods; and, from around 2000BC, a startling cultural advance is demonstrated by the presence of shards of pottery. This is a clear guide to the highly developed culture of these southern tribes, as the art of fashioning clay

vessels and baking them was not discovered for a further eight centuries over most of North America.

Cultivation began around 1000BC, giving rise to the emergence of crude irrigation schemes in the Lake Okeechobee area of central south Florida. Advances in the tribes' ability to feed themselves led to something of a population explosion, and settlements gradually appeared across the entire peninsula. Estimates of the aboriginal population around the time of the arrival of the Spanish vary enormously, with a median of about 10,000 spread throughout the state and divided into tribes. The peoples included the Timucuans in the central and northern areas and the Apalachee in the north and east Panhandle region. Tampa Bay was settled by the Tocobega, while warring Calusas hunted the southwest coast and Tequestas controlled the Everglades and southeastern shores.

A rich culture Jean Ribaut, a French Huguenot who led an expedition to the territory, described the Indians in the mid-16th century as 'of tawny colour, hawk nosed and of a pleasant countenance'. They wore light deerskin coverings, coloured earrings made from inflated fish bladders, and the men sported intricate tattoos.

Remnants of a proud culture

Ribaut was impressed by Indian hunting methods – disguised in deerskins and horns, they could sneak right up close to their prey for the kill.

Tribal government was administered by chieftains advised by elders and priests. Animal sacrifices were made to appease the sun god, and they also sacrificed first-born children in a demonstration of fealty to the tribal chief. Human bones discovered in burial sites, up to 6,000 years old, form another information-gathering source besides the earlier middens. Reserved for important figures, these burial mounds increased in size and ingenuity until they became massive earthworks visible for miles around, landmarks on complex road and canal systems which developed along similar lines to those of the ancient Aztec and Mayan civilisations of South and Central America.

The beginning of the end Florida's native people were highly developed, but the writing was on the wall for them with the arrival of the early explorers. Their ships brought slave traders and European ailments such as measles, chickenpox and venereal diseases against which the native population had no defence, and to which they would eventually succumb altogether.

■ **When Spanish explorer Juan Ponce de León set sail from his base in Puerto Rico on 3 March 1513, he was looking for the lost island of Bimini and its legendary fountain of eternal youth. A month later he landed near the site of present-day St Augustine on Easter morning, and named the new territory *La Florida*, after the Spanish Eastertide Feast of Flowers, *Pascua Florida* .....■**

De León's explorations led him around the Keys (from the Spanish for island, *cayo*) – which he named *Los Martires* as they reminded him of a chain of martyred men – and up the west coast of the peninsula to Charlotte Harbor (Fort Myers), where he was met by ferocious natives shouting in Spanish. Whether the Spanish words had been learnt from contacts with South American Indians or forays by slave hunters is not known.

The first attempt to colonise Florida was a disaster. De León returned in 1521 with 200 settlers and missionaries, but their settlement was attacked before the foundations were complete, and the Spanish retired to Cuba where de León died from an arrow wound.

Exploring the past

<< Italian map-maker John Cabot may have been the first European to see Florida when he sailed down the North American coast on a charting mission for King Henry VII of England. Although he never set foot ashore, 16th-century maps of Cabot's voyages appear to confirm that he sighted the Florida peninsula. >>

Dreams of gold In 1528, Pánfilo de Narváez landed in Tampa Bay with a force of 400 men. They trailed north into the Panhandle in search of gold, leaving instructions for their ships to join them. Disease and Indian raids took a heavy toll, the ships never turned up, and the remnants of the expedition took to sea in makeshift boats from which there were only four survivors (who reappeared in Mexico some eight years later). There were still dreams of undiscovered pots of gold when Hernando de Soto fielded a further expedition in 1539. Setting out from Tampa Bay in March of that year, de Soto led his 1,000 battle-hardened *conquistadores* and fortune-seekers deep into the interior. They ventured as far as North Carolina and Alabama, where de Soto died of a fever on the Mississippi after three years of fruitless searching. The promise of gold was wearing a little thin. It is now believed that any gold the native Indians possessed had probably been recovered from Spanish shipwrecks along the coast.

European inroads The next attempt to establish a permanent Spanish settlement on the peninsula fell to Tristan de Luna y Arellano. This nobleman and veteran of several campaigns, sailed into Pensacola Bay with a total of 1,500 soldiers, priests and craftsmen in 1559. Their luck was no better, and the combination of Luna's short-sighted management, crippling food shortages and a violent hurricane forced them to retreat in 1561. By this time, although the Spanish had signally failed to establish a foothold on their vast new territory, their presence was being felt in a far more long-reaching and insidious fashion. European diseases were laying waste the native American population, and raids by slave traders from strongholds in the West Indies forced the native Americans from their traditional homelands. Within 200 years, the original inhabitants of Florida would no longer exist.
For a record of these lost Floridians, we are indebted to the French. Spurred on by Spain's failure to colonise, French explorer Jean Ribaut made several forays along the Florida coast. In 1564, a colony of Huguenots founded a settlement on the St Johns River, Fort Caroline. Here, Ribaut and his chart maker, Jacques le Moyne, compiled a fascinating account of the local tribes with detailed descriptions of native

Philip II of Spain took great interest in his American lands

dress, customs and practices illustrated by le Moyne (see page 35).
This French Protestant enterprise proved too much for Spanish Catholic pride, and Philip II despatched Pedro Menéndez de Avilés to dislodge the French. Menéndez landed south of the St Johns on 28 August 1565, the feast of St Augustine. Soon after, the Huguenot outpost was razed to the ground.

> **<<** Menéndez was also charged by Philip II with ensuring the New World embraced Catholicism; he set about his task with unprecedented patience and humanity. Although the immediate effect was many dead Jesuit priests, by the 17th century the Indian Catholic reserves were models of peaceful community life. **>>**

St Augustine grew to become the oldest continuously inhabited settlement in the United States – despite numerous attempts by hostile raiders, England's Sir Francis Drake included, to remove it from the face of the earth.

■ **On learning of Menéndez's rout of the French colonists, Philip II of Spain declared it was wholly justifiable 'retribution ... upon the Lutheran pirates', which would act as a lesson to all. However, Spain's problems with foreign fortune-hunters, particularly those on the high seas, were only just beginning ....■**

The plunderers plundered

Throughout the 16th and 17th centuries, Spanish treasure fleets laden with gold, silver, copper and precious stones plundered from Spain's West Indian and South American colonies, ploughed slowly homeward around the southern tip of Florida. They attracted buccaneers like bees to honey. Attacking the lumbering galleons from smaller, swifter craft, pirates could easily escape with their booty and hide out in the impenetrable maze of coastal mangrove swamps, or play hide-and-seek around the Florida Keys.

<< Potential profits far out-weighed dangers, as Francis Drake soon discovered. He returned from a successful foray to the New World with Spanish booty worth some £1.5 million, was knighted by Queen Elizabeth I in the docks at Deptford and despatched straight back to colonise north America – all the while continuing to deny any hostility towards Spain. >>

Booty from a treasure ship

Disaster at sea The treasure ships had numerous natural hazards to face as well, including treacherous tides, knife-edged coral reefs concealed in the shallows and violent storms which could descend with little warning. On 4 September 1622, a fleet of Spanish galleons, guarded by men-o'-war, upped anchor in Havana harbour and sailed for home. They included the *Nuestra Señora de Atocha* and the *Santa Margarita*, both lying low in the water, weighed down by their priceless cargoes. By the following evening, they and six other vessels lay at the bottom of the Florida Straits in the wake of a hurricane which also killed 550 men. It was some 350 years before king of the salvagers, Mel Fisher, located the site and its fabulous golden bounty, now on show in Key West (see page 102) and elsewhere.

Black Caesar's domain The Keys had long been a haven for smugglers and pirates, and there are more wrecks cluttering up the reefs here than anywhere else around the coast. Some, no doubt, fell prey to natural disasters, but many others are said to have been lured to their fate by false signals, the victims of legendary pirates such as the truly unlovable Black Caesar. Reputed to be an escaped Negro slave, Black Caesar distinguished himself by capturing small vessels single handed from his base just north of Key Largo. He then graduated to the post of trusted henchman to the notorious Edward Teach, alias Blackbeard.

Caesar's lust for jewels and wanton cruelty gave him such a fearsome reputation that the authorities were forced to act. Lieutenant Robert

Pirates sharing spoils. From A Book of Pirates, *1905*

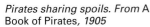

Maynard eventually captured Teach's ship, the *Queen Anne's Revenge*, flying the Jolly Roger flag, in 1718. Teach was killed in the battle, and Black Caesar was brought back in chains to Virginia, where he was hanged.

Gasparilla The East Coast area around Fort Pierce and Vero Beach is another fruitful spot for salvagers – 11 vessels of the Spanish Plate Fleet went down in 1715. On the Gulf Coast, gold coins have been washed ashore at Naples after heavy storms, and there was certainly plenty of shipping and pirate action around Tampa Bay and the Charlotte Harbor area. This is where legendary mutineer-turned-buccaneer, José Gaspar – 'affectionately' known as Gasparilla – carved his violent niche into Floridian folklore.
Captiva Island is said to have been named after one of his more repellent exploits – the capture of the Spanish Infanta and her escort of 11 Mexican maidens in 1801. Having landed on the island, Gaspar handed the captive maidens over to his crew and claimed the Spanish princess for himself. When she refused to co-operate, he had her summarily executed – just one of a hundred similarly gory tales of rape, pillage, torture and murder.

> **<<** Fact or fiction? According to local storytellers, José Gaspar was a high-ranking gentleman who staged a bloody mutiny on the Spanish galleon Florida Blanca in 1785. As Gasparilla, he terrorised passing sea traffic for the next 37 years, and captured or sank some 36 ships between 1784 and 1795 alone. **>>**

Gaspar's freedom of the seas lasted until 1822, when an American warship masquerading as a British trader lured his pirate ship into hot pursuit, then revealed its true colours with a blast from a concealed gun battery. Realising the game was up, Gasparilla committed suicide by leaping overboard. The day of the big time Florida pirates was almost over, though the Lafitte brothers and the mysterious Tavernier were still harrying American shipping from south of the border well into the 19th century.

During the 17th century, British slavers made frequent raids into Spanish territory to capture native Floridian Indians. The people were highly prized for the training they had received from their Spanish masters, though they were not slaves but servants, or free men, living in segregated reserves .....

Native opportunists Raids were becoming more daring by the beginning of the 18th century, and the slavers were now assisted by Creek Indians from Alabama, Georgia and the Carolinas. Many of the Creeks stayed on, occupying former Spanish farmlands and native Indian territory. For deserting their own tribes in the north, they became known as *Seminoles* from a Creek word meaning 'runaways' or 'wanderers'.

When Spain and Britain concluded the Seven Years War with the Treaty of Paris in 1763, Britain received Florida in exchange for Cuba. As the Spanish sailed away with the remnants of the aboriginal population, the British moved in with their Creek allies, and the two communities co-existed amicably enough.

Vast tracts of land were swiftly annexed and granted to settlers, together with financial inducements. Rice, sugar cane and indigo plantations were carved out of the fertile soil by Black slaves, and many Blacks were assimilated into Indian communities through servitude and marriage.

Spanish reoccupation Britain was mistress of Florida for only 20 years. With British reserves severely depleted by the 1776 American War of Independence, Spain saw a golden opportunity to reclaim her lost American territory, landed a force at Pensacola, and captured West Florida in 1781. Four years later, the Second Treaty of Paris saw Florida back in Spanish hands – but it was to bring its old conqueror little joy.

The Seminoles largely ignored Spanish jurisdiction and soon found their land claims being disputed by a steady flow of white settlers from the north. Indian migrants continued to move south, and escaped Negro slaves from the southern states sought refuge in Spanish territory, incurring the wrath of Georgia's powerful planters.

The First Seminole War Tension built up along the border, and relations between the Seminoles and the Americans deteriorated to a point where General (later President) Andrew Jackson leapt upon the flimsiest pretext to thunder into Florida and extract a bloody revenge by the Suwannee River. This was the First Seminole War of 1817–18.

Desperate measures In 1819, Spain cancelled her $5 million debt to the United States, and left for good, opening the door for a further influx of white settlers. In 1823, an attempt was made to restrict the Seminoles to a single four million-acre reservation in central west Florida, but it failed. The Removal Act of 1830 sought an even more drastic solution, with the forced migration of all Seminoles to reservations in Arkansas, west of the Mississippi. Senior chieftains journeyed west to view the land in 1832, but after just one chief had agreed to sign away his tribal lands, the process was halted by the arrival of Osceola.

The Second Seminole War A young brave of striking good looks and immense pride, Osceola was widely respected, and he succeeded in uniting the various tribes to fight the Second Seminole War which

Traditional scene of Seminole family life. Today's Seminoles are largely tourist attractions

lasted seven long and bloody years (see also page 43). His capture, by trickery, while negotiating under a flag of truce in 1837, prompted a considerable public outcry. He died a year later, incarcerated in Fort Moultrie, South Carolina.

> << Although he was, in fact, part European, Osceola had all the pride of a full-blooded Indian. One of his main grievances against the Americans was the slavers' kidnapping of his wife Che-cho-ter (Morning Dew) – who, herself, had a trace of Negro blood. This was an insult to his tribe and family that he could never forgive. >>

Osceola's place was taken by Chief Coacoochee (Wild Cat), but the Seminole spirit was broken, and the United States' superior manpower and weaponry won out.

Surrender and survival Some 3,000 Seminoles travelled the 'Trail of Tears' across the Mississippi in 1842. Led by Chief Billy Bowlegs, a handful of renegades slipped into the Everglades and continued to harry odd settlers, and the army, into the Third Seminole War of 1855. They finally surrendered in 1858, and the chief was escorted west. A further 300 Seminoles melted back into the Everglades, and later emerged to trade alligator skins, deerhides and small amounts of produce. It is their descendants who comprise the present-day native American population of around 1,500 Seminoles, and the smaller 500-strong Miccosukee group.

■ **When Spain cancelled her debt to Washington by relinquishing control of the Florida peninsula in 1819, General Andrew Jackson was appointed the territory's first governor. 'Old Hickory' (Jackson was reputed to be as tough as this very hard wood) arrived to take up his post in 1821, but only remained three months before high-tailing back to Washington, where he eventually made it to president in 1828 .....■**

A central government One of the most important questions facing the Floridians was where to establish their state government seat. The two major settlements, Pensacola and St Augustine, were three weeks' journey apart at opposite sides of the peninsula. In 1832, two scouts were sent out on horseback, one from each of the principal towns, and they met midway between the two, in the rolling hills of northern Florida. It was here that the town of Tallahassee was built.

By 1824, Florida's early legislative councils were convening in three log cabins near the site of the present-day Capitol building in Tallahassee. These were replaced by a two-storey masonry structure in 1826, but as Florida moved towards statehood, a larger and more impressive building was felt appropriate. Congress found $20,000 and commissioned a Capitol, which was completed just in time to welcome the new state government on 3 March 1845.

Union guns at Fort Brady in the American Civil War

Settlement and slavery During the 1820s, land grants and financial inducements encouraged a steady stream of white settlers to northern Florida, where they planted cotton, rice, tobacco and sugar cane, greedily snatched former native American lands, and suborned free Blacks to slavery. The port of Jacksonville, founded in 1821, helped open up the interior as pioneers ventured down the St Johns River, set up trading posts and grew indigo and citrus fruits. Down in the Keys, pirates gave way to wreckers (some could see no difference) and they were joined by immigrants from the Caribbean who contributed their distinctive architecture and planted pineapples, bananas and mangoes.

One of Florida's early senators, David Levy Yulee, was also Caribbean born. His sugar plantation and mill near Homosassa on the West Coast, employed 1,000 slaves. As in other southern states, slavery was the backbone of the plantations, and it is estimated some 25,000 slaves laboured under the yoke of 'King Cotton' in Florida.

> << Cotton turned little Apalachicola into the third largest port on the West Coast during the 1830s, but the town is best remembered for Dr John Gorrie's ice-making machine, invented here in 1848. It led, eventually, to the development of air conditioning and refrigeration. >>

The Castillo de San Marco, St Augustine, Florida's most historic fortress

Florida's population almost doubled from 34,370 to 66,500 between 1830 and 1845. Skirmishes between the native American and white settlers became more frequent and bloody, and government efforts to forcibly deport the Indians by the Removal Act of 1830 resulted in the Second Seminole War (1835–42). It cost 1,500 white American lives and untold native American casualties. Fort Lauderdale, Fort Myers and Fort Pierce were all founded in response to the war, and the total bill ran to more than $40 million (see also pages 40–1).

The Civil War During a brief respite, the first cross-state railroad was built between Fernandina and Cedar Key to open in 1861. But Florida had barely recovered from its internal conflicts, when pressure from wealthy plantation owners ensured that the 16-year-old state seceded from the Union on 10 January 1861. Allied to the pro-slavery Confederate southern states, Florida went to war against the Union ... and lost. Florida's main role in the Civil War

<< Florida still takes pride in its Confederate history. After the war ended, many senior Confederate figures were forced to flee, among them Secretary of State Judah P Benjamin. He took refuge with Major Robert Gamble on his plantation at Ellenton, near Tampa. Today, the house has been immaculately restored as the J P Benjamin Memorial (see page 204). **>>**

was as a food provider for the Confederate army, though Key West, among other places, remained loyal to the North and became a vital staging post for Union troops. The Confederates won a battle at Olustree, near Lake City; and Tallahassee made the record books as the only Confederate capital east of the Mississippi not to fall to Union forces, when a 'cradle and grave' troop of old men and boys successfully repelled the northerners at the Battle of Natural Bridge in March 1865. But, two months later, the Union flag was run up above the State Capitol after General Robert E Lee surrendered the Confederate cause at Appomattox.

■ **At the end of the Civil War, President Andrew Johnson appointed a provisional government to oversee the 'Reconstruction' of Florida. It was to be some 20 years, however, before the the state started to flourish with the coming of the railways .....■**

Black rights A constitutional convention met in October 1865, the secession order was annulled, and laws were introduced to safeguard Blacks' civil rights. But the changes were largely cosmetic and, although the state government eventually bowed to pressure to include the Negro population in its political processes, the requirements for those seeking high office would automatically disqualify most Negro candidates.

There were some exceptions, however. When the vote was granted to all male citizens of Florida aged 21 and over (including Negroes) in 1868, Jonathan C Gibbs, Florida's first black Cabinet member, was elected and later appointed Secretary of State in 1869. Born of free parents in Philadelphia, Gibbs came to Florida after the Civil War to serve as a Presbyterian missionary.

Meanwhile, nine-tenths of Florida's Blacks were back working in the fields. The active role of the Ku Klux Klan in the 1870s perpetuated most of the old injustices, though Harriet Beecher Stowe, whose anti-slavery epic *Uncle Tom's Cabin* had done so much to rally the abolitionists when it was published in 1852, did note that Florida's 'freemen' were better off than in neighbouring states.

Opening up the state Despite the threat of yellow fever and malaria, the bad communications and other assorted ills, there were still plenty of settlers keen to make a go of it in Florida's wide open spaces.

Citrus plantations were all the rage, and in 1881 the state sold four million acres of Central Florida to Hamilton Disston, who set about draining land in the Kissimmee and Caloosahatchee valleys for building settlements and for farming.

<< By the 1870s, even tourists were venturing into the interior of Florida – albeit from the civilised confines of luxury steamboats plying the St Johns River. >>

The railroad barons In the 1880s, two businessmen were to transform the state with railroads. Henry B Plant pioneered a cross-state railroad to Tampa on the Gulf Coast; Henry M Flagler decked the Atlantic Coast with a necklace of luxurious resort hotels which would eventually stretch from Jacksonville to Key West, linked by his East Coast Railroad.

State land grants in exchange for development were a powerful incentive for the railroad builders, and Plant received 5,000 acres of virgin territory per mile for the 75-mile stretch of track between Kissimmee and Tampa. In 1884, he made it into Tampa with just 63 hours to spare on the contract, and began work on a $3.5 million extravaganza, the 500-room Tampa Bay Hotel.

Wider connections Plant also added to his growing transport system with a steamship service to Key West and Cuba. In 1885, Vincente Martinez Ybor transferred his Cuban cigar-making industry from Key West to Tampa Bay; and that same year inventor Thomas Edison found a good spot beside the Caloosahatchee river at Fort Myers, down the coast from Tampa, where he built himself a winter home. Tampa's Cuban connection made it a hotbed of anti-Spanish propaganda, and in 1898 Teddy Roosevelt and his Rough Riders rode into town *en*

44

Locomotives old and new

route for the Spanish-American war in Cuba. A young British journalist, Winston Churchill, covered the news story from the comfort of Plant's hotel.

East coast splendour Though Plant was a prime mover in the development of Florida, the transition to a fashionable winter vacation area was largely due to the efforts of Henry M Flagler. Honeymooning in St Augustine in the early 1880s, he was disappointed at the lack of facilities, and determined to bring the resort up to standard by founding the magnificent Spanish-Moorish-Revival' style Ponce de Leon Hotel, which opened in 1888. The Hotel Ormond at Ormond Beach followed in 1890, painted yellow with a green trim – the East Coast Railroad colours. The Royal Poinciana opened at Palm Beach in 1894.

During the winter of 1894–5, a terrible freeze destroyed citrus plantations as far south as Fort

<< Though the Ponce de Leon Hotel is now a college, and the Hotel Ormond and Royal Ponciana have disappeared, there is one exceptional reminder of the days when Florida's Atlantic Coast was the premier winter playground of Vanderbilts, Rockefellers and the leisured classes. The Breakers at Palm Beach, originally a Flagler creation, was rebuilt in the 1920s after a fire, and its seven-storey Italian Renaissance style façade, lofty ceilings and magnif-icent furnishings are still a sight to behold. **>>**

Lauderdale. Miami pioneer Julia Tuttle grabbed the opportunity to send Flagler a bouquet of orange blossom, untouched by the freeze further north, and persuaded him to continue his East Coast Railroad to Miami in 1896. Continuing to the southern tip of the state, Flagler eventually reached Key West in 1912, a year before his death.

■ **In 1912, when Henry Flagler steamed into Key West aboard his 'Railroad that went to the Sea', it was the culmination of a dream. This had been a romantic project from the start; and it had cost Flagler very-dearly .....**■

The last 156-mile section of the East Coast Railroad system, from Homestead south of Miami down through the Keys, took seven years and several millions of dollars to complete. But, somehow, anything seemed possible in Florida at the beginning of the new century.

Creating new land Entrepreneur Carl Fisher arrived in Miami as Flagler was celebrating. He found New Jersey horticulturist John Collins battling with a failed avocado plantation which he was trying to turn into a residential development on a strip of sand three miles out in Biscayne Bay. Fisher advanced Collins $50,000 to develop the land in exchange for a 200-acre plot as security. They completed a wooden bridge across to the mainland, the longest in the country at the time, and Fisher started a dredging operation in 1915, which would almost double the size of the island, known as Miami Beach.
As the mangrove wilderness was tamed, elegant hotels sprang up along the beach; shopping malls, golf courses and tennis courts provided recreational distractions in the rapidly landscaped setting. Across the bay, industrialist millionaire James Deering built himself a magnificent mansion, Villa Vizcaya; further up the coast, self-taught architect Addison Mizner was enchanting the well-to-do with his Spanish-Mediterranean inspired creations in Palm Beach. By the 1920s, Florida was well and truly on the map, and everybody wanted a little piece of it.

Real estate madness It was with a sense of adventure that the first 'tin can tourists' motored down the length and breadth of the country in their shiny new Fords, Oldsmobiles

and Packards. A shortage of hotels could not deter them. They set up tented cities on the beach, and dined out of tin cans. And they were easy fodder for the squadrons of silver-tongued salesmen who had hastened south as rumours spread of a real estate mania that was to get so crazy that the Marx Brothers even made a film about it – *Coconuts*. Street-corner opportunists, the 'binder boys', made fortunes overnight reselling options on undeveloped lots to the uninitiated. Massive advertising campaigns involving unheard-of sums of money further fuelled the dreams of the winter-bound northern workforce, who promptly streamed south to invest in a little Florida sunshine.

The entrepreneurs George Merrick, founder of America's first planned city, spent $3 million in a single year advertising his Coral Gables development in Miami. This was one of the finest results of the Land Boom era, and one of the most enduring. Merrick's French, Dutch, South African and Chinese 'villages' are still regarded as one of the most desirable residential neighbourhoods in Miami (see page 54).
Inspired by the success of Carl Fisher's dredging operation at Miami Beach, one Charlie Rodes tackled the swamps of Fort Lauderdale. By dredging a series of parallel channels, he raised a neat clutch of 'finger islands' which turned the city into an 'American Venice' – and earned Rodes a fortune. Meanwhile, Addison Mizner was doing so well in Palm Beach, that he and his brother, Winston, snapped up 16,000 acres of land around the fishing hamlet of Boca Raton. In 1925, they ran a fulsome advertising campaign incorporating the slogan 'I'm the

Greatest Resort in the World!', and sold $26 million worth of contracts before they had built a single Venetian-style bridge.

>> The Land Boom also hit the West Coast. Real estate manipulator Wilson Fuller wrote a book describing his experiences in St Petersburg, where his creative practices allowed him to transform a single investment of $50,000 into $270,000 in a few simple moves. Just down the coast, in Sarasota, circus king John Ringling, threw causeways across the bay to Longboat Key, his barrier island development, where he built an attractive shopping district to save his wife and guests the trouble of journeying to Palm Beach. >>

Florida's sunshine has drawn visitors for more than 100 years

End of a dream The Land Boom reached its height in 1925, but by 1926 Mizner's Boca Raton was decried as 'Beaucoup Rotten'. A couple of banks collapsed in the spring, Miami was hit by a hurricane, and real estate-crazed investors came down to earth with a bump when they took stock of their precious plots. Some plots were under water in swamps, others buried beneath mosquito-infested mangrove thickets. A drastic hurricane swept across the lower edge of the state in 1928, leaving more than 2,000 people dead and millions of dollars worth of property destroyed. The final straw was the stock market crash of 1929, which marked the start of the Depression era.

■ **The collapse of the Land Boom and the ensuing great Depression left a string of paper millionaires turned paupers – and an unpleasant taste in the mouths of many investors .....**■

But Florida was to suffer less than most. While the rest of the country was locked in gloom, one of the few bright spots on the horizon was Florida itself: the promise of sunny skies and palm-fringed beaches still worked a tantalising magic.

The 1930s After a quiet start, the 1930s were actually a time of expansion for the state. Hardest hit by the crash, Miami was also the first to recover, and new building programmes were a confident sign that the city was on the road to recovery. Miami Beach blossomed with the first flush of art deco hotels, and embraced Streamline Moderne style a few years later.

The elegant Hialeah Park Race Track

High-rise drama in Miami

DUPONT PLAZA

48

opened in 1931 to celebrate the legalisation of pari-mutuel betting (whereby winning gamblers share the total wagered on a race). This drew a large and enthusiastic following to the greyhound tracks as well as the jai-alai frontons (literally the walls against which this pelota-like game is played). On a less encouraging note it also attracted the attention of organised crime, and the likes of Al Capone, who retired to a heavily guarded estate on Palm Island where he died in 1947. With no income tax nor inheritance tax, and not to mention the climate, Florida was also a haven for more legitimate retirees.

During the mid-1930s, the state benefited from a number of wide-ranging Federal aid programmes. Land reclamation, public buildings, transport and communications were all covered by the brief, as well as cultural, educational and welfare projects. When Flagler's former Overseas Railroad was destroyed by the Labor Day hurricane of 1935, Federal relief workers picked over the ruins and built the Overseas Highway. Meanwhile, the Florida Emergency Relief Agency (FERA) worked together with local residents to gentrify Key West into a suitably *recherché* haunt for literary types (see page 104).

Tourists and astronauts By the early 1940s, Florida's population of two million was outnumbered by the annual tourist influx. To cope with increased demand, between 1945 and 1954 more hotel rooms were built in Greater Miami alone than in the rest of the US. In 1959, the nation's first scheduled domestic jet air service opened between New York and Miami, and a new generation of 'tin can tourists' took to the skies.

International Drive, Orlando

Jet airliners were not the only hardware streaking across Florida's wide blue yonder. The Cape Canaveral Air Force Station, midway up Florida's Atlantic coast, was chosen by the newly established National Aeronautics and Space Administration (NASA) as a testing ground for its early satellite and rocket programmes in 1958. Later NASA built its own facility near by, and world attention was focused on the Kennedy Space Center's monitors for the historic Apollo 11 moonwalk, when Neil Armstrong carried mankind one step further into the future.

The Disney phenomenon The Mouse arrived in 1971. Preparations for Mickey Mouse's Florida début began quietly in the early 1960s, when Walt Disney targeted the state – and specifically Orlando – as the ideal site for his new venture. Good communications, sunshine and a high tourism profile were all plus factors, but the greatest attraction of all was the spread of undeveloped land.

Appalled by the tacky commercial sprawl which had sprung up around his Californian Disneyworld, Disney was determined to control the surroundings on this project. Executives were sworn to secrecy as agents began to buy land. By the time an announcement was made in 1965, Disney had amassed a 28,000-acre site, twice the size of Manhattan; as yet only one quarter of it has been developed. Magic Kingdom opened in 1971, Epcot Center in 1983, and Disney-MGM Studios in 1989. Together they comprise the world's number one tourist destination, and attract over 20 million visitors a year.

Into the future Florida continues to grow from strength to strength. The tourist dream born in the 1880s is a vital industry of the 1990s, while improved communications have drawn new life-blood from the commercial world. There is no let-up in the stream of new residents arriving to take up their place in the sun, and the recent realisation that conservation is the way ahead will ensure that the next generation will have something to look forward to.

MIAMI

Stretched luxuriantly along the glittering blue water-front of Biscayne Bay, Miami is a palm-fringed beach resort, bustling gateway to Latin America, financial powerhouse, and notorious drugs and crime den with a dubious pedigree which stretches even further back than Al Capone, who died at 93 Palm Island in 1947. Today Greater Miami covers an area of 2,040 square miles, and numbers 1.9 million residents, but when Yankee industrialist's wife Julia Tuttle arrived by mailboat in 1875, all she found was the remains of Fort Dallas, a Seminole Indian trading post and a few scattered plantations around the bay. After a terrible frost in the winter of 1894–5 decimated citrus groves as far

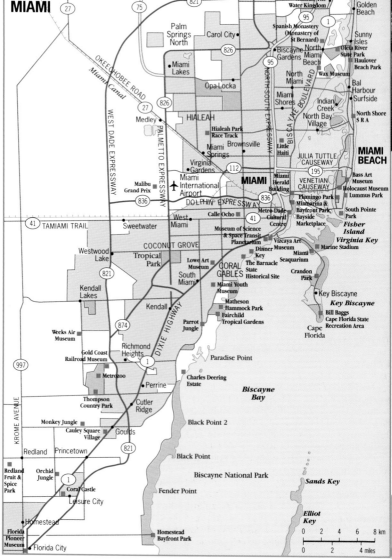

MIAMI

Atlantis, The Water Kingdom
Golden Beach
Spanish Monastery (Monastery of St Bernard)
Sunny Isles
Oleta River State Park
Haulover Beach Park
Palm Springs North
Carol City
Biscayne Gardens
North Miami Beach
Wax Museum
Bal Harbour
Surfside
Miami Lakes
Opa-Locka
North Miami
Miami Shores
Indian Creek
North Bay Village
North Shore SRA
HIALEAH
Medley
Hialeah Park Race Track
Little Haiti
JULIA TUTTLE CAUSEWAY
MIAMI BEACH
Miami Springs
Brownsville
Virginia Gardens
Malibu Grand Prix
Miami International Airport
MIAMI
Miami Herald Building
VENETIAN CAUSEWAY
Bass Art Museum
Holocaust Museum
Lummus Park
Flamingo Park
Miamarina & Bayfront Park,
South Pointe Park
Fisher Island
Metro-Dade Cultural Centre
Bayside Marketplace
Calle Ocho
West Miami
TAMIAMI TRAIL
Sweetwater
Museum of Science & Space Transit Planetarium
Virginia Key
Marine Stadium
COCONUT GROVE
Dinner Key
Vizcaya Art Museum
Miami Seaquarium
Westwood Lake
Tropical Park
Lowe Art Museum
The Barnacle State Historical Site
CORAL GABLES
Crandon Park
South Miami
Miami Youth Museum
Kendall Lakes
Key Biscayne
Bill Baggs Cape Florida State Recreation Area
Matheson Hammock Park
Fairchild Tropical Gardens
Kendall
Parrot Jungle
Cape Florida
Weeks Air Museum
Gold Coast Railroad Museum
Richmond Heights
Paradise Point
Metrozoo
Perrine
Charles Deering Estate
Biscayne Bay
Thompson Country Park
Cutler Ridge
Monkey Jungle
Cauley Square Village
Goulds
Black Point 2
Redland
Princetown
Black Point
Redland Fruit & Spice Park
Orchid Jungle
Coral Castle
Black Point
Biscayne National Park
Sands Key
Leisure City
Fender Point
Homestead
Elliot Key
Florida Pioneer Museum
Florida City
Homestead Bayfront Park

OKEECHOBEE ROAD
Miami Canal
WEST DADE EXPRESSWAY
PALMETTO EXPRESSWAY
NORTH-SOUTH EXPRESSWAY
BISCAYNE BOULEVARD
DOLPHIN EXPRESSWAY
DIXIE HIGHWAY
KROME AVENUE

0   2   4   6   8 km
0   2   4 miles

51

south as Palm Beach, Mrs Tuttle sent a bouquet of unfrosted citrus blossom to railway baron Henry Flagler and persuaded him to extend his railroad south to Miami, where it arrived in 1896.

At the turn of the century, monied northerners discovered a subtropical paradise at the end of the line and began building elegant winter retreats, such as James Deering's magnificent **Villa Vizcaya**. George Merrick transformed his father's citrus grove into the elegant Mediterranean-style **Coral Gables** development; while Carl Fisher and John Collins built causeways and landscaped an avocado plantation on an offshore island to form Miami Beach.

The 1920s Land Boom and the advent of 'tin can' tourism saw Miami's population explode from 30,000 to 100,000 in just five years; then confidence tricksters, a devastating hurricane in 1926, and the 1929 Depression marked the end of an era.Development continued, however, and the Work's Project Administration moved into Miami Beach in the 1930s, dressing it in the height of art deco fashion. Palatial resort hotels followed in the 1950s; and during the 1980s, concrete and glass landmarks dramatised the Downtown skyline.

Inner city rejuvenation has seen a cultural revolution in music and the arts; world-class sporting events cram the calendar; and an average year-round temperature of 75.9°F ensures the city's 15 miles of beaches are enduringly popular. Miami's Hispanic population has also sparked a revolution which has not only lent the city an exotic Latin aura, but has also transformed it into a thrusting cosmopolitan city which is now a centre for Latin American issues.

Miami's Neighbourhoods

Re-evaluation of the tastes of the 1930s has brought new life to Miami Beach's Ocean Drive

Art Deco District A 20th-century national historic district, Miami Beach can boast the largest collection of art deco architecture in the world. From Sixth Street north to 23rd Street, and from Ocean Drive west to Lenox Avenue, some 800 significant buildings are enclosed within this one square mile. A 1980s facelift has so rejuvenated parts of the district as to recall its glorious 1930s and 1940s heyday. **Ocean Drive**, facing the beach, is a showcase strip of elegant hotels: the **Streamline Carlyle**, the **Leslie**, and the 70-room **Cardozo**, where Frank Sinatra strutted his stuff in the 1950s movie *A Hole in the Head*. On weekends today, crowds of bright young things pack the numerous watering holes and bring traffic to a standstill beneath a gaudy halo of neon.

The building boom started after World War I with a flourish of Mediterranean Revival architecture relying heavily on borrowed romantic styles from the past, typified by the Venetian-influenced **Amsterdam Palace** (116 Ocean), with its massive stone portal, courtyard and barrel roof tiles – said to have been shaped over Cuban workmen's thighs!

During the transitional classical art deco period, elaborate decorative features appeared, often depicting natural subjects – palms and flamingos in the case of Florida, which earned this style the title 'tropical deco'. The 1930s heralded a brand new age of mass production, exciting new building materials and streamlined aerodynamics. These were celebrated in the Moderne style with geometric motifs, rounded-off corners, horizontal racing stripes, and the use of friezes, pediments and columns to highlight bold vertical planes. The **Park Central** and **Imperial** (640 and 650 Ocean) combine a wealth of these tricks of the trade. During restoration, at least one art deco rule was deliberately flouted: the original restrained colour schemes were replaced by powder pinks, sunset oranges, lavenders, deep turquoises and sea greens, which brilliantly define the intricacy and the-harmony of the designs. (See also walk on page 56.)

Coconut Grove When Doctor Horace P Porter opened his Cocoanut (sic) Grove Post Office in 1873, there were only two coconut palms in the grove. However, the name caught on when the Town of Coconut Grove was incorporated in 1919, and a plentiful supply of palm fronds now dapple the sidewalks, shopfronts and outdoor cafés of this pleasantly Mediterranean-type neighbourhood. Bordering Biscayne Bay, Coconut Grove lies a 10-minute drive south of downtown Brickell Avenue. Its villagey atmosphere has long attracted visiting artists and writers, while Everglades conservationist Marjorie Stoneman Douglas has lived here since 1926.

Coconut Grove was the product of a friendship between early settlers Charles and Isabella Peacock, and Yankee visitor Ralph Middleton Munroe. Munroe encouraged the Peacocks to establish a small hotel in 1884, which prospered with the arrival of Henry Flagler's railroad 12 years later. Rustic camps sprang up along the bayfront, and Munroe built his own home, **The Barnacle**, now a state historic site. The Peacock Inn expanded, and soon employed a number of Bahamian immigrants who constructed their distinctive wood-frame 'conch' houses along Charles Avenue. Their contribution is celebrated in style every June when the lively **Goombay Festival** takes place, complete with processions, 'junkanoo' bands and street stalls. On the corner of Charles Avenue, the decorative 1920s **Coconut Grove Playhouse**, opened as a cinema in 1926, is now home to one of south Florida's leading theatre companies.

Festivals are big in the Grove. The annual three-day Arts Festival in February attracts some 700,000 visitors. Its offerings include demonstrations, lectures, live jazz and tempting food stalls. Another crowd-puller is October's Banyan Arts & Crafts Festival, and during the same month, the Columbus Day Regatta sees 65 vessels compete in 21 classes over a weekend. In December there is the crazy King Mango Strut Parade, and in mid-April foodies will find the Seafood Festival irresistible.

53

Gleaming smiles and chrome in Coconut Grove

MIAMI

In a moment of inspiration, George Merrick transformed an obsolete quarry into a delightful swimming hole, and created the Venetian Pool at 2701 DeSoto Boulevard, Coral Gables. Around the astonishingly blue lagoon, which is fed by a natural spring, there is a beach, bridges, waterfalls, islands and caves. Low red-roofed buildings house changing rooms and a courtyard café. The Miami Opera performed here (in the drained pool) in 1926, and swimming stars Johnny Weissmuller and Esther Williams have also made appearances.

Down on the waterfront, Dinner Key Marina boasts the old art deco Pan American terminal building; while James Deering's **Villa Vizcaya** and the **Museum of Science and Space Transit Planetarium** sit face to face on the northern boundary of the Grove. Boutiques, galleries and restaurants line Main Highway and Commodore Plaza; Mayfair-in-the-Grove and CocoWalk on Grand Avenue have more of the samef.

Coral Gables At the height of the 1920s Land Boom, developer George Merrick laid the foundations of America's first planned community, his 'City Beautiful', Coral Gables. Almost 70 years later, Merrick's exclusive 12-square-mile estate remains one of the most prestigious neighbourhoods in town. Between broad main boulevards, quiet tree-lined streets wind past villas and walled compounds, fountains and plazas, and green open spaces. **Coral Gables House**, on Coral Way, was Merrick's boyhood home.

A pet project of Merrick's was the development of **The Villages**. Although he never travelled, he gave these enclaves architectural styles ranging from traditional French town houses and mini châteaux, to colonial Dutch South African, and the oriental detail of the Chinese Village. The community was entered by gateways like the imposing Puerto del Sol at the junction of Douglas Road and Tamiami Trail. Among the highlights are the Spanish Mediterranean-style City Hall on Miracle Mile (which issues driving tour maps of the district), and Merrick's stunning **Biltmore Hotel**, on Anastasia, built at a cost of $10 million, and recently refurbished.

The University of Miami was founded on land donated by Merrick, and its **Lowe Art Museum** (1301 Stanford Drive) exhibits the fine Kress Collection of Renaissance and baroque art (*Open*: Tuesday to Saturday 10.00–17.00hrs, Sunday 12.00–17.00hrs. Information, tel: (305) 284 3535.).

Colonnade Building, Coral Gables

Downtown A mixture of gleaming skyscrapers, cultural centres, building sites and Latin discount stores, Miami's Downtown district is on the way up after several decades of neglect. Downtown spans both sides of the Miami River, with its main thoroughfare, Flagler Street, running east-west from the bayfront.

Two important arts centres on Flagler are the 1920s **Gusman Center for the Performing Arts** (174 E Flagler) which plays host to the highly regarded New World Symphony and Philharmonic Orchestra of Florida, as well as an annual Film Festival; and the **Metro-Dade Cultural Center** (see page 62). Shoppers are well catered for in a variety of major stores and small shops on Flagler, but pride of place goes to the attractive **Bayside Marketplace**. Parking is a problem, so use the cheap and efficient Metromover transport system.

Little Haiti Tucked between Biscayne Bay and Interstate-95, north of 46th Street, this area was once known as Lemon City. Haitian immigrants arriving in Miami in the 1980s remoulded the district with ethnic food stores, Creole restaurants and brightly painted shopfronts such as those in the two-block stretch along 54th Street from Miami Avenue to NE 2nd Avenue. There is also a lively springtime Haitian Carnival.

Little Havana Since the 1960s, Cuban refugees and immigrants have been resettling in Miami. They have imported their language, customs, hopes and heroes to this 3.5-acre district just west of Downtown, and infused it with a distinctive Latin flavour. SW 8th Street, better known as Calle Ocho, is the commercial heart of the district, and the place to find a good Cuban sandwich or a window full of votive statues; buy a handrolled cigar from **El Credito**, at No 1108, or check out the action in **Domino Park**, on the corner of 15th Street. A night out in a Cuban restaurant is a taste experience, and the annual March fiesta is one of Miami's biggest and best street parties.

A meal in itself, a Cuban sandwich is constructed on a heroic scale. Locals gather on the sidewalk outside the sandwich shop windows sipping tiny cups of Cuban coffee while they wait for their sandwiches to be built. Long, crusty loaves of Cuban bread are split and piled high with ham, pork, Swiss cheese and pickles, then baked in a pizza oven and finished off with lashings of mild-to-hot peppery sauce.

55

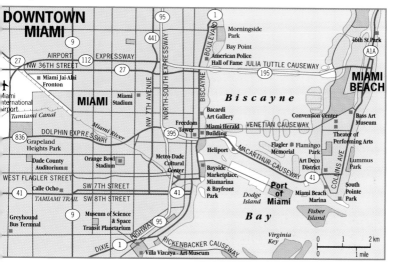

DOWNTOWN MIAMI

Morningside Park
Bay Point
American Police Hall of Fame
JULIA TUTTLE CAUSEWAY
46th St Park
MIAMI BEACH
AIRPORT EXPRESSWAY
NW 36TH STREET
Miami Jai-Alai Fronton
Miami International Airport
Tamiami Canal
MIAMI
Miami Stadium
Biscayne
Bacardi Art Gallery
Convention Center
Bass Art Museum
Miami River
DOLPHIN EXPRESSWAY
Grapeland Heights Park
Freedom Tower
Miami Herald Building
VENETIAN CAUSEWAY
Theater of Performing Arts
Dade County Auditorium
Orange Bowl Stadium
Metro-Dade Cultural Center
Heliport
Flagler Memorial
Flamingo Park
Art Deco District
Lummus Park
WEST FLAGLER STREET
SW 7TH STREET
Bayside Marketplace
Miamarina & Bayfront Park
Port of Miami
Miami Beach Marina
South Pointe Park
Calle Ocho
TAMIAMI TRAIL SW 8TH STREET
Dodge Island
Fisher Island
Greyhound Bus Terminal
Museum of Science & Space Transit Planetarium
Bay
Virginia Key
RICKENBACKER CAUSEWAY
Villa Vizcaya - Art Museum

0   1   2 km
0   1 mile

Walk Through the Art Deco District

From the Trolley Bus stop on Ocean Drive at 11th Street, take a quick detour up Ocean Drive as far as No 1116.
Amsterdam Palace is an unusual Mediterranean-Revival edifice.

Walk back to 1036 Ocean.
The **Adrian Hotel** is worth a stop for its stuccowork façade.

Turn right on 10th Street.
The **Essex Hotel**, at Collins, has a beautifully restored art deco interior. Opposite, the **Fairmont Hotel** is one of L Murray Dixon's neon extravaganzas. Check out the façade of the enormous **Washington Storage Building** on Washington Avenue.

Continue on 10th Street, then turn left on Pennsylvania Avenue.
The Milfred (936 Pennsylvania)

boasts an extravagant glass block and Vitralite doorway. Next door, at **No 928**, is a rare pre-art deco house. There are two wonderfully gaudy restored apartment houses at **810** and **813 Pennsylvania**.

Turn left on 8th Street, down the side of the old Blackstone Hotel.
Note the **Tiffany Hotel**'s futuristic neon tower at Collins.

Back on Ocean, turn right for the Beacon Hotel (720 Ocean) and Park Central (640 Ocean). Then head north along Ocean.
Do not miss the **Waldorf Towers, Café des Arts, Breakwater,** and **Edison**.

Pastel colours characterise the restored façades of Miami's Art Deco District

Walk Coconut Grove

The walk starts at the Trolley Bus halt on Main Highway.
The first stop is the **Coconut Grove Playhouse** (3500 Main Highway), rebuilt in 1927, after the hurricane of the year before. Its attractive Spanish rococo façade boasts elaborate stuccowork, parapets and twisted barleysugar columns.
Charles Avenue was the home of the Grove's first black community founded in the 1880s. Note the traditional Bahamian 'conch' architecture.

Continue on Main for five minutes to the corner of Devon Road on the right.
The ivy-draped **Plymouth Congregational Church** was erected in 1916. Palms flank a 400-year-old walnut and oak door from the Pyrenées, and there is a pretty garden cloister.

Return from Devon Road along Main.
The Barnacle (3845 Main), built by pioneer Coconut Grove resident and naval architect Ralph Munroe in 1891, has an authentic period interior and overlooks the bay.

Further up Main, take a left on to Commodore Plaza.
This shopping mecca has two great galleries: **Carlos**, at 3162, for colourful Haitian art (prices from $25); and **Hendrix Collection Inc**, at 3170, for native American art, furniture and jewellery.

Continue along Main to CocoWalk and The Mayfair on Grand Avenue for boutiques galore.

The Barnacle, with its 5-acre grounds, is a gracious reminder of Coconut Grove's early days

One for crime buffs: the US' largest police museum

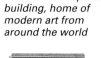

▶▷▷ American Police Hall of Fame
3801 Biscayne Boulevard
More than 10,000 law enforcement-related exhibits, the most extensive collection in the US, are located in the former Miami FBI headquarters. You will see police vehicles, weaponry, jail cells, stocks and a pillory (for hands-on experience of old-fashioned justice), and sobering sights such as an authentic electric chair.
Open: daily 10.00–17.30hrs.

▶▶▷ Atlantis, The Water Kingdom
2700 Stirling Road
South Florida's only water theme park, out at Hollywood, this is the place to chill out on a hot day. Rides and slides include the Black Out tube slide, White Water rapids ride, a seven-storey Slidewinder with nine slides, plus speed pools with Olympic swimming lanes and diving platforms.
Open: late June to August, daily 10.00–22.00hrs; April to June, September and October, weekends 10.00 –17.00hrs; closed winter.

The Bacardi Imports building, home of modern art from around the world

▶▷▷ Bacardi Art Gallery
2100 Biscayne Boulevard
North of Downtown, the gallery occupies the unusual 1930s blue-and-white mosaic tiled Bacardi Imports building, and offers a good programme of contemporary exhibitions by local and international artists. For current information, tel: (305) 573 8511.
Open: Monday to Friday 09.00–17.00hrs.

▶▶▷ Bal Harbour
9700 Collins Avenue, Miami Beach
This is an exclusive, beautifully laid out shopping mall with a handful of notable European designer boutiques joining the ranks of top American stores Saks Fifth Avenue, FAO Schwarz and Neiman Marcus.

Open: Monday, Thursday and Friday 10.00–21.00hrs; Tuesday, Wednesday and Saturday 10.00–18.00hrs; Sunday 12.00–17.00hrs.

▶▷▷ Bass Art Museum

2121 Park Avenue, Miami Beach

Housed in an elegant 1930s Streamline former library, the Bass displays a permanent collection of Renaissance, baroque and rococo art works. It also hosts contemporary exhibitions of American and international art and travelling exhibits. For details of Sunday jazz programmes, tel: (305) 673 7533.

Open: Tuesday to Saturday 10.00–17.00hrs; Sunday 13.00–17.00hrs.

▶▷▷ Bayfront Park

100 Biscayne Boulevard

Downtown's breathing space, the 32-acre Bayfront Park skirts the shoreline from Bayside Marketplace around towards the cruise ships in the Port of Miami. Joggers pound past the palm trees, and there is an amphitheatre which hosts popular open-air concerts. Plaques around the **John F Kennedy Memorial Torch of Friendship** represent Miami's friendly ties with Latin and South America: the gap in the row is for Cuba, which will be added at the demise of the communist Castro regime.

▶▶▶ Bayside Marketplace

401 Biscayne Boulevard

Right on the bay, fronting the Downtown district, this is one of Miami's newest and busiest attractions. Over 140 shops ranging from wacky gift stores to popular clothing outlets like **Esprit** and **The Gap**, ethnic South American crafts stalls, cheap sunglasses-sellers and sports outfitters vie for attention. Entertainment is provided by street performers, and there are plenty of bars and coffee shops.

The dockside bustles with charter boats heading off on trips around the bay. Bayside is also the terminal for the Old Town Trolley Buses (services every half-hour from 10.00 to16.00hrs) which provide tours with commentary around the Coconut Grove and Coral Gables neighbourhoods, and Miami Beach, (see **Excursions**, page 69). Live music at night makes for a great atmosphere, and there is a choice of international cuisine including Chinese, Thai, Italian, Mexican and, of course, good old American burgers. The shops may close at 22.00hrs, but the daiquiris flow far into the night on weekends.

▷▷▷ Black Heritage Museum

Miracle Center, 3301 Coral Way

Black people have a long and chequered history in Florida.

Today, blacks form an integral part of the Floridian population and this museum, housed in the Miracle Center shopping mall, includes a variety of exhibits from all aspects of black history, including African carvings, items of black American art and craft, and pieces of local historical interest.

Open: Monday to Friday, 11.00–16.00hrs; Saturday and Sunday, 13.00–16.00hrs.

The first black person to set foor in Florida was known as Little Steven, and was part of a Spanish expedition in 1527. Later, runaway slaves found refuge in the swamps, where their lives became entwined with those of the Seminoles. Though some blacks were recorded as property owners by the middle of the last century, segregation was to follow, holding sway until the 1950s.

Entertainment on the Bayside

While building Coral Castle, Edward Leedskalnin shifted some 1,100 tons of rock singlehanded and furnished his 'castle' with rock fittings, including a nine-ton swinging gate.

60

Masts bristle in Dinner Key Marina

▶▷▷ Cauley Square Village
22400 Old Dixie Highway
Just off US1 at Goulds, south of Miami, the 10-acre 'square' was built by pioneer developer William H Cauley in the 1920s, on Henry Flagler's Overseas Highway railroad route to Key West. The village's little cottage homes have been lovingly restored and now house a labyrinth of art and antiques galleries, craft shops, second-hand and contemporary fashionshops and twee tea rooms.
Open: Monday to Saturday 10.00–16.30hrs.

▶▶▷ Charles Deering Estate
16701 SW 72nd Avenue
Charles Deering's 360-acre waterfront preserve on Biscayne Bay could not be more different from his brother James' elegantly manicured Vizcaya estate. Purchased by the County in 1985, it has now been opened as a country park with acres of virgin mangroves, pinelands, palms and tropical hardwood hammock (the name given to ground raised above the original swamp). Tours of the grounds can be made on foot or by tram, and twice a day there is a 3˘-hour guided canoe trail. Deering's stone mansion and a timber-framed hotel, which was the original property on the estate, are both being restored and are open to visitors.
Open: weekends only 09.00–17.00hrs. Information, tel: (305) 235 1668.

▶▷▷ Coral Castle
28655 S Dixie Highway, Homestead
On the northbound lane of US1 (at SW 286th Street), this bizarre monument was created between 1925 and 1940 by a lovesick, five-foot tall, 97lb Latvian, Edward Leedskalnin, as a memorial to the fiancée who jilted him.
Open: daily 09.00–21.00hrs.

▷▷▷ David Kennedy Park
S Bayshore Drive and Kirk Street
This is a favourite spot with Coconut Grove's fitness freaks, who pound around the bayshore vita (fitness) course. As well as bike paths and walking trails, there is boat rental and a children's playground.

▶▷▷ Dinner Key Marina
3400 Pan American Drive
Another Coconut Grove hang-out, this was where early residents used to set out on boat picnic expeditions, hence the name. Today the busy marina boasts several bars with a view, and there is boat and windsurfer rental, plus charter fishing operators.

▶▶▷ Fairchild Tropical Gardens
10901 Old Cutler Road, Coral Gables
More than 80 acres of lawns and lakes comprise the largest botanical gardens in the continental US. In the Fairchild, visitors are allowed to touch, smell and explore the exhibits and the grounds planted with exotic species from around the globe. There is a constant rustle of palms with fragrant frangipani, flowering shrubs, trees,

vines and bromeliads, and special mangrove, rainforest and Everglades areas. Enjoy a two-mile tram ride, inspect the Rare Plant House, find a snack in the café, or take a picnic to adjacent Matheson Hammock Park (see page 73).
Open: daily 09.30–16.30hrs.

▷▷▷ Freedom Tower
600 Biscayne Boulevard
Not open to the public, but impossible to miss, the 1925 Freedom Tower, built to house the *Miami News*, was modelled on the Giralda Tower in Seville, Spain. Across from Bayfront Park, it earned its present name as a refugee processing centre for more than 600,000 Cuban exiles during the 1962 crisis.

▶▷▷ Fruit and Spice Park
24801 SW 187th Avenue, Redland
More than 500 varieties of exotic fruits and spices gathered from every corner of the earth flourish in the 20-There are guided tours at weekends, a gift shop, and tours of the local historical district.
Open: daily 10.00–17.00hrs.

▶▷▷ Gold Coast Railroad Museum
12450 SW 152nd Street
This fine collection of historic locomotives in South Miami includes a plush former presidential rail car, the *Magellan*. With weekend train rides around the 68-acre site, this is definitely a must for train buffs.
Open: Monday to Friday 10.00–15.00hrs; Saturday and Sunday 10.00–17.00hrs.

▶▶▷ Haulover Beach Park
10800 Collins Avenue
On a spit of land north of Miami Beach, the park offers a two-mile stretch of hotel-free seashore with golden sands, Atlantic surf, nine holes of golf, deep-sea fishing, picnic areas with barbecue facilities, boat rental and walking trails.

A cool vista in Fairchild Tropical Gardens

61

MIAMI

Although it is a replica, HMS *Bounty* is no fake. The ship has sailed over 70,000 miles since her launch in 1960, including a maiden voyage to Tahiti where Fletcher Christian's famous 1787 mutiny was re-created for the big screen with an all-star cast which included Marlon Brando and Trevor Howard.

Scene (almost) of the famous mutiny

Hialeah

Hialeah is a distinctly sporting annexe of Miami, northwest of the city along Okeechobee Road. **Hialeah Park Race Track** (2100 E Fourth Avenue) is one of the most beautiful courses in the world. Built in 1931, it was a winter racing mecca, frequented by society bigwigs who travelled in daily from their estates in Palm Beach. The ivy-covered, French-style clubhouse, the stables and the paddock areas are open to the public on non-race days, along with the palm-fringed gardens.

The racing season lasts for only two months of the year: either January and February, or March and April. During this time, breakfast is served at the track. (For more information, tel: (305) 885 8000.)

Hialeah's other sporting draw is the **Miami Jai-Alai Fronton** (3500 NW 37th Avenue), where spectators not only observe but bet furiously on the action of the world's fastest game, a version of pelota (see page 83).

In the centre of the 1.5-mile Hialeah race track, the world's largest flock of domestic flamingos parades gracefully, and makes forays across the infield in a cloud of pink- and black-tipped feathers.

HMS *Bounty*
401 Biscayne Boulevard

Built for MGM's 1962 classic, *Mutiny on the Bounty*, this replica of a fully rigged 18th-century vessel is anchored at Bayside Marketplace, dressed for the tourist trade with a crew of all-American pirates.
Open: Monday to Friday 10.00–17.00hrs.

Key Biscayne
See facing page.

Metro-Dade Cultural Center
101 W Flagler Street

One of Downtown's most celebrated architectural showpieces, Philip Johnson's Mediterranean-style complex houses the **Center for the Fine Arts**, the **Historical Museum of Southern Florida**, and the state-of-the-art **County Library**. The museum offers an interesting glimpse into Floridian history, plus a good programme of special events and tours.
Open: Tuesday to Saturday 10.00–17.00hrs; Thursday, 10.00–21.00hrs; Sunday, 12.00–17.00hrs.

Key Biscayne

■ Once a haunt of wreckers and hunters, this former coconut plantation in Biscayne Bay is a favourite weekend retreat for Miami's urban dwellers. It is linked to the mainland by the Rickenbacker Causeway, which forms an impressive curve across the bay. .....■

The new high-level bridge replaced the old Rickenbacker Causeway bridge, which is now a pier for fishermen. The causeway affords a terrific view of Downtown Miami *en route* to Virginia Key, Key Biscayne's sister island.

Virginia Key The roadside is lined by a narrow strip of sand known as Hobie Beach, fringed by Australian pines, with parking for fishermen, windsurfers and other watersports enthusiasts. The **Miami Seaquarium** is on Virginia Key; and another major attraction is the **Miami Marine Stadium**, which stages 'Pops by the Bay' summer concerts, international rowing regattas and powerboat racing.

Path of the moon Bear Cut Bridge makes the short hop to Key Biscayne. The name comes from the Indian *Bischiyano*, meaning 'Favourite Path of the Rising Moon'. However, the southern tip of the island was named Cape Florida by early explorer Ponce de León in 1513.

Crandon Boulevard runs the length of this island, where Richard Nixon once set up his alternative White House. In the northern section, the lush 500-acre **Crandon Park** offers picnicking facilities, a haven for joggers and 2.5 miles of public beach. The oceanside is lined with luxury hotels and condominiums, and first-class resort facilities include one of the finest 18-hole golf courses in the country, plus a tennis complex which plays host to international tournaments.

Away from it all The southern tip of the island is given over to the **Bill Baggs Cape Florida State**

Recreation Area. This 406-acre preserve is the site of Florida's oldest lighthouse, founded in 1825. A dizzying 122-steps spiral staircase climbs up the brick structure to an observation post with a grand view of the bay and the elevated holiday homes of Stiltsville. Below, there is a reconstructed New England-style keeper's cottage with period furnishings.

By the beach area, edged by pines and sea grapes, a concession stall sells snacks and bait and rents tackle, snorkels, bicycles and windsurfers. The best fishing is from the bayside sea wall, with a chance of hooking snook, bonefish or grouper. There are walking trails, good birdwatching and turtles nesting in season.

Cape Florida Lighthouse

63

Siesta-time for one of Metrozoo's inhabitants

High jinks at Miami Seaquarium

▶▶▶ Metrozoo
12400 SW 152nd Street, Kendall
Florida's beneficent climate is ideally suited to Metrozoo's purpose of re-creating natural habitats. One of the largest cageless zoos in the US, its 280 acres of simulated African jungle and veld, and Asian and European forests is home to some 2,800 animals. A two-mile monorail circuit spans the four different 'continents' and an aviary, with stops along the way. Highlights of the Metrozoo are the rare white Bengal tigers and the permanent koala exhibit.
Open: daily 10.00–17.30hrs (last tickets 16.00hrs).

▶▶▶ Miami Seaquarium
4400 Rickenbacker Causeway
Founded in 1955, the Seaquarium is home to a terrific variety of marine life from dolphins and sea lions to rescued manatees and turtles. There are shows, touch tanks and boardwalk exhibits such as 'Faces of the Rain Forest', and the 'Lost Islands Wildlife Habitat', which has a nesting area for giant turtles and several species of sea birds. However, the star attractions are undoubtedly the performers: Sally the sea lion, Lolita the killer whale, and the most famous dolphin of them all, Flipper (the Flipper movies and TV shows were filmed here). The shows in the 2,500-seat stadium are exemplary, combining a little gentle education, polished performances and an abundance of good humour. Allow a full half-day to take in all the shows. There is also a gift shop and refreshment stops, and there are baby strollers are available.
Open: daily 09.00–18.30hrs.

▶▷▷ Miami Youth Museum
5701 Sunset Drive, South Miami
A fun option for the young, this museum has plenty of hands-on exhibits designed to stir up the spirit of investigation. **Kidscape**, a mini-neighbourhood, allows small children to see the world on their scale.
Open: Monday to Friday 10.00–17.00hrs; Saturday and Sunday 12.00–17.00hrs.

▷▷▷ Miccosukee Indian Village/Airboat Tours
30 miles west of Miami on Tamiami Trail (US41)
Definitely a tourist trap, but the airboat tours into the Everglades are an experience. Alligator-wrestling has its fans, and there are demonstrations of native crafts, a museum and a gift shop.
Open: daily 09.00–17.00hrs.

■ **Florida is a great place for kids. Although most families make a beeline for the theme parks, Miami has a lot to offer parents and children too. There are the beaches;. resort hotels devise programmes for children; restaurants welcome them; and many attractions are deliberately geared to their needs .....■**

The **Miami Youth Museum**, for instance, is all about magic and fantasy with a load of excellent hands-on exhibits. On the science front, no budding Einstein or astronaut should miss the **Miami Museum of Science and Space Transit Planetarium**, packed with animal, electrical and mineral exhibits, plus the world's largest flight simulator.

Animal magic Southern Florida's sunny climate has given local zoological parks the edge on many of their colder weather cousins. Top favourites are **Metrozoo**, **Monkey Jungle** and **Parrot Jungle**, where carefully re-created habitats provide a home-from-home for thousands of exotic species. In addition to on-site playgrounds, bathing facilities (Monkey Jungle) and children's petting areas, frequent animal shows aim to educate as well as entertain.

Across the Rickenbacker Causeway, **Miami Seaquarium** is another must. Education is a top priority here, too: ecologically aware marine exhibits include rescued manatees and great shows which combine snippets of fascinating data with amazing feats. Visiting toddlers can be pushed around in the comfort of special dolphin-shaped strollers which are available at the entrance.

Water, water everywhere Waterbabies are in luck on Miami's beaches. Gently sloping sandbars extend for several hundred yards before reaching deep water, so there is plenty of shallow swimming and paddling. Public beaches are well supplied with concession stalls, shaded picnic facilities, and sun umbrella and deckchair hire. The **Bill Baggs State Recreation Area**, on Key Biscayne, is an excellent spot for a family day out, with a beach, bait for sale and tackle hire, plus bikes and trikes for exploring the woodland trails or windsurfers for a spree on the ocean wave.

Or head for Miami's fun-packed waterpark, **Atlantis, The Water Kingdom**, a little way out of town, at Hollywood. The **Venetian Pool**, in Coral Gables, is more sedate, but ideal for young children.

Sporting choice Junior sports fans can sample baseball action when the Baltimore Orioles come to town for spring training; preview games are played in March and April. American football notables, the Miami Dolphins, pack Joe Robbie Stadium during the September to December season.

For more local colour, the Miami Jai-Alai Fronton features this fast and furious Basque sport.

Weekend Intinerary

Day one Old Town Trolley Magic City Tour from Bayside Marketplace. Stop off at Vizcaya and the Museum of Science and Space Transit. Lunch in Coconut Grove. Continue on Trolley via Coral Gables back to Bayside Marketplace for shopping and sunset drinks. Dinner in Little Havana.

65

Day two Old Town Trolley Miami Beach Tour from Bayside Marketplace. Stop for brunch in the Art Deco District. Return to Bayside for a Biscayne Bay Cruise.

Older children might enjoy a few hours under sail on the Bay

Most subtropical orchids grow on trees, so you need to look up to see their flashes of brilliant colour high up in the treetops. They are, however, not parasites but epiphytes – their trailing aerial roots gather water and food released by tree bark after rain. Many orchids are scented, and they come in an amazing variety of colours – from speckled camouflage-brown, flame orange, lemon yellow, purple and pink to purest white.

Sign language: an inmate of Monkey Jungle

▶ ▶ ▶   Monkey Jungle
14805 SW 216th Street

A family-owned concern, Monkey Jungle has a unique feature in its free-ranging monkey colony. Joe Dumond moved to Florida from Connecticut in 1933, and released six macaques into a 10-acre hardwood hammock intending to study their behaviour. When money for his scientific studies dried up during the Depression years, he opened the project to visitors, but the monkeys resented the intrusion and adopted an agressive stance. Rather than lock up the monkeys, Dumond decided to cage the visitors instead, and built a network of covered walkways through the jungle habitat.

Breeding programmes and studies of primate behaviour are still an integral part of the work here, and the inhabitants (like the visitors) are drawn from around the world - Africa, Asia and South America. However, many animals are still caged, such as the graceful, acrobatic gibbons; black spider monkeys, apparently sporting Beatles' haircuts; beautiful black-and-white colobus monkeys whose fringed pelts were once highly prized for African ceremonial costumes; and dainty, orange-maned golden lion tamarins. The swimming pool area is a good spot for mother-and-toddler bathing parties; plus there are shows throughout the day.

Open: daily 09.30–17.00hrs.

▶ ▶ ▶   Museum of Science and Space Transit Planetarium
3280 S Miami Avenue

This hands-on museum with more than 150 touchable exhibits and live demonstrations sets out to win over kids from the word go.

For starters, there is an intriguing onslaught of echo tubes, momentum machines (save ice-cream for later), plus a host of lasers and things that flash in the dark. In the Body Action area plenty of older children can be

found testing their muscle flexibility and endurance. Casting a dramatic image in the Shadow Box is a hot favourite, and the outdoor Wildlife Center is a haven for damaged birds who are rehabilitated before being released back into the wild.

The separate Planetarium (combination ticket) is a tribute to the wonders of space travel, boasting the world's largest flight simulator, fantastic multi-media astronomy and laser shows (for information, tel: (305) 854 2222). The Observatory is free and is open on weekend evenings, weather permitting.

Open: daily 10.00–18.00hrs.

▶▷▷   Orchid Jungle
26715 SW 157th Avenue, Homestead
Signposted off US1, the Fennell family's orchid business was founded in the 1880s. There are over 100 species of orchid native to Florida, and around 8,000 examples flourish in this natural setting beneath a leafy canopy.
Open: daily 08.30–17.30hrs.

▶▶▶   Parrot Jungle
11000 SW 57th Avenue, S Miami
Set in magnificent jungly gardens filled with gorgeous flowering plants and palms (all carefully labelled for horticulturists), Parrot Jungle has been in operation since 1936. From humble beginnings, the 30-acre wildlife habitat now supports around 1,100 rare and exotic birds, alligators, giant tortoises and koi fish. Many of the birds are free-flying, returning home at night for food. There are shows at regular intervals which feature talking, cycling and numerically gifted prodigies. Even some of the less intelligent occupants are also stars, such as the gawky flamingos which brighten up the title credits of *Miami Vice*. The gift shop is laden with 'parrot-phernalia', and there is a snack bar.
Open: daily 09.30–18.00hrs.

▶▷▷   South Pointe Park
Washington Avenue at Biscayne
On the southern tip of Miami Beach, this 17-acre park is a popular recreational spot with a beach and vita course. Fishermen are welcome, and there is a children's playground, picnic areas and barbecue grills. Concerts are staged at an amphitheatre.

▶▷▷   Spanish Monastery
16711 W Dixie Highway
Founded in Segovia, Spain in 1141, the former Monastery of St Bernard was spotted by newspaper magnate William Randolph Hearst while on an art-buying trip to Europe in the 1920s. He shipped it across the Atlantic to add to his vast San Simeon estate in California, but when Floridian customs officials replaced the blocks in the wrong cases the project was abandoned. The painstaking five-year task of piecing it all together was undertaken 25 years later, and the eminently satisfactory result now houses a medieval art collection.
Open: Monday to Saturday 10.00–17.00hrs; Sunday 12.00–17.00hrs.

Week's Itinerary

Day one and Day two As weekend itinerary (see page 65).

Day three Miami Seaquarium; relax on Key Biscayne.

Day four Parrot Jungle; picnic in Matheson Hammock Park; Fairchild Tropical Gardens.

Day five Hialeah; cool off at Atlantis, The Water Kingdom.

Day six Everglades National Park, Main Visitor Center, near Homestead; return via Coral Castle.

Day seven Metrozoo; Weeks Air Museum; and shopping in Cauley Village Square.

Companionship in Parrot Jungle

68

Villa Vizcaya, a bit of Italy under American skies

▶ ▶ ▶ **Villa Vizcaya**

3251 S Miami Avenue

On the northern boundary of Coconut Grove, Villa Vizcaya is one of Miami's premier attractions. The fabulous neo-Renaissance villa was built as a winter residence for industrialist James Deering between 1914 and 1916. A great admirer of European architecture and style, Deering was also an avid collector. When he began work on Vizcaya, he despatched young designer, Paul Calfin, to Europe, and between them they furnished the house with carpets from Portugal, ceilings from Italy, chandeliers from France, Roman statuary and antique treasures from the finest periods of European design. The building itself is the work of F Burrell Hoffman, a mere 29 years old at the time, who created an elegant northern Italian-style villa built around a courtyard.

The house is now the Vizcaya Art Museum. Each of the 34 rooms on display represents a particular ideal, such as the gracious 18th-century English-style Adams Library featuring a concealed door in the bookcase; the magnificent Rococo Salon and the Renaissance Hall. The grounds were landscaped with a combination of Italian- and French-pattern formal gardens which lead down to Biscayne Bay and a Venetian waterlanding, while the entire estate is surrounded by a native hammock of mature tropical hardwoods.

Refreshments are available in a pleasant chintzy café-restaurant, and there is an up-market gift shop.

Open: daily 09.30–16.30hrs.

▶ ▷ ▷ **Weeks Air Museum**

14710 SW 128th Street

Out at Tamiami Airport, this is just the place to check out the history of flight pre-World War II. The Weeks is dedicated to the preservation and restoration of historic planes, and there are 35 on display including Mustangs, Pipers and baby Boeings, plus a wide variety of engines and propellers. There are good scale models, video booths and a gift shop.

Open: daily 10.00–17.00hrs.

Boat Tours, Rental and Charter

Bayside Cruises, Bayside Marketplace (tel: (305) 888 3002 or (800) 327 9600). There are 90-minute cruises on Biscayne Bay, daily departures year-round every two hours from 13.00–21.00hrs. Also half- or full-day deep-sea fishing charters for individuals and groups. Reservations required.

Club Nautico of Miami Beach, International Yacht Harbor, 300 Alton Road (tel: (305) 673 2502 or (800) NAUTICO). Full-, half-day and hourly powerboat rental at three Miami locations: Miami Beach, Coconut Grove and N Bayshore Drive (Downtown).

Easy Sailing, Dinner Key Marina, Coconut Grove (tel: (305) 858 4001 or (800) 780 4001). Sailboats and power-boats from 19 to 135ft. Sailing lessons available; on-board catering by request; deep-sea fishing charters.

Island Queen Sightseeing Tours, Bayside Marketplace (tel: (305) 379 5119). There are 90-minute narrated cruises featuring Millionaires' Row and cruise ships in the Port of Miami. Daily departures at 11.00, 14.00, 16.00 and 17.30hrs, and also 19.00hrs at weekends; disco cruises 21.30 and 23.30hrs. Luxury yachts for charter.

Nikko Gold Coast Cruises, Haulover Marina, 10800 Collins Avenue, Miami Beach (tel: (305) 945 5461). Year-round daily departures on a variety of cruises around the bay; also excursions to the Everglades and Fort Lauderdale.

Bus and Trolley Bus Tours

American Sightseeing Tours, 11077 NW 36th Avenue (tel: (305) 688 7700 ext 280 or (800) 367 5149). Good choice of half- and full-day city tours, including the Art Deco District, shopping and nightlife excursions. Reservations required.

Go America Tours, 17070 Collins Avenue, Miami Beach (tel: (305) 945 7036 or (800) 273 8680). Half- and full-day city attractions tours, plus trips to the Everglades and Florida Keys. Reservations required.

Old Town Trolley, a fun way to take in Miami's sights

Why not take a mini-cruise to the Bahamas for the ultimate day out. SeaEscape, 1080 Port Boulevard, Pier 6 (tel: (305) 379 0000 or (800) 327 2005), offer mini-cruises from one-day excursions to the Bahamas to a couple of hours 'to nowhere' around the bay. There are buffet meals, entertainments and full casino facilities to be enjoyed, and all at a bargain price.

Old Town Trolley of Miami, Bayside Marketplace (tel: (305) 374 8687). Based outside Bayside Marketplace, with pick-up points all along the route, this is a great way to see the sights and stop off at the attractions. The 90-minute **City Magic** tour covers all the main sights in Downtown, Coconut Grove and Coral Gables with departures every 30 minutes from 10.00 to 16.00hrs. A less frequent **Miami Beach** tour (also 90 minutes) departs every two hours between 10.45 and 16.45hrs. Ticket holders can get off at any stop along the route and rejoin a later service, but check the times of the last trolley and remember to collect a boarding pass from the driver.

Cycling and Motorcycling

Several neighbourhood districts of Miami are well suited to a gentle cycle ride, but do not set out without adequate protection from the sun, and remember to drink plenty. **Miami Beach Bicycle** is found at 923 W 39th Street (tel: (305) 531 4161). Pedal around the Art Deco District until it is time for a swim or an ice-cold drink in one of the trendy cafés along Ocean Drive.

Explore the parks and paths of Key Biscayne on two wheels from **Mangrove Bicycle**, 260 Crandon Boulevard (tel: (305) 361 5555); or wheel around Coconut Grove with a bike from **Dade Cycle**, 3216 Grand Avenue (tel: (305) 444 5997). For more adventurous types, there is a 14-mile bayside bike trail following Old Cutler Road around Biscayne Bay.

Homesick easyriders should hasten to **Tourwings of America**, 340 NE 183rd Street (tel: (305) 653 8868). Cruising and touring bikes are available for hire by the day, week or month; organised South Florida tours are bookable two months in advance.

One of the more unusual ways of getting around

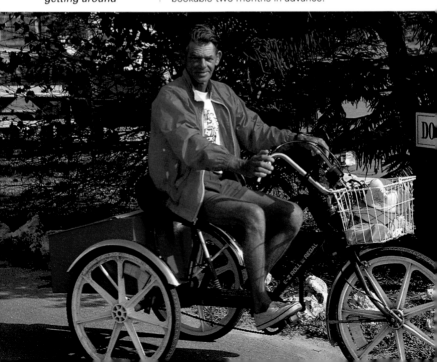

Driving Tours

Miami is so vast that visiting a handful of major sights can turn into a day trip. One scenic drive is the S Bayshore Drive–Main Highway–Old Cutler Road route around **Biscayne Bay** *en route* to the popular South Miami attractions near Homestead. **Miami Beach** is easily explored by car from the art deco delights along Ocean Drive to Bal Harbour, the ritzy hotels and beaches of upper Collins Avenue. The only way to get a real feel for **Coral Gables** is through a car tour; maps are available from the Coral Gables City Hall on Miracle Mile. Or drive through **Little Havana** on Calle Ocho (SW 8th Street).

Beyond the Greater Miami city limits, two superb National Park sites are an easy day trip away. **Biscayne National Park** (nine miles east of Homestead) is a 181,550-acre aquatic preserve with glass-bottomed boat and dive tours. Several gateways provide access to the famous **Everglades National Park** (see pages 90-1). The eastern entrance and park headquarters are 10 miles southwest of Homestead; the northern entrance at Shark Valley lies 25 miles west of downtown Miami via the Tamiami Trail (US41).

The **Gold Coast** begins just north of Miami with A1A providing a slow route along the coast and fast Interstate-95 thundering north–south a few miles inland. The yachts and shops of **Fort Lauderdale** can be reached in under an hour; and exclusive **West Palm Beach** is well worth a day's outing.

(For car rental information, see page 84.)

Rickshaw Tours

Majestic Rickshaw, Coconut Grove (tel: (305) 443 6571). A Coconut Grove night-time speciality: hail a bicycle rickshaw on Grand Avenue or Main Highway between 20.00 and 02.00hrs for a spin around the block, or take a moonlit flit along the bayshore.

Walking Tours

Art Deco Welcome Center, 661 Washington Avenue, Miami Beach (tel: (305) 672 2014). The Miami Design Preservation League's headquarters welcomes visitors to the famous Art Deco District. The 90-minute Saturday morning tours depart at 10.30hrs, or by request for groups; there is also a gift shop with books, maps, posters and souvenirs.

Dade Heritage Trust, 190 SE 12th Terrace (tel: (305) 358 9572). Based south of Downtown, the Trust is dedicated to the preservation of local historic properties. It organises cultural heritage events and offers tours – telephone for schedules.

Historical Museum of Southern Florida, 101 W Flagler Street (tel: (305) 375 1492). Tours galore from walking and cycling excursions to moonlit gourmet canoe trips balance fun with insight. Call for prices and schedules.

Beaches

■ **By the mid-1970s, Miami Beach was almost beachless. The twin actions of construction work on the island and erosion by the ocean had brought hotels and other buildings literally to the water's edge .....■**

The city called for the cavalry, and between 1977 and 1981, the US Army Corps of Engineers mounted a vast $51 million beach reconstruction operation dumping millions of tons of sand along the oceanshore to form a 300-foot-wide stretch of beach. From Sunny Isles in the north to South Pointe Park, the 10-mile strip is divided into a series of beaches each with its own character. Key Biscayne and its island neighbour, Virginia Key, offer a further four miles of beach space; there is Oleta River State Recreation Area north of the city, and the oceanfront Matheson Hammock Park in the south.

Miami Beach and North Miami

South Pointe Park Washington Avenue. Not the best beach, but there's good fishing and snorkelling from the 300-foot pier (beware of currents). There are also picnic areas with barbecues, footpaths, a vita course, a children's playground and a scenic view of the Port of Miami across the bay.

First Street Beach The hot spot of Miami's surfing culture, packed with bright young things on boards. A beach bar-restaurant pumps up the volume, and there is volleyball for voyeurs.

Lummus Park Sixth to 14th Streets. Sandwiched between the art deco delights of Ocean Drive and the not-very-deep-blue-sea. Windsurfing and deck chair rentals; refreshments; playground.

21st Street Beach Start of the two-mile **Miami Beach Boardwalk**, this is a favourite with the gay community, where topless Europeans are less likely to stand out. Unofficially, topless bathing is more or less tolerated between First Street Beach and Surfside. Refreshments; hunky lifeguards.

35th Street Beach Hemmed in by high-rise buildings, this little beach is relatively peaceful. Refreshments; good swimming.

46th Street Beach Overlooked by the monster Fontainebleau Hilton, the boardwalk ends here. A happy-go-lucky crowd of watersporters from Miami University make their presence felt; refreshments; excellent swimming.

Northshore State Recreation Area 79th to 87th Streets. A 40-acre oasis of subtropical vegetation and sandy shores, this offers picnic areas with barbecues, playground, one-mile bike trail, vita course, fishing and boat rental.

Surfside Beach 93rd Street. Quieter neighbour of Bal Harbour area beaches which fill up with wealthy northerners in the winter. Fine swimming.

Haulover Beach 10800 Collins Avenue. Often overlooked, but well worth the trip, Haulover combines beach, dunes and parkland with a full range of facilities including picnic areas, playground, walking trails, vita course, boat rental, tennis and golf.

Sunny Isles 163rd to 192nd Streets. Two miles of blustery beach with windsurfer, jet-ski and sailboat rentals. Fishing from the pier; refreshments.

Oleta River State Recreation Area 3400 NE 163rd Street. On the mainland, with good swimming from a man-made beach. There is also a 1.5-mile bike trail, canoeing, boating

and picnic facilities, plus a chance to see dolphins, manatees and land mammals.

Key Biscayne, Virginia Key and South Miami

Bill Baggs Cape Florida State Recreation Area Key Biscayne. On the southern tip of the island, this preserve has ocean beaches, a historic lighthouse, walking trails, windsurfer and bike hire, fishing on the bayside, picnic areas and refreshments (see also page 63).

Crandon Park 400 Crandon Boulevard. Parkland and beach at the northern end of Key Biscayne, with picnicking facilities, refreshments, playground, biking trails, vita course and boat rental. A great favourite with Cuban families on the weekend.

Hobie Beach Rickenbacker Causeway. Windsurfers and surfboaters skim across the bay

Running for the big one: surfing is the archetypal Florida sport

around the causeway, then rendezvous with their picnics on narrow, pine-fringed strips of sand along the roadside. You will find picnic tables, refreshments, and all manner of watersport equipment hire.

Virginia Key Beach At the bottom end of the island, running northeast from the causeway, this area has picnic facilities with barbecues, walking trails, plus a number of secluded coves edged by woodlands.

Matheson Hammock Park 9610 Old Cutler Road. A beautiful bayside beach in a country park south of Coral Gables. On offer are picnic tables, refreshments, a playground, walking trails among the mangroves, a vita course, fishing, boat rental from a little marina, golf and tennis.

Shopping

Shopping is big news in Miami, and big is definitely beautiful when it comes to the city's numerous shopping malls. Neighbourhood shopping is fun too, with a kaleidoscope array of fashion boutiques, small galleries and speciality stores designed to amuse and entertain passing browsers as well as serious spenders.

Miami's beach culture is reflected at every turn – itsy-bitsy teeny-weeny bikinis, colourful beach towels and oceans of tanning preparations are widely available. The subtropical surroundings have also spawned a flourishing business in Florida kitsch, with flamingo and palm tree motifs decorating everything from T-shirts and tableware to flashing flamingo Christmas tree lights.

Downtown going north Downtown's pride and joy is **Bayside Marketplace**, 401 Biscayne Boulevard (see also page 59). This 16-acre waterfront site combines shopping with live entertainment and international dining opportunities. The latest fashions and hottest sportswear rub price tags with great crafts and gift items. Look out for brightly coloured South American appliqué cotton jerseys, jewellery and leather items, as well as funky Floridian fantasies.

Part of the Omni hotel complex, **Omni International Mall**, 1601 Biscayne Boulevard, has been somewhat overtaken by Bayside. However, it still has a good range of 125 shops and restaurants, plus a wonderful gilt carousel which is a sure-fire hit with junior shoppers.

On the bargain trail, take a detour to the **Fashion District**, NW Fifth Avenue between 24th and 29th Streets, where cut-price designer clothes, accessories and locally made fashions are offered at factory outlet shops and discount stores. Another Downtown attraction is **Decorators' Row**, 40th Street between Miami Avenue and NE Second Avenue. Meanwhile, shoppers in North Miami can sample some 200 department stores and boutiques overflowing from the **Aventura Mall**, 19501 Biscayne Boulevard.

74

The Lincoln Road shopping area, one of Miami Beach's older malls

Miami Beach On Miami Beach, the Art Deco District is a shopper's delight. Trawl **5th Street** for microscopic swimwear, fun jewellery and cute little ceramic deco buildings to take home. A historic gem in its own right, **Espanola Way** features a clutch of alluring antiques stores and small galleries crammed with 1930s and 1940s furniture, furnishings and Streamline-style kitsch. For something more up to date, do not miss the **South Florida Art Center**, 800–1000 Lincoln Road Mall. It is a showcase for weird and wonderful contemporary sculpture, paintings and design, contrasted with a few antiques. Big spenders should head straight for **Bal Harbour**, 9700 Collins Avenue (see also page 58). A limo's length from Millionaires' Row, the darlings of European design along with America's top stores, including Florida's largest Neiman Marcus, cater to well-heeled residents and visitors alike in an elegantly landscaped setting. North Miami Beach is home to the three-level **Mall at 163rd Street**, 1421 NE 163rd Street, the world's first Teflon-coated indoor mall.

Coconut Grove Coconut Grove's metamorphosis from hippy to hip has made it a front runner for sunglasses capital of the world. These Florida essentials have been raised to an artform and a whole fleet of chic optical boutiques can be found anchored amid the fun atmosphere of the Grove.

Cascades of greenery, Mexican-tiled fountains, 60 up-market boutiques, restaurants and several smart late-night clubs inhabit exclusive **Mayfair-in-the-Grove**, 2911 Grand Avenue. A further galaxy of trendy nightspots, bars and café-restaurants are perched above two levels of boutiques at the Grove's latest 'in' place, **CocoWalk**, 3015 Grand Avenue. The clothes-conscious will find everything from Westernwear to lingerie posing on the shelves; there is a good book and map store too. **Main Highway**, the main street, is crammed with both everyday and outlandish fashions, poster and card shops, great T-shirts and amazing kids' stuff.

Another favourite shoppers' haunt is **Commodore Plaza**, which boasts some great galleries selling colourful South American and Haitian art, American Indian jewellery, ethnic furnishings and toys.

Coral Gables going south Between LeJeune and Douglas, **Miracle Mile** is the main shopping district in Coral Gables. This two-block stroll is lined with antique shops, galleries, boutiques and interior design emporiums. For something a little more affordable, head for the modernistic **Miracle Mile Center**, 3301 Coral Way.

South of Coral Gables, the **Dadeland Mall**, 7535 N Kendall Drive, is the largest mall in the southeast with five department stores, 175 shops and a well-stocked food court. Also in the Kendall area, **Falls Shopping Center**, 8888 Howard Drive, boasts Miami's only Bloomingdales, and a further 60 prestigious stores are set in tropical surroundings.

Not a traditional mall, but a good place to shop, **Cauley Square Village**, 22400 Old Dixie Highway at Goulds, offers cutesy crafts and curios in an attractively restored historic district.

Mobile stalls sell cheap and cheerful souvenirs

Food and Drink

Variety is the spice of life, and this is the only rule to keep in mind when dining out in Miami. Diverse cuisine from Argentinian to West Indian, via Brazilian, Cuban, French, Greek, Haitian, Spanish and Thai, is served up in an equally diverse spread of eateries. Fresh fruit and vegetables are produced locally; steak is trucked in from the ranches of Central Florida; fish and shellfish arrive fresh every day on the docks; and adventurous eaters can look out for exotic Florida specialities like alligator meat and Everglades frogs' legs.

Stop for a meal The gourmet's day begins with breakfast, normally served between 07.00 and 11.00hrs. It usually consists of a sticky glazed Danish pastry and sweet fruit muffins; a less sugary alternative is a bagel or buttered English muffin. Late breakfast at a café table on the sidewalk is a popular feature along Miami Beach's Ocean Drive and in Coconut Grove, where eggs Benedict and a plate of fresh fruit accompany a leisurely session with the morning paper.

Lunching has become a lost art in many North American cities, but Miami's Latin and European inhabitants have ensured that it remains an important feature of their day. Between 11.30 and 14.00hrs, power lunchers weigh up the menu in Downtown haunts like the **Oak Room**, while the snacking population grabs a double-decker bus-size Cuban sandwich piled high with ham, pork and cheese. Snacking is big in Miami – everywhere there are concession stalls, juice bars, delis and healthfood shops. Cubans eat late, but dinner is a running buffet in Miami, which starts with cut-price 'early bird' saver menus at 17.00hrs, and lasts until the Latin restaurants and late-night cafés switch off the stove at around 24.00 or 01.00hrs – though most dining spots do not take orders after 22.00hrs. However, there are several 24-hour chain diners, usually found near busy truck routes such as US1.

Choosing where to eat This is almost as confusing as choosing what to eat. Perhaps the first consideration is price, and fortunately Miami is well supplied with restaurants, bistros and cafés in every price range.

Some of the best value dining is found in the neighbourhood shopping malls, where a choice of restaurants is augmented by a good range of bargain-priced fast food concessions. These are ideal for families, and dishes from several different serveries can be eaten in the seating areas provided; alcohol can be bought at the bar and taken to the table. Cafeterias, coffee shops and fast food restaurant chains extend their hospitality with 'bottomless' cups of coffee, and over-generous portions which often necessitate the use of a doggie bag, produced as a matter of course by the waitress. For fast service sit at the bar, or to eat elsewhere order a 'take out'.

Eating Cuban Inexpensive Cuban cuisine is one of the highlights of dining Miami-style. Throughout the day, Cuban sandwiches and thick, sweet thimbles of *café Cubano* keep the world going round; another delicious treat is *fritas,* spicy mini-hamburgers with minced pork,

There's no need to waste a lot of time over a meal

Bayside bar in Miami

garlic and paprika added to the traditional beef. For an early evening snack, experiment with *tapas*; there are several bars and restaurant lounges on Little Havana's Calle Ocho (SW 8th Street) where they will make up a mixed platter of the savoury specialities for novice *tapas* enthusiasts to try. There is plenty of time to taste everything – dining rooms in the Latin quarter do not fill up until around 22.00hrs.

Menus usually carry English-language descriptions of the various dishes, and favourites include: *sopa de frijoles negros*, traditional black bean soup; *arroz con pollo*, roast chicken with saffron rice; *arroz con camarones*, rice with shrimps; *piccadillo*, spicy minced meat with pimento, olives and raisins; and *palomilla*, thin Cuban steaks. *Tostones*, fried green plantain, or *platanos*, ripe plantains, are popular accompaniments.

Top of the scale Sunset in Miami is thoughtfully accompanied by Happy Hour, which brings some of the most expensive views in town within reach of most pockets between 17.30 and 19.30hrs. Miami is casual, but many up-market establishments do not permit blue jeans and request a jacket and tie.

For a special meal, Coral Gables is considered the city's gastronomic centre with a raft of exclusive restaurants; while some of Miami's top hotels boast elegant dining rooms. Perhaps an art deco treasure like the **Café des Arts** on Ocean Drive would fulfil your romantic dream; or candlelight and a violin serenade at the Grove's affordable **Trattoria Pampered Chef**. Foodies should look out for 'New World' cuisine, the latest taste sensation, which weds aspects of Mediterranean, Hispanic and Caribbean cuisines with local produce, creating a feast of unusual but delicious combinations.

No mistaking what this bar is selling

As the sun sets behind the Downtown skyline, Miami prepares for another night on the town, while cocktail shakers and conductors' batons set the pace. Miami's major performing arts venues are in the Downtown district, with outposts in Miami Beach and Coconut Grove; the Beach and the Grove (as they are known to *aficionados*) are also the main nightspots.

When it was first switched on in the 1930s, Miami Beach's art deco neon lighting knocked the socks off locals and northern visitors alike. After dark, Ocean Drive is still an electrifying sight. For real magic do not miss: The Crescent, 1420 Ocean; The McAlpin, 1424 Ocean; and The Fairmont, 1000 Collins. The Waldorf Towers, 860 Ocean, has a pseudo lighthouse; and the nearby Breakwater sports an impressive ship's prow.

78

Cocktails, clubs, comedy and discothèques Starting in Coconut Grove, **Regine's**, Grand Bay Hotel, 2669 S Bayshore Drive (tel: (305) 858 9500), is an old favourite with spectacular bay views and a sophisticated Euro-set following, and **Stringfellows**, Mayfair-in-the-Grove, 3390 Mary Street (tel: (305) 446 7555), caters to a similar crowd in a glamorous state-of-the-art nightclub. **Monty Trainor's**, 2560 S Bayshore Drive (tel: (305) 858 1431), is casual with good live music and waterfront views, while there is live music, reggae, calypso and great people-watching at the **Zanzibar**, 3468 Main Highway (tel: (305) 444 0244). For a friendly neighbourhood bar with an eclectic jukebox and sports on TV, try the **Tavern in the Grove**, 3416 Main Highway (tel: (305) 447 3884). **Improv at Coconut Grove**, CocoWalk, 3015 Grand Avenue (tel: (305) 441 8200), offers an impressive comedy showcase bill, as does **Coconuts Comedy Club**, Peacock Café, 2977 MacFarlane Road (tel: (305) 446 CLUB).

Downtown after dark tends to be a little more refined, though not in the case of **Coco Loco's**, Sheraton Brickell Point, 495 Brickell Avenue (tel: (305) 373 6000), where the disco terrace bumps and grinds to Top 40 and Latin sounds. The **Oak Room**, Hotel Inter-Continental, 100 Chopin Plaza (tel: (305) 577 1000), is more typical, with jazz and a piano bar in clubby English-style surroundings. **Tobacco Road**, 626 S Miami Avenue (tel: (305) 374 1198), has a great reputation for live R&B.

Bathed in neon, celebrities and surfies stalk the sidewalk cafés, hole-in-the-wall clubs and power discos of Miami Beach's fashionable Art Deco District. **Penrod's Beach Club**, 1 Ocean Drive (tel: (305) 538 1111), is a surfie-beach-party hang-out with Top 40 and rock 'n' roll; art deco-style **Luke's Miami Beach**, 1045 5th Street (tel: (305) 531 0464), has three stages featuring jazz and disco. **Fifth Street International Club**, 429 Lenox Avenue (tel: (305) 531 1910), induces disco fever with Progressive and reggae nights, but if you want to stay cool in the pool, listen to live R&B and jazz at **Tropics International**, 960 Ocean Drive (tel: (305) 531 5335). There is more jazz as well as special events at the **Music Room**, 804 Ocean Drive (tel: (305) 531 0392), a New York-style speakeasy. **Club Nu**, 245 22nd Street (tel: (305) 672 0068), is the Beach's ever-fashionable celebrity nightspot; while **Club Tropigala**, Fontainebleau Hotel, 4441 Collins Avenue (tel: (305) 672 SHOW) stages exotic dinner shows and revues in lavish surroundings.

Classical music Responsible for luring world-class artists to the city, the Concert Association of Florida, 555 17th Street, Miami Beach (tel: (305) 535 3491), hosts the annual **Prestige Series of Concerts** at the **Dade**

Live music is easy to find in Miami after the sun goes down

Dale County Auditorium offers a programme of opera during the winter months

County Auditorium, 2901 W Flagler Street (tel: (305) 854 7890). The auditorium is also home to the **Greater Miami Opera**, one of the largest permanent companies in the US. Two orchestras are based at the Gusman Center for the Performing Arts, 174 E Flagler: the **Florida Philharmonic Orchestra** (tel: (800) 226 1812) hosts a full October to May season of classical music, pops and children's programmes; and the gifted young musicians of Michael Tilson Thomas's **New World Symphony** (tel: (305) 673 3331) offer a broad repertoire of classical and contemporary works.

Dance Former principal dancer Edward Villella directs the **Miami City Ballet**, Dade County Auditorium, 2901 W Flagler Street (tel: (305) 532 4880), in a highly acclaimed programme of classical and contemporary choreography. And as evidence of Miami's multicultural society, flamenco flourishes at the **Ballet Flamenco la Rosa**, 1008 Lincoln Road, Miami Beach (tel: (305) 672 0552).

Film Each February the **Miami Film Festival**, 444 Brickell Avenue (tel: (305) 377 3456), hits town with an eight-day extravaganza featuring the latest homegrown and international screenings, all on show at the Gusman Center for the Performing Arts.

Theatre National and regional premières, experimental productions, comedy and musical reviews are the stock in trade of the excellent **Coconut Grove Playhouse**, 3500 Main Highway (tel: (305) 442 4000). The **Greater Miami Broadway Series**, Jackie Gleason Theater of the Performing Arts, 1700 Washington Avenue, Miami Beach (tel: (305) 673 8300), features touring productions of hit Broadway shows. Also, the University of Miami's drama department stages four productions a year at the **Ring Theater**, 1380 Miller Drive, Coral Gables (tel: (305) 284 3355).

Accommodation

Beachfront luxury or beachfront bargain, accommodation in Miami comes in all shapes and sizes. The city boasts some 53,000 guest rooms in an impressive variety of hotels, motels, inns and spas. Luxurious world-class resorts can offer a full range of recreational activities, five-star dining and spectacular views, while even the humblest motel generally provides air-conditioning, TV, telephone and a pool.

Most visitors are here for the sunshine, and sunshine means the beach, so – not suprisingly – Miami Beach is where most of the city's hotels are found. Exclusive neighbourhoods like Coral Gables, Key Biscayne, and lively Coconut Grove also have their share of up-market accommodation, as does Downtown, which features several spectacular modern hotel complexes aimed at the corporate sector with prices pitched correspondingly high.

Miami's peak season lasts from 15 December to Easter. Christmas and Easter are very busy, and even in summer it can be difficult to find a room over the Independence Day (4 July) celebrations, and Labor Day weekend (beginning of September). A Greater Miami area resort tax of five per cent is added to hotel bills, and there is an additional six per cent sales tax.

Keeping down the cost Miami Beach offers the greatest choice of accommodation both in style and price range. The central, and most expensive, section of the Beach — from Lincoln Road to Surfside and Bal Harbour – is known as 'Hotel Row'. Further north, the Sunny Isles beaches front 'Motel Row', where prices are more reasonable and considerable discounts can be found during the summer season. Motel rates can drop by up to 50 per cent between May and December, though the increase in summer visitors from Europe and South America is changing this.

South of Hotel Row, the newly restored and increasingly popular Art Deco District offers some real gems, with moderate prices but less of a seasonal price swing. For real budget travellers, Miami's only youth hostel is located here in the Clay Hotel, 1438 Washington Avenue, Miami Beach (tel: (305) 534 2988).

Bed and breakfast accommodation is in short supply in the Miami area, but for a list of what is available from Coconut Grove to private homes in the more distant reaches of Dade County, contact: **Bed and Breakfast Accommodations**, PO Box 262, South Miami, FL33243 (tel: (305) 661 3270).

There are several money-saving tips to bear in mind when choosing accommodation: the view, for example, can make a considerable difference to the bill. Beachfront vistas, and even a side view of the ocean, may add as much as 25 to 50 per cent to the price of a room.

Many hotels and motels make no charge for children under 18 sharing a room with their parents, and the excellent range of suite or apartment hotels offering a separate bedroom and living area makes this an ideal cost-cutting arrangement. Ask about **family plans**; a minimum stay may be required.

Self-catering accommodation, both rooms and suites,

Miami Beach's art deco hotels are stylish places to stay

*Stay at an Ocean
Drive hotel for fine
sea views*

are known as **efficiencies**, and generally provide a range of sleeping arrangements, bathroom, fridge and cooking facilities (often a microwave). When booking accommodation, always inform the hotel of your estimated time of arrival. After 17.00hrs, room reservations will be cancelled if the hotel is not warned. Check-out is normally 11.00hrs.

Luxury and style If cost is no object, several of Miami's finest hotels deserve a special mention. Half a mile of Miami Beach's golden shoreline is overlooked by the sweeping façade of the deluxe **Fontainebleau Hilton Resort and Spa**, a 1950s monument and a favourite with visiting personalities. Across the way, the **Eden Roc Americana** features a scrumptiously re-created New York deli among the marble and chandeliers; while the **Doral Ocean Beach Hotel** boasts a superbly equipped AquaSport Center and free transport to the country club facilities of its sister establishment, the equally fabulous **Doral Resort and Spa**.

*One of the restored
Art Deco District
hotels*

Art deco delights include the **Cardozo**, **Essex House**, and **Park Central**. In Coconut Grove, operatic tenor Luciano Pavarotti's split-level suite, complete with baby grand piano, is available at the **Grand Bay Hotel** when the maestro is out of town; or survey the bay from the rooftop pool at the all-suite **Mayfair House Hotel**.

A Coral Gables landmark, George Merrick's recently refurbished **Biltmore Hotel** may reopen; or there is the supremely elegant **Hotel Place St Michel**, also built in the 1920s. Key Biscayne's jewels are the sporty 300-room **Sonesta Beach Hotel and Tennis Club**, and the **Sheraton Royal Biscayne Beach Resort & Racquet Club**, which has a list of facilities as impressive as its name suggests. Without doubt, Downtown's finest is the towering, ultra-deluxe **Omni International**.

■ **Miami is sports-mad. From surf to stadium, the city's sporting calendar is packed with local and world-class events. There are plenty of opportunities for golfers, joggers, horseback riders, tennis players and watersports fanatics to follow their chosen hobbies every day of the year .....■**

There is even a 24-hour sports hotline which updates the news and scores every 10 minutes (tel: (305) 976 3300).

Fishing Casting a line into the ocean or Biscayne Bay is a favourite form of relaxation among the locals, and there are any number of causeways and bridges with catwalks and official fishing piers to make life easier. Sea fishermen should note, however, that they will need a saltwater fishing licence. Popular spots are **Bill Baggs State Recreation Area** on Key Biscayne, **Haulover Beach Park** and **Sunny Isles** on Miami Beach.

Golf The Greater Miami Convention and Visitors' Bureau publishes the *Golf is Greater in Miami* list of around 30 public and private courses in the area. There is a variety of nine- and 18-hole courses operating year-round; green fees vary, and advance reservations are recommended in winter. **Key Biscayne Golf Course**, 6700 Crandon Boulevard (tel: (305) 361 9129) is rated one of Florida's best public courses. Golfers can also test their skills on the famed 'Blue Monster' at the exclusive **Doral Resort and Country Club**, 4400 NW 87th Avenue (tel: (305) 594 0954), which hosts the Professional Golf Association's (PGA) Doral Ryder Open each spring.

Horseback riding About 12 miles west of Downtown is a small enclave of stud farms which breed Arabs, Apaloosas and Pasofinos, and there are several riding stables. Call in advance: **Jimaguas Ranch**, 12201 SW 80th Street (tel: (305) 271 4289); **North Forty Farm**, 12201 SW 45th Street (tel: (305) 227 1859); or **Santa Barbara Ranch**, 12450 SW 72nd Street (tel: (305) 596 0704).

Jogging Bayside parks are plentiful and popular, and many offer a vita course as well as scenic jogging trails. Favourites include: **Haulover Beach Park**, 10800 Collins Avenue, Miami Beach; **Crandon Park**, 4000 Crandon Boulevard, Key Biscayne; **Matheson Hammock Park**, 9610 Old Cutler Road, south of Coral Gables; and Downtown's **Bayfront Park** on Biscayne Boulevard.

Spectator sports The game that Miami has made its own is *jai-alai* (pronounced hi-li). Devised by teams of Spanish Basques three centuries ago, the world's fastest game was introduced to Miami via Cuba. The *pelota* (ball) is propelled at speeds of up to 175mph with the aid of *cestas* (curved wicker slings) attached to

Horse-racing takes place at Hialeah Race Track, Gulfstream Park Race Track and Calder Race Course in Miami

players' hands, and the betting is as furious as the play at **Miami Jai-Alai**, 3500 NW 37th Avenue (tel: (305) 633 6400).

More traditional, but no less exciting, National Football League challengers, the Miami Dolphins pack **Joe Robbie Stadium** (JRS), 2269 NW 199th Street (tel: (305) 620 5000), during the September to December season; and hot new basketball team Miami Heat fight it out at the **Miami Arena**, 721 NW 1st Avenue (tel: (305) 577 HEAT), from September until April. There is horse-racing at **Hialeah Park**, E 2nd Avenue and 32nd Street (tel: (305) 885 8000); **Calder Race Course**, 21001 NW 27th Avenue (tel: (305) 625 1311); and **Gulfstream Park**, US1 and Hallandale Beach Boulevard (tel: (305) 944 1242); and greyhound racing at **Biscayne Kennel Club**, 320 NW 115th Street (tel: (305) 754 3484); or **Flagler Kennel Club**, 401 NW 38th Court (tel: (305) 649 3000). Speed merchants should not miss the **Miami Grand Prix**, which screams around the Downtown streets each spring.

Watersports The **Rickenbacker Causeway** on Virginia Key is the watersports focus of Miami. Enthusiasts can waterski, rent windsurfers, surfboats and jet-skis along this narrow strip of sand. Surfing is a Miami Beach speciality, with the biggest waves around **Haulover Beach** and **South Pointe**; there is also windsurfer rental at various locations along the Beach.

Resort hotels offer watersports facilities; one of the best is the AquaSport Center at **Doral Ocean Beach Resort**, 4833 Collins Avenue (tel: (305) 532 3600). Scuba-diving and snorkelling excursions, equipment hire and instruction can be arranged by **R J Diving Ventures**, 15560 NE 5th Avenue, Miami Beach (tel: (305) 940 1182); and **Diver's Paradise**, 4000 Crandon Boulevard, Key Biscayne (tel: (305) 361 3483). For swimming, see **Beaches**, pages 72–3.

The Orange Bowl, Miami's home of sport and centre of activities during the Orange Bowl Festival

Summer diving is ideal in the seas off Miami

Practical Points

Airport and transfer Miami International Airport is located eight miles west of Downtown. Overseas flights arrive at the International Satellite Building which is linked to the main terminal by an automated shuttle. A currency exchange, 24-hour information desk, duty-free shops, luggage lockers, restaurant and snack bar facilities are located on the upper level.

Taxi and shuttle bus ground transportation is available from the lower level concourse. The 15- to 20-minute taxi ride to Downtown costs $12 to $15; south Miami Beach (14 miles) takes 25 minutes, and costs around $25; northern Miami Beach costs $25 to $30. Reasonably priced 24-hour **SuperShuttle** buses run door-to-door services to all destinations within the Greater Miami area every 15 to 20 minutes with fares costing $5 to $18 (for reservations, tel: (305) 871 2000).

Car rental Miami's car rental agencies are based out near the airport, and offer free shuttle bus transportation from the terminal to the parking lots. Rates are very reasonable in Miami; advance reservations are advisable in winter, and be prepared to queue if several international flights have just arrived. For further details, see **Travel Facts**, page 264.

Crime Miami is no better and probably no worse than most large cities. Areas to avoid are Overtown and Liberty City, but the best advice is to be alert. Do not walk along dark, unpopulated streets at night; lock car doors when travelling; ask for directions at public places, such as gas stations, and not from passers-by; keep cash in a moneybelt; and if you are attacked, do not resist. Cocaine and crack are *not* for sale in the hotel lobby.

Getting around As already mentioned, car rental is cheap, but Miami also has a very good public transport system.

By car Miami's attractions are spread out over a large area, so a car makes good sense. The city is laid out on the grid system with four quadrants (NW, NE, SW and SE) divided by Miami Avenue and Flagler Street. Numbered avenues run north to south, and streets run across from east to west. There is a network of expressways which make travelling from one side of town to the other, or even around it, fast and direct. Note, however, that Downtown parking is in short supply.

In Coral Gables, all the streets have names and it is very difficult to get around without a map (from the City Hall, on Miracle Mile). Hialeah has its own grid. Parking is impossible or expensive Downtown, but metered parking is widely available elsewhere.

By public transport Over 25,000 people use Metro-Dade County's public transport system every day. The elevated **Metromover** (or 'People Mover') circuit serves a 26-block area of the Downtown district. Fully automated cars operate every 90 seconds daily between 06.00 and 24.00hrs, and connect with Metrorail at Government Center station. **Metrorail** has 21 stops on its 20-mile journey from South Dade to Hialeah. Trains run every 15 minutes (eight minutes at peak times) daily between

Policeman on the beat on Miami's streets

06.00 and 24.00hrs. **Metrobus** operates 65 routes around the city and suburbs daily from 04.30 to 02.15hrs; Miami's commuters use the peak-hour **Tri-Rail** service. For information on all services, tel: (305) 638 6700 (06.00–23.00hrs).

By taxi Not cheap, but often necessary for non-drivers, Miami's taxis do not cruise the streets looking for fares. Allow time to call one of the following:
Central Cab Service, tel: (305) 534 0694
Diamond Cab Company, tel: (305) 545 7575
Metro Taxi, tel: (305) 888 8888
Yellow Cab Company, tel: (305) 444 4444

Hotel reservations The Central Reservations Service, 7001 SW 97th Avenue, Suite 205, Kendall (tel: (305) 274 6832 or (800) 950 0232) provides a free 24-hour reservation service for all hotels in the Greater Miami area.

Media There are two daily papers printed in Greater Miami, the *Miami Herald* and its Spanish-language edition *El Miami Herald*, plus another major Hispanic paper, *Diario Las Americas*. Other national dailies are available at news-stands and from vending machines. The monthly *Miami/South Florida* features a listings section.

Tourist information The Greater Miami Convention and Visitors Bureau, 701 Brickell Avenue, Suite 2700, Miami FL33131 (tel: (305) 539 3000 or (800) 283 2707), publishes *Destination Miami*, an excellent brochure with useful information on sights and services within the area. Individual districts also have their own Chambers of Commerce (listed in the telephone directory) which can supply maps and information.

Metromover, Downtown's light-rail mass-transit system, the easiest way of getting around this part of town

THE KEYS AND EVERGLADES

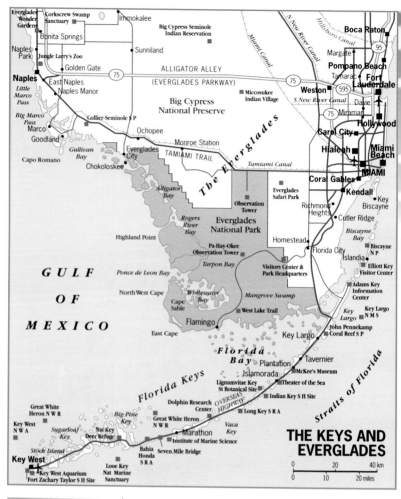

THE KEYS AND
EVERGLADES

| 0 | | 20 | | 40 km |
| 0 | 10 | | 20 miles | |

A useful tip on driving in the Florida Keys: the Overseas Highway (US1) is the only road route between Key Largo and Key West. Some sections of the drive are single lane in each direction, and speed limits (maximum 55mph) quite rigorously enforced. It is best to leave aside a whole day to make the trip with stops along the way (non-stop around two and a half hrs). Traffic at weekends and holiday times can be a bumper-to-bumper nightmare.

An hour's drive south of Miami, the Florida Keys angle off the peninsula in a spectacular chain of islands set in shimmering blue-green seas. This is the American Caribbean, where brilliantly-coloured tropical birds and plants flit and flourish along the roadside, exotic fish dart about the only living coral reef in the continental US, and tourism is the name of the game.

Indians were the islands' first inhabitants, until the fierce Calusas were replaced by equally inhospitable pirates and wreckers. Key West was a notorious haunt of nautical lowlife until the US Navy cleaned it up in 1821. A miraculous feat of early 20th-century engineering, Henry Flagler's 'Railroad to the Sea' reached Key West in 1912, only to be destroyed by a hurricane in 1935. It was replaced by the Overseas Highway (US1), which earns its name from the 42 bridges – including the famous **Seven Mile Bridge** – that carry traffic down the 113-mile roadlink from Key Largo to Key West. **Key Largo** is the largest of the 31 islands, synonymous with Bogart, Bacall and hurricanes, where two superb marine parks

THE KEYS AND EVERGLADES

87

offer excellent diving opportunities and glassbottomed boat trips. **Islamorada** is the 'Sport Fishing Capital of the World'; **Marathon**, the hub of the Middle Keys; and laid-back **Key West** marks the end of the line, just 90 miles north of Havana, Cuba. Places within the Keys section are located using the Mile Markers (MM) which begin at Mile Marker 126, just south of Florida City, and finish in Key West.

Florida City is also a jumping off point between the nation's largest aquatic park, **Biscayne National Park**, stretching out into the Atlantic, and the main entrance to the **Everglades National Park**, above Florida Bay. On the Atlantic side, manatees, sea turtles, snorkellers and divers are frequent visitors to the shallow coastal waters of Biscayne Bay. To the west, the Everglades has been designated a World Heritage Site. Both are an easy day trip from Miami, though nature lovers will probably want to spend more time here. There are accommodations and camping facilities in the Everglades National Park, at Florida City and in Homestead.

Big Cypress National Preserve

Oasis Ranger Station, Tamiami Trail (US41 east of Monroe Station)

Big Cypress extends to the north of the Everglades National Park in a 2,400-square-mile wedge of wet and dry prairie, marshlands, slash pine and hardwood hammocks. It is about one-third covered with cypress trees, deciduous conifers which can tolerate standing in water for long periods of time. Bald cypresses can grow to heights of over 100 feet; the more common dwarf variety rarely tops four feet. Big Cypress is a favourite home for alligators, bobcats, deer, rare black bears and a few remaining Florida panthers. Spectacular bird life includes the Everglades kite which feeds exclusively off apple snails found in the preserve.

The main drainage swamp southwest of Big Cypress is **Fakahatchee Strand**, which is a separate State Preserve area. It contains the largest stand of native royal palms in North America, and a rare concentration and variety of epiphytic orchids.

Just west of Copeland on SR29, **Jane's Memorial Scenic Drive** is a 20-mile dead-end excursion into the backwoods, where a boardwalk gives access to an impressive virgin cypress stand. Unusual wildlife in this region includes the mangrove fox squirrel and Everglades mink.

Road access is provided by the testing **Loop Road** (CR94) from Forty Mile Bend (just west of Shark Valley) to Monroe Station, which is paved for 13 miles of its 24-mile route. There is also **Turner River Road** (CR839), a graded dirt track running due north to Alligator Alley (but note: rented-car drivers are not insured here); and hiking trails from the Oasis Ranger Station.

Big Cypress National Preserve, a contemplative view

▶▶▶ **Biscayne National Underwater Park**

Convoy Point, SW 328th Street (9 miles east of Homestead)

The park boundaries encompass some 181,500 acres of Biscayne Bay of which 96 per cent is under water. The remaining four per cent represents an 18-mile chain of 44 keys hemmed in by tangled mangroves and surrounded by dazzling azure sea.

Brackish water trapped in the mangrove roots plays host to an enormous variety of life. Just offshore, live coral reefs teem with a kaleidoscope array of creatures in waters from 10 to 60 feet deep. Hundreds of species of fish, sponges and soft corals thrive in Biscayne Bay, and manatees frequent the warm shallows. Fishing is exceptional, with snapper, snook and barracuda among the most common varieties of catch.

The mainland Visitor Center is at Convoy Point, and ranger stations are located on Elliot Key and Adams Key. Self-guided walks on the keys include a boardwalk and short nature trail one-third of a mile east of the Elliot Key Visitor Center. An old road runs the length of the island (7 miles), and rangers lead hiking programmes during the winter months. Most of the park is only accessible by boat. Boat launches are found at Homestead Bayfront Marina, and at Black Point Marina. Elliot Key has a 66-berth harbour, and there are anchorages off the keys. Canoe rentals are available at Convoy Point: this is an ideal way to explore and birdwatch along the mainland mangrove shoreline.

Elkhorn Reef is a good site for inexperienced snorkellers; other popular sites include **Schooner Wreck Reef** and **Star Coral Reef**. Daily three-hour glassbottomed boat tours, four-hour scuba and snorkelling trips to the reefs and Sunday afternoon jaunts to Elliott Key can be reserved through **Biscayne Aqua-Center** (tel: (305) 247 2400), who will also arrange equipment rental for independent divers.

Park open: 08.00hrs–dusk.

Park headquarters information: tel: (305) 247 2044 (PARK).

Visitors to Florida's wet wilderness areas are confined to boardwalks

▶ ▶ ▶ **Everglades National Park**
The Everglades region starts at Lake Okeechobee, where a freshwater river six inches deep and 50 miles wide begins to creep seaward, but the national park preserve (1.4 million acres) only commences below the Tamiami Trail (US41), extending south to the tip of the peninsula, and west to the Gulf of Mexico. The best time to visit is the winter dry season when low water levels make wildlife spotting easier as animals and birds concentrate around the deeper pools and sloughs for food. In spring, temperatures rise uncomfortably and during the summer wet season, as water levels rise, wildlife ranges further afield, and blood-thirsty clouds of mosquitoes descend. West of Homestead, is the most popular access point, with the main Visitor Center. Walking trails off the road between here and Flamingo on Florida Bay explore six different ecosystems which contribute to the overall Everglades habitat – the Anhinga and Gumbo Limbo Trails are favourites. Follow the trails with an experienced guide.

Tram tours depart daily from the northern **Shark Valley** entrance on a 15-mile circuit which is also open to hikers and bikers. To the west, the **Gulf Coast Ranger Station** provides back country camping permits and access to the Ten Thousand Islands.

Entrances and Information Centers
Main Entrance Park Headquarters Information Center (tel: (305) 247 6211), 10 miles southwest of Florida City and Homestead via SR9336. The Center presents a 15-minute introductory film on the ecology of the park at regular intervals. Free information brochures, and park activity schedules including details of boat tours, guided walks, canoe rentals. Within the park, the **Royal Palm Interpretive Center** is the start point for several ranger guided walks, and **Flamingo Visitor Center** provides information on accommodations, camping, sightseeing cruises, charter fishing boats and bicycle rentals.

Vista of Everglades wetlands

Open: Information Center daily 08.00–17.00hrs; Park 24hrs. Admission ticket valid for one week.

Northern Entrance/Shark Valley Information Center, (tel: (305) 221 8776), 35 miles west of downtown Miami via Tamiami Trail (US41). Tram tour departures (reservations recommended December to March (tel: (305) 221 8455), nature trail, and bicycle rental.

Open: daily 08.30–18.00hrs.

Western Entrance/Gulf Coast Ranger Station, (tel: (813) 695 3311). Near Everglades City; 80 miles west of Miami on CR29 via Tamiami Trail (US41). Marine and shore life displays, maps, information on boat tours and canoe rentals.

Open: daily in winter 08.00–17.00hrs; reduced hours in summer.

General Information

Accommodation 102 rooms and 24 cottages in **Flamingo Lodge**, Box 428, Flamingo, FL33030 (tel: (305) 253 2241).

Boating Excellent on Florida Bay, and in the Ten Thousand Islands; canoe trails around Flamingo and Everglades City. Boat and canoe hire from the **Flamingo Marina** (tel: (305) 253 2241); and **Sammy Hamilton**, Everglades City (tel: (813) 695 2591 or (800) 445 7724).

Camping Official campsites are available at Flamingo, Long Pine Key and Everglades City. Permits must be obtained from ranger stations for overnight stays in the 48 back country sites.

A mangrove, the only tree that can extract fresh water from salt and thus flourish along the coast

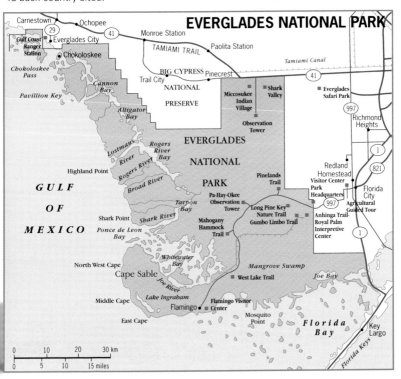

EVERGLADES NATIONAL PARK

Everglades Ecology

A month before the Everglades National Park was dedicated by President Truman in December 1947, 'writing woman' Marjorie Stoneman Douglas published *The Everglades: River of Grass*. With a single phrase she transformed many people's understanding of the Everglades from pestilential swamp to a living entity with a vital role to play in the ecology of southern Florida. A founding member of the Friends of the Everglades campaign in 1969, she became a leading lobbyist in the conservation field during her 80s and 90s, and still lives in Miami's Coconut Grove.

Native Americans called the region *Pa-Hay Okee*, 'grassy waters'; it is an apt description. Vast and mysterious, a carpet of waterlogged saw grass punctuated by cypress swamps and hardwood hammocks, the Everglades stretch to the horizon criss-crossed by secretive waterways. Before 1842, this was virgin territory, and until the 1970s most settlers saw it as a challenge to be overcome, tamed, drained and reclaimed into 'useful' land. But the Everglades already had their uses. The region was a perfectly balanced ecosystem, and its unique habitat supported myriad species of native flora, land fauna and aquatic creatures which relied upon it for their existence.

The Everglades' subtropical climate is the key to its success. There are two distinct seasons: the summer rains, followed by the winter dry period, and this ancient pattern of deluge and drought is essential to the well-being of the entire region, not just the Everglades themselves.

The dry season The shorter days of October and November herald the start of the dry season in southern Florida. As the waters recede animals and birds are forced to congregate and feed around the remaining deepwater sloughs (large pools). This is the mating season, but if water levels are too low, and there is insufficient food, mating will not occur.

The rainy season When the rains begin in May and June, the withered brown sawgrass pushes up new shoots, algae and plankton flourish around its roots, mosquito larvae, tadpoles and small fish start filling out the lower end of the food chain, and animals and birds disperse from dry season refuges to rear their young. Water is the Everglades' lifeblood. The summer downpours bring 60 inches of rain during an average year, and as Lake Okeechobee overflows and the prairies flood the water starts to move imperceptibly towards the sea. It flows at a rate of around half-a-mile a day, and in the course of its journey it will gradually drop some 15 feet before the invisible 50-mile-wide river discharges into Florida Bay.

Disappearing water But the river's progress is no longer natural, nor assured. The completion of the Tamiami Trail in 1928 allowed lumber barons to log the Everglades' cypress hammocks; they were followed in the 1940s by oil explorers. Ranchers to the north drained tracts of wet prairie for pasture, and contractors along

the East Coast have reclaimed vast acreages of land for housing and industrial development. Irrigation channels for agricultural projects, chemical pollution and the heavy demand for fresh water from cities such as Miami have blocked the free flow of water, and although the authorities have recognised the need to supply the Everglades with water in order for them to survive, they pay scant attention to the natural cycle. Releasing excess water in the dry season does little to alleviate the problem; whereas a significant proportion of the wet season floodwaters will evaporate and clouds of moisture from the Everglades will release their contents further north where the rain is needed.

Wildlife in peril Another pressing reason to preserve the Everglades is its treasury of plant and animal life. Some 2,000 diverse plant species, some 45 of which are found nowhere else in the world, rely on the sunlight and rainfall of southern Florida. The dazzling flocks of snowy egrets and pink-feathered roseate spoonbills recorded by celebrated naturalist painter John James Audubon in 1832 have dwindled to just a handful of birds (flamingos have sadly vanished from Florida's waters, so any large pink-plumaged bird seen will be a roseate spoonbill). Wood storks, herons, bald eagles and ospreys; the Everglades mink, Florida panther, manatees, American crocodiles and green sea turtles are also threatened. They will disappear forever should short-sighted politicians and developers continue to 'tame' the Everglades.

Boats for touring the Everglades

At least 10 times a year, the 'Sport Fishing Capital of the World' puts money where its mouth is in the form of fishing tournaments. Starting with January's Presidential Sailfish Tournament, hardly a month goes by without a chance for deep-sea fishermen to test their skills against other sportsmen as well as tarpon, marlin, permit, bonefish, and sailfish. For information, contact: Florida Keys Fishing Tournaments, PO Box 435, Summerland Key, FL 33042 (tel: 800-54 FISH 91).

 Islamorada

Named islas moradas (purple isles) by the Spanish, Islamorada is a collection of pine-fringed islands including Windley and Upper and Lower Matecumbe Keys. Rumour has it that early explorers found here great concentrations of Janthina janthina, a violet sea snail – hence the 'purple'. Others reckon it came from the beautiful orchid trees. Today, Islamorada is chiefly known as the Sport Fishing Capital of the World.

Indian Key Historic Site and San Pedro Underwater Archaeological Preserve, *access by boat at MM 78.5.* A 12-acre ocean-side island, Indian Key was once a thriving wreckers' community. However, local Indians reacted to threats by the white settlement leader, John Housman, by burning it to the ground in 1840. The main attraction now lies offshore in the form of the *San Pedro,* an 18th-century Spanish galleon lying in 18 feet of water. It is the centrepiece of the Key's first underwater archaeological sanctuary, which was unfortunately not set up in time to prevent seven poured concrete cannons being added to the gun deck for effect. Sections of the wooden hull and piles of ballast rock are a haven for a wide variety of marine life, and make for great warm water diving. A no-fishing policy is strictly enforced. For details of the boat schedule, write to PO Box 1052, Islamorada, FL 33036 (tel: (305) 664 4815).

Theater of the Sea, *MM 84.5* The world's second oldest marine park, created in pools and lagoons formed by Flagler's railroad excavations, this is still a popular stop on the Overseas Highway. Continuous tours run throughout the day introducing visitors to all manner of underwater creatures from sea urchins to sharks, plus a dolphin boat ride and sea lion and dolphin show. For details and reservations on the **Dolphin Adventure-Swim**, tel: (305) 664 2431.
Open:: daily 09.30–16.00hrs.

Coral Reefs

■ **Coral reefs are built by polyps, primitive soft-bodied relatives of the sea anemone and jellyfish, which secrete limestone to form an exterior skeleton. They cannot survive temperatures below 68°F, so are confined to warm seas .....■**

Polyps feed on tiny phytoplankton which they snare with stinging cells on their tentacles, and they also receive oxygen and nutrients from algae within their bodies. In return the algae extract carbon dioxide for photosynthesis and give coral its colours. Hard coral grows slowly as each generation builds on the skeletal deposits of its ancestors. A large brain coral can take centuries to build; branching coral may manage around three inches a year.

Inner reefs Known as patch reefs, these develop in shallow waters where the wave action is less marked. They comprise the more delicate formations such as sea fan, mountain star, whips and plumes of soft corals, and the unnervingly lifelike brain coral. Angelfish, wrasse, tang, damsels, butterfly fish and spiny lobster are some of the more colourful inshore residents; further out, barracuda and shark are known to cruise around massive out-crops of staghorn and elkhorn coral. Every nook and cranny is a potential hiding place for camouflaged moray eels who dart out from murky crevices to snap up unsuspecting victims.

A friendly habitat Corals are functional as well as beautiful. They form a vital breakwater diffusing the destructive force of storm-whipped seas, and provide a safe anchorage for molluscs, sea anemones, barnacles and sponges. Colourful parrot fish graze on coral, biting off chunks with their powerful beaks, and grinding it up to extract polyps and algae. Fish nibbling on corals produce more than 2.5 tons of sand per acre annually. Seagrasses grow on the sandy bottom, and in turn create a food source and sympathetic environment for turtles, manatees and thousands of other marine plant and animal species.

Threats to the system The delicate ecosystem of a coral reef is easily damaged. Boat anchors, propellers and careless divers are an obvious threat. More insidious is chemical run-off from the mainland, and drifting oil from deep-sea shipping lanes. Pollution and sediment from dredging operations can smother living coral polyps, destroy the lower end of the food chain and, as a result, gradually threaten the entire reef population.

95

Milleflora dichotoma: *fire coral*

THE KEYS AND EVERGLADES

Conch (pronounced 'conk') is a rubbery mollusc much beloved of Keys chefs, who subject it to a full gamut of culinary uses from basic conch fritters and chowder to more up-market variations, such as conch cevice, cured with fresh Key lime juice. But a 'conch' is also a native Keys resident born and bred. You become an honorary 'fresh-water conch' when you have lived in the Keys for seven years or more.

▶▶▶ Key Largo

Across Blackwater Sound, Key Largo is the northernmost island linked to the mainland by the Overseas Highway. At 30 miles long, though less than two miles wide, it is the largest of the Keys, and achieved widespread fame as the setting of 1948 screen classic *Key Largo*, with Humphrey Bogart and Lauren Bacall. Cinema buffs still seek out the coral rock 'Key Largo Hotel', and there is a further treat in store for nostalgic types in the original steel-hulled *African Queen*, moored by the Holiday Inn at MM 100, which starred alongside Bogart and Katherine Hepburn in 1951.

Key Largo's present-day claim to fame lies in the spectacular John Pennekamp Coral Reef State Park and Key Largo National Marine Sanctuary (see below), where some of the nation's premier dive sites attract thousands of visitors every year. More than 25 local dive outfits provide daily excursions, equipment hire and tuition. November brings Key Largo's biggest annual event in the shape of **Island Jubilee**, a four-day festival of special events with music, food and crafts stalls in **Harry Harris Park**, off US1 at MM 92.6. Accommodations in Key Largo are plentiful and varied; reservations are advisable in winter and at weekends.

Dolphins Plus, *off US1 at MM 100* Divers in the Key Largo area often have tales to tell of encounters with playful bottlenose dolphins, and there are several marine research facilities in the Keys which offer a chance to swim with these friendly and intelligent creatures. This low-key establishment is dedicated to educating visitors as well as providing a memorable experience, and a pre-swim orientation seminar explores the marvels and myths attached to the dolphin. Participants in the encounter sessions must be swimmers with some experience of using a mask and flippers.

Open: two sessions daily. Information: PO Box 2728, Key Largo, FL33037 (tel: (305) 451 1993).

John Pennekamp Coral Reef State Park, *MM 102.5*, America's first underwater park, and the adjoining Key **Largo Coral Reef National Marine Sanctuary** total some 178 nautical square miles of the Atlantic Ocean. Warmed by the Gulf Stream, the coral reefs and seagrass beds support more than 500 species of fish, 55 varieties of coral and around 27 types of gorgonians, marine life forms such as sea anemones. It is a fabulous undersea world that is a major attraction for scuba divers and snorkellers, but the park is also accessible to non-swimmers through the excellent aquariums and displays in the Visitor Center, and with the help of glassbottomed boat trips out to the main reef areas. Popular dive sites include **Molasses Reef**, with tunnels and towering coral formations including elkhorn, staghorn, star and brain coral; **French Reef** and its Christmas Tree Cave; the **Benwood Wreck**, a freighter torpedoed in 1942; **Grecian Rocks**; and the *Christ of the Deep* statue in 25 feet of water at **Dry Rocks**. There are several daily dive boat departures; windsurfer, sailboat and canoe rentals are available from the sandy beach area; a campsite is available.

Open: Visitor Center daily 08.00—sunset. Boat tours, scuba and snorkel trips, dive shop rentals, tel: (305) 451 1621.
Park postal address: PO Box 487, Key Largo, FL 33037 (tel: (305) 451 1202).

Key Largo Undersea Park, *MM 103.2* Set in an acre-wide lagoon, the park offers a wide range of diversions for scuba divers, snorkellers and even non-swimmers. Beneath the lagoon, snorkellers can observe scientists in the Marine-Lab Undersea Habitat perform underwater research projects; marine archaeologists search for shipwrecks; and marine artists create bizarre 'seaworks' in conjunction with the ocean. There is also a museum and huge aquariums, and this is the home of a six-compartment underwater hotel, **Jules Undersea Lodge** (tel: (305) 451 2353). Tuition is available for first-time snorkellers, and the lagoon is an ideal learning enviroment.
Open: daily 09.00–17.00hrs. Charge for tours and equipment hire.

Kimbell's Caribbean Shipwreck Museum, *MM 102.5* Hundreds of shipwrecks lie off the Florida Keys and Caribbean islands, and the Shipwreck Museum has gathered artefacts from several major sites including the 1733 Fleet, the *Concepcion*, and Mel Fisher's *Atocha* (see page 102). Ingots, Spanish 'pieces of eight', gold Mexican escudos, even counterfeit coins, magnificent costume jewellery, glassware and pottery are all displayed alongside a quick look at pirate history through literature and art. Treasure hunting maps and books are on sale.
Open: daily 10.00-17.00hrs.

Amateur photographers should not be afraid to try their skill under water to record the beauties of a coral reef. As well as purpose-built underwater cameras, waterproofing housings are sold which will protect most types of normal camera, and even videos, to depths of up to 35 feet. The best time to shoot below the surface is between 10.00 and 14.00hrs when the sunlight is strongest; at depths below 10–20 feet use a flash. For the best results get close to the subject and, if possible, use a wide angle lens.

Rescued from the sea: finds in Key Largo's Shipwreck Museum

Local 'conch' architecture was introduced to Key West by Bahamian settlers in the early 19th century. Houses were built from imported hardwoods or salvaged lumber and set on coral rock piles out of danger from flooding; roofs were designed to channel rainwater into cisterns for storage. During the Classic Revival period, symmetrical façades adorned with columns, pediments and gables were all the rage, and many houses still sport marvellous gingerbread detailing. Windows and doors were protected from sun and rain by wooden louvred blinds, and other local adaptations developed into a distinctive vernacular style.

Although JJ Audubon did not live, or even stay in Audubon House, he did paint there. During his visit in 1832 he spent his days recording the spectacular Keys birds.

Audubon House: the nursery

▶ ▶ ▷ Key West

The 'Southernmost City in the United States', Key West is a captivating blend of intimacy and exploitation, laid-back locals and international sunseekers, leafy back-streets and tourist trolleys.

A racy history of pirates and wreckers laid the foundations of the town, and by the 1890s Key West was the largest and wealthiest city in Florida. Sponge diving and cigar making were flourishing industries, and tourism arrived on board Henry Flagler's $50 million 'Railroad that went to the Sea', which reached Key West in 1912. From the seeming disaster of the 1935 hurricane, Key West was saved by the Emergency Relief Administration, which replaced the railroad with tarmac and launched a cunning plan to turn the city into a resort for authors and artists in need of a little sunshine. Ernest Hemingway was already here, and it did not take long for a cultural colony to spring up alongside the revitalised tourist industry.

To get a feel for Key West, jump aboard the **Old Town Trolley**, 1901 N Roosevelt Boulevard, or one of 14 stops around town (daily 08.55–16.30hrs). **Duval Street** is the heart of downtown, a mile-long shopper's dream packed with boutiques interspersed with bars and eateries, including Hemingway's favourite watering hole, **Sloppy Joe's**, 201 Duval. Do not miss sunset at **Mallory Square**; and for something a little offbeat, check out turtle racing at **Land's End Village** on Wednesday nights.

Audubon House and Gardens, *205 Whitehead Street* This beautiful house was built by prosperous wrecker John H Geiger in 1830. Engravings of of John James Audubon's wonderful bird illustrations are hung extensively around the house. Borrow a guide to the lovely tropical garden which is practical as well as decorative . *Open*:: daily 09.30–17.00hrs. Information, tel: (305) 294 2116.

Curry Mansion Inn, *511 Caroline Street* Home of Florida's first millionaire, William Curry, who made his fortune in the wrecking and lumber businesses, this is one of the loveliest buildings in town. The original homestead was the rear of the house, erected in 1855; then Milton Curry added the gracious façade in 1899. The restored interior has been exquisitely furnished with period antiques, Tiffany glass and scattered rugs on the highly polished floors. There are patchwork quilts on brass beds, a pool table in the attic and an enviable view from the roof.
Open: daily 09.00–17.00hrs. See also **Directory**.

East Martello Museum and Art Gallery,*3501 S Roosevelt Boulevard* During the 1840s, the US Army began work on a series of coastal defences to protect Key West, including downtown Fort Zachary Taylor (see below) and, later, two Martello towers. The towers were not even fully completed when construction was halted by the introduction of rifled cannons which rendered the old brick-built fortifications obsolete. Now the East Tower, the only remaining example of its type on the US eastern seaboard, houses an eclectic little local history museum featuring local industries, Flagler's railroad, and a welter of nautical memorabilia. Climb to the top of the citadel for a panoramic view of the town. There is a little gallery hung with works by local naïve artist Mario Sanchez, who creates jaunty carved and painted wooden 'pictures', and there is a good selection of local history books and pamphlets available in the gift shop.
Open::daily 09.30–17.00hrs.

Fort Zachary Taylor State Historic Site, *Truman Annex (entrance at west end of Southard Street.)* Founded in 1845, the fort took 21 years to complete as its builders battled against yellow fever, hurricanes and straightforward isolation. While most of Florida supported the Confederacy, this fort was controlled by Union forces during the Civil War. Today the grounds offer Key West's only sizeable area of public beach, which is furnished with a good supply of barbecue grills and picnic tables. A small museum traces the fort's history and weaponry.
Open: daily 08.00–dusk.

The largest coastal fortress in the US encircles the island of Garden Key in the Dry Tortugas, 60 miles west of Key West. Fort Jefferson was founded in 1851. Its eight-foot-thick walls rise 50 feet high with three gun tiers, and its 70-foot wide moat was once patrolled by sharks and barracudas. The fort is only accessible by boat or sea plane from Key West. The plane trip is spectacular; and on arrival you can enjoy a sand beach and diving, and watch turtles and birds.

Big guns in retirement at Fort Zachary Taylor

Walk Exploring Key West

Start outside the 1891 Florida Bank Building on the corner of Duval and Front Streets. Turn left on Front Street.

Mel Fisher's Maritime Heritage Society occupies a site at the top of Whitehead Street; its glittering treasure trove salvaged from Spanish wrecks is a sight to behold. A stone's throw across the way, lovely **Audubon House**, at Whitehead and Greene Streets, has an equally beautiful garden where ornithologist John James Audubon set up his easel in 1832. Reluctant to stay ashore for fear of contracting yellow fever, he nevertheless spent many fruitful days sketching the diverse birdlife around the gardens. Opposite Caroline Street, there is a detour through Truman Annex to President Truman's **Little White House**.

From Whitehead, turn left on Caroline Street; passing several typical 19th-century Key West-style houses. Then turn right on to Duval Street.

Halfway down the block, the **Oldest House Wrecker's Museum**, 322 Duval, is a historic gem filled with antiques and curios. The volunteer guides are happy to answer questions and have a fund of interesting local anecdotes to liven up a visit.

A left on Eaton Street reveals another clutch of attractive historic homes; then turn left again on to Simonton Street, named for Key West's founder, John W Simonton.

The T-Shirt Factory, 316 Simonton, sells great T-shirts at outlet prices. Then stop by the **Pelican Poop Shoppe**, 314 Simonton, and ask for a tour of the amazing **Casa Antigua** hidden garden behind the shop. **Key West Handprint Fabrics**, 201 Simonton, is a popular stop with shoppers. They give free tours of their print workshops, and sell an enormous range of colourful Hawaiian-style shirts, pretty print frocks, linen and furnishing fabrics.

Take a left on Greene Street, and left again down Ann Street.

At the bottom of the lane, stop off at the gorgeous **Curry Mansion Inn**, 511 Caroline. The façade is a work of art, and although the owners operate a bed and breakfast business, visitors are welcome to inspect the lovingly restored interior for a small charge. The last stop is back on Duval: a restorative drink at **Sloppy Joe's**, in the relocated premises of Hemingway's favourite bar.

Wrecker's licence in the Oldest House Wrecker's Museum. This was once a lucrative trade

Hemingway House, *907 Whitehead Street* Built in the mid-19th century by naval architect Asa Tift, this fine Spanish Colonial-style house was bought by Ernest Hemingway in 1931. He and his second wife, Pauline, decorated the interior with a comfortable hodgepodge of furnishings and mementoes gathered on trips to Spain, Africa and Cuba. Hemingway penned the bulk of his greatest novels and short stories in an airy study above the carriage house, which was joined to the main building by a catwalk. Very appropriate too, as an extensive colony of cats, introduced by the writer, still have the run of the house and gardens. Look out for their enormous feet – some have as many as eight toes – a genetic hiccough which attracted Hemingway's attention when he adopted his first feline from a passing sea captain. A ceramic cat by Picasso in the master bedroom was a gift from the artist. The swimming pool, a $20,000 folly fed by two salt-water wells, was the first in Key West. Regular guided tours provide a wealth of interesting detail and anecdotes about Hemingway.
Open: daily 09.00–17.00hrs. Information, tel: (305) 294 1136.

Key West Aquarium, *1 Whitehead Street* The original Florida Keys attraction, this aquarium opened in 1932. In glass-fronted aquaria which line the walls particularly decorative residents include peppermint and banded coral shrimps and feathery sea anemones. Check tour

Hemingway-fever hits town in July, when hundreds of Ernest Hemingway look-alikes converge on Key West for the annual Hemingway Days Festival. The week-long celebration of the writer's life includes seminars, look-alike contest, fishing competitions and story-telling. Later in the year, the October Fantasy Fest is wild. Hotels and businesses organise theme décor, and locals slave over lavish costumes for the big parade. Make hotel reservations well in advance.

The Aquarium, opened in 1932, was Key West's first ever tourist attraction

For a great view, climb the 88 steps to the top of Key West Lighthouse

and shark feeding schedules; also conches in a touch tank, and shark and turtle pens on the dock.
Open: daily 10.00–18.00hrs.

Key West Lighthouse Museum, *938 Whitehead Street* For a bird's-eye view of Key West look no further than the lighthouse. It's an 88-step ascent to the viewing balcony; another 10 steps lead to the light itself. The present edifice was built to a height of 66 feet in 1847–8, and replaced an earlier wooden structure. A further 20 feet were added in 1894. At ground level, the former Keeper's Quarters, panelled with rock-solid Dade County pine, were shared by the keeper and two assistants, each with a separate entrance. Now it houses memorabilia from past keepers, including Mary Bethel, who took the job over from her husband in 1908, and operated the station for 14 years with the help of her children.
Open: daily 09.30–17.00hrs.

Little White House Museum, *111 Front Street* Tucked in the Truman Annexe, part of the old naval station, this was President Harry S Truman's alternative White House. He took 11 working holidays here during his six years of office. The house dates from 1890, when it was the waterfront home of the base commander. Recently refurbished in1940s style, it contains several Truman era relics such as his custom-made poker table with shell cases for ashtrays.
Open:: daily 09.00-7.00hrs.

Mallory Square Pier, *off Wall Street* Key Westers don't just watch the sun go down, they celebrate it. Locals and visitors alike gather on the dockside at Mallory Square to watch the fiery sun slide into the Gulf of Mexico, and sample some man-made spectacles too. Street entertainers roll up in force: washboard strummers and bongo bashers set feet tapping, while jugglers, mime artists and unicyclists fill their hats with dollar bills and coins from the crowd; meanwhile, the Cookie Lady peddles her wares from a bicycle basket.

Mel Fisher Maritime Heritage Society, *200 Greene Street* 'Today's the day!' is Mel Fisher's motto, and it kept him going through 16 years of determined exploration before he finally hit the jackpot with the discovery of the Spanish galleon *Atocha* in 1985. There had been several handy finds in the meantime, but nothing to match the $200 million in gold, silver and jewels which sank off the Keys in 1622. Artefacts include everyday items such as majolica earthenware, weapons and the remains of a pitch pot used to prepare caulk for repairing leaks in the ship's hull. And then there is real treasure: gold and silver tableware, emeralds from the Muzo mines of Colombia, and fabulous jewellery like a 12-foot-long wedding chain which weighs 4.5lb and is valued at a mere $500,000. Silver ingots and ballast rock are heaped in a replica hull; there are coins galore; and a hole in the wall with a gold bar which visitors can handle. Take in the video presentation; and do not miss Fisher's personal haul displayed around the back from

the souvenir shop. There are original authenticated finds and replica jewellery for sale – at a price.
Open: daily 10.00–17.15hrs.

Mosquito Coast Kayak Guides, *1107 Duval Street* A great way to get to grips with nature in the Keys, this is a must for naturalists and outdoorsmen; experience is not necessary. Knowledgeable guides lead escapist tours into the back country, exploring mangrove islands and crystal clear waters teeming with birds, tropical marine species and other wildlife.
For information and reservations for daily trips, tel: (305) 294 7178. Snorkelling gear supplied.

Wrecker's Museum, *322 Duval Street* Built around 1829, 'the Oldest House in Key West' is a fine example of early Key West architecture with its distinctive maritime flavour. The interior is lined with horizontal planks reminiscent of a ship's hull, while furnishings and artefacts trace the history of the 19th-century wrecking industry and the one-time owner of the house, Captain Francis B Watlington. The original outdoor kitchen is the last in the Keys. Look out for the misaligned 'landlubber's tilt'; in the captain's office; and the unusual ship's hatch in the attic.
Open: daily 10.00–16.00hrs.

Mallory Square Pier, where the dramatic sunset is the big event of the day

Between Olivia and Angela Streets, Key West City Cemetery is a surprising repository of local 'conch' humour. Alongside a litany of quirky nicknames, there are some distinctly irreverent postscripts, such as B P Roberts' 'I told you I was sick', and one honest widow's revenge: 'At least I know where he's sleeping tonight'. If it all looks a little disorganised, blame the local bedrock which has left several stone caskets resting above ground. And shortage of space means an estimated 100,000 people have been buried in the 15,000 plots.

103

CLOSE-UP

Hemingway and Others

■ **When novelist John Dos Passos rode Flagler's 'Railroad That Went to the Sea' into Key West in the 1920s, he later described it as 'one of the most exhilarating experiences of my life; coming into Key West was like floating into a dream'. .....■**

It was Dos Passos' recommendation that lured Ernest Hemingway to the island in 1928, and marked the beginning of a long and fruitful association between Key West and many leading 20th-century American writers.

Fishing and booze When Hemingway arrived, with his second wife Pauline, he was at pains to play down his role as a writer, and launched himself into the macho antics of the local seafaring community with enthusiasm. From turn-of-the-century boomtown, Key West was on the decline. Its population had dropped from 22,000 in the town's heyday to around 10,000, and the stream of winter tourists dried up with the 1929 Stock

Hemingway's House, Key West

Market crash. Fortunately for 'Papa' Hemingway, Prohibition meant nothing in Key West. The exploits (and wares) of Cuban rumrunners supplemented fishermen's tales of mighty marlin, tarpon and wily bonefish and lent local bars an alluring pioneer flavour with a spice of fascinating yarns. Hemingway's fishing trips became legendary, and one of his favourite fishing cronies Joe Russell, was also the proprietor of Sloppy Joe's bar.

A place to write Pauline's uncle bought the house at 907 Whitehead Street (see page 101) as a belated wedding present for the couple in 1931. In between trips abroad, Hemingway returned here to write *For Whom the Bell Tolls, A Farewell To Arms, The Snows of Kilimanjaro* and *Death in the Afternoon* among others. The three stories comprising *To Have and Have Not* are his only fiction with an American setting. In 1936, Hemingway met journalist Martha Gellhorn in Sloppy Joe's. She would become his third wife, and precipitate his move to Cuba in the 1940s.

A literary haven The Emergency Relief Administration's post-hurricane scheme to attract the cultural classes to Key West has been a wild success: seven Pulitzer Prizes have been awarded to a succession of visiting and resident writers. In the late 1930s, poet Elizabeth Bishop spent a brief sojourn in Key West; Robert Frost, Gore Vidal and Kurt Vonnegut Jr all enjoyed a respite from northern winters in the town; and playwright Tennessee Williams lived quietly near Duncan and Leon Streets from 1949 until his death in 1983.

▶▶▷ **Lower Keys**

The magnificent **Seven Mile Bridge** marks the transition from the Middle to the Lower Keys. Built in 1982, the present structure is actually 110 feet short of seven miles, but affords dazzling views over the bay and ocean sprinkled with tiny jewel-like isles. Beaches in the Keys are a rarity, but just across the bridge Bahia Honda State Recreation Area (see below) boasts beautiful white sand beaches and excellent swimming. A large area of **Big Pine Key** has been declared a deer refuge to preserve the few hundred remaining Key deer, an endangered species. In the middle of the refuge, Blue Hole is the largest body of fresh water in the Keys. Accessible from Big Pine, Little Torch, Ramrod and Summerland Keys, the Looe Key National Marine Sanctuary (see below) is another diver's delight. **Cudjoe Key** is the home of the US government's Zeppelin-lookalike 'Fat Albert', which hovers aloft on the lookout for illegal drug traffickers.

Bahia Honda State Recreation Area, *MM 37* The Spanish named the key for its deep harbour(*honda*), and now Bahia Honda is the southernmost state recreation area and a favourite break point on the Overseas Highway. Stop off for a swim or a picnic; the sandy shore has been ranked among the top one per cent of the nation's beaches in a recent survey. Pelicans, egrets, herons and terns are frequently spotted; botanists may find several rare plants on the nature trail. There is a boat ramp, camp ground, and some of the best tarpon fishing along the coast.
Open: daily 08.00hrs to sunset.

There's good swimming at Bahia Honda

At Looe Key, numerous local dive operators make trips out to the reef and arrange equipment hire. Divers will need certificates, but anyone can snorkel. For more information, contact: Dolphin Marina, Little Torch Key, MM 28.5, tel: (305) 872 2685
Cudjoe Gardens Marina and Dive Center, Cudjoe Key, MM 21, tel: (305) 745 2357
Looe Key Dive Center, Ramrod Key, MM 27.5, tel: (305) 872 2215
Underseas Inc, Big Pine Key, MM 30.5, tel: (305) 872 2700 or 800 446 LOOE.

105

A GATOR NAMED ALLIG

THERE ONCE WAS A GATOR NAMED ALLIG,
WHO LIVED IN A PLACE CALLED BLUE HOLE.
SOME PEOPLE FED HIM WHILE OTHERS THEY SWAM,
BUT MOST OF THE WATER WAS HIS DINNER BOWL.

SO ALLIG GREW BRAVER WITH EACH PASSING WEEK,
AND NO LONGER CALLED HIS VISITORS SIR.
HE MISTOOK A YOUNG MISS FOR HIS USUAL FISH,
AND ONE MORNING BEFORE BREAKFAST ALLIG-ATE-HER.

ALLIGATORS ARE WILD ANIMALS AND
SHOULD BE TREATED AS SUCH. SWIMMING
OR FEEDING THE ALLIGATORS IS PRO-
HIBITED FOR YOUR PROTECTION.

Looe Key National Marine Sanctuary *6.5 miles off Big Pine Key at MM 30* This 51/3-square nautical mile marine preserve is one of the most popular dive sites along the Keys. The sanctuary surrounds a well-developed section of coral reef and several different undersea habitats from seagrass beds and patch reefs to sand flats. Excellent water clarity and moderate sea conditions make for satisfying snorkelling on the surface, while the wide range of depths within the park make it equally exciting for beginners and for experienced divers. There are thousands of brilliantly-coloured piscine inhabitants swimming around elkhorn, staghorn and pillar coral formations; delicate soft coral sea fans and sea whips sway gently in the current. In addition to the reef, there are wrecks to explore, including that of British frigate HMS *Looe* which struck the reef and sank here in 1744.
Open: daily.

National Key Deer Refuge and Blue Hole, *Big Pine Key, 1.5 miles west at MM 30.5* It is estimated that around 250 to 300 Key deer remain on Big Pine Key and scattered over 16 surrounding islands, but around 60 to 70 are killed by motorists every year – speed limits are strictly enforced on Big Pine Key. Key deer are the smallest sub-species of the Virginia white-tailed deer, just 24–28 inches high; fawns weigh only around 2-4lbs at birth. They feed off native plants and berries, and although they can tolerate a small amount of salt water in their diet, fresh water is essential. There is a short nature trail, and the best time to spot deer is early morning and in the evening. The fawning season is April to June; and look out for traces of antler velvet in late August and early September.

Blue Hole is an old limestone quarry at the heart of the Key Deer Refuge. Material for most of the roads on Big Pine Key was removed from here, and the quarry's fresh water supply is vital to the the Key deer's survival. Although some salt water seeps into the lower levels of Blue Hole, freshwater species that thrive happily in its depths include bass, blue gills, mosquito fish and alligators. There are one or two surprise residents, too, such as goldfish abandoned by disenchanted owners. Herons, cormorants, ducks and moorhens can congregate here, even the occasional osprey in search of a quick snack.
Open: daily 08.00hrs–dusk.

Perky Bat Tower, *Sugarloaf Key, off US1 at MM 17* When Righter C Perky set up a fishing camp here, the mosquitoes were such a menace that he built this quirky louvred bat tower in 1929, one of the stranger offerings on the National Register of Historic Places.

▷▷▷   **The Middle Keys**
The Middle Keys stretch southwest from the region's second longest bridge, the 21/3 mile Long Key Bridge, to the famous Seven Mile Bridge, near Marathon. Along the way, **Conch Key** has a rustic (if not rusty) fishing dock area, and its picturesque cluster of whitewashed cottages is a popular subject with photographers; **Duck**

Key once thrived as a salt producer; **Grassy Key** is not particularly verdant, but offers another opportunity for dolphin encounters at the **Dolphin Research Center**, MM 59 (telephone reservations, tel: (305) 289 0002); and **Crawl Key** was named for the turtle pens, or *kraals*, used to store live turtles until they were converted into soup or jewellery in the heartless days BC (Before Conservation). Marathon is a well-developed small town with an airport, shopping malls, a marina, golf course and public beach, plus a wide range of accommodations, campsites and trailer parks.

Museum of Natural History of The Florida Keys and Crane Point Hammock, *50, Marathon* The copper doors of this woodland museum, alive with fish and reef life, are a feature in themselves, and beyond there is a fascinating insight into the unique natural history of the Keys. User-friendly information panels explain local geology, geography, history and wildlife; exhibits include a Skylab photograph of the region, reef dioramas, and tales of shipwrecks at sea. An outdoor area is especially designed to appeal to children; and a quarter-mile nature trail explores the surrounding hammock. **Crane Point** covers some 63 acres, habitat of a wide range of tropical vegetation and 10 endangered animal and plant species. Among the mangroves, palms and hardwood trees, an exposed pit reveals ancient ocean fossils predating man's association with the Keys which runs back over 5,000 years. Evidence of pre-Columbian and prehistoric Indian habitation have been found in the grounds, as well as the remains of a Bahanian village. *Open*:: Monday to Saturday 09.00-17.00hrs, Sunday 12.00-17.00hrs.

107

Seven Mile Bridge, between Marathon and Sunshine Key

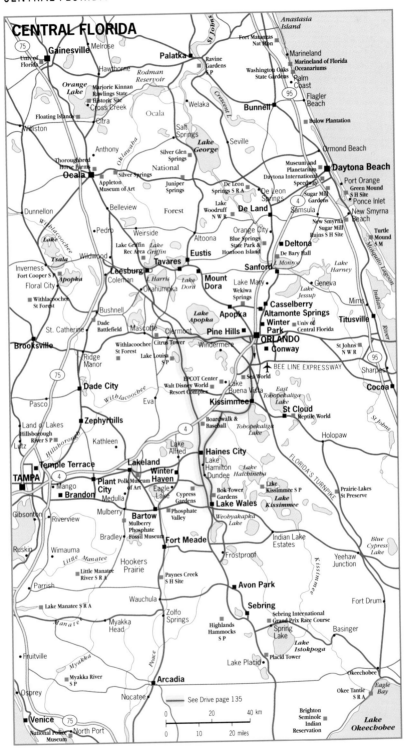

108

CENTRAL FLORIDA

Univ. of Florida

Gainesville

Melrose

Palatka

Ravine Gardens S P

Fort Matanzas Nat Mon

Marineland

Marineland of Florida Oceanariums

Washington Oaks State Gardens

Palm Coast

Hawthorne

Rodman Reservoir

Welaka

Crescent

Bunnell

Flagler Beach

Orange Lake

Marjorie Kinnan Rawlings State Historic Site

Cross Creek

Floating Islands

Williston

Citra

Ocala

Salt Springs

Lake George

Seville

Bulow Plantation

Ormond Beach

Anthony

Silver Glen Springs

Oklawaha

National

Museum and Planetarium

Daytona International Speedway

Daytona Beach

Port Orange

Green Mound S H Site

Ponce Inlet

Thoroughbred Horse Farm

Ocala

Silver Springs

Appleton Museum of Art

Juniper Springs

De Leon Springs S R A

De Leon Springs

Sugar Mill Gardens

Samsula

New Smyrna Beach

Dunnellon

Belleview

Forest

Lake Woodruff N W R

De Land

New Smyrna Sugar Mill Ruins S H Site

Turtle Mound S M

Withlacoochee

Pedro

Weirside

Altoona

Orange City

Blue Springs State Park & Hontoon Island

Deltona

De Bary Hall

Mosquito Lagoon

Lake Tsala

Wildwood

Lake Griffin Rec Area

Lake Griffin

Eustis

Sanford

L Monroe

Lake Harney

Lake Jessup

Geneva

Inverness

Fort Cooper S P

Floral City

Apopka

Leesburg

Tavares

L Harris

Lake Dora

Mount Dora

Lake Mary

Wekiwa Springs

Casselberry

Altamonte Springs

Winter Park

Titusville

Mims

Coleman

Okahumpka

Lake Apopka

Apopka

Univ of Central Florida

Bushnell

Dade Battlefield

Mascotte

Clermont

Pine Hills

ORLANDO

Conway

St Johns N W R

95

Brooksville

Withlacoochee St Forest

Ridge Manor

Citrus Tower

Lake Louisa S P

Windermere

BEE LINE EXPRESSWAY

Sharpes

75

Dade City

Withlacoochee

Eva

EPCOT Center

Walt Disney World Resort Complex

Sea World

Lake Buena Vista

Cocoa

Pasco

Zephyrhills

Kissimmee

East Tohopekaliga Lake

St Cloud

Reptile World

St Johns

Land o' Lakes

Hillsborough River S P

Lutz

Kathleen

4

Boardwalk & Baseball

Tohopekaliga Lake

Holopaw

TAMPA

Temple Terrace

Mango

4

Lakeland

Winter Haven

Lake Alfred

Haines City

FLORIDA'S TURNPIKE

Plant City

Polk Museum of Art

Eagle Lake

Lake Hamilton

Dundee

Lake Hatchineha

Lake Kissimmee S P

Prairie Lakes St Preserve

Brandon

Medulla

Cypress Gardens

Bok Tower Gardens

Lake Kissimmee

Gibsonton

Mulberry

Bartow

Phosphate Valley

Lake Wales

Riverview

Bradley

Mulberry Phosphate Fossil Museum

Fort Meade

Weohyakapka Lake

Ruskin

Wimauma

Little Manatee

Hookers Prairie

Frostproof

Indian Lake Estates

Blue Cypress Lake

Yeehaw Junction

Parrish

Little Manatee River S R A

Paynes Creek S H Site

Kissimmee

Fort Drum

Lake Manatee S R A

Manatee

Wauchula

Zolfo Springs

Avon Park

Myakka Head

Sebring

Sebring International Grand Prix Race Course

Basinger

Fruitville

Myakka

Myakka River S P

Peace

Highlands Hammocks S P

Spring Lake

Lake Istokpoga

Osprey

Lake Placid

Placid Tower

Okeechobee

Eagle Bay

Arcadia

Nocatee

See Drive page 135

Brighton Seminole Indian Reservation

Okee Tantie S R A

Lake Okeechobee

Venice

75

North Port

National Police Museum

0   20   40 km

0   10   20 miles

Contrast is a recurring theme throughout Florida, but never more so than in the Central region. Cane fields, citrus groves, cartoon characters, cowmen – Central Florida has it all, and yet most visitors come for one thing only...

Orlando is the region's first city. Settled as a fortress during the Seminole Wars, it developed into a relatively prosperous citrus and cattle town, ringed with lakes, and earned its nickname 'The City Beautiful'. When Walt Disney selected Florida as the location for his second theme park in the 1960s, Orlando was the perfect site, with good transport and communication links close to undeveloped land.

Today, Walt Disney World is the world's biggest tourist attraction, attracting millions of visitors every year. Despite the inevitable onslaught of tourist-related industries and tacky spin-offs, Orlando itself retains much of its character: there are pleasant open spaces around the city, and areas such as **Winter Park**, which have been swallowed by the suburbs, offer a pleasant escape with a couple of excellent small museums, up-market shopping and boat rides on Lake Osceola. Orlando is within easy reach of both the east and west Florida coasts: **Kennedy Space Center** (pages 192–3) is an hour's drive east; while the Gulf of Mexico, **Tampa** (pages 226–9) and **St Petersburg** (page 216) lie 90 minutes west.

Citrus country stretches west and south of Orlando. **Lake Wales** is renowned for its annual Passion Play, and there are two marvellous gardens near by: Bok Tower Gardens, and Cypress Gardens, near Winter Haven. **Arcadia**, 65 miles west of Okeechobee City, is in the heart of cattle country. Façades straight out of a Western movie line the main drag, and it is wall-to-wall blue jeans and stetsons during the All-Florida Championship Rodeo. Once a vital link in the Everglades ecosystem, beautiful **Lake Okeechobee** has been dangerously tamed, but it is still a haven for birdwatchers and fishermen.

Journey north from Orlando, and there is **Ocala**, surrounded by beautifully turned-out thoroughbred stud farms. It boasts a fine art museum on the edge of town, and the vast expanses of Ocala National Forest. Rolling hills and ranches girdle historic **Gainesville**, which has hardly been touched by tourism. Sports fans flock here to support University of Florida football supremos, the mighty Gators.

Arcadia

Take a detour off SR70 for a quick look at this sleepy cattle town. Past the imposing **De Soto County Courthouse**, downtown **Oak Street** has been restored, and the old rail **Depot** houses a one-room museum plastered with ageing photographs and bits of riding tack. There are no chic boutiques here, but **Mercer's Western Store Inc**, 29 W Oak, sells cowman kit such as Resistol and Stetson headgear, cowboy boots, belts and ladies' leather Annie-Get-Yer-Gun skirts. It is worth continuing on down Oak to see some of the lovely old houses beyond the shopping district.

North on SR17, **Peace River** is a shallow waterway where **Canoe Outpost** (tel: (813) 494 1215) rents out equipment to the adventurous. On SR72, just east of Sarasota, **Myakka River State Park** is one of the state's largest parks at 28,875 acres. The wilderness preserve can be explored on foot, on horseback, by tram, or by boat trips on the Myakka River as it flows through the park. Cottontail rabbits, deer, alligators and red-shouldered hawks all make their home in the varied terrain.

 Gainesville

Surrounded by cattle ranches, stud farms and Florida-style rolling hills, Gainesville is home to the University of Florida and its Gators football team. Both leave an indelible mark on this quiet town, where bicycle power and gracious fraternity halls adorned with Greek lettering survive alongside brazen alligator logos and pick-up trucks. The Downtown shopfronts around University Avenue and Main Street have been restored, and the brick-paved

Lake Alice, near Gainesville

streets and sidewalks dotted with outdoor cafés make this a good place to stop off for a while.

In the University campus, the **Florida Museum of Natural History**, Museum Road (*open*: Tuesday to Saturday 10.00–16.00hrs; Sunday 13.00–16.00hrs), deals with Floridian history in several interesting displays. The skeletons of prehistoric creatures, together with bronze casts of a sabre-toothed tiger and giant upright sloth, are particularly fascinating. Wall displays in the Florida Heritage section give a good potted history of early Cracker settlers and the Land Boom era, and there are books on native American Indians in the gift shop.

Not far away, the **Samuel P Harn Museum of Art**, Hull Road at SW 34th Street (*open*: Tuesday to Friday 11.00–17.00hrs; Saturday 10.00–17.00hrs; Sunday 13.00-17.00hrs), is a dramatic new campus feature with a fine semi-permanent collection of American, Oceanic, African and pre-Columbian arts, plus contemporary works. There is another art gallery at the University of Florida.

On the outskirts of town, the scenic and unusual **Devil's Millhopper State Geological site**, 4732 NW 53rd Avenue (*open*: daily 09.00hrs–dusk), is a 500-foot wide, 120-foot deep sinkhole (caused by natural subsidence) festooned with lush plants and giant ferns, which are cooled by a dozen little waterfalls. At the **Fred Bear Museum**, Archer Road at Interstate-75 (*open*: Wednesday to Sunday 10.00-18.00hrs), a 20th-century bowman has built up a sizeable collection of big game trophies and hunting artefacts.

▶▷▷ **Kissimmee**

A popular vacation base south of Orlando and a few minutes from Walt Disney World, Kissimmee has one foot in the present and the other firmly planted in its cattle town origins. The centre of town, **Broadway**, still has its historic shopfronts and country hardware stores – such as **Makinson's**, with its bullet-riddled old tin sign in the shape of a horse. There are cattle auctions at the **Livestock Market** on Wednesdays. **Lake Front Park** edges Lake Tohopekaliga (better known as Lake Toho), where there are boat rentals and fishing tackle hire from **Lake Toho Marina**, 101 Lakeshore Boulevard (tel: (407) 846 2124).

Between Interstate-4 and the town centre, US192 is known as Irlo Bronson Memorial Highway: it is also called the 'Tourist Trap Trail'. **Water Mania**, 6073 Irlo Bronson, has more to offer than its waterslides; there is an 8,100-square-foot maze, mini-golf and arcade games for those who do not want to get their feet wet. **Old Town**, 5770 Irlo Bronson, is a nostalgic concoction of brick-lined streets and period architecture stuffed with shops, eateries, a Ferris wheel and museums of wood-carving and wooden trains. The **Elvis Presley Museum** is also here, exhibiting the largest collection of the King's possessions outside Graceland. A short distance down the trail, **Xanadu**, 4800 Irlo Bronson, depicts a prototype 'home of the future', and Kissimmee is also home to **Tupperware World Headquarters**, US441, which offers free tours. Kissimmee has various other attractions apart from those mentioned here.

In 1928, New York authoress Marjorie Kinnan Rawlings moved to Cross Creek, a quiet rural community, where she bought a small homestead and settled down to learn about backwoods Cracker life. The fruits of her labours were a series of fascinating novellas, including *The Yearling*, which won her a Pulitzer Prize. Her home, the Marjorie Kinnan Rawlings State Historic Site, lies 21 miles southeast of Gainesville on SR325 (*open*: Thursday to Monday 10.00–11.30hrs, 13.00–16.00hrs). It has been preserved just as she left it, with an ancient typewriter on the porch, rum by the fireplace and tinned food on the shelves.

Monument to the US at Kissimmee

A large proportion of Florida's $7.8 billion equine industry is kicking its heels around Marion County, and several Florida Thoroughbred Breeders' Association members welcome visitors. Call ahead and book an appointment: Monday, Good Chance Farm (tel: (904) 245 1136); Tuesday, Florida Stallion Station (tel: (904) 629 4416); Wednesday, Bridlewood Farm (tel: (904) 622 5319); Thursday, Live Oak Stud (tel: (904) 854 2691); Friday, Ocala Stud Farm (tel: (904) 237 2171); Saturday and Sunday, Ocala Breeders' Sales Company & Training Center (tel: (904) 237 2154) (early morning workouts 07.00–09.00hrs).

▶ ▷ ▷ Lake Wales

North of Lake Wales, on ALT27, it is worth making a short detour west to **Chalet Suzanne**, a rambling country hotel-restaurant with craft shops and a home-made soup business. It is not just any old soup – this stuff is so popular that it even accompanied the crew of *Apollo 15* to the moon in 1973.

A few miles south, again off ALT27, do not miss beautiful **Bok Tower Gardens**, CR17 (*open*: daily 09.00–17.00hrs). The 128-acre gardens are a mass of azaleas, camellias, magnolias and ferns, shaded by slender palms, pines and oaks. The centrepiece is a 205-foot pink and grey marble and coquina tower boasting a 53-bell carillon which chimes half-hourly from 10.00hrs, with a full daily recital at 15.00hrs.

Another favourite local attraction is 'mysterious' **Spook Hill** on North Avenue. Take the car out of gear at the white line and it will appear to roll uphill. The annual two-month run of the **Black Hills Passion Play** has proved a springtime crowd-puller. Performances take place in an outdoor amphitheatre (for information, tel: (813) 676 1495).

▶ ▷ ▷ Mount Dora

On the shores of Lake Dora, 20 miles north of Orlando, this picturesque village is a favourite haunt of antiques collectors. The Chamber of Commerce, 341 Alexander Street, provides walking maps of the restored Downtown antiques district, and a neighbouring clutch of decorous Victorian mansions. One of the finest is the impressive 1893 Steamboat Gothic-style **Donelly House**, on Donelly Street. The **Royellou Museum**, off Baker Street, displays antique sabres in the old Town Fire Station.

Silver Springs near Ocala has the largest group of artesian wells in the world

►►► Ocala

Of the 600-plus thoroughbred horse farms in the state, 400 can be found in Marion County. Every road to Ocala is lined with miles of neat white-painted railings and grassy paddocks in which glossy horses graze peacefully. At the centre of town, **Town Square Park** is a bright patch of green surrounded by shops, a few café-restaurants, and the Chamber of Commerce (which supplies details of local attractions).

Don Garlit's Museum of Drag Racing, 13700 SW 16th Avenue (*open*: daily 10.00–17.00hrs), is overflowing with trophies and record-breaking automobiles. **Silver Springs**, one mile east of Ocala via SR40 (*open*: daily 09.00–17.00hrs), is yet another Floridian phenomenon, augmented by glass-bottomed boat rides, jungle cruises, jeep safaris and not-to-be-missed robotic dinosaurs. Do not miss out on nearby **Wild Waters** family water park either (*open*: April to May daily, and September weekends 10.00–17.00hrs; June to August daily 10.00–19.00hrs).

The Appleton Museum of Art, at 4333 E Silver Springs Boulevard (seven miles east of Interstate-75), is a most unusual regional art museum. The collections were amassed by Chicago industrialist and Ocala horsebreeder, Arthur I Appleton. The stunning Italian travertine marble museum building houses 6,000 exhibits (up to 4,000 of which are on permanent display), spanning 5,000 years of civilisation. Ancient Greek and Etruscan pottery and bronzes precede the brilliant peacock blue glazes of Persia, while African ceremonial masks and woodcarvings lead into an array of votive figurines. Look for the fantastic water bottles from South America, intricate Japanese ivories, extraordinarily detailed Chinese jade and coral carvings, Burmese wall-hangings and Tiffany lamps aglow with dragonflies. *Open*: Tuesday to Saturday 10.00–16.30hrs, Sunday 13.00–17.00hrs.

▷▷▷ Okeechobee

Right down at the southern extent of the central region, **Lake Okeechobee** is the second largest expanse of fresh water in the US. It covers 750 square miles, but is only around 14 feet deep. **Okeechobee City**, at the northern end of the lake, is not much of a city, but it was the site of a major battle won by the Seminole Indians, and a commemorative monument to this victory stands by US98, south of the town.

It is possible to drive right around the lake, with stops on the eastern side at **Port Mayaca**, and at **Pahokee State Recreation Area** for picnicking, camping and boat rentals. The lake is popular with birdwatchers, and with fishermen on the trail of largemouth bass which appear on every menu and (stuffed) on almost as many walls. The southern end of the lake is sugar country, where the vast **Belle Glade mill** produces some 2,000 tons of raw sugar daily. The levee alongside US27 was built after the disastrous 1928 hurricane which devasted the southern shores. **Clewiston** is a sugar town with a side line in cabbage palms.

Along the northwest lakeshore, the road traverses **Brighton Seminole Indian Reservation**.

Ancient American exhibit in Appleton Museum of Art

ORLANDO

For a great escape, travel back in time to the leisurely steamboat era and relax on a cruise down the St Johns River aboard a replica of an 1880s steamer. Based at Sanford (18 miles north of Orlando), *Grand Romance* offers luncheon and dinner cruises over three or four hours, and a two-day cruise which plies the full 150 miles of waterway to Jacksonville (for information and reservations, tel: (407) 321 5091).

Orlando...or land where the theme parks grow. Not content with the world's number one attraction, **Walt Disney World**, Orlando can boast a wealth of additional attractions from water parks to historical museums, and from themed restaurants to botanical gardens. Take time out for a riverboat cruise, or a stroll by lovely **Lake Eola** with its remarkable fountain. There is accommodation to suit every pocket; look out for good deals in the Kissimmee area.

▶ ▷ ▷ Cartoon Museum
4300 S Semoran Boulevard, Ste 109
This compact gallery-style museum is a real find for cartoon buffs. The wide-ranging collection contains thousands of examples from comic books, magazines and newspapers, and includes several rarities. Not recommended for children under 11.
Open: Monday to Saturday 11.00–18.00hrs; Sunday 11.00–16.00hrs.

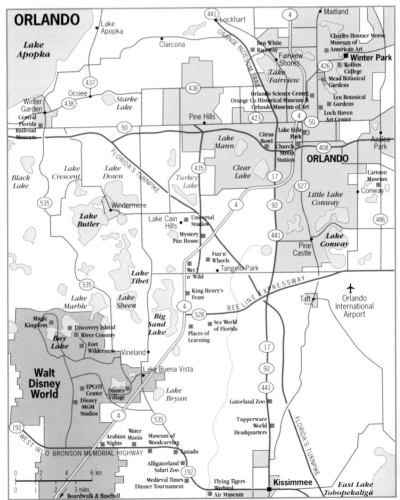

▶▶▶ Church Street Station
129 W Church Street

Located in a newly renovated section of downtown Orlando, Church Street Station is a complete shopping, dining and entertainment complex where the good times roll morning to night every day of the year. The old red-brick Orlando and Strand Hotels, together with the Purcell Building, flank both sides of Church Street and boast a host of shopping places, five restaurants and six entertainment venues.

The **Exchange Shopping Emporium's** 50 speciality shops include fashion and gift boutiques: check out collectables and memorabilia in **Commander Ragtime's Post Exchange**; and souvenirs in the **Bumby Emporium.** The underground **Wine Cellar** has a bar, and stocks around 4,000 bottles of wine for tastings and retail sales.

On the food front, the choice is enormous: enjoy up-market dining at **Lili Marlene's Aviator Pub and Restaurant**; experience great value at **Crackers Oyster Bar**; or grab some fast food from the **Exchange Food Pavilion**. Deli sandwiches and hot dogs at **Rosie O'Grady's Good Time Emporium** are served up with a side order of Dixieland jazz and a handful of can-can girls. The **Cheyenne Saloon and Opera House** features thigh-slapping country and western entertainers, and a Texas barbecue-style restaurant.

Rock and rollers will feel at home in the **Orchid Garden Ballroom**, there is folk and blue grass at **Apple Annie's Courtyard**, disco fever at **Phineas Phogg's Balloon Works**, and a combination of fun, food and games to entertain all-comers at Commander Ragtime's (see above). As if all this was not enough, there are around 10 street parties every year, celebrating such events as Hallowe'en, and great value weekly specials along the lines of **Nickel Beer Nite** (Wednesday 17.30–19.00hrs) at **Phineas Phogg's,** which delivers a glass of draught beer for a nickel.
Open: daily 11.00–02.00hrs.

Eat, shop, and be entertained at Orlandos Church Street Station complex

Fun 'n' Wheels, theme park for fast movers

▶▷▷ Fun 'n' Wheels
International Drive and Sand Lake Road (SR482)
A family attraction with a choice of go-cart tracks
suitable for all ages, bumper cars and (perfect for a hot
day) bumper boats. The latest addition is **Tank Tag**,
played in two-seater miniaturised tanks that compete on
a customised battlefield. There is also a Ferris wheel, a
video arcade and a waterslide. A second location at
Osceola Square Mall (SR192), Kissimmee, offers similar
carting opportunities, but fewer side attractions. Both
have snack bars and Kiddie Ports.
Open: summer, daily 10.00–24.00hrs; winter, Monday to
Friday 16.00–23.00hrs, weekends 10.00–24.00hrs.

▶▶▷ Gatorland
14501 S Orange Blossom Trail (US441)
Just north of Kissimmee, a monster alligator jaw marks
the entrance to the 55-acre 'Alligator Capital of the
World'. Here you will find 5,000 alligators and crocodiles,
and a breeding marsh area which can be observed safely
from a raised boardwalk. There are daily alligator shows
in the 'Wrestlin' Stadium', 'Gator Jumperoo' displays
and feeding times. Other attractions include the
Flamingo Lagoon, monkeys, deer and snakes. You can
sample gator meat cuisine, and pick up alligator skin
souvenirs in the gift shop if your conscience allows.
Open: daily 08.00–dusk.

▶▷▷ Leu Botanical Gardens
1730 N Forest Avenue
Fifty-six acres of lush gardens in the heart of Orlando
make this just the place for a quiet stroll. Take plenty of
time to explore the camellia and azalea woods, the orna-
mental flowering tree garden, sweet-scented Mary
Jane's Rose Garden, and the native wetland garden
down by Lake Rowena. The floral clock is a popular
attraction, there is an Orchid Conservatory, and there are

tours of **Leu House**, a carefully restored turn-of-the-century farmhouse.
Open: daily 09.00–17.00hrs.

▶ ▷ ▷   **Mel Fisher's World of Treasure Museum**
8586 Palm Parkway, Lake Buena Vista
Renowned for his treasure hunting successes off the Florida Keys, Mel Fisher has imported a fraction of the loot from his Key West base to dazzle visitors at this new facility in the Vista Center shopping complex over by Walt Disney World. Silver goblets, gold coins and precious emeralds recovered from Spanish shipwrecks are guaranteed to impress.
Open: daily 10.00–21.00hrs.

▶ ▷ ▷   **Mystery Fun House**
5767 Major Boulevard
Just across from Universal Studios, the recently refurbished Fun House does it with mirrors. There are 15 'Chambers of Surprise', including an Indiana Jones-inspired Forbidden Temple, and a laser game called 'Starship Omega'. Play mini-golf with 'The Wizard', or try the video games in what is one of Orlando's largest games rooms. A free trolley bus service operates between the Fun House and International Drive.
Open: daily 10.00–22.00hrs.

▶ ▷ ▷   **Orange County Historical Museum**
812 E Rollins Street, Loch Haven Park
A few minutes north of downtown Orlando, this museum provides an interesting history of the region which early white settlers called Mosquito County before citrus groves were planted here in the 1880s. Artefacts date back to the original Timucuan Indians, and there is a pioneer kitchen and an old fire station.
Open: Tuesday to Friday 09.00–17.00hrs; Saturday and Sunday 12.00–17.00hrs.

▶ ▷ ▷   **Orlando Museum of Art**
2416 N Mills Avenue
The museum's renowned pre-Columbian gallery – which opened in 1979 – houses 250 pieces, dating from 1200bc to ad1500. Permanent collections of African and 20th-century American art are displayed on a rotating basis, and changing exhibits from other international and private collections cover a range of periods and styles.
Open: Tuesday to Thursday 09.00–17.00hrs; Friday 09.00–21.00hrs; Saturday and Sunday 10.00–17.00hrs.

▶ ▷ ▷   **Orlando Science Center**
810 E Rollins Street
Next door to the Historical Museum, the Science Center is both museum and planetarium. Hands-on participation is encouraged throughout the complex which has exhibits on health, physical sciences and natural history. There are daily multimedia space shows in the John Young Planetarium, and popular weekend 'Cosmic Concerts'.
Open: Monday to Thursday 09.00–17.00hrs; Friday 09.00–21.00hrs; Saturday 12.00–21.00hrs; Sunday 12.00–17.00hrs.

Around South Orlando's International Drive, there are some amazing bargains to be had. An attraction in its own right, Belz Factory Outlet, 5401 W Oakridge Road, houses 80 outlet stores selling discounted fashions, electronics, books and toiletries. This is the place to pick up Disney character T-shirts at prices around *three-quarters* less than the official souvenir shops. Bargain World, 6454 International, offers great deals on sportswear and souvenirs, and International Discount Golf & Tennis, 5684 International, will kit out sporting types with top-name equipment.

▶ ▷ ▷   Sea World of Florida
7007 Sea World Drive

Opened in 1973, this is the world's most popular marine life park. It is huge – 135 acres of marine stadiums, lagoons, aquariums, botanical gardens, restaurants and cafés – and deserves a whole day to explore.

A good place to start is at the 20-minute **Window To The Sea** multimedia presentation in the Sea World Theater. Visitors get a look behind the scenes and a brief introduction to the various park residents. The round of shows begins with the **Whale and Dolphin Discovery Show**, or with wacky antics from Clyde and Seamore, stars of the **Sealion and Otter Stadium**. A performance by **Shamu** the killer whale is a must.

Who says it never snows in Florida? The **Penguin Encounter** manufactures freezing conditions for its inmates, who can be seen waddling around Arctic wastes and swimming under water. **Terrors of the Deep** provides an assemblage of barracudas, sharks and razor-toothed moray eels. To recover, visitors over 21 can refresh themselves with a free beer at the Anheuser-Busch Hospitality Center.

Open: daily 09.00–19.00hrs, extended in summer.

▶ ▷ ▷   Turkey Lake Park
3401 Hiawassee Road

Southwest of downtown Orlando, this 60-acre lakeside park offers beaches, swimming pool, hiking trails, a cycle trail, a 200-foot fishing pier, canoe rentals and a children's playground and petting zoo.

Open: daily 09.30–19.00hrs.

▶ ▶ ▶   Wet 'n' Wild
6200 International Drive

At this state-of-the-art water park, one of the latest is the $1.5 million children's water playground with scaled down versions of adult rides like **Mach 5**: the 'grown-ups' version features 2,500 feet of twists and turns. Nerves of steel are required for **Black Hole** as riders rocket down a 500-foot descent in pitch darkness enlivened by space-age effects. Consider **Der Stuka**, the highest and fastest speed slide in the world, or thunder down the six-storey-high **Blue Niagara**.

Open: daily except January to mid-February. For schedules, tel: (407) 351 WILD or (800) 992 WILD.

Encounter penguins at Sea World of Florida

There are plenty of thrills for swimmers at Wet 'n' Wild

■ **Serious competition for Disney-MGM Studios, Universal Studios' $60-million Florida facility (Interstate-4 at the Florida Turnpike) is a force to be reckoned with, and many rate the recently added Back to the Future ride as the best in Orlando. The 444-acre site houses the largest motion picture studio outside Hollywood, with around 50 attractions and 40 individual movie street sets. To do the studio justice, you should take two days to explore it; if you only have a day to spare, start early with a carefully considered plan of what you intend to see and do .....■**

The rides A light breakfast is advisable before hot favourite **Back to the Future** – four minutes of 21-million jigowatt, stomach-churning action in Doc Brown's back-up DeLorean with OMNIMAX screens. Or brave a New York **Kongfrontation** with one mean 35-foot, 13,000lb ape. Universal's **Earthquake** is indeed 'The Big One' – it has been recorded at an earth-shattering 8.3 on the Richter scale. Ride a San Francisco subway train through a maelstrom of fire, flood and crashing masonry; then subside with a bowl of chowder and some sour dough bread on the Fisherman's Wharf street set. On the other hand, skip the snack if the **Funtastic World of Hanna-Barbera** is the next stop – highly recommended cartoon japes and a bumpy ride on the trail of Dick Dastardly and Muttley. The cast of **Ghostbusters** includes 14 larger-than-life ghosts, the Stay-Puft Marshmallow Man, tons of slime and some 'spooktacular' effects. **ET Adventure** goes for the cute vote with an ET-in-a-basket on the front of every bicycle, and singing flowers – good entertainment for small children, but not exactly a thrill a minute.

In between rides There are plenty of other things to see and do. **The Gory, Gruesome & Grotesque Horror Picture Make-Up Show** revives the truly horrible

metamorphosis of man to insect from *The Fly* among others; TV hopefuls can try out as Executive Producer on an episode of *Murder, She Wrote Mystery Theater*; or star alongside Leonard Nimoy and William Shatner of *Star Trek* fame in the **Screen Test Home Video Adventure**. Catch the **Wild, Wild, Wild, Wild West Stunt Show**; learn a thing or two from **Alfred Hitchcock: The Art of Making Movies**; and turn the kids loose at **Nickelodeon** or **American Tail: Fievel's Playland**.
Open: daily 09.00hrs; closing times vary (tel: (407) 363 8628).

A set at Universal Studios

WALT DISNEY WORLD

(map)

Orlando

Lake Sheen
Lake Mabel
South Lake
Pocket Lake
Big Sand Lake

WINTER GARDEN-VINELAND ROAD
APOPKA-VINELAND ROAD

Reedy Lake
Magic Kingdom
Bay Lake
Contemporary Resort
Discovery Island
Grand Floridian Beach Resort
Seven Seas Lagoon
Pioneer Hall
River Country
Magnolia Golf Course
Disney Inn
Monorail Station
Palm Golf Course
Polynesian Resort
Fort Wilderness
Eagle Pines Golf Course
Bay Lake
Vineland

Lake Buena Vista
The Crossroads of Lake Buena Vista
Lake Buena Vista Golf Course
EPCOT CENTER DRIVE
Spaceship Earth
EPCOT Center
Disney's Village Resort
World Showcase
Disney Village Marketplace
Pleasure Island
WDW Swan, WDW Dolphin
BUENA VISTA
Caribbean Beach Resort
Typhoon Lagoon
Disney - MGM Studios Theme Park
WORLD DRIVE
Reedy Creek
Bonnet Creek
Kissimmee

4
528
Exit 28
Sea World
Exit 27
Exit 26
536
535
192
4
Exit 25
192

0   1   2km
0   1mile

120

▶▶▶ Walt Disney World

It is another world – no doubt about it. A 28,000-acre site housing three theme parks, two water parks, 21 resorts, 99 holes of golf, horseback riding, sandy lakeside beaches, dinner shows, a nightclub park, and enough good times to last a lifetime. Mickey Mouse is out to play, and the whole world (so it seems in peak season) follows suit. Young and old can happily exchange the everyday for the fantasy of **Magic Kingdom**, the futuristic vision and international flavours of the **Epcot Center**, and a sprinkling of stardust in the Tinseltown setting of **Disney-MGM Studios**.

Admission Tickets are valid for one park for one day. For two- or three-day visits separate tickets have to be bought each day; however, a Passport could prove more flexible and better value. **Four-day All Three Parks Passports, Five-day Super Passports**, and **Annual Passes** cover multiple entry to all three main parks over the named period; the Five-day Super Passport also covers unlimited admission to River Country, Typhoon Lagoon, Discovery Island and Pleasure Island for seven days from the first date stamped.

Opening hours During the low season, **Magic Kingdom** and **Disney-MGM Studios Theme Park** are generally open 09.00–19.00hrs; hours can be extended until 22.00–24.00hrs in summer and during peak holiday periods. **Epcot Center**'s opening times of 09.00–21.00hrs are also extended seasonally. For daily schedules, tel: (407) 824 4321.

When to go The busiest days are Monday to Wednesday at **Magic Kingdom** and **Epcot Center**; Wednesday to Friday at **Disney-MGM Studios**. If you visit at Christmas, Easter or during the summer vacation, expect crowds and long waiting times in all the parks. The best time to plan a trip is from September to early November, or on either side of the Easter holiday peak period, up until early June. In summer when the park stays open late, the evening is a good time to catch a lot of the rides with minimum queuing time. Be warned, however, that eateries are very busy at 11.30–13.30hrs and 17.00–19.30hrs. Eating late saves a lot of time.

On the following pages, the various theme parks within Walt Disney World are described alphabetically by theme park. Individual attractions are described alphabetically within the parks.

Spectromagic at Walt Disney World

Earfel Tower in the evening: a unique silhouette

Disney-MGM Studios Theme Park Presenting sheer entertainment, from the tips of the Mickey Mouse ears perched on the water tower to the shops and eateries of Hollywood Boulevard, Disney-MGM Studios has proved so popular that it is growing all the time. Many new features due to be added in the next few years, include a musical production of Andrew Lloyd-Webber's **Noah's Ark**, **Roger Rabbit's Hollywood**, and **Dick Tracy Crimestoppers**. There is a nightly **Sorcery in the Sky** fireworks show. Guest services provide showtime schedules and details of celebrities taking part in the **Star Today** programme.

Backstage Studio Tour This ride is a must, but try to get here first thing or later in the afternoon. The backstage shuttles run right through production, a market garden's worth of trees and shrubs in waiting, then the wardrobe, camera, props and lighting departments before emerging by a backlot street with houses like the Golden Girls' Miami bungalow, and a star car-parking lot. There are great special effects in Catastrophe Canyon (passengers on the left will get wet); then on to a New York City street set re-created in fibreglass. There is a wait before Inside the Magic, the one-hour walking tour with visits to a special effects area and sound-stages.

The Great Movie Ride Housed in a replica of Grauman's Chinese Theater in Hollywood, audio animatronic figures do their best to re-create great moments from film classics, such as Gene Kelly getting drenched in *Singin' in the Rain*, and Bogie and Bacall in *Casablanca*. Though there's commendable attention to detail, this is a disappointing ride.

Here Come the Muppets! Kermit, Miss Piggy, Fozzie Bear, Gonzo and the Electric Mayhem Band strut their

Star Tours

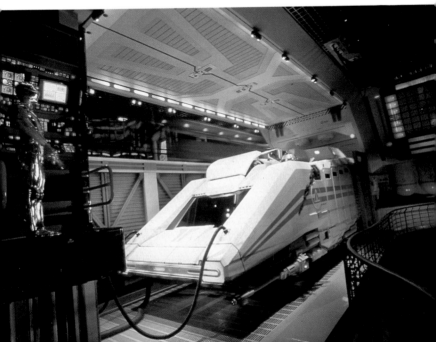

stuff in this thoroughly enjoyable show. At the opposite side of the park, by the delectable **Miss Piggy Fountain**, there is another chance to see Jim Henson's creations in **Muppet Vision 3-D**.

Hollywood Boulevard A 1930s and 1940s pastiche of California Deco and Streamline Moderne, this is the 'Hollywood that never was and always will be'. Shopping is the name of the game along the Boulevard, though browsing is perhaps better advised. **Sid Cahuenega's One-of-a-Kind** stocks movie-bilia, fanzines, glitzy costume jewellery, Indiana Jones jackets and copies of Judy Garland's red-sequinned slippers from *The Wizard of Oz*. Starstruck movie buffs can also pick up authentic memorabilia – at a price.

Indiana Jones Epic Stunt Spectacular Plenty of fire, brimstone and death-defying live stunt work, but also an intriguing look at the tricks of the trade. Volunteers from the audience take part in scenes from *Raiders of the Lost Ark*; the rest of the crowd feels the heat of the explosive finale.

Magic of Disney Animation Hugely popular, this fascinating walk through the Animation Building lays bare every stage of the animation process: story and character development, effects, inking and painting, camera work and the final edit. From Robin Williams' side-splitting introduction to animation basics, right through to the final presentation in the **Disney Classics Theater**, this is one of the best attractions in the park.

Monster Sound Show Audience volunteers add to the general hilarity as sounds are matched with actions. Despite the miracles of modern science, coconut shells still make great hoofbeats, and after the show visitors can test their ingenuity and vocal cords in the **Soundworks**.

Star Tours Hang on to your seats, stomachs and spectacles for this bone-shaking trip through space in an out-of-control Starspeeder vehicle on hire from *Star Wars* travel agent duo R2D2 and C3PO. This intergalactic awayday is not for the faint-hearted.

SuperStar Television Taking audience participation to new heights, here visitors get a chance to feature alongside television characters in some of the most popular shows. On a stage re-created from the early days of live television, members of the audience, duly costumed and made up, get to perform in episodes from *I Love Lucy*, *The Golden Girls*, *General Hospital* or *Cheers*. Though the participants cannot see the complete picture, the audience can through the miracle of 'bluescreen' editing which mixes live action with historic film clips.

Theater of the Stars Check showtime schedules for this open-air bandshell, which stages all-singing, all-dancing musical tributes to the golden age of Hollywood. Disney characters take the various roles, and it is all good fun.

Add an extra-special dimension to a Central Florida holiday with a hot-air balloon flight, and soar over Walt Disney World. Balloon trips can be arranged through Central Florida Balloon Co (tel: (407) 895 1686), Orange Blossom Balloons (tel: (407) 239 7677), or Rise and Float Balloon Tours (tel: (407) 352 8191). For extra lift, sample Rosie O'Grady's Champagne Balloon Flights, or ride a 'blimp' from Virgin Airships (tel: (407) 841 8787).

Disney-MGM Studios really do make films and television shows right here. The soundstages visited on the Backstage Tour provide proof virtually every day. The All New Mickey Mouse Club is one Florida-based production, and there are plans aflipper to return a certain dolphin to the screen in a new movie to be filmed here.

Epcot Center
Adapted from Walt Disney's vision of an 'experimental prototype community of tomorrow', Epcot Center consists of: **Future World**, which explores the role of communications, transport, agriculture and energy, and delves into the realms of the imagination; and **World Showcase**, which tackles the world about us, re-creating the sights and smells of far-off places such as Britain and Beijing, all bathed in uncharacteristic Floridian sunshine. Dining out in one of the ethnic restaurants is a real treat; make reservations first thing at the **Worldkey Information Service** screens at Earth Station, Epcot's information centre – beneath the landmark silver geosphere of Spaceship Earth.

Future World
Communicore East and West Both buildings house a variety of corporate sponsored exhibits looking at subjects as diverse as information gathering and energy efficiency. **Epcot Computer Central** (East) is riveting for computer literate youngsters.

Horizons Time-travel to the 21st century, and a world of holographic telephones, robotic farm-workers, free-floating space and ocean colonies.

Journey into Imagination Pursue the source of creativity with Figment the dragon, lots of jolly songs, dancing laser beams and fantasy landscapes. Also Michael Jackson's made-for-Disney 3-D *Captain Eo*; and hours of hands-on fun at **The Image Works**.

The Land Food, glorious food is under the microscope on a boat trip through an amazing experimental greenhouse. There are also walk tours, a film show and swinging condiments at the **Kitchen Kabaret**.

Living Seas Fascinating study of man and the sea. Take in the introductory film; plumb the depths on the **Caribbean Coral Reef Ride**; check out the videos and hands-on exhibits in **Seabase Alpha**.

Spaceship Earth A ride through the development of earthling communications. Wonder at the hieroglyphics, smell Rome burn, and be dazzled by science.

Wonders of Life Ricochet through the bloodstream on the **Body Wars** ride, or experience a day in the life of a 12-year-old boy in **Cranium Command**. Also included are fitness testing machinery, comedy theatre from the **Anacomical Players** and hands-on health education.

World of Motion and Universe of Energy These focus attention on the history of transportation and energy sources respectively.

World Showcase
American Adventure A generously proportioned Classical-Revival mansion houses a 30-minute animatronic show, which celebrates the 'spirit of America' from the Pilgrim Fathers to John Wayne. Attractive souvenirs from **Heritage Manor Gifts**.

Canada A Rocky Mountain, a totem pole and a flourish of native trees precede the CircleVision 360 presentation, *O Canada!* Buy up lumberjack shirts and maple syrup from **Northwest Mercantile**.

China A flourish of bamboo and the colourful **Gate of the Golden Sun** front a dazzling world of ornate green

124

Venice at the Epcot Center

Reservations are an absolute must at any of the Epcot Center restaurants. However, each of the two 'Worlds' has a couple of good snack stops which can save the day.

A favourite Future World filler is Farmers Market in The Land pavilion; some of its fresh produce is supplied by the on-site experimental greenhouse. Or try Pure and Simple for muffins and yoghurt shakes in Wonders of Life.

and gold curved roofs, carp-filled lily ponds and one of the Showcase's top features, a CircleVision 360 journey through China.

France *Belle époque* Paris in the shadow of an Eiffel Tower (to scale): a Pont des Arts-esque bridge, a sidewalk café, a poster-plastered kiosk and a deliciously scented bakery. Very chic shopping and some serious cuisine at **Chefs de France**.

Germany Fairytale façades, oompah music, red geraniums, lederhosen, and a pungent and unmistakable whiff of sauerkraut from the **Biergarten Restaurant** all add up to a very convincing scene.

Italy Venice's St Mark's Square and the Doge's Palace re-created in extraordinary detail. Bask in the piazza, then sample the pasta at **Alfredo di Roma** (the genuine article).

Japan Inscrutable as ever, the Japanese pavilion is a vision of tiered pagoda roofs, bonsai, monkey puzzle trees and enormously elegant but difficult-to-fathom music and dance demonstrations.

Mexico Explore the **Mayan Temple**, then relax with a beer and a burrito while sombreroed mariachi bands entertain on the lakeshore.

Morocco Enjoy a wander around the bazaar, and take time to admire the cool, tiled courtyards of the **Medina** (Old City). Constructed by Moroccan artisans, this is one of the most impressive buildings in the Showcase.

Norway Ride a Viking vessel into Norse history and the midnight sun.

United Kingdom Half-timbered façades, old red telephone boxes and warm beer in a traditional pub are just the ticket; but Anne Hathaway's Cottage taken over by a tea shop? It is just not cricket!

At World Showcase, there are delicious spring rolls and *dim sum* at China's Lotus Blossom Café; or go for an all-American Adventure at Liberty Inn, and enjoy bowls of chilli, hot dogs, hamburgers and apple pie.

■ **For information in advance, send for a helpful Vacation Guide from Guest Letters, WDW, PO Box 10040, Lake Buena Vista, FL 32830-0040. Hotel, campground, show and ticket reservations can be made through Central Reservations, PO Box 10100, Lake Buena Vista, FL 32830-0100 (tel: (800) 647 7900). The office is open daily 08.30–22.00hrs. Each park has its own information centre located near the entrance which supplies guidebooks and maps. There is an Information Line (tel: (407) 824 4321) and Guest Relations help (tel: (407) 824 4500). Details of services and facilities are given below .....■**

Children and babies Thoughtfully provided **Baby Services** facilities in all three parks offer feeding and changing rooms, and on-site sales of useful items such as nappies, food and baby bottles. Pick up child name-tags at the information centre and hire strollers for a small fee. Snacks can make queuing waits more bearable. Lashings of suncream and a hat are well advised.

Disabled visitors Special parking areas and 'handicap vans' with platforms for loading wheelchairs are provided on request. A WDW *Guidebook for Disabled Guests* details additional facilities and makes helpful suggestions.

Sports WDW has three golf courses: **Magnolia**, **Palm** and **Lake Buena Vista Golf Course**. For information and reservations, tel:

(407) 824 2270. Green fees are halved after 15.00hrs. Equipment hire, tuition classes and private lessons can be arranged.

Tennis courts can be booked at the **Contemporary Resort** (tel: (407) 824 3578), **Grand Floridian Beach Resort** (tel: (407) 824 2438), the **WDW Swan** and **WDW Dolphin** (tel: (407) 934 6000), **Disney Inn** (tel: (407) 824 1469), and **Village Clubhouse** (tel: (407) 828 3741). There is no charge at the last two locations, nor at **Fort Wilderness Campground** where courts are allocated on a first-come-first- serve basis. Equipment and tuition are available.

Transportation WDW is 20 miles southwest of Orlando, off **Interstate-4** and **US192**. From the airport, take the **Beeline Expressway (US528)**. WDW has its own internal bus, monorail and water transport systems which are free to guests staying in WDW hotels and Passport holders. Ferries and the monorail between the Transportation and Ticket Center (TTC) and Magic Kingdom are covered by one-day Magic Kingdom tickets; otherwise one-day unlimited transportation tickets are on sale. There is a small fee for car parking; make a note of the number and row of your space before taking a shuttle bus to the park entrance.

Magic Kingdom

The first of the three Walt Disney World parks to open (in 1971), the 100-acre Magic Kingdom site is based on the original Disneyland design. Mickey Mouse lords it over singing bears, pirates, Cinderella and a host of fun-loving characters from the magical world of Disney cartoons. At 15.00hrs every day the **Main Street Parade** is a must; get there early for a good spot on the route. During summer's extended park hours, thousands of twinkling lights and optical effects electrify twice-nightly **SpectroMagic** displays. Maps and information are available from **City Hall** at the bottom of Main Street, near the entrance.

Adventureland Crazy colonial architecture, Moorish minarets, exotic plants and tropical juice bars take second place to the action-packed fun on offer here. Explore the roomy, vine-covered **Swiss Family Robinson Treehouse**, which has a great view of the park from its crown; then hop aboard a launch at the last outpost river landing for a steamy **Jungle Cruise** down the Nile and up the Amazon jungle. **Pirates of the Caribbean** is the favourite ride in Adventureland, so be prepared to queue: it is well worth it for a rollicking encounter with one-eyed buccaneers, treasure troves and a sighting of the world's first raid by pirates under the influence of audio animatronics. Crooning flowers and chattering totem poles join the **Enchanted Tiki Birds** in a tropical serenade. Less enchanting is the fact that it lasts 35 minutes and there is no escape: over-long for children, but the air-conditioning is bliss.

Fantasyland In the style of the Brothers Grimm, Disney classics cornered in Cinderella's Castle include the Mad Tea Party, Dumbo the Flying Elephant, Mr Toad's Wild Ride and Peter Pan's Flight. There are several fun rides for small children, including **Cinderella's Golden Carousel**, although the 3-D **Magic Journeys** film might

127

Contemporary Resort, one of many places to stay in the theme park

Main Street USA, a trip back to a Victorian era

be a bit scary for the very young. There is a popular sea monster hunt on board a Jules Verne submarine in **20,000 Leagues Under the Sea**, and hundreds of song and dance dolls in national costume entertain at **It's a Small World**. This is the obvious place to raid the toy shop, though prices are on the steep side.

Frontierland Here you will find boardwalks and a brass-railed saloon where the **Diamond Horseshoe Jamboree** is packed with dance-hall belles revived from some long-lost gold-rush town. An all-singing, all-dancing **Country Bear Jamboree** is quite entertaining, too. **Tom Sawyer's Island** offers old Fort Sam Clemens, Injun Joe's Cave and the Magnetic Mystery Mine, and there is a runaway train charging down **Big Thunder Mountain**. **Splash Mountain** is a recent hair-raising addition: a log flume ride with a 45-degree drop and speeds of nearly 40mph.

Liberty Square Culture shock is guaranteed here after a visit to Frontierland's Wild West. While half the country was whooping it up in the local saloon, the other half built gracious colonial-style homes, embroidered flags and brewed great chutney. Brush up on American history with lectures from audio animatronic presidents in the **Hall of Presidents** (children are often less impressed than their parents). There is a relaxing cruise through history on a sternwheel steamer (complete with dancing girls) at **Liberty Square Riverboats**; or paddle your own Davy Crockett canoe. The most popular ride in this land is the **Haunted Mansion**. After gravestone humour has provided a diversion from the queue, sidle past creepy greeters, take time to check out the horror wallpaper, and climb aboard a doom buggy. Although the start is unimpressive, the trailing cobwebs and shrieking holograms ensure that this soon develops into a rip-roaring ride.

Main Street USA The hub of Magic Kingdom from which the other lands radiate, **Cinderella's Castle** is the focus of Main Street. With more than a hint of mad King Ludwig of Bavaria's turreted folly Neuschwanstein, this 180-foot fantasy castle is the first taste of what is to come.

Main Street re-creates a pristine Victorian village of 'olde worlde' shopfronts and colour co-ordinated floral displays, barber's shop quartets, ice-cream parlours and hot dog stalls with striped awnings. The shops are real, and sell antiques, gifts and fancy foodstuffs.

Watch glass ornaments being made by hand, or plunder the serried ranks of Mickeys, Minnies, Donalds and Plutos in the Disney souvenir outlets. The scent of freshly baked croissants and cookies from the **Bake Shop** makes it hard to concentrate, but do not hurry away too soon. There is a **Penny Arcade** with authentic old-fashioned games and venerable 'moving pictures' created by a roller of cards turned by hand. Vintage Disney cartoons get an airing in the **Main Street Cinema**, while the Walt Disney Story has a tale to tell about the great man himself, including letters from admiring presidents and the (seven) dinky Oscars won by Snow White and the Seven Dwarfs. A handy introduction to the Kingdom is a ride on the **Walt Disney World Railroad**.

Mickey's Starland There is no mistaking Mickey's little red car parked in the driveway of Mickey and Minnie's little cartoon house. Take a peek into Mickey's bedroom, then be sure to catch **Mickey's Starland Show** with a whole cast of Disney characters zipping through a jaunty programme which culminates in a good old sing-along.

Starland is a favourite photo-call opportunity tricked out with miniature shopfronts and Disney topiary, a tree-house, a doll's house and animal encounters at **Grandma Duck's Farm**. Special entertainments like puppet shows and jugglers appeal to children, or they can get just a *little* bit lost in the **Mouskamaze**.

Tomorrowland The trouble with a tomorrowland built in the 1970s is that it is already looking distinctly yesteryear. However, there are plans to revamp the complex by 1996. The best reason to stop off here is **Space Mountain**, a terrific roller-coaster ride which rockets through the darkness past meteors and shooting stars. Children under seven years old or 44 inches in height must be accompanied by an adult; this is a rough ride, so accessories like cameras and spectacles should be glued on. Goodyear's **Grand Prix Raceway** is also popular: its mini racing cars plug around four 2,260-foot tracks. Real rack-and-pinion steering and disc brakes require more control skills than might be expected. Of the other attractions, **American Journeys** takes a 360-degree CircleVision tour of the US with flying sequences realistic enough to induce air-sickness, **Mission to Mars** is introduced by a 1960s space puppet and features alarming bucketing chairs, and **Carousel of Progress** delivers 20 minutes on the changes wrought by electricity. At this point, escape to Fantasyland via the aerial **Skyway**.

The steel and fibreglass fantasy of Cinderella's Castle

Two faces of WDW: a 'medieval' town fronts futuristic Spaceship Earth

Other WDW attractions include:

Discovery Island

A back-to-nature corner in Walt Disney World, this 11-acre island in Bay Lake is the perfect antidote to a couple of hectic days in the theme parks. The attractions here are 100 per cent natural, though to create the luxuriant jungle surroundings, palms, bamboo and hundreds of varieties of exotic flora were imported to the site, then planted around winding paths, boardwalks and habitats for a multitude of animals and birds.

Avian Way is one of the largest walk-through aviaries in the world, covering almost an acre. The brilliant plumage of its breeding colony of scarlet ibis is spectacular. There are also African crowned cranes, stately white peacocks and all manner of singing, chattering and fluttering residents. Outsize trumpeter swans can be found down by **Trumpeter Springs**, leggy flamingos at **Flamingo Lagoon**, rescued brown pelicans at **Pelican Bay**, and performing macaws at **Parrots' Perch**.

Among the wildlife to look out for are marsh rabbits and Patagonian cavies (members of the guinea pig family) – approach slowly and quietly, and it is possible to get quite close to them. The giant Galapagos tortoises are a favourite, though often mistaken for boulders. There is no swimming on Discovery Island, but sunbathing is allowed on the beach. Picnickers are welcome, and a snack bar provides ice-creams and cold drinks.

Open: daily 10.00–18.00hrs; summer season, 10.00–19.00hrs. Daily admission tickets, and combination tickets with River Country; admission is also covered by Super Passports.

Fort Wilderness

The official WDW campground with some 1,190 woodland sites, Fort Wilderness is also an excellent activities centre, though use of many of the facilities is restricted to guests staying in WDW-owned properties. Campsite reservations can be made through **Central Reservations** (tel:(407) 934 7639 – some sites are prepared for real canvas campers, others for trailer campers, and there are 363 fully equipped Fleetwood Trailers for rental. These make a great alternative form of budget accommodation. They have two configurations: two double beds and a bunk; or two doubles.

When it comes to what to do, there are no end of diversions at Fort Wilderness, from boating to walking. The 315-foot-long sandy beach on **Bay Lake** is a good place to work on a Florida tan, though its use is restricted to WDW guests. Near by, sailboats, pedal boats and whizzy little Water Sprites can be rented from the marina. Daily fishing excursions are arranged on the lake, and anglers can try their luck after largemouth bass on the placid canals around the camp domain. Basic fishing gear is on sale at the trading posts, or there is equipment hire from the Bike Barn.

The **Bike Barn** is the obvious place to hire a bicycle – there are tandems too for the well balanced. Canoe rentals are perfect for a quiet paddle around the canal system (daily rentals are very good value). Joggers and fitness fanatics will find a scenic vita course circuit; basketball, tennis, volleyball and tetherball facilities are also on hand.

For a touch of animal magic, visit the **Petting Zoo** behind Pioneer Hall. It contains mostly barnyard animals, but the pony rides are popular with young children. For adults and children over nine, there are daily horseback trail rides, which are open to non-WDW guests as well. Even non-riders usually enjoy a visit to the **Horse Barn**, where Disney's champion Percheron horses relax from their theme park duties.

Evening entertainments include the **Hoop-Dee-Doo Musical Revue** (see panel), a popular **Campfire Program** with a sing-along, Disney cartoons and movies, and the summertime **Marshmallow Marsh Excursions**, which involve roasting far too many marshmallows and watching the **Electrical Water Pageant**.

There is never a spare seat in the house for the rollicking Hoop-Dee-Doo Musical Revue dinner show at Fort Wilderness. This is family entertainment at its best, and reservations for the three daily shows (17.00, 19.30 and 22.00hrs) should be made several months in advance at least. Enjoy the verve and energy of the Pioneer Hall Players, along with the generous barbecue-style banquet of ribs, chicken, corn on the cob and strawberry shortcake which arrives at intervals during the two-hour show. To book seats, write to or telephone Central Reservations.

River Country

The smaller of WDW's two water parks (see also **Typhoon Lagoon**), River Country occupies a corner of Bay Lake at Fort Wilderness and boasts a vast 330,000-gallon pool which has been transformed into an adventure-packed 'swimmin' hole' that Huck Finn and Tom Sawyer would have swapped all their marbles for. **Bay Cove** has been kitted out with rope swings, a ship's boom and assorted other constructions off which to jump, dive and generally splash down.

The **Whoop 'n' Holler Hollow** has two corkscrew flume rides for high-speed water-batics; sit up for a vaguely controlled descent, lie back for the greased lightning effect. Two waterslides provide a brief flurry of foaming water and then dump their contents in the pool with an unceremonious splash. For something a little less traumatic, try **White Water Rapids**. Despite its ominous title, this tube ride makes its descent in a series of curvaceous chutes and pools which slow the process down somewhat. On the other hand, there is always a nice, flat, dry piece of sand beach to seek out. In summer, River Country can be extremely busy; one of the best ways to enjoy it is in the late afternoon after a day's sightseeing.

Open: daily 10.00–17.00hrs; Easter week, 09.00–18.00hrs; summer season, 09.00–20.00hrs; closed January. Admission by one- or two-day tickets (reduced after 15.00hrs), combination tickets with Discovery Island, and Super Passports.

Typhoon Lagoon

So the story goes, a typhoon once swept through this 56-acre lagoon resort, and examples of its legendary ferocity are all around: a ship stranded aloft Mount Mayday, huts held together with rope and roofs thatched by whole trees. But everything else here works, from the wave machine to the ice maker.

The centrepiece is the **Lagoon**, with 4-foot waves that crash on to the surrounding sand beaches every 90 seconds. **Castaway Creek** describes a lazy 2,100-foot tube ride around the lagoon – it takes about 25 minutes. There are places to stop along the route, and a dripping rain forest section. Scale Mt Mayday for a spot of **Humunga Kowabunga** – two 214-foot waterslides that send willing victims rocketing down the mountainside and through a series of caves at speeds of up to 25mph. Three storm slides – **Jib Jammer**, **Rudder Buster** and the quaintly named **Stern Burner** take a moderately less hair-raising route down to pools around the lagoon. There are also three raft adventures, one of which can accommodate four people at a time.

Rent fins and a mask to explore fascinating **Shark Reef**. This 326,000-gallon saltwater coral reef environment is teeming with exotic marine life including colourful butterfly fish, angel fish, tangs, and odd-looking but harmless nurse sharks. Small children are likely to get particular enjoyment from **Ketchakiddie Creek**'s scaled-down water zone.

Open: daily. For schedules, tel: (407) 824 4321. Admission by one- or two-day tickets, and also with Super Passports.

Walt Disney World Village and Pleasure Island

Just off Interstate-4 in Lake Buena Vista, and conveniently close to Hotel Plaza, Walt Disney World Village offers recreational activities, shopping, dining, entertainment and plenty of car-parking space.

Shop-till-you-droppers will have a field day at **Disney Village Marketplace**, an attractive complex of boutiques and gift shops, with family-orientated dining at the casual **Pompano Grill**, or one of an assortment of fast food, pizza and sandwich outlets. The biggest Disney merchandise shop in the world, **Mickey's Character Shop** is also located here. Pick up Floridian souvenirs from **Conched Out**, swimwear, sportswear and bright cotton fashion gear at **Resort Wear Unlimited**, great folksy items at the **Great Southern Country Craft Co**, or plan for a traditional Yuletide at **Christmas Chalet**. There's usually something on around the **Captain's Tower** whether it's a book signing or a fashion show.

Connected to the Village by footbridges, **Pleasure Island** is Disney World's home of late-night entertainment, though its shops, restaurants and cinemas remain open all day. Of the six nightclubs, **Mannequins** is wild, with a state-of-the-art lightshow, bubble machines and a display of dancing dummies – oops, mannequins – from which it takes its name. Get down for a country and western evening at **Neon Armadillo**, try not to fall over the rollerskating waitresses at **XZFR Rock & Roll Beach Club** which features a nostalgic line in live bands playing hits from the 1950s up to the present day, or sample the alternative groove at **Cage**.

There are two alternatives to dancing: have a drink, listen to an outrageous bedtime story and explore the junk-strewn **Adventurers Club**; or let the funny men (and women) take the strain at the **Comedy Warehouse**.

Open: daily; shops 10.00–24.00hrs; restaurants 11.30–24.00hrs; clubs 19.00–02.00hrs. Admission only after 19.00hrs (includes entry to all clubs).

If the kids hate to shop, pack them off to Lake Buena Vista Marina, where they can hire pedal boats and Water Sprites, or let them losse in the playground near the Village Stage.

133

Pirates of the Caribbean

ORLANDO

Do not miss a stroll around the lovely campus of Rollins College (Holt Avenue, Winter Park). By the entrance, a Walk of Fame features stones from the birthplaces and homes of famous people. There is a Spanish Mediterranean-style College Chapel, and the Cornell Fine Arts Museum, which houses collections of European Old Masters, 19th-century American paintings, sculpture, modern prints and graphics, and Indian artefacts (*open:* Tuesday to Friday 10.00–17.00hrs; Saturday and Sunday 13.00–17.00hrs).

An English-looking corner of Cypress Gardens

▶ ▶ ▶   Winter Haven

The actual town of Winter Haven has little to recommend it, though the Boston Red Sox undergo spring training here every year, and there is a **Water Ski Hall of Fame**, 799 Overlook Drive (*open:* Monday to Friday 10.00–17.00hrs). However, just outside town is one of Central Florida's biggest attractions – **Cypress Gardens** (*open:* daily 09.00–18.00hrs; extended in summer). Here are cataracts of bougainvillea, waterlily pads the size of picnic tables, 500 types of roses, scented lilies and gardenias, 2 million multi-coloured chrysanthemums for the November **Mum Festival**, and 5,000 red, white and pink poinsettias on display at Christmas. In addition, there is a water ski show on the lake, acrobatic demonstrations, an elaborate model railroad, costumed southern belles, boat rides and **Island in the Sky**, Kodak's 153-foot revolving observation platform.

▶ ▷ ▷   Winter Park

Founded as a winter resort just north of Orlando at the turn of the century, Winter Park is a delightful half-day excursion. Strike off down Morse Boulevard to Lake Osceola for a **Scenic Boat Tour** (daily 10.00–16.00hrs). Lake Osceola and Lake Virginia are linked by leafy canals, and edged by impressive houses. The **Charles Hosmer Morse Gallery of Art**, 133 E Welbourne Avenue (*open:* Tuesday to Saturday 09.00–16.00hrs, Sunday 13.00–16.00hrs), is a must for its superb collection of Tiffany glass, much of it rescued from a fire at Louis Comfort Tiffany's home in Long Island. Glorious stained glass windows filled with roses, and fruit and vegetable 'still lives' are shown alongside jewellery, lampshades, ornaments, and examples of unusual ' drapery' glass (folded when still soft). Other art nouveau artists with work on display include Lalique, Emile Gallé and Maxfield Parrish.

Drive Flowers and Farms in Central Florida

See map on page 108.

This drive makes a comfortable day's outing from Orlando, heading out among the citrus groves to visit two stunning gardens near **Lake Wales**: first, **Bok Tower Gardens**, with its famous carillon bells; then **Cypress Gardens**, which combines acres of scenic floral displays with rides and a waterski spectacular.

From Orlando, there are two routes south to ALT27 at Haines City. The main route takes Interstate-4 south to the Baseball City exit (10 miles from Walt Disney World), then a further 9 miles on US27. A more scenic route via Kissimmee follows US17 South/92 West (25 miles), where it joins ALT27 South.
South of Haines City is a pleasant drive though **Lake Hamilton** and **Dundee** in the heart of citrus country. The glossy, dark green groves are at their best when covered in blossom during the spring, and when the fruit is ripe around Christmas time. Along the roadside, farm stalls groan with fruit and garden produce.

On the outskirts of Lake Wales, take CR17A east for half a mile.
Bok Tower Gardens were donated to the American people by Dutch immigrant Edward W Bok in 1929. The lovely gardens surround an elegant marble tower and local landmark sited on one of the highest points of the Florida peninsula. (For details of the gardens and **Lake Wales**, see page 112.)

Return to ALT27. Turn left into Lake Wales, and proceed to the traffic lights at Central Avenue. A left turn here leads down to a lake and the short detour to Spook Hill; or turn right for US27 (1 mile). At US27 turn right (north) for 5.5miles; then left on to SR540 West for 4 miles.
Cypress Gardens promises all-round family entertainment from flower power to hang-gliding stunts (see **Winter Haven** on facing page).

US27/Interstate-4 leads back to Orlando. For an extended trip, continue north on US27 for 35 miles to Clermont. Continue uphill for a quarter of a mile from the intersection with SR50.
Ahead is another Central Florida landmark, **Citrus Tower** (*open:* daily 08.00–18.00hrs). The 226-foot-high observation deck gives unparalled views over 2,000 square miles. There are also tours of the citrus groves, a candy factory and marmalade making.

Return to Orlando via SR50 East (23 miles).

Sails on Lake Wales

THE GOLD COAST

Sun, sea, sand and palm trees on the Gold Coast

GOLD COAST

0   10 km

0   10 miles

- Jonathan Dickinson S P
  - Blowing Rocks Beach
- Tequesta — Jupiter Inlet
  - 95 Jupiter
- **North Palm Beach** — **Juno Beach**
- **Palm Beach Gardens** — J D MacArthur Beach S P
- **Riviera Beach** — Palm Beach Shores
- **West Palm Beach** — Flagler Museum
  - **Palm Beach**
- Haverhill Norton Gallery of Art
- Palm Springs — **Lake Worth**
  - Lantana
    - Lantana Park
- **Boynton Beach**
  - Ocean Ridge
  - Gulf Stream
- **Delray Beach**
- Morikami Museum — Highland Beach
  - Spanish River Park
  - Red Reef Park
- **Boca Raton**
  - South Beach Park
- **Deerfield Beach**
- Margate — Butterfly World
  - Lighthouse Point
- **Pompano Beach**
  - Hugh Taylor Birch S R A
- Tamarac
  - 95
- Oakland Park
- **FORT LAUDERDALE**
  - John U Lloyd Beach S R A
- Davie — Dania
- **Hollywood**

See Drive Page 153

FLORIDA'S TURNPIKE

Hillsboro Canal

Flamingo Gardens

Golden sun, golden sand and golden opportunities are the stuff the Gold Coast is made of. A package holiday mecca and rich man's retreat, it spreads its wares along a narrow coastal strip between two very different cities bordered by the Atlantic Ocean and the Everglades.

At the southern extreme, **Fort Lauderdale** is one of the fastest growing cities in the state, a flashy high-rise success story built on a maze of inner-city canals carved from the swamps. A few minutes' drive from the glittering Downtown skyscrapers, Fort Lauderdale beach, 3.5 miles long, is lined with swish resort hotels, condominiums, beachfront motels and a minor miracle – 180 acres of natural preserve fronting the shore. This only goes to show that Fort Lauderdale does have some soul. It also has 40,000 yachts, reef diving and sport-fishing. The city is expanding west, reclaiming land with a rapacious enthusiasm which is turning small country towns like horse-mad Davie into suburban satellites.

Davie is the Gold Coast's very own Wild West show. While surfies are riding the Atlantic rollers, the residents of Davie are more likely to be testing their skills at steer-wrestling or bronco-riding at the Thursday night Jackpot Rodeo.

Head north of Fort Lauderdale, and more than a dozen oceanside communities stretch out along A1A fronted by a strip of golden sand. **Pompano Beach** is a noted sport-fishing centre, named for a fishy gourmet delicacy found in the waters off its shores. At **Deerfield Beach**, there is a chance to explore an unspoilt oasis of coastal hammock where armadillos can be seen trotting across the nature trail into the undergrowth.

Then there is **Boca Raton** with its superb beach parks and small but perfectly formed Museum of Art. 'Pretty in pink' is the motto of this exclusive community, where elegant villas are painted to resemble strawberry ice-cream, polo is the name of the game, and shopping is best left to the professionals. Palm Beach architect Addison Mizner planned to build the 'Greatest Resort in the World' here, but was cheated of his dream by the collapse of the 1920s Land Boom. Although Mizner only

managed to complete one hotel, the town has honoured its founder with a wealth of Mediterranean-inspired architecture in the same fashion – painted with lashings of pastel pink, naturally – and it is well worth a visit. For a change of pace, **Delray Beach** is a good shelling spot, and has a hidden treasure in its peaceful Japanese gardens.

As if to emphasise their differences, the Gold Coast's other main focal point, the island community of **Palm Beach,** is not expanding anywhere. Railway king Henry Flagler founded West Palm Beach on the mainland specifically to keep the riff-raff out of his exclusive resort, and that is the way the present-day residents intend to keep it, even though most of them only visit for three months of the year. An hour's drive north of Fort Lauderdale by car, Palm Beach is light-years apart in style. While the *nouveaux riches* of the former are charging about on their yachts to the sound of screamin' reels, the seriously rich of the latter are planning charity croquet tournaments and packing picnic hampers for the polo.

Palm Beach wins all the landscaping points, but **West Palm Beach** is not without its attractions, and it is the place to look for an affordable hotel in this neck of the woods. Its Norton Gallery of Art is a must for culture vultures, and polo, African safari and Everglades adventures are all to be had in the vicinity. **Juno** and **Jupiter** sound like Space Coast satellites, but turtle-watching is more common than star-gazing in these relaxed beach communities at the northern extent of the Gold Coast. Jupiter is Burt Reynolds' home town, where the film star's father runs his tack and feed store.

Sport is big on the Gold Coast. As well as spectator sports like polo, jai-alai and greyhound racing, there are superb tennis and golf facilities throughout the area. Keen sportsmen and sportswomen should investigate the excellent resort sporting packages on offer, with particularly competitive rates available during summer. The traditional off-season accommodation savings are a major attraction, and seniors will also find special deals.

*Boardwalk in Boca
Raton's oceanfront
Red Reef Park*

 Boca Raton

Boca Raton's name dates back to the Spanish explorers who called it 'rat's mouth' for the razor-sharp rocks guarding the bay. It was during the 1920s Land Boom, that Palm Beach architect Addison Mizner gathered a coterie of blue-chip backers, including the Vanderbilts and Elizabeth Arden, to launch a luxury 16,000-acre project that was to be an American Venice with a Grand Canal, a beachfront hotel, an inn, a lagoon with gondolas, a casino and a cabaret. The superb Cloister Inn was completed (now the swish **Boca Raton Resort and Club**), but the project collapsed with the Boom, though a wealth of pink Mediterranean-inspired architecture is still in keeping with Mizner's plan.

Boca Raton is booming again. The 'Winter Capital of Polo' is well supplied with elegant new shopping malls, restaurants and golf, as well as drama, musicals and revues at the **Caldwell Theater** (tel: (407) 241 7432), and five miles of superb ocean beaches. Special events include the **Mizner Festival** (April to May), which celebrates the town's heyday with shows, art and craft exhibitions, and concerts like the jazzy **Meet Me Downtown** event; and **Boca Festival Days** (August).

Boca Raton Museum of Art *801 W Palmetto Park Road*
Well worth a stop for art lovers, this small museum features themed exhibitions which change every six weeks or so. From humble beginnings as an arts society gallery, its transition to a museum has relied on donations, and the collection ranges from works by Andy Warhol and David Hockney to African and pre-Columbian artefacts. The only permanent exhibit is the **Mayers Collection** of drawings, sketches and minor works by late 19th-century and 20th-century artists. As a condition of the bequest, lighting is low and the air-conditioning icy, but brave the temperature for Picasso, Matisse, Seurat, Degas and Modigliani among others.
Open: Monday to Friday 10.00-16.00hrs, Saturday and Sunday 12.00–16.00hrs.

Mizner Park *Mizner Boulevard* This Mizner-inspired shopping, dining and entertainment complex is the latest pink extravanganza to emerge in Boca Raton. The epitome of up-market shopping, this is where art galleries, jewellers, bespoke shoemakers and boutiques cater to local squillionaires, while their chefs can pick up designer spaghetti and four different colours of peppercorns. It is a great free show for browsers. There are shaded benches for surveying the scene, cinemas, an open-air amphitheatre, and plans are in the pipeline to open the **World Museum of Cartoon Art** (moving from New York) in Mizner Park, complete with 75,000 original cartoons, plus over 100 hours of animated videotapes. A wide choice of eateries runs the gamut from chi-chi salads to hearty grilled sandwiches, via Bavarian, Italian and seafood specialties.

Red Reef Park *1111 N Ocean Boulevard (A1A)* Straddling A1A, the 67-acre park offers almost a mile of pristine ocean-front beach bordered by a dense strip of palms, palmettos, sea grapes and Australian pines. There is good swimming and snorkelling around offshore rocks and reef formations, and in an artificial reef area. Picnicking facilities with tables and barbecue grills are provided, and there is also a golf course and plenty of car parking. Surf fishing is a favourite pastime.

About 20 acres of the park has been set aside for the **Gumbo Limbo Nature Center**, which encourages visitors to learn a bit more about their surroundings. Across A1A from the beach, the visitor centre houses interpretive displays, touch tanks and saltwater aquariums for turtles. A boardwalk trail through the tropical hardwood hammock leads to a 50-foot observation tower, and there are Saturday morning guided walks (small charge) which range from beachcombing with an expert to exploring the varied native flora and fauna which inhabit the preserve. In June and July, night-time turtle walks take place on the beach.
Open: daily 08.00–22.00hrs (Park); Monday to Saturday 09.00–16.00hrs (Gumbo Limbo).

The sea grape is a native, saltwater-tolerant shrub occurring naturally in coastal hammocks and along beaches in the southern part of the state. Early settlers used the distinctive round, leathery leaves as emergency note – paper, as plates and even as headgear. The fruit was harvested to make wine and jelly, and the flowers rank in importance with those of black mangroves as nectar-producers for honey. The sea grape is now protected.

139

Pink is the theme colour in elegant Boca Raton

The old wooden cottage that houses Singing Pines Children's Museum

Royal Palm Polo Sports Club *Clint Moore Road* Every spring, polo players from the world over converge on the Gold Coast, when Boca Raton's Royal Palm, one of the region's major clubs, hosts the annual $100,000 International Gold Cup Tournament at the end of March. Games are played at the club every Sunday from January to mid-April at 13.00 and 15.00hrs. For general admission and box seats, pay at the ground; for advance reservations for tailgate car parking, tel: (407) 994 1876. Free non-spectator car parking areas.

Singing Pines Children's Museum *498 Crawford Road (off Palmetto Park Road, beyond City Hall)* The museum occupies an octogenarian Cracker cottage reckoned to be the oldest wooden structure in Boca Raton. It is a great rainy day option or a treat for children who will enjoy a couple of hours play-acting in the shopping room, the Pioneer kitchen or a Seminole *chickee*, and drawing or playing games.
Open: Tuesday to Saturday 12.00-17.00hrs.

South Beach Park *400 N Ocean Boulevard (A1A)* This is another lovely section of beach, but less developed than popular Red Reef and Spanish River. Walkways cut through the dense coastal undergrowth; life-guards patrol 09.00–17.00hrs; good swimming and some snorkelling.
Open: daily.

Spanish River Park *3001 N Ocean Boulevard* Boca Raton's award-winning 46-acre city park occupies both sides of A1A with three tunnels linking the parking areas to a 1,850-foot strip of sun-soaked ocean beachfront. Nature trails explore an undeveloped natural hammock and woodland preserve, and picnickers will find plenty of tables and barbecue grills. Bicycle trails and a boat dock are provided, and there is good fishing on the Intracoastal Waterway. A two-level observation tower overlooks the park and the coast, and affords a good view of the city.

Addison the Architect

■ **Addison Mizner was an unlikely candidate as the most influential architectural stylist in South Florida. A 20-stone ex-prize fighter and retired miner, he rolled into Palm Beach in 1918, and is credited with introducing the 1920s vogue for Spanish-style architecture. .....■**

Everglades Club Mizner's first venture, the Everglades Club in Palm Beach, was a collaboration with Paris Singer, scion of the sewing machine fortunes. Intended as a convalescent home for World War I veterans, it bears a strong resemblance to a Spanish monastery with a battery of medieval turrets and wrought-iron curlicues. The end of the war saw it swiftly redesignated as a private club, which it remains today. Its eye-catching design was an instant hit, spawning a host of imitations, and its architect was signed up immediately to build winter residences for wealthy Philadelphia socialites – Stotesburys, Vanderbilts and Wanamakers.

Spain in the New World Mizner studied the Old World architecture of South America and traced it back to its roots in Spain. Conscious of the broad blue Florida sky as the only backdrop for his designs, he created bold pastel outlines and incorporated elegant courtyards surrounded by cool arcades. Red barrel roof tiles topped second-storey galleries, fountains played into tiled pools and decorative mosaic murals added a Roman-Mediterranean touch. Interiors featured lofty vaulted ceilings with exposed beams hewn from mature pecky cypress. Buying trips furnished his creations with the trappings of Old Spain, and Mizner also set up local factories to reproduce ironwork, tiles and furniture – the accessories for his buildings – in the correct Mediterranean style.

End of a dream In 1925, with the Land Boom in full swing, Mizner embarked on a lavish scheme to

<< The pecky cypress has a pitted, streaky appearance, and when attacked with wire brushes, blow torches and acids, then stained, it looks suitably antique **>>**

transform 16,000 acres around Boca Raton into a dream resort. 'I am the Greatest Resort in the World,' boasted the immodest advertisements, and they netted $2 million-worth of contracts on the first day of sales. Six months later, the Boom was over, a devastating hurricane and a trail of dirty deals had renamed the project 'Beaucoup Rotten', and Mizner was penniless. One enduring memorial to Mizner's fantasy resort is his $1.25 million Cloister Inn (now the Boca Raton Resort and Club), believed to be the most expensive 100-room hotel built in its time – and it is truly fabulous.

Mizner Park, where the millionaires do their shopping

▶ ▶ ▷ **Butterfly World**

Tradewinds Park South, 3600 W Sample Road, Coconu Creek

Located southwest of Deerfield Beach and the Florid Turnpike, this provides an unusual opportunity to be dazzled by the insect world, and it is a popular outing with children as well. On a 2.8-acre site, some 2,000 butterflies from more than 100 species live their shor lives in the sort of ideal conditions that mean they some times survive for two whole weeks – about twice the normal time for a butterfly in the wild. First stop past the entrance is a look at the laboratory where thousands o larvae and pupae are visible at various stages o development. Behind the scenes, Butterfly World is a fully-fledged butterfly breeding farm which aims to supply collectors with specimens, some of which are becoming endangered in the wild.

The first of the huge screened aviaries is **North American Butterflies**, reserved for native species; the second, **Basket Walk**, allows visitors to watch the emerging pupae; and the third enclosure, the **Tropica Rain Forest** is a dramatic 30-foot-high constructior equipped with observation decks, waterfalls, ponds and tunnels where thousands of gossamer-winged creatures from around the world form a dazzling pattern of shifting colours. Do not forget your camera to catch the momen when a butterfly lands on one of your party (brigh yellow T-shirts appear to be popular). There are wate gardens and displays of butterfly-attracting plants for the garden in the grounds; there is also an **Insectarium and Museum**, and plenty of butterfly souvenirs in the gif shop.

Open: Monday to Saturday 09.00–7.00hrs, Sunda 13.00–17.00hrs.

▶ ▶ ▷ **Davie**

Way out west in Broward County, but a mere 10 mile from downtown Fort Lauderdale, Davie is another worlc It would be unfair to call Davie a 'one horse town', as boasts enough hitching posts to secure the 7th Cavalry This is a town with horses on the brain, where ever McDonalds have got the idea loud and clear and provid a 'ride-thru' service for locals who believe in taking thei food at a gallop. The local Town Hall boasts swinging saloon doors and a bristling display of imported cact while the 5,000-seat **Davie Rodeo Arena**, 6591 SW 45th Street, provides live action in the 'Jackpot Rodeo every Thursday night at 20.00hrs. Steer-wrestling, calf roping, bareback riding, and bronco- and bull-riding a find a place on the programme, and for a touch of class no self-respecting cowboy should miss the **Florid State Championship Rodeo** sponsored by the Florida Cowboys Association each November/December (te (305) 581 0790 for details). Armchair cowboys and cow girls can shop for authentic gear alongside the real thing at South Florida's largest purveyor of Western wear **Grif's Western Wear**, 6211 SW 45th Street, whic stocks boots, hats, pearl-buttoned shirts, jeans and saddles of every description.

There are a couple of other outdoor attractions near by which are listed below.

An old-time cowman from Davie

Everglades Holiday Park and Campground, *21940 Griffin Road* On the eastern edge of the vast Everglades swamplands which stretch right across the state to the Gulf of Mexico, the park allows a brief Glades experience complete with alligators and airboat rides. Powered by aircraft propellers, these metal framed contraptions zip across the shallow marshes, giving a ringside seat for viewing all the weird and wonderful native flora and fauna on offer. Forty-five-minute narrated airboat tours depart every 30 minutes from 09.00–17.00hrs, and there are self-drive craft for hire. A replica Seminole Indian village hosts a stopover and provides entertainment in the form of alligator wrestling. The park's campground has 100 sites for tents and trailers. For information, tel: (305) 434 8111.
Open: daily.

Flamingo Gardens, *3750 Flamingo Road (north off Griffin Road)* There is a bit of everything at this popular attraction, and a tram ride explores the 60-acre site, which was one of the county's earliest citrus groves. In addition to the glossy citrus trees, still much in evidence, there is a native hammock area, an arboretum, mature oaks and 19 huge Champion trees. Bromeliads and orchids flourish among the tropical scenery, and rare gingers and heliconias make an impressive display. Alligators, crocodiles, monkeys and otters all represent the animal kingdom, plus a squawking, chattering and brilliantly coloured array of exotic birds including the flamingos which give the park its name. Children will enjoy the petting zoo, and other attractions include a small historical museum, a natural craft and book store, and the annual **Plant Affair West and Landscape Design Show** in October.
Open: daily 09.00–17.00hrs.

143

A coastguard on the look-out for trouble

▷▷▷ **Deerfield Beach**

Just a mile south of Boca Raton city limits, Deerfield Beach is one of the few remaining strips of Gold Coast shoreline still of interest to shell seekers, but its best-kept secret is **Deerfield Island Park**. Only accessible by boat, the 56-acre island sits in the middle of the Intracoastal Waterway at its junction with the Hillsboro Canal. There is a free boat service from the dock at the end of Riverview Road (off SR810 by the Chamber of Commerce) on Wednesdays and Saturdays. A stone's throw from the hurly-burly of A1A and the coastal developments, this little pocket of virgin wilderness offers two beautiful nature trails with a chance to see armadillos and grey foxes in the wild. The Coquina Trail parallels the Intracoastal Waterway to a rocky bluff, while the Mangrove Trail is a raised boardwalk through areas of black, red and white mangroves and around a wooded swamp.

Open: daily 08.00hrs–dusk.

▶▷▷ **Delray Beach**

A pleasant seaside town with a broad main thoroughfare, Atlantic Avenue, stretching out to the west, Delray was settled in 1901. The early residents included the Yamato Colony of Japanese pineapple farmers. The main attraction here is the **Morikami Museum and Japanese Gardens** at 4000 Morikami Road (tel: (407) 499 0631). These tranquil gardens make a lovely picnic spot, and the complex offers a fascinating insight into Japanese art and traditions. In the museum, antique *netsuke* carvings are collected, together with contemporary prints, musical instruments and folk crafts such as origami (paper folding). Learn about the tea ceremony and the ancient skill of bonsai culture (growing dwarf trees), and try to attend one of the four traditional Japanese seasonal festivals celebrated here: **Hatsume Fair** (February), **Bon Festival** (August), **Bunka No Hi** (November), and **Japanese New Year** (December/January).

Open: Tuesday to Sunday 10.00–17.00hrs. For festival information, tel: (305) 495 0233.

Mangrove swamp: Deerfield Island Park is one of the places where it is possible to see this strange landscape

Gold Coast Beaches

■ Hitting the beach is an all-important ingredient of any Florida holiday, and visitors to the Gold Coast will find themselves spoilt for choice. And, hard to believe though it is, a couple of wilderness beaches do still exist along this highly developed coastline. .....■

Fort Lauderdale area Even in downtown Fort Lauderdale, it is possible to find a tiny enclave of natural beach accessible from the Hugh Taylor Birch State Recreation Area. It is surrounded by a further 3.5 miles of city beach, though the backdrop is a rather less scenic series of high-rise hotels and condominiums. A short distance south of Fort Lauderdale, **Hollywood Beach** (on A1A) is a five-mile mirage of golden sand and swaying palm trees – except it really does exist. It runs into leafy **North Beach Park**, which has shady picnic areas, an observation tower and sea turtle tanks. The quietest municipal beach area around here is little **Dania Beach**, off Oak Street; but then **John U Lloyd Beach State Recreation Area** is 12 times the size with a nature trail through a coastal hammock, manatee-watching and good fishing on the Intracoastal Waterway. Drive north from Fort Lauderdale, and there is **Pompano Beach** with its fishing pier; while **Deerfield Beach** (seefacing page) is a good spot for beachcombing.

Boca Raton area The first of the Boca Raton beaches is **South Inlet Park**, also the most secluded, and a good bet for peace and quiet during the week. Next up, **South Beach Park** (see page 140) is relatively undeveloped, in fact positively backward compared with neighbouring **Red Reef Park** (see page 139), which boasts a golf course and nature centre across A1A. **Spanish River Park** (see page 140) is another family-orientated beach park with nature and bicycle trails. **Delray Beach** (see facing page) is a good spot for shelling, and

there is a great little beach at **Lantana Park**. Both are *en route* for Palm Beach.

Palm Beach area A narrow 6-mile strip of sand borders the ocean at Palm Beach, but for some spectacular seashore head north to **John D MacArthur Beach State Park** (see page 157), which is a favourite nesting ground for sea turtles in summer. Continue north to **Juno Beach** (see page 158), and it is the same story, though parking can be tricky here. **Blowing Rocks Beach** on Jupiter Island is not a good place to swim, but the scenery is marvellous; venture on to **Jupiter Beach Park** for excellent swimming and walks along the shore.

Quiet beach, Fort Lauderdale

THE GOLD COAST

The magnificent new $53-million Broward Center for the Performing Arts at 624 SW Second Street provides world-class facilities for opera, theatre, ballet and concerts in Fort Lauderdale, and is the place to catch Broadway productions. Artists as diverse as Itzhak Perlman, Marvin Hamlisch and Branford Marsalis have appeared there. The Parker Playhouse, 707 NE Eighth Street also hosts top-of-the-line Broadway and occasional pre-New York productions.

▶ ▶ ▶ Fort Lauderdale

The most popular beach resort in the state, Fort Lauderdale also prides itself on being the 'Yachting Capital of the World' (40,000 registered craft), the 'Tennis Capital of the World' (birthplace of Christine Evert), and the 'Venice of America' (300 miles of navigable waterways). Less appealing is the nickname 'Fort Liquordale', from the days when rum runners kept the town generously supplied with liquor during Prohibition. In the 1950s, droves of college students on Easter vacation revived the 'Liquordale' image, inspiring the 1960 beach bimbo movie *Where the Boys Are*, until the legal drinking age was raised. Despite the drop in spring business, Fort Lauderdale breathed a sigh of relief as it got on with the job of promoting its attractions as a year-round family tourism destination.

Early days The first known white settler, Charles Lewis, created a plantation by the New River in 1793. Later, Major William Lauderdale came south to establish a small fort, the first of three, for the protection of local settlers during the Second Seminole War in 1838. Ohio steelworker Frank Stranahan was next on the scene. He set up an overnight camp for the Bay Biscayne Stage Line at Tarpon Bend in 1893 and also established a trading post which became a focal point for the development of Fort Lauderdale. For a few years, his main customers were the Seminole Indians who traded pelts, alligator hides and egret plumes for provisions. The arrival of Flagler's East Coast Railroad in 1896 created a mini boom. Soon there were enough children to justify a school teacher, Ivy Cromartie, who later married

Intracoastal yacht off Fort Lauderdale

OAKLAND PARK BOULEVARD 816
Middle River North Fork
Paddlewheel Queen
811
Wilton Manors
Middle River South Fork
A1A
Lazy Lake
1
Middle River
WILTON DRIVE
Hugh Taylor Birch State Recreation Area
ATLANTIC BLVD
N OCEAN BLVD
Intracoastal Waterway
838 SUNRISE BOULEVARD 1
Parker Playhouse
Holiday Park
War Memorial Auditorium
Bonnet House
FORT LAUDERDALE
NE 3RD AVENUE
AVENUE
FEDERAL HIGHWAY
Fort Lauderdale Historical Society
Museum Museum of Art
LAS OLAS BOULEVARD 842
Museum of Discovery and Science
Stranahan House
Bahia-Mar Yacht Basin
New River
International Swimming Hall of Fame
ANDREWS
Turpon River
FEDERAL HIGHWAY
Jungle Queen
Voyager Sightseeing Tram
DAVIE BOULEVARD

147

Ocean World Dolphin Show
17TH STREET
Stranahan River
SEA BREEZE BLVD
Ft Lauderdale Beach
A1A
84
BROOKS MEM CAUSEWAY
PORT ROAD
Port Everglades
0   ½   1km
0   ½mile
595 Snyder Park
Fort Lauderdale-Hollywood International Airport
John U Lloyd State Recreation Area
FORT LAUDERDALE

Stranahan. Other local communities sprang up: tomato-farming Danes in **Dania**, to the south; Swedes, **Hallandale** and **Pompano,** to the north, favoured by Georgians and North Carolinians.

Florida's governor, Napoleon Bonaparte Broward, launched his much-vaunted plan to drain the Everglades in 1906, and the Roaring Twenties heralded a massive programme of land reclamation in the New River swamps, and the foundation of **Hollywood-by-the-Sea** by developer Joseph Young, who was also the visionary behind **Port Everglades**, now the second largest cruise port in the world. The collapse of the Land Boom put an end to all this until 1947, when another canal dredging and landfill project raised further communities.

In the 1990s, Greater Fort Lauderdale's population of around 1.2 million is growing all the time. A $670-million urban redesign programme for the decade includes redevelopment of the beachfront, and a **Riverwalk** which will link the city's past and future as it follows the course of the New River from historic **Stranahan House** to the brand-new **Broward County Performing Arts Center**. On the accommodation front, a total of 30,000 hotel rooms come in all prices, ranging from swanky deluxe resorts to great value beachfront motels and small lodgings. Free weekday Trolley Services operate around Downtown and the Las Olas Boulevard shopping district; and do not miss a chance to ride in a water taxi.

Bonnet House, *900 N Birch Road* All it takes is one short telephone call to be admitted to this ravishing private estate: anyone with a love of beauty, the arts, and a certain idiosyncratic style should make that call.

Bonnet House, named for the yellow Everglades lilies which flourish on the 36-acre downtown site, is the legacy of two artists, Frederic Clay Bartlett, and his third wife, Evelyn. Bartlett designed the gracious two-storey plantation house in 1919. A luxuriantly planted central courtyard, broad verandas and outdoor walkways integrate the house with its natural surroundings. Examples of Bartlett's artwork – murals, frescos, canvases – are everywhere. Evelyn Bartlett's paintings hang in a small gallery, and the orchid house was her special preserve. Animals and birds feature constantly around the estate, from the carousel beasts and menagerie of wood carvings in the courtyard to the free-ranging monkey colony and gracious black and white Australian swans. Tours of the grounds with their hardwood hammock, mangroves and freshwater lagoon are made by golf buggy, and lemonade is served informally on the veranda.

Open: by appointment May to November, Tuesday, Thursday, Sunday, tel: (305) 563 5393.

Fort Lauderdale Historical Society Museum, *219 SW Second Avenue, Himmarshee Village district* Information panels and photographs explain architectural trends and the development of the area. Read up on the 1920 construction kings; see Mizner's plans for the proposed (but not built) Ritz Carlton hotel; and don't miss the views of Fort Lauderdale from 1920 to 1948, showing the river marshes transformed into America's Venice.

Just down the street **King-Cromartie House**, 229 SW Second Avenue, illustrates a typical pioneer home furnished as it would have looked in the early 1900s. There is a question mark over who is going to operate the house after 1992: ask at the Historical Society for details.

Open: Tuesday to Saturday 10.00–16.00hrs, Sunday 13.00–16.00hrs.

Fort Lauderdale claims to be the 'Yachting Capital of the World'

■ **Standing on reclaimed Everglades marshland, Fort Lauderdale bears the proud title of 'Venice of America'. However, with over 300 miles of navigable inland waterways, Fort Lauderdale and Broward County actually outstrip Venice by quite a long way. .....■**

It all began with Governor Napoleon Bonaparte Broward who won his political ticket on a promise to drain the Everglades for agricultural land. In 1906, true to his promise, he began a dredging programme on the New River at Sailboat Bend, employing brothers Reed and Thomas Bryan, and settlers who had worked on the Panama Canal. The Bryan brothers built homes here which now form the historic **Chart House Restaurant** (self-guided tours Tuesday to Sunday). The veterans of Panama called the first settlement on reclaimed land Zona, later to be renamed **Davie** after a local cattle baron.

In 1912, the North New River Canal reached Lake Okeechobee, creating a brief fad for cross-state steamboat cruises to Fort Myers, but heavy silt closed the canal in 1921. In the same year, Messrs Hortt, Dye and Stilwell, inspired by Carl Fisher's Miami Beach land reclamation, dreamed up a landfill operation for a stretch of mangrove swampland between the New River and the Intracoastal Waterway. They christened it Idlewyld, and it now forms part of downtown Fort Lauderdale.

Building an American Venice

Idlewyld's success was the cue for seed store merchant and real estate investor Charlie Rodes to enter the arena. Using a Venetian land-building technique known as 'finger-islanding', he dredged a series of parallel canals from central Las Olas Boulevard towards the river, and created narrow peninsulas with landspoil from the channels. Each peninsula had a central dead-end road with waterfront plots to either side, and this grid of exclusive little fingers of land was called Venetian

Isles. It remains the most sought after real estate in the city.

<< Parking problems are a thing of the past in Fort Lauderdale. Forget the car and take to the canals with the city's water taxi service. The service will pick up direct from a wide variety of hotels, restaurants, and sights including Stranahan House, Ocean World and the Galleria Mall (allow 10 minutes). There is a fixed one-way rate, and good value unlimited use day passes. Guided tours of the New River (Saturday 10.30hrs) are highly recommended. (For information and bookings, tel: (305) 565 5507.) >>

Take to water transport

Get away from the city bustle in Hugh Taylor Birch State Recreation Area

Hugh Taylor Birch State Recreation Area, *3109 E Sunrise Boulevard* Generations of Fort Lauderdale residents and visitors have reason to be grateful to Hugh Taylor Birch, provider of 180 acres of city centre parkland. A green oasis sandwiched between the seafront hotels of Atlantic Boulevard and the Intracoastal Waterway, the park is the ideal antidote to life in the mainstream, with walking trails, picnic areas, canoe rentals, boating, a vita course, and an underpass to a section of ocean beach. A 1.75-mile circuit round the park can be walked, jogged or driven. Off the beaten track, the quarter-mile **Beach Hammock Trail** leads off into the natural hammock and mangrove areas.

There are around 524 species of plant growing here such as the flaky red-limbed gumbo limbo, or 'tourist tree'; feathery Australian pines; dense belts of mangroves; predatory strangler figs; and a mass of flowering plants which attract flocks of outsize butterflies. Racoons, squirrels, marsh rabbits and owls can be spotted by eagle-eyed explorers, and wading birds frequent the lagoon and shores of the Intracoastal Waterway. This is also a good fishing spot. Near the entrance, a visitor centre housed in Birch's last residence provides a brief introduction to the park's history, flora and fauna with a short film and exhibits. *Open*: daily 08.00hrs–dusk.

International Swimming Hall of Fame, *1 Hall of Fame Drive (off E Las Olas)* Remember Mark Spitz and all those gold medals? And did you know the legendary Johnny Weissmuller was a champion swimmer before he became King of the Apes? In addition to celebrating the feats of Olympic heroes, the Hall of Fame features aquatic art, films, exhibits of technical equipment used in professional racing, historical data and records, even swimwear through the years – from woollen bathing costumes more likely to sink than swim to sleek modern racing gear. The neighbouring **Aquatic Complex** has two Olympic pools and diving facilities.

For information on opening times, tel: (305) 462 6536.

Jungle Queen, *Bahia-Mar Yacht Center, Ocean Drive (A1A)* The Jungle Queen riverboats are a great way to explore the city and its environs, albeit in a distinctly touristy fashion. Three-hour narrated Sightseeing Cruises depart twice daily (10.00 and 14.00hrs) for a trip up the New River through Downtown and into the edge of the Everglades. After a glimpse of the river frontage of the city's most exclusive neighbourhoods, it is time for a wander around a purpose-built Indian village offering souvenirs, caged birds and alligator wrestling.

For a full-day trip (09.15–17.15hrs), there is a jaunt down to Miami. Or sail up the New River on a four-hour **Barbeque Ribs and Shrimp Dinner Cruise** which docks at an island for an 'all-you-can-eat' spread and entertainment in the shape of a vaudeville revue. For information and reservations, tel: (305) 462 5596.

Museum of Art, *1 E Las Olas Boulevard* Designed by Edward Larabee Barnes and opened in 1986, the museum is an impressive showcase for its extensive collections of 19th- and 20th-century American and European art. There are also collections of African and pre-Columbian artefacts, and changing exhibitions which focus on specific periods and art forms. During September and October, the gallery displays the pick of entries for the M Allen Hortt Memorial Competition, South Florida's most prestigious art prize, and one which attracts a terrific diversity of mediums.

A browse in the Museum Store is highly recommended: great cards, posters and art books; unusual gifts and handcrafted jewellery.

Open: Tuesday 11.00–21.00hrs, Wednesday to Saturday 10.00–17.00hrs, Sunday 12.00–7.00hrs.

An easy way of seeing the sights

The second largest cruise port in the world, Port Everglades has a five-star fleet of 25 ocean liners. For a brief experience of life on the ocean wave, two local cruise line operators offer day trips to the Bahamas, daytime cruises and dinner cruises with casino action and live entertainment. For details, contact: Discovery Line, tel: (305) 921 5788; or SeaEscape I, tel: (305) 379 0000 or (800) 432 0900.

THE GOLD COAST

Museum of Discovery and Science, *401 SW Second Street* A $30-million project opened in autumn 1992, this is going to be a blockbuster with youngsters. Packed from floor to ceiling with hands-on exhibits, a five-storey-high six-channel sound IMAX cinema, and special programmes of exhibits and events, it is often busy with school parties during term time. Themed exhibits put the 'fun' into 'functional' with displays like the **Body Works** where mums and dads sneakily test their reactions while kids test their strength and pounding hearts. **Kidscience, Space Base, SoundTracks** and **Technology** all provide plenty to see and do, from bending beams of light to a spot of sensory deprivation. One of the highlights is the walk-through **Florida Ecoscapes display** with a series of simulated Florida habitats. Space freaks should not miss the **Manned Maneuvring Unit** space ride (not for the weak of stomach); there is Laser Pinball; and young children can enjoy the **Florida Sunshine Grove** harvest-to-market exhibitions. The self-service café is a useful pit stop, and there is a museum store.
Open: Tuesday to Saturday 10.00–17.00hrs, Sunday 12.00–17.00hrs.

Ocean World, *SE 17th Street (off A1A)* Any trip to Florida should feature at least one marine park, and Ocean World is a good place to start. The stars of the show are bottlenose dolphins, whose high jinks and underwater acrobatics make for great family entertainment, while cheeky sea lions provide light relief. The continuous round of shows at this compact park also includes exotic birds demonstrating their mastery of human skills from polite conversation to riding a bicycle. You can 'enjoy' shark feeding sessions, watch alligators bask in their pools, and also pet some of the dolphins and meet baby 'gators. A passenger boat, *Miss Ocean World*, makes regular departures on sight-seeing trips past the palatial mansions on the New River, and into Port Everglades for a look at the cruise ships and naval vessels lining the docks.
Open: daily 10.00–18.00hrs (last tickets 16.30hrs).

Dolphins in their element in Fort Lauderdale's Ocean World

Drive **Fort Lauderdale to the Palm Beaches**

See map on page 136.

Two main routes run the length of Florida's East Coast: fast Interstate-95, and the seaside route A1A. Palm Beach makes an excellent day trip from Fort Lauderdale, and a good way to see more of the area is to take a gentle drive up A1A. The trip back via Interstate-95 can be undertaken in less than an hour later in the day.

From the junction with Sunrise Boulevard, drive north on Atlantic Boulevard (A1A) for 7 miles to Pompano Beach.
Pompano Beach is fêted as the 'Swordfish Capital of the World' with a list of record catches quite as long as one of those fishermen's tales. Its 1,080-foot **Municipal Pier** is a popular spot with anglers, and during winter there is a well-supplied Farmers' Market.

The Intracoastal Waterway appears to the left at Hillsboro (2 miles); to the right, luxuriant greenery conceals wealthy beachfront villas.
If it is a Wednesday or Saturday, and there is time to spare, the intersection with **SR810** at **Deerfield Beach** is the cue to turn left for the boat service to **Deerfield Island Park**, a 56-acre natural preserve on the Intracoastal Waterway (see page 144).

Continue on A1A, for a short distance to the junction with Camino Real at Boca Raton.
Founded by 1920s architect and developer Addison Mizner, **Boca Raton** is well worth a detour off A1A for a taste of its palm-fringed elegance (see pages 138–41).

Turn left on to Camino Real, and follow the old canal route past the de luxe Boca Raton Resort and Club to the junction with Federal Highway; turn right. Ice-cream pink Royal Palm Plaza Mall is just one

Boca Raton shoppers' haven near the junction with Palmetto Park Road. Turn right here, and rejoin A1A opposite South Beach Park, along a stretch of tree-lined roadside which continues most of the way to Highland Beach, and Delray Beach (8 miles).
An unusual detour at **Delray Beach** is the **Morikami Museum and Japanese Gardens** (see page 144).

A1A continues up the coast to Palm Beach. After 16 miles the road divides: both A1A and the right-hand fork, South Ocean Boulevard, intersect with Royal Palm Way, which crosses the Intracoastal Waterway to West Palm Beach and Interstate-95.
(See **Palm Beaches**, pages 161–9.)

You can get away from it all

Shipwrecks and Reefs

■ **The Gold Coast does not get its name from its miles of sandy beaches, its millionaire residents or year-round sunshine. The gold in question comes from the sea. .....■**

154

Spanish treasure During the 17th and 18th centuries, Spanish treasure fleets laden with bounty from the New World started the journey homeward hugging the South Florida coastline. Their efforts to avoid offshore storms were often to no avail, and many vessels were tossed on to the reefs or sank with their priceless cargoes of gold, silver and precious stones. One of the most notable losses was the sinking of 11 vessels off the coast between Vero Beach and Fort Pierce, north of Palm Beach, on the night of 30 July 1715. The Spanish began their own salvage operation immediately, and it continued for some years; more recently the renowned Florida marine treasure specialists Real Eight and Treasure Salvors Inc, have made a more comprehensive sweep.

Natural reefs The needle-sharp underwater rock formations which plagued the Spanish off the Gold Coast are the upper reaches of South Florida's three-tiered network of natural reefs, which extend 220 miles northwards from the Florida Keys. It is the largest natural reef area in North America, and home to a magnificent variety of marine life. Depths range from 12 feet to around 120 feet within half a mile of the shore. The water's low temperature is around 72°F in winter, and visibility averages 70–100 feet the year round. Pollution and careless divers have taken a toll of the living reef in the Fort Lauderdale area, but strict controls are now enforced to prevent any further damage.

A sea change One of the most interesting developments aimed at preserving this natural habitat has been the growing trend for creating artificial reefs: shipwrecks are back in fashion. These modern-day

Cave diving

shipwrecks are intentional, and more than two dozen derelict freighters and other vessels have been sunk off the coast of Broward County in recent years. Virtually any solid object, from a concrete piling to a buoy, will serve as a focal point for fish. Something as substantial as a ship can harbour an entire aquatic community, and as the soft and hard corals adhere to its steel plates, the hull is soon transformed into a veritable pillar of this community. The 'ocean reafforestation' programme began in the mid-1980s with a couple of deep diving sites including a 435-foot freighter, the *Lowrance* (at 200 feet), and two Tenneco oil platforms (at 60-150 feet). Since then, artifical reefs have been interspersed with live reef areas at depths between 15 and 400 feet, with the purpose of entertaining divers and snorkellers of all abilities, and also to attract deep-sea game fish such as tuna and sailfish from the nearby Gulf Stream. One of the most notorious wrecks is the 200-foot German freighter *Mercedes I*, which beached itself on the pool terrace of a Palm Beach socialite during a Thanksgiving Day storm in 1984. After a thorough clean-up and four years in 100 feet of water a mile off Fort Lauderdale beach, its coral growths are flourishing and a resident barracuda welcomes visitors. Snorkellers will find angel fish, sergeant majors,

butterfly fish, sea turtles and octopus – all now common around the rejuvenated reef.

Air mystery The likelihood of discovering a new wreck is pretty remote, but that is not to say it is impossible. One recent find by treasure hunters was a clutch of five World War II Avenger aircraft in some 700 feet of water 10 miles from Fort Lauderdale's beach. The discovery prompted speculation that the 'Lost Squadron' of Bermuda Triangle fame had been located finally, but the Avengers were from a different flight group, so the mystery continues.

Dive packages One great plus for divers visiting Fort Lauderdale is that the Broward County reefs are a lot less crowded than the Keys. Another is a range of excellent value hotel/diving packages offered by local operators. Check out what is on offer from: **Lauderdale Diver**, 1334 SE 17th Street Causeway, Fort Lauderdale, FL 33316 (tel: (305) 467 2822 or (800) 654 2073); and **Pro Dive**, Bahia Mar Resort and Yachting Center, A1A, Fort Lauderdale, FL 33316 (tel: (305) 761 3413 or (800) 772 DIVE). Both operate fully-equipped dive boats (additional charge for scuba equipment hire). Reef trips are also open to divers and snorkellers not taking part in hotel packages.

Every October jazz lovers and musicians from across the country converge on Fort Lauderdale's satellite town, Hollywood, to celebrate the Hollywood Jazz Festival. The three-day rave takes place in Young Circle Park. November sees the East Coast's biggest film festival and market here, the slightly confusingly named Hollywood Film Festival, featuring ten days of major motion picture premierès, free film seminars, galas and the Alamo Film Competition.

Riverwalk River frontage is prime real estate in Fort Lauderdale, and access has always been the prerogative of property owners. The Riverwalk development will change all this by providing a stretch of Downtown pedestrian footpath along the New River, planned to extend from Stranahan House to the historic Himmarshee village area, and on to the Broward Center for the Performing Arts. Landscaped with trees and native plants, Riverwalk has outdoor cafés, picnic tables in gazebos and park benches for relaxing.

Stranahan House, *335 SE Sixth Avenue (Las Olas at New River Tunnel)* Frank Stranahan was despatched to manage an overnight camp on the Lantana–Lemon City road early in the 1890s. He set up a trading post for the local Indians and ran a ferry operation from his New River Camp, which became a popular sportsmen's retreat with the arrival of the railroad in 1896. In 1900 Stranahan married the local school teacher, Ivy Cromartie, and a year later started to build a property on the banks of the New River. Stranahan House was the result, a homely Pioneer residence that has been beautifully restored in the style of 1913–15, with fine examples of Victorian furniture, mementoes and photographs of the early days. Guided tours give an account of life in turn-of-the-century Fort Lauderdale, the Boom years and how Ivy preserved the house until her death in 1971.
Open: Wednesday, Friday and Saturday 10.00–15.30hrs.

Voyager Sightseeing Tram, *600 Seabreeze Boulevard* Make city orientation easy with a 90-minute narrated tram tour around town, pinpointing 60 unusual and historic places of interest along the 18-mile route. The tour departs from near Bahia Mar Yacht Center. For information, tel: (305) 463 0401.

Stranahan House, Fort Lauderdale

Walk John D MacArthur Beach State Park

At 10900 SR703 (A1A), North Palm Beach, this barrier island park was donated to the state in 1981. It has plenty to offer and great walks along the undeveloped seashore.

Start at the visitor centre on the western side of the peninsula. There are displays and a video presentation, illustrating the park's plant and animal communities.

Take the 1,600-foot boardwalk across Lake Worth Cove to the coastal hammock on the Atlantic shore. A trail winds through the gumbo limbos, strangler figs and cabbage palms to MacArthur Beach. This is a prime nesting ground for loggerhead, green and leatherback turtles from May through August. There are special ranger-led turtle walks in June and July. Swimming, snorkelling and shell collecting are permitted along the 2-mile beach, and walkers may see pelicans, sandpipers, terns and other wading birds which inhabit the coastline. Serious birdwatchers should spend time scanning the mangrove-edged cove for rare roseate spoonbills, osprey, herons and ibis.

Back on the western side of the cove, there is another nature trail through a tropical hammock.

Open: daily 08.00hrs–dusk.

157

Walk Jonathan Dickinson State Park

Situated at 16450 SE Federal Highway (US1), Hobe Sound (5 miles north of Jupiter), this is one of southern Florida's larger parks at 10,328 acres. The site is named after an English Quaker who survived a shipwreck in 1696, and made it back to St Augustine. Beneath Hobe Mountain (all 86 feet of it), the park's main attraction is the Loxahatchee River, Florida's only undeveloped natural waterway, which winds through the swamps and mangroves, providing refuge for manatees and a breeding ground for rare Southern bald eagles. There are areas of sandpine scrub, pine flatwoods, and a great diversity of plant life. Deer, marsh rabbits, otters and snakes can be spotted, and alligators bask on the riverbank.

A nine-mile hiking trail and choice of shorter trails explore the preserve, and rangers lead walking tours from the Trapper Nelson Interpretive Site year round.

The 30-seat *Loxahatchee Queen* river-boat makes two-hour cruises up the river; there are canoe and rowboat rentals, a campsite and cabins. For information, tel: (407) 546 2771.

Open: daily 08.00hrs-dusk.

Osprey (Pandion haliaetus)

Turtle-talk at Juno Beach

▷▷▷ **Juno Beach**

off A1A

Once the administrative seat of Dade County, which stretched all the way down to Miami in 1889, Juno is a sleepy little town of less than 2,000 inhabitants. Its main claim to fame is **Loggerhead Park**, named after the sea turtles which come ashore to lay their eggs here each summer. The **Marinelife Center of Juno Beach** (*open*: Tuesday to Saturday 10.00–15.00hrs) is the centrepiece of the park, housing natural history and marine life displays with a special emphasis on the sea turtles. There is a turtle nursery where baby turtles are raised in saltwater tanks and then released into the surf, and museum staff conduct turtle walks along the beach during the June to July nesting season.

▶▶▷ **Jupiter**

The oldest settlement in Palm Beach County, Jupiter was founded in 1838 during the Second Seminole War. The name originated with the Jobe Indians who populated the region before the Spanish and English speakers, whose tongues transformed it into Jupiter. The settlement became the northern terminal of the Lake Worth Railroad in 1888, other stops along the line including Mars, Venus and Juno. The little terminal was bypassed by Flagler's East Coast Railroad, but a small settlement remained around the landmark **Jupiter Lighthouse** (completed in 1860), and passed almost unnoticed until the 1950s, when popular singer Perry Como began to sign off his radio and television shows with: 'I'm going home to a little bit of heaven called Jupiter, Florida'. Home-grown movie star Burt Reynolds lives in Palm Beach these days, but his father minds the **Burt Reynolds Ranch Tack and Feed Store**, 16133 Jupiter Farms Road (2 miles west of the Florida Turnpike), which also has a petting zoo.

Jupiter Theater, *1001 E Indiantown Road* Formerly the Burt Reynolds Jupiter Theater, even without its big name prefix this is an excellent dinner theatre. Stars of the stage and screen are often lured here to appear alongside professional casts in a year-round cycle of plays and revues. For information, tel: (407) 746 5566.

Loxahatchee Historical Museum, *Burt Reynolds Park, 805 N US1* Housed in a purpose-built museum, costumes, utensils, period photographs and information panels illustrate Pioneer life along the Loxahatchee River. Other subjects include Flagler's railroad; shipwrecks; and Seminole Indian life (there are authentic thatched *chickee* huts in the grounds). The natural hammock area around the museum is being laid out with boardwalk trails and interpretive displays. On Sunday afternoons, the museum opens two other properties. A small historical museum in the red-painted 105-foot **Jupiter Lighthouse** is one. **Dubois House,** the other, is a typical Pioneer home built on top of an Indian shell mound in the late 1890s (guided tour).
Open: Tuesday to Friday 10.00–16.00hrs, Saturday and Sunday 13.00–16.00hrs.

▶▶▷　**Jupiter Island**
Turn off A1A on to CR707 for Jupiter Inlet Colony at the southern tip of the island, and the town of Jupiter Island to the north. These two élite residential communities have attracted the likes of Jacqueline Kennedy (after President John F Kennedy's assassination in 1963), George Bush's mother and Perry Como – who forgot to mention that his 'little bit of heaven' was rather richer and more secluded than downtown Jupiter.

Blowing Rocks Preserve, *CR707* Get here early to find a parking space and explore the preserve before the trippers arrive. Your visit should be timed to coincide with high tide when fountains of spray are pushed up through blowholes in limestone outcrops along the rocky shoreline. A hardwood hammock borders the dunes where sea grapes, palmetto and cabbage palms combine with colourful, hardy wild flowers and saltwater-resistant sea oats to anchor the sand. Woodpeckers and warblers, pelicans and osprey can all be seen.
Open: daily 06.00–17.00hrs.

Between May and August, hundreds of female sea turtles make an annual pilgrimage to Florida's southeast coast where they come ashore to lay their eggs in the sand.. It is thought the females return to nest on the same beach from which they hatched. Loggerhead, green and leatherback turtles all frequent the Florida shores. The leatherback is the most distinctive – capable of growing up to 6.5 feet in length and weighing 1,300lb, it does not have a hard shell.

Royal tern, seen around the coast

Henry Flagler

■ **Henry Morrison Flagler was born in Hopewell, New York, on 2 January 1830. The son of a struggling Presbyterian minister, he left home at the age of 14, and sought work with relations in Ohio; by 1852, he was a partner in their grain and distillery business. .....■**

When a venture into the profitable Michigan salt industry was wiped out by the Civil War, Flagler moved to Cleveland where he recouped his fortunes and made the acquaintance of another bright young Cleveland businessman, John D Rockefeller, owner of a small oil company. In 1867, Flagler and an Englishman, Samuel Andrews, became Rockefeller's partners. Together they launched an American legend, the Standard Oil Company, in 1870.

The East Coast Railroad Flagler originally visited Florida in the early 1880s with his first wife. After her

East Coast Railroad carriage

death, he married again (there would be three wives in all), and honeymooned with his new bride in St Augustine. The old-world charm of the city (founded by the Spanish in the 1560s), the winter sunshine and the enormous development potential captured Flagler's imagination. He chose young architects John M Carrere and Thomas Hastings to design him a fabulous Spanish/Moorish-style hotel, the Ponce de Leon, which opened in St Augustine in 1888. To save his customers from the indignity of abandoning their comfortable Pullman cars at Jacksonville, taking a ferry across the St Johns River, and roughing it on the rickety local railway, Flagler bought up the existing railroad, converted it to standard gauge and built a railbridge over the river.

Now committed to his vision of creating an 'American Riviera' along Florida's East Coast, Flagler began building hotels and buying out local railroads, extending his line down to Titusville and Cocoa in 1893 and Palm Beach in 1894. Then Miami pioneer Julia Tuttle convinced him he should continue to Miami in 1896.

A dream fulfilled The greatest challenge was still to come – the 156-mile engineering feat which took Flagler's 'Railroad to the Sea' down the Florida Keys. Three thousand workmen toiled over seven years to carve a path through marsh and jungle, built bridges and viaducts, and connected islands and hundreds of coral reefs until the first official train made the journey into Key West on 22 January 1912. Flagler was on board, and announced: 'Now I can die happy; my dream is fulfilled'. He died on 20 May 1913.

▶▶▶ Palm Beach

Palm Beach has been cited as 'an example of what God would do if He had money'.

This place is all about serious money. It owes its fortunes to a typical Gold Coast occurrence – a shipwreck. In 1878, a Spanish brigantine, the aptly named *Providencia*, foundered off the coast with a cargo of 20,000 coconuts. A handful of settlers planted the coconuts, named the settlement after them, and the resulting swathe of tropical palms inspired Henry Flagler to create an élite winter resort here, marked by the opening of the Royal Poinciana Hotel in 1894, since demolished.

The Mizner vision In 1918, Addison Mizner arrived in town with a vision of his own. The former miner launched his career with the Spanish Revival-style **Everglades Club** on Worth Avenue. Liable to omit such tiresome necessities as kitchens from his house plans, Mizner was in his element when designing public places. The 300 blocks of **Worth Avenue**, one of the world's most exclusive shopping streets, is a typical Mizner creation of elegant boutiques decorated with a sprinkling of outdoor staircases, wrought ironwork, tropical shrubs and vines. This is where the great and the good gather for lunch during the winter season.

Palm Beach practicalities Anyone can visit Palm Beach, but to feel at home on Worth Avenue, or slip into The Breakers for a cocktail, it helps to dress up. Car parking is – at a guess, deliberately – hard to come by, and the Palm Beach traffic cops are tireless. Meters are limited to one or two hours, but Whitehall has its own parking lot.

The Royal Poinciana was the largest resort hotel in the world and possibly the biggest wooden structure ever built. A second hotel, the Palm Beach Inn, opened in 1896. Later renamed The Breakers, it was twice destroyed by fire and rebuilt. The 1926 version, at 1 County Road, is an Italianate marvel. The railway magnate was so taken by the place, he built Whitehall, a magnificent 'cottage' for his third wife, on the landward side of the island in 1901. Here he entertained Rockefellers, Astors, Vanderbilts, Dame Nellie Melba and Woodrow Wilson in regal style.

161

The suitably palm-shaded entrance road to Palm Beach

THE GOLD COAST

162

The battle to keep Palm Beach exclusive and genteel, started by its founder Henry Flagler, continues unabated. A series of municipal by-laws ban washing a car in public, hanging out a washing line, and – horror of horrors– jogging bare-chested.

Flagler had the builders construct the frescoed ceiling of the Marble Hall in the Whitehall mansion 8 feet lower than the original designs, so he would 'feel at home'.

Henry Morrison Flagler's magnificent Whitehall mansion

Bethesda-by-the-Sea Church, *141 S County Road* Built in 1927, southeast Florida's first Protestant church is a little gem of Spanish-Gothic restraint amid the opulence. It has some lovely stained-glass windows. Behind the church are the quiet **Cluett Memorial Garden**s.
Gardens open: daily 08.00–17.00hrs.

Henry Morrison Flagler Museum, *Coconut Row* The Whitehall mansion, Henry Flagler's wedding present to his third wife, Mary Lily Kenan was designed by John Carrere and Thomas Hastings, architects of Flagler's grandiose Ponce de Leon Hotel in St Augustine. The classic two-storey villa by Lake Worth took just 18 months to build at a cost of $2.5 million. It is now a museum. The interior is a monument to historic European styles, some 55 lavishly furnished, gilded and patterned rooms crammed with paintings, porcelain and antiques most of which are originals from Flagler's time. Portraits of Flagler and his granddaughter, Jean Flagler Matthews, who rescued the building from demolition in 1959, hang in the impressive Marble Hall. Mary Flagler was an accomplished singer; her portrait graces the opulent Music Room, with its acreage of highly polished parquet and French windows to the South Porch, a favourite setting for musical tea parties. The magnificent Louis XV Ballroom was also designed to spill out into the Courtyard. Renaissance France was the inspiration for the superb Dining Room: take time to admire the extraordinary detail of the coffered ceiling created with gilded wood carvings inset with dainty papier mâché. Of the bedrooms, the English Arts and Crafts Movement chamber was a novel addition, and the combination of matching wallpaper and fabric in the Yellow Roses Room was also an innovation.
Open: Tuesday to Saturday 10.00–17.00hrs, Sunday 12.00–17.00hrs.

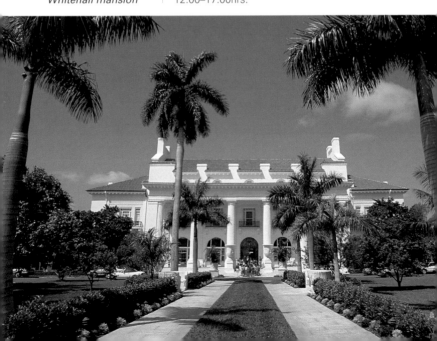

The Hibel Museum, devoted to the work of Edna Hibel

Hibel Museum of Art, *150 Royal Poinciana Plaza* The late Ethelbelle and Clayton B Craig were very keen on Edna Hibel's artwork. Their extensive collection of her paintings, lithographs and sculpture is now displayed in an attractive modern gallery which claims to be the only non-profit-making museum devoted to a lone, living female artist. The distinguished Ms Hibel (born Boston, 1917) has a light, sketchy style which is used to effect in portraits, landscapes and nudes. Look out for travelling exhibitions and film shows, and there are free promenade concerts here on the second Sunday of each month from November to May. For information, tel: (305) 833 6870.
Open: Tuesday to Saturday 10.00–17.00hrs, Sunday 13.00–17.00hrs.

Palm Beach Bicycle Trail, Pedal power is a great way to explore Palm Beach, excellent for taking a leisurely look at some of the more imposing mansions. Most of the streets are shaded by outsize palms, and, of course, the terrain is as flat as a pancake – this is Florida after all. The official breezy bike trail parallels Lake Worth, opposite the mainland. You can venture further afield to S Ocean Boulevard and along the ocean side of the island. Bikes can be rented from the **Palm Beach Bicycle Trail Shop**, 223 Sunrise Avenue (tel: (407) 659 4583), *open* daily 09.00–17.30hrs.

Society of Four Arts Gardens, *Four Arts Plaza* In the grounds of this venerable cultural institution off Royal Palm Way, take time to relax in a series of enclosed gardens filled with plants, trees and the odd carp pond. The centrepiece is the **Philip Hulitar Sculpture Garden**. There is also an art gallery which hosts monthly exhibitions, a library, plus a theatre with a music and dance programme. For information, tel: (407) 655 7226. *Open*: Monday to Friday 10.00–17.00hrs; also Saturdays, November to April.

As befitted a champion of rail travel, Henry Flagler had his own railway carriage, *The Rambler,* which has come to rest in the garden of his former home, Whitehall. It has been immaculately restored to its original glory with the help of photographs from the Flagler era. Oak panelled, plumply upholstered and fitted with carpets and chandeliers, it even boasts a copper-lined shower, and tiny private kitchen with a wood-burning stove, a sink and an ice box for preparing refreshments *en route*.

■ **As befits one of the world's top holiday destinations, the Gold Coast does not just rely on its miles of sandy beach to occupy visitors. There is a wealth of opportunity for sporting types to indulge in their favourite pursuits from golf and tennis to sportfishing .....■**

Armchair sports fans will have a field day too, with the frenetic excitement of jai-alai and top drawer polo. There is even baseball when the New York Yankees pitch up for spring training at Fort Lauderdale's Yankee Stadium, 5301 NW 12th Avenue (tel: (305) 776 1921), and the Atlanta Braves brave West Palm Beach Stadium, 1610 Palm Beach Lakes Boulevard (tel: (407) 683 6100).

Golf Greater Fort Lauderdale boasts 51 courses, while Boca Raton alone has 25 green, pleasant and suitably challenging venues for keen golfers. In the Fort Lauderdale area several top resorts offer all-inclusive golfing packages including: **Rolling Hills Golf Resort** (tel: (305) 475 0400); **Bonaventure Resort and Spa** (tel: (305) 325 3535); and **Palm Aire Spa**

Jai-alai, Cuban-type pelota

Resort and Country Club in Pompano Beach (tel: (305) 972 3300). For notable non-residential courses, try **Deer Creek**, Deerfield Beach (tel: (305) 421 5550); and the City of Fort Lauderdale Municipal Golf Course (tel: (305) 735 2256). Around Boca Raton, there is the **Boca Raton Municipal Golf Course** (tel: (407) 483 6100), and oceanfront **Red Reef Golf Course** (tel: (407) 391 5014). Palm Beach has Fazio-designed **Emerald Dunes** (tel: (407) 684 GOLF), and 45 championship holes at the **Palm Beach Polo and Country Club** (tel: (407) 798 7000). For both golf and tennis try the new **PGA National Resort and Spa** (tel: (407) 627 2000)

Jai-alai Introduced to Miami by Cuban immigrants, this fast and furious spectator sport (see page 83) is featured at two Gold Coast sites: **Dania Jai-Alai**, 301 E Dania Beach Boulevard/A1A (tel: (305) 426 4330), Tuesday to Saturday 19.15hrs, matinees; and **Palm Beach Jai-Alai**, 1415 45th Street, West Palm Beach (tel: (407) 844 2444), November to May, Monday to Saturday 19.00hrs. Games last 15 minutes with a 10-minute break in between - used by spectators to place complicated bets - and there are a dozen or so games each evening.

Polo It should be no suprise that the Gold Coast is the winter home of this princely pastime; the good news is that it does not cost a fortune to watch. The season runs from December/January into April, and attracts a host of celebrity fans, which makes star-spotting almost as riveting as the polo action itself. For a good look at both, check out the weekend action at **Royal Palm Polo**

164

Sports Club, 6300 Clint Moore Road, Boca Raton (tel: (407) 994 1876); and **Palm Beach Polo and Country Club**, 13198 Forest Hill Boulevard, West Palm Beach (tel: (407) 798 7040). A game consists of teams of four horses and riders competing over six seven-minute chukkers (periods). If the teams are tied at 3:3, there is a sudden-death decider.

Tennis With inspiration in the form of local legend Christine Evert, tennis freaks will find facilities galore, with 550 local courts in the Fort Lauderdale area. Contact the **City of Fort Lauderdale Parks and Recreation Department** (tel: (305) 761 2621). Boca Raton has some distinctly stylish courts. Try the **Boca Del Mar Tennis and Golf Club** (tel: (407) 392 8118), **Boca Raton Bath and Tennis** (tel: (407) 994 1889), or **Memorial Park** (tel: (407) 391 7489).

Polo: a Palm Beach speciality

In West Palm Beach, there is **Gaines Park Tennis Center** (tel: (407) 659 0735), and the fabulous **Palm Beach Polo and Country Club** (tel: (407) 798 7040); or ask advice from the **Palm Beach Recreation Department** (tel: (407) 964 4420).

Sportfishing Fort Lauderdale's **Bahia Mar Yacht Center** is packed with charter fishing boats like the *Chula Vista* (tel: (305) 462 3250), *Lady Pamela II* (tel: (305) 761 8045), and *Moby Dick VII* (tel: (305) 561 0171). But the top fishing spot is probably Pompano Beach, where the **Fish City Charter Fleet**, 2629 N Riverside Drive (tel: (305) 943 8222) operates around a dozen charter vessels on the trail of marlin, pompano, shark and sailfish.

Tennis is an ace Gold Coast sport

West Palm Beach, once Palm Beach's poor relation, is now an important business centre

▶ ▶ ▶   West Palm Beach

If Palm Beach was born with the proverbial silver spoon in its mouth, West Palm Beach was the poor relation. The workers and the commercial and industrial services required to keep Henry Flagler's élite resort running smoothly were conveniently housed out of sight across the Intracoastal Waterway. However, it was West Palm Beach that became the administrative seat of Palm Beach County when it was created in 1909, and it has developed as a business centre for law, accounting and brokerage firms, while building a new reputation for computer and electronics manufacturing.

Downtown West Palm Beach has two excellent museums and a small zoo, but its other attractions are widely spread: Lion Country Safari (see page 167), and the prestigious Palm Beach Polo and Country Club (see page 168–9), for instance, are both situated a fair drive out to the west. In the north, the Port of Palm Beach at Riviera Beach is home to **Crown Cruise Lines**, who offer day trips to the Bahamas and coastline cruises (for information, tel: (407) 845 2101).

Singer Island is another fine resort and residential out-post with a magnificent municipal beach on the ocean. Sewing machine heir Paris Singer, together with Waldorf founder Harry Kelsey, began developing the island as a resort in 1925. The project was abandoned after the 1926 hurricane, and development was delayed until after World War II. **Palm Beach Shores** is a particularly exclusive enclave, and the lakefront marina has one of the largest charter fishing fleets in the area.

Fishermen will find plenty of action around the Palm Beaches. Sportfishing charters are available from Boynton Beach, Lantana and Riviera Beach, as well as Palm Beach Shores. Keen anglers can try their luck from the fish camps out at Lake Okeechobee, which is teeming with largemouth bass, or, closer to home, Lake Worth is renowned for its fishing.

Festivals are a feature of West Palm Beach. January sees the South Florida Fair, then foodies should not miss Palm Beach Seafood Festival (held in February or March – tel: (407) 659 9841 for information). The four-day Sunfest in May is one of the region's biggest events, with non-stop jazz, arts and crafts, foodstalls, puppet shows, dance demonstrations and more. The Florida Heritage Festival, and the cultural delights of the month-long Palm Beach Festival (throughout the Palm Beaches) are in November, while Holidayfest, at the beginning of December, ushers in the Christmas festivities.

Arthur R Marshall Loxahatchee National Wildlife Refuge, *off US441/SR7 (west of Boynton Beach)* The closest entrance to the Everglades from the Palm Beaches, this 220-square mile sawgrass and hammock preserve is a haven for a tremendous variety of native wildlife, and has a 7-mile wilderness canoe trail. From the visitor centre, a boardwalk trail extends above an area of cypress swamp where there is a chance to spot alligators; the marshland trail leads to a 20-foot lookout tower above a pond which is frequented by herons and other waterfowl. For a different perspective, **Loxahatchee Everglades Tours** offer narrated airboat tours of the Refuge from their base at the Hillsboro Recreation Area, 14900 W Lox Road (12 miles south). Tours depart daily 09.00–17.00hrs; boat rentals and fishing tackle rental are also available from a concession stand.
Open: 30 minutes before dawn to 30 minutes after dusk. (Note: bring mosquito repellent.)

Dreher Park Zoo, *1301 Summit Boulevard* This modest parkland setting is home to some 500 animals and birds from 100 different native and exotic species. Among the miscellaneous reptiles, a petting zoo and a small collection of butterflies, a sinuous Florida panther (on the endangered list) steals the show.
Open: daily 09.00–17.00hrs.

Lion Country Safari, *W Southern Boulevard (SR80)* For a fun family day out, take a safari beyond the Florida Turnpike, and visit this 500-acre African wildlife park complete with elephants, rhinos, bison, wildebeest, giraffes and chimps, as well as lions. The park was opened in 1967 as the nation's first drive-through 'cage-less' zoo, and the 1,000-plus animals are now well established; and, though it is not the Serengeti, the brilliant Florida sunshine is a good substitute for the real thing. Convertible cars are not allowed, but the park rents out zebra-striped hardtops for a low hourly rate. The 8-mile circuit takes around an hour with plenty of photo stops.
After the drive, the **Safari World Park** offers a further chance for animal encounters and fairground rides. Enjoy a cruise on the *Safari Queen* or navigate a pedalboat around the lagoon with its monkey islands and flamingo colony; meet a llama in the Petting Zoo; see alligators and snakes in the Reptile Park; walk the Nature Trail; and cluck over recent arrivals in the Animal Nursery. There is an on-site café, pet kennels, and an adjacent campground with a swimming pool.
Open: daily 09.30–17.30hrs.

Norton Gallery of Art, *1451 S Olive Avenue* An outstanding small gallery founded by Chicago industrialist Ralph H Norton in 1941, the Norton's extensive collections are divided into four main areas. The **French Collection** is broadly representative of the late 19th- to early 20th-century Impressionist and Post-Impressionist era with works by Monet, Matisse, Pissarro and Renoir, also Chagall, Dufy and Picasso. Echoing its European counterpart, the **American Collection** includes works by

A few blocks south from the Norton Gallery are the Ann Norton Sculpture Gardens at 253 Barcelona Road (*open:* Tuesday to Saturday 12.00–16.00hrs). The three-acre gardens are devoted to the work of Ralph H Norton's wife, Ann Weaver. Her sculptures have been beautifully arranged against a luxuriant back-drop of native plants (many specifically chosen for their popularity with wild birds) and 150 varieties of palm trees. You can see small sculpture pieces in wood and marble in Norton's former studio.

Striking sculpture on the Norton Gallery of Art

Ernest Lawson, John Sloan and Winslow Homer from the earlier period, and continues up to to the present day via Edward Hopper, Georgia O'Keefe and Jackson Pollock. Bronzes, jade carvings, Buddhist sculpture and peerless ceramics occupy a gallery devoted to the **Chinese Collection**; and the fine **Sculpture Collection** embellishes a patio garden with works by Henry Moore, Maillol and contemporary American sculptor, Duane Hanson.

The museum's reputation enables it to secure some of the best travelling art shows circulating the US, and there is a varied exhibition programme which highlights established artists and new discoveries. Concert and film presentations are also on the agenda. There is a 3,000-volume art reference library, and a good gift store. *Open*: Tuesday to Saturday 10.00–17.00hrs, Sunday 13.00–17.00hrs.

Palm Beach Polo and Country Club, *13198 Forest Hill Boulevard* On a Sunday afternoon in winter, everybody who is anybody in Palm Beach County packs a picnic and heads for the polo ground. The Palm Beach Polo and Country Club is one of the world's classiest polo venues, where international teams like Les Diables Bleus compete for the prestigious USPA Rolex Gold Cup, and $100,000 World Cup titles, in the 5,000-seat stadium. The Prince of Wales has been known to wield a mallet here, and visiting polo fans have numbered Dustin Hoffman, Calvin Klein, Sylvester Stallone and Larry

Hagman among their ranks. Visitors can also watch backfield practice matches during the week (Tuesday to Saturday), and sign up for week-long beginners' or players' polo clinics from February through April.

Polo is not the only spectator sport on offer at the club: a 125-acre landscaped equestrian complex hosts the annual **Winter Equestrian Festival.** Olympic with a range of events which traditionally include a World Cup qualifying competition. Meanwhile, golfers can take up the challenge of 45 championship holes devised by some of the top names in the golfing world. Ron Garl and Jerry Pate put their heads together over the Dunes Scottish links-style course; the new Cypress course is the work of Pete and P B Dye; and George and Tom Fanzio were responsible for the challenging nine-hole course. The club's five-star tennis facilities provide 20 clay, two grass and two hard courts. There are residential golf and tennis packages, and professional instruction. For information tel: (407) 798 7000.

South Florida Science Museum, *4801 Dreher Trail North* This provides a terrific children's day out, with lots of hands-on exhibits, flashes, crackles and surprises. Adults who never grasped the basics, let alone the principles of physics, will learn more in an hour of chasing a seven-year-old around here than they did in their entire school careers. All the usual skeletons and dioramas are here, but take a break to wander through the glossy tropical Native Plant Center. The Light and Sight Hall unleashes the true spirit of investigation.

The **Aldrin Planetarium,** at the heart of the museum complex, takes spectators on a journey through the solar system out into the galaxy and around the universe on most days. Laser concerts (Fridays 20.00 and 21.00hrs) are another popular feature, and the 16-inch Newtonian Reflector telescope in the Gibson Observatory is one of the largest in the state. Earthlings can get a close-up peek at the planets on Friday evenings (20.00–22.00hrs), weather permitting.

Open: Tuesday to Sunday 10.00–17.00hrs.

Gold Coast Shopping

■ When a *USA Today* worldwide survey discovered that the single most popular holiday pursuit is shopping, the Gold Coast was taking note. Department stores, discount malls, designer boutiques and flea markets abound – shop-oholics should be issued with a health warning...and several pairs of walking shoes .....■

Fort Lauderdale Downtown Fort Lauderdale's finest shopping street is chic **Las Olas Boulevard**, a delightfully landscaped district of pretty designer boutiques, art and antiques galleries and a choice of elegant little café-restaurants which are just the ticket for recuperating after a tough morning scrutinising price tags. **The Galleria**, on E Sunrise Boulevard near the beach, is a magnificent three-storey modern mall featuring 150 shops and restaurants including top-notch stores Nieman Marcus, Jordan Marsh and Saks Fifth Avenue, plus Brookes Brothers, Polo/Ralph Lauren and The Disney Store.

Fashion in Palm Beach

Head out west of Downtown to the Plantation district, where the cool marble and granite precincts of **The Fashion Mall**, 321 N University Drive, boast a further 100 shops anchored by Lord & Taylor and a Food Court serving steaks, Chinese take-aways, slices of pizza Italian-style and deli snacks. Lord & Taylor also have a **Clearance Center** near by which offers the store's off-season merchandise at greatly reduced prices; periodical sales knock a further 40–50 per cent off already discounted price tags. Bargain hunters should make the trek out to **Sawgrass Mills**, 12801 W Sunrise Boulevard (9 miles), the world's largest discount mall with more than 200 manufacturers and retail outlets, plus brand-name discounters who slash prices on designer brands by up to 70 per cent. Athlete's Foot, Sears and Van Heusen all have their own discount stores, and there are electrical goods, toiletries, books, toys and fashions at amazing prices. Another bargain-basement shopping opportunity is the 75-acre **Fort Lauderdale $wap Shop**, 3291 W Sunrise Boulevard, which also has a Farmers' Market with local produce, fairground rides and daily circus performances.

For specialist shopping, Dania's **Antiques Row**, on US1, is a great place to browse for china, glass, furniture, silverware and jewellery. Souvenir seekers might fancy a trip to the **NFL Alumni Store**, 4460 N US1, which stocks all kinds of American football gear from caps and shirts to helmets.

Boca Raton Shopping is a way of life in Boca Raton, as is the colour pink.

Fashionable **Royal Palm Plaza**, N Federal Highway at Palmetto Park Road, has been nicknamed 'Pink Plaza' for the strawberry ice-cream hue of its Spanish-style stucco buildings. Eighty up-market boutiques, gift shops and speciality stores range around elegantly landscaped courtyards and ornate fountains. The kids will find hands-on fun in the **Children's Science Explorium**, and the **Little Palm Theatre**; and Jan McArt's Royal Palm Dinner Theatre is also tucked away here. (Note how the US 'theater' has been Europeanised to show just what a classy area this is!) A delicate shade of salmon-pink distinguishes **Mizner Park**, the latest shopping marvel to hit town (see page 139). **Town Center Mall**, 6000 W Glades Road, has lured the likes of Louis Vuitton and Laura Ashley to join Bloomingdale's and The Sharper Image in its Mediterranean-inspired complex. The Museum Store and Nature Company provide a rather more down-to-earth influence. For a more intimate shopping experience, there is the **Crocker Center**, Military Trail at Town Center Road; and open-air shopping at nearby **Glades Plaza**.

Palm Beaches One of the world's most exclusive shopping streets, **Worth Avenue**, is in Palm Beach.

You can buy souvenirs at the top end of the market

Glittering with style, sophistication and a recently opened branch of the fabulous New York jewellers, Tiffany's, it derives much of its charm from the landscaped sidewalks and Mediterranean-style architecture designed by Addison Mizner over 70 years ago. Along the street, around the courtyards and down narrow pedestrian alleyways, some 200 speciality shops and department stores, art galleries and gourmet restaurants cater to a rarified clientele.

Moving from the historic to the brand new, West Palm Beach's latest shopping extravaganza is the $150 million **Gardens Mall**, PGA Boulevard. Beneath a glass atrium, trees and ponds line the walkways, and 170 shops and restaurants fill the complex, along with big department stores, such as Bloomingdale's, Saks Fifth Avenue and Sears. **Palm Beach Mall**, Palm Beach Lakes Boulevard, is another tasteful collection of skylights, shrubs, department stores and boutiques. The county's only discount mall, **Palm Beach Outlet Center**, 5700 Okeechobee Boulevard, has been situated well out west, near the Florida Turnpike.

EAST COAST

0 ⌐ 20 km
0 ⌐ 10 miles

GEORGIA

Fort Clinch S P
Amelia **Fernandina**
Island **Beach**
Little Talbot
Island S P
Zoo
JACKSONVILLE
Fort • Mayport
Caroline • Atlantic Beach
Jacksonville
Mandarin • **Beach**

95

South Ponte
Vedra Beach

Castillo de
St San Marcos
Augustine Alligator Farm
Anastasia I

Fort Matanzas

Marineland • **Marineland of Florida**
Oceanariums
Palm Coast **Washington Oaks**
State Gardens
Bunnell • Flagler Beach

Ormond Beach
Daytona
Beach Daytona International
Speedway

4
New Ponce de Leon
Smyrna Inlet Lighthouse
Beach

E Harney

Canaveral
National
Seashore

Titusville
John F Kennedy
Space Center
Merritt Merritt Island
Island N W R
Cocoa C Canaveral
Rockledge • Cape Canaveral
Cocoa Beach
Patrick Air
Force Base
• Satellite Beach
• Indian Harbour
Melbourne • Indialantic
• Melbourne Beach
Palm Bay

95 Sebastian Inlet
S R A &
Blue McLarty Museum
Cypress Sebastian
Lake Pelican Island
Indian River
Gifford Shores
Vero Beach

Jack Island
St Lucie State Preserve
Fort Pierce Fort Pierce Inlet
S R A &
Pepper Beach
Elliott Museum *Hutchinson
Island*

Jensen Beach
Stuart Gilbert's Bar
House of Refuge
Hobe Sound
Hobe Sound N W R
J Dickinson *Jupiter I*
S P

See Drive page 197

The East Coast covers an area north from the top of the Gold Coast to St Mary's River (the border with Georgia). It is a 300-mile stretch of the mainland, largely protected by a string of lush barrier islands. Here, the Floridas of past and present are juxtaposed in a series of historic old towns and modern beach resorts, ancient Indian shell mounds and 20th-century space wizardry.

The East Coast is where it all began, when Spanish explorer Ponce de León first stepped ashore near present-day St Augustine in 1513. This area now calls itself the 'First Coast', and includes Jacksonville, on the St Johns River, where French Huguenots established a settlement in 1564. Hearing this, Philip II of Spain despatched his lieutenant Pedro Menéndez de Avilés to teach the French a lesson, and a brutal massacre of the shipwrecked French at Matanzas Bay ('bay of slaughter') left the Spanish to claim the territory by the founding of St Augustine in 1565. Though the mosquito-infested swamps of the east coast were of little value, St Augustine was a strategic link in the maritime defence of Spanish treasure fleets, and a prime target for English attacks. The town was razed by Sir Francis Drake in 1586, was attacked again in 1702, and the English actually moved in for 20 years in 1763.

War and tourists By the early 19th century, sugar, citrus and indigo plantations were starting to appear around Indian River and the Halifax River (as the Intracoastal Waterway is known near Fort Pierce and Daytona respectively), but the outbreak of the Seminole Wars, followed by the Civil War, led many settlers to abandon their plantations. Business picked up again in the 1870s, and the first trickle of tourists drifted down to the railhead at Jacksonville, and continued south by boat down the St Johns River, or along the coast to St Augustine, Ormond Beach and Rockledge.

When Standard Oil millionaire Henry Flagler determined to develop Florida's East Coast as a 'Southern Newport' winter resort for wealthy Philadelphia socialites, the trickle became a torrent, and Flagler ferried them south on his railroad and put them up in his own hotels.

Jacksonville is the original gateway to Florida. Flagler's seaside hotel at Atlantic Beach was the start of today's Jacksonville beaches resort area, and the city recovered from a devastating fire in 1901 to emerge as an important industrial and trading port, the insurance capital of the south and a vibrant cultural centre. The St Johns River meanders through the city, past Jacksonville University, where composer Frederick Delius once lived on a citrus plantation, and squeezes around a narrow bend to divide the Downtown district in half. Much-maligned for the stench of its wood-pulp mills near Interstate-95, Jacksonville's attractive centre, with its Riverwalk and water taxis, and the neighbouring beaches certainly justify a detour.

A short distance north, near the Georgia border, historic **Fernandina** has seen eight national flags struck over its picturesque old town centre. Today it is a haven for antiques browsing, for beach lovers and also has a busy shrimping fleet.

The longest continually inhabited settlement in the US, **St Augustine** is hailed as 'America's Oldest Town'. Pensacola was colonised earlier, but the settlers abandoned their encampment, and St Augustine has the 'Oldest House', 'Oldest Wooden School House', a historic fort, and a tourist park on the spot where Ponce de León is reckoned to have made his first footfall, making him the first European on North American *terra firma* during the era of the Early Explorers. St Augustine's old Spanish Quarter has been well preserved and there are beaches near by, all of which combine to make the town a pleasant stopover.

Further south, **Daytona** is the 'Birthplace of Speed', where Malcolm Campbell piloted his *Bluebird* into the record books. Driving on the beach is still permitted, but a 10mph speed limit restricts modern-day fliers, and Daytona is now a popular, modern beach resort.

The **John F Kennedy Space Center** is NOT called Cape Canaveral. The third biggest attraction in Florida, home of America's space shuttle programme, is very particular about its title, and is at pains to point out that Cape Canaveral is a lump of sand. The Kennedy Space Center is the centrepiece of the **Space Coast**, which also offers a choice of good value, family-orientated resorts and amazing wildlife flourishing in the shadow of the launch pad. The sinking of the treasure-laden Spanish Plate Fleet off Vero Beach in 1715, has nicknamed this section of Atlantic oceanfront the 'Treasure Coast'. **Fort Pierce** is the largest town on the mainland, but the real attractions here are the relaxed resorts, golden beaches, watersports and diving opportunities.

The Birthplace of Speed

■ **At the close of the 19th century, en-trepreneur Henry Flagler built a grand hotel (the Ormond) on a superb 23-mile stretch of beach north of Daytona. He could hardly have envisaged that the golden sands would become one of the world's most famous racetracks, and his hotel a pit stop for early automobile enthusiasts .....■**

Henry Ford, Louis Chevrolet and Harvey Firestone were all lured south by the winter sunshine, but it was R E Olds, of Oldsmobile fame, who staged the first oceanside race across the hardpacked sands in 1902. He and Alexander Winton clocked a mind-boggling 57mph as they tore down the beach; a year later the top speed was over 65mph, and by 1905 speeds had passed the 100mph mark. In 1907, Fred Marriott recorded 197mph in a Stanley Steamer, before crashing into the surf.

The original 'track' began on Ormond Beach, at Granada Avenue, and ran south for 12 miles to Daytona Beach proper.

Faster and faster The beach track celebrated its finest hour in 1935, when Sir Malcolm Campbell set the last land speed record on the beach as he raced his Rolls-Royce powered *Bluebird* to 276mph. Motorbikes had also joined the fray, piloted by the likes of Glen Curtis.

After a quiet few years, beach racing was back on target in the southern beach area in the 1950s, but its popularity became a problem: large crowds and construction along the seafront made it too dangerous, and the action was moved to **Daytona International Speedway**, Bill France Boulevard (off Volusia) in 1959, the year of the first Daytona 500. The '500' is the most famous of eight-plus major car and motorcycle events staged annually at the high-banked, oval race track, and the centrepiece of February's 14-day **Speed Weeks** extravaganza. On non-race days, there are short guided tours of the track and pit area.

<< For a potted history of auto racing on the beach and the part it played in the development of the automobile industry (including a replica of a Stanley Steamer), drop into the **Birthplace of Speed Museum**, 160 E Granada Boulevard (*open:* Tuesday to Saturday 10.00–17.00hrs). There are more memorabilia and great photographs at the **Halifax Historical Museum**, 252 S Beach Street (open: Tuesday to Saturday 10.00–16.00hrs). >>

Pit crew in action in Daytona

Daytona

The 'World's Most Famous Beach' is 23 miles long, up to 500 feet wide, and an unsightly parking lot. But then Daytona's love affair with the automobile is a historic tradition. The Daytona Beach resort area, which stretches down the peninsula from Ormond Beach to Ponce Inlet, is the largest resort area on the East Coast, welcoming 8 million visitors annually. The season kickstarts in February with the famous formula and stock car **Speed Weeks** at the Daytona International Speedway. Several thousand leather-clad bikers transform Main Street into a 24-hour chrome carnival in March's **Motorcycle Week**, followed in April by hordes of northern students celebrating Spring Break. With over 16,000 hotel rooms and rental apartments, Daytona is well prepared for these regular invasions.

There is no shortage of other diversions – the beach itself is a giant amusement park, and driving on to the hard-packed sands is just the beginning. Concessions cater for every type of watersport: jet-skis, windsurfers, surf boards and sailboats are all easily available. The **Boardwalk** is an old-fashioned amusement gallery, and there are aerial gondola rides on **Main Street Pier**. Jai-alai and greyhound racing are popular local spectator sports. For a spot of culture, check out the impressive **Ocean Center**; the London Symphony Orchestra appears every other year at the **Peabody Auditorium**; and free beachside concerts take place at the **Bandshell** in Oceanfront Park. Natural delights include trails, boating and fishing at **Tomoka State Park**, N Beach Street; **Sugar Mill Gardens** in Port Orange; and **Dixie Queen Riverboat Cruises** (tel: (904) 255 1997) on the Halifax River (or Intracoastal Waterway).

The Casements *25 Riverside Drive (at Granada)* Named for its casement windows, the present-day Ormond Beach Cultural & Civic Center was built in the early 1900s and purchased by oil magnate John D Rockefeller in 1918.

Various Rockefeller-related artefacts have been gathered together here, including his wicker beachchair with its glazed portholes. There is an exhibition gallery on the ground floor, and an extraordinary collection of scouting memorabilia crammed into the attic.

Open: tours available Monday to Friday 10.00–14.30hrs, Saturday 10.00–12.00hrs.

For a couple of winters, Rockefeller had taken over an entire floor of his friend and business partner Henry Flagler's Ormond Hotel across the street, but, learning that he paid more than other guests, he moved to The Casements, a modest clapboard house, returning every winter until his death in 1937.

Daytona Beach, one of the East Coast's most popular resorts

Amateur historians will find plenty to enjoy at the Halifax Historical Museum, 252 S Beach Street, Daytona (*open:* Tuesday to Saturday 10.00–16.00hrs). Indian artefacts here include a 600-year-old Timucuan dugout canoe. There are also Spanish relics found in local plantation ruins, a 1909 time capsule, and auto history memorabilia. Pride of place must go to the enchanting, and marvellously detailed wooden model of the Boardwalk as it looked in 1938.

Museum of Arts and Sciences, *1040 Museum Boulevard* This classy modern museum really does have something for everyone – exhibits range from a giant ground sloth skeleton to a collection of Cuban art! The 13-foot-high sloth hangs out in the prehistory section, and dates from about 130,000 years ago. Hands-on specimen drawers offer fossils, puzzles, and even a mammoth tooth and a giant ostrich egg for inspection.

The main art gallery houses changing themed exhibitions using exhibits from the permanent collections. These might include African and pre-Columbian artefacts, Christian icons, American and European decorative arts and touring exhibits. There is a gallery devoted to arts in America, with paintings, furniture, silver, needlework and sculpture.

The Cuban Foundation Collection was donated to the city by General Batista in 1952. Portraits and landscapes record 200 years of Latin American history in vivid style. A set of precise Eduardo Laplante lithographs depicting plantation life is typical of those commissioned by landowners who never visited their investments. Folk art, jewellery, ceramics and photographs also play their parts.

Open: Tuesday to Friday 09.00–16.00hrs, Saturday and Sunday 12.00–17.00hrs.

Ponce Inlet Lighthouse, *Peninsula Drive, Ponce Inlet* Set at the southern end of the Daytona peninsula, this 1887 red brick lighthouse is now working again, and affords great views up and down the coast from the top of its 203-steps spiral staircase. Below, is a keeper's

Giant sloth, Daytona Museum of Arts and Sciences

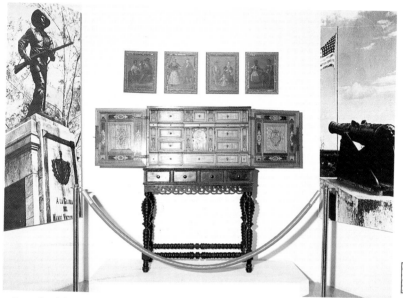

cottage furnished 1890s-style, and a small museum of nautical memorabilia. The fishing village of Ponce Inlet is renowned for its seafood restaurants, and there are picnic areas, a children's playground, a marina and a quiet beach in adjacent **Ponce Inlet Park**, Atlantic Avenue.
Open: daily 10.00–16.00hrs.

Nostalgic corner in the Daytona Museum of Arts and Sciences

▶▶▷ Fort Pierce
Named after a military outpost constructed by Colonel Benjamin Kendrick Pierce in 1838, Fort Pierce was incorporated in 1901, and grew into a small but prosperous fishing port surrounded by citrus groves. Indian River citrus is still renowned for its quality, but the town now has a different primary role, that of a popular resort area at the heart of the Treasure Coast. It has achieved this in a pleasantly relaxed fashion. The business district remains on the west bank of the Intracoastal Waterway (called **Indian River** here), while holidaymakers have a choice of fine sandy beaches on the barrier islands of North and South Hutchinson, which extend to either side of Fort Pierce Inlet. North of the inlet is surfing favourite **Fort Pierce Inlet State Recreation Area**, and **Pepper Beach**; nature-lovers should seek out well-concealed **Jack Island State Preserve** (off A1A), a 630-acre mangrove island with nature trails and superb birdwatching. To the south, try **Stuart Beach**; and snorkellers can explore the glassy-smooth waters around **Bathtub Reef**.

Elliott Museum, *825 NE Ocean Boulevard, Stuart* At the southern end of North Hutchinson Island, this is an interesting stop right on A1A. It is named after American inventor Sterling Elliott, the man who, for example, put four wheels on a bicycle and came up with a quadricycle. Here you will find Indian artefacts, antique

toys, a row of old-fashioned stores imported from Massachusetts, and a terrific collection of vintage bicycles, motorbikes and cars, including a Stanley Steamer, and a 1922 Rolls-Royce Pall Mall Phantom.
Open: daily 13.00–16.00hrs.

Gilbert's Bar House of Refuge, *301 SE MacArthur Boulevard, Stuart* A mile south of the Elliott Museum, this 1875 sailors' refuge was provided by the US Life Saving Service, forerunners of the Coast Guards. The ground floor rooms are simply furnished, and a small museum contains antique nautical paraphernalia and primitive life-saving equipment.
Open: Tuesday to Sunday 13.00–16.00hrs.

A stone's throw from the ocean, the white clapboard building known as Gilbert's Bar House of Refuge had a permanent keeper who scoured local beaches looking for stranded sailors whose vessels had foundered on Gilbert's Bar reef.

Harbor Branch Oceanographic Institution, *5600 Old Dixie Highway* This is a non-profit-making research and education facility involved in marine sciences and ocean engineering. The visitor centre shows introductory videos, together with related displays and exhibits; tours include a close-up look at working research ships and submersibles (when in port), laboratories and aquaculture facilities. More fascinating than fun.
Visitor centre open: Monday to Friday 10.00–16.00hrs; tours at 11.00 and 13.00hrs. (For revised schedule information, tel: (407) 465 2400.)

Vero Beach is a distinctly bijou community 20 miles north of Fort Pierce; just the spot for a little up-market shopping in the boutiques and galleries along beachfront Ocean Drive. Do not miss the intriguingly wacky hotel-restaurant, The Driftwood Inn and Resort on 3150 Ocean Drive (tel: (407) 231 0550). Dreamed up by entrepreneur Waldo Sexton, it was built in the 1930s from driftwood, beachcombing treasures, flea market finds and art works salvaged from house sales.

St Lucie County Historical Museum, *414 Seaway Drive* In a park at the eastern end of South Bridge, this museum provides a pleasant introduction to local history. The entrance is a replica East Coast railroad station. There is the restored Cracker-style 1907 Gardner House, a 1919 American LaFrance fire engine, turn-of-the-century stores, and a reconstructed Seminole Indian encampment. You can also see military hardware from Old Fort Pierce, and artefacts from Spanish shipwrecks.
Open: Tuesday to Saturday 10.00–16.00hrs, Sunday 12.00–16.00hrs.

Savannas Wilderness Area, *1400 E Midway Road* Close by Indian River, Florida's last intact freshwater lagoon system is preserved within the Fort Pierce city limits. The 550-acre park consists of a fragile marsh and uplands ecosystem with a rich diversity of plant and animal life. Fishing and boating are permitted on the canal system, and other facilities include a campsite, botanical garden, children's playground and petting zoo.
Open: daily 08.00hrs–dusk.

UDT-SEAL Museum, *3300 N A1A (at Pepper Park)* This is a real-life adventure story featuring the US Navy's World War II Underwater Demolition Teams (UDT) and their modern-day successors, the Sea, Air and Land Teams (SEAL). In 1943, this beach area was chosen as the training site for the Navy's élite wartime frogmen, and the museum pays tribute to this usually secretive branch of the armed forces. An impressive array of military exhibits, diving equipment, demolition apparatus, weapons, and photographs tells the story.
Open: Tuesday to Saturday 10.00–16.00hrs, Sunday 12.00–16.00hrs.

►►► Jacksonville

Capital of the 'First Coast' (see page 172), Jacksonville is flourishing – the 15th largest city in the US in terms of population, and the biggest of them all in terms of area. It is a pity that the city authorities make such a thing of this as it is not actually a good sales pitch, and anyway, in reality, much of the overblown 'city' is as yet undeveloped. Still, Jacksonville has plenty to offer family holidaymakers, historians and visiting culture vultures.

The city's roots are deep. A party of French Huguenot soldiers and settlers, led by René de Goulaine de Laudonnière, founded **Fort Caroline**, one of the earliest European colonies in North America, on the banks of the St Johns River in 1564. Native Timucuan Indians helped them construct a rough fort, but the Spanish did not take kindly to 'foreign' occupation of their New World territories, and ousted the French before establishing their own settlement at St Augustine, 60 miles further south. Jacksonville was named after General Andrew Jackson, and was laid out on the site of Fort Caroline around 1822. Extending both sides of the St Johns River, it prospered as a river port, and then as one of the earliest Florida tourist destinations with the arrival of the railroad. At the end of the 19th century, Henry Flagler built a hotel (now gone) at **Atlantic Beach**, part of Jacksonville's 15-mile stretch of sandy beachfront.

The Downtown district is compact, but divided by the river. To the north, the business district empties into **Jacksonville Landing** for shopping, dining and entertainment. Ferry services run shuttles from here to the south bank, where a **Riverwalk** meanders past street entertainers, hot dog stands and the fountains of **Friendship Park**. As the river curves south, the attractive **Riverside** district, to its west, home of up-market shopping enclaves and the lovely **Cummer Gallery of Art** leads off.

179

Jacksonville: 20th-century skyline of a historic city

Cultural treats in Jacksonville include the programme at the gloriously kitsch **Florida Theatre** (tel:(904) 355 5661). Painstakingly restored to its 1920s grandeur, it has earned a spot on the National Register of Historic Places, probably despite rather than because this is where Elvis Presley made his first stage appearance. Classical music fans should listen out for the **Jacksonville Symphony Orchestra** (tel: (904) 354 5547), while jazz lovers are treated to one of the world's largest free jazz events, October's annual three-day **Jacksonville Jazz Festival**, in Metropolitan Park.

Cummer Gallery of Art, *829 Riverside Avenue* If you need an excuse to visit the attractive Riverside district, then this is it. One of the Cummer's greatest attractions is its lovely gardens, a mixture of formal Italian and English landscaping which stretches down to the water's edge, interspersed with serene ponds and brick pathways between the plants and trees.

The recently refurbished and extended gallery space houses over 2,000 works of art dating from today right back to the 5th century. There are notable Oriental collections featuring delicately carved Japanese *netsuke*, Chinese jade and porcelain, Old Masters, contemporary painting and sculpture, and the Wark Collection of 18th-century Meissen tableware, one of the largest publicly displayed collections of its kind in the world.

Open: Tuesday to Friday 10.00–16.00hrs, Saturday 12.00-17.00hrs, Sunday 14.00–17.00hrs.

Fort Caroline National Memorial, *12713 Fort Caroline Road (off SR10)* Historic site of de Laudonnière's French Huguenot colony, this park has a scale model of the original fort, three walking trails and several pleasant picnic spots. A granite marker commemorates French

The St Johns River is the focal point of the city, and a great sightseeing opportunity. Several companies operate Water Taxi services between Jacksonville Landing and the Riverwalk, and also provide trips to Jacksonville Zoo. If there is romance in the air, why not take a gondola (tel: (904) 642 6357)? Riverwalk Cruise Lines (tel: (904) 398 0797) offer lunch and dinner sightseeing cruises with commentaries and musical entertainment; and River Entertainment Inc (tel: (904) 396 2333) also make evening sorties in the *Annabel Lee* paddleboat.

180

On the beach at Jacksonville

explorer Jean Ribaut, and is a good place to look out for bottlenose dolphins in the river. One mile southeast of Fort Caroline, the Theodore Roosevelt Area has been designated a Timucuan Ecological and Historic Preserve, encompassing 35,000 acres of wetlands, river systems and historic sites, and a two-mile hiking circuit through maritime hammock forest and salt marsh.
Open: daily 09.00–17.00hrs.

Jacksonville Art Museum, *Boulevard Center Drive* On the south side of Downtown, this museum combines a permanent collection of art old and new with a constantly changing programme of visiting and themed exhibitions. Notable collections of pre-Columbian artefacts and Oriental porcelain share the billing with contemporary graphics, photography and excellent multimedia shows, lectures and workshops.
Open: Monday to Friday 10.00–16.00hrs (Thursday until 22.00hrs), Saturday and Sunday 13.00–17.00hrs.

Jacksonville Beaches, *(12 miles east via US 90/SR10)* Jacksonville's Atlantic beaches were established as a resort area with the arrival of the railroad in the 1880s. Fifteen miles of dazzling sand, sun and fun link the three distinct beachfront districts of **Atlantic Beach**, **Neptune Beach**, and **Jacksonville Beach** (together with its southern annexe, **Ponte Vedra Beach**). The first two are both bordered by residential communities, and are somewhat quieter than the more commercial Jacksonville Beach section, which offers shopping and sports facilities.
The official beach season opens in April with a round of festivals and entertainments celebrating the end of winter; Floridians reckon it is all over by September, though there are enough sunny days in October to tempt more hardy northern types. Watersports enthusiasts will find a host of beachfront surf shops renting surfboards and sailboards; boat rentals for waterskiing and diving are available from **Club Nautico**, 2305 Beach Boulevard (tel: (904) 241 2628). **Jacksonville Beach Pier** is a great spot for fishing, well supplied with tackle rental and bait shops.

Jacksonville Landing, *Independent Drive* Downtown's shopping, dining and entertainment complex, the horseshoe-shaped festival marketplace sits on the north bank of the St Johns River, below Main Street Bridge. During the day, the $50-million mall is a shopper's delight, packed with temptations from evening wear to tennis gear via speciality gifts and jewellery; **Banana Republic**, **The Gap** and **Footlocker** are among the well-known names. The **Food Hall** caters to all tastes including Japanese, Mexican and Italian, plus generous deli sandwiches. As the sun sets upriver, the Landing is transformed with weekly entertainments in the central courtyard, live bands and DJ-hosted shows at **Fat Tuesday** and **T-birds Dance Club**; sports fans can catch big games on the big, big screen at **Hooters**, which also boasts an outdoor terrace on the river.
Shops open: Monday to Saturday 10.00–21.30hrs, Sunday 12.00–18.00hrs.

181

Shells are a popular souvenir. You can also pick up your own from the beach – but be aware of the restrictions

On the African veldt at Jacksonville Zoo

Jacksonville Zoological Park, *8605 Zoo Road (off Heckscher)* A fun way to get to the zoo is to take a river shuttle from Downtown. Water comes in handy around the zoo as well, where it is used to secure the inhabitants behind moats in preference to cages. The 61-acre site houses over 700 animals and birds in a variety of habitats. Ostriches, elands and Thompson gazelles scamper around the African veldt, there is a boardwalk trail, and the Okavango African river village has a petting zoo of enchanting pygmy goats, dwarf zebu and horses – a major hit with children. Check out the outdoor aviary; ride a camel, an elephant or a miniature train; take a cruise on the *Jacksonville Zoo Sundowner,* and catch animal shows at weekends.
Open: daily 09.00–17.00hrs.

Kathryn A Hanna Park, *500 Wonderwood Drive* A 450-acre beachfront park south of Mayport Naval Station, this is a highly recommended alternative to the main public beaches. Dunes crested with sea oats stretch forever a mile along the shore, while behind the beach woodland hiking and bicycle trails explore the nature preserve, which also encompasses over 60 acres of fresh-water lakes. As well as good fishing, there are lakeside picnic tables and barbecue grills (picnic supplies are available from the park campers' store), summer concessions, and 300 campsites (for information, tel: (904) 249 4700/2316).
Open: daily 08.00hrs–dusk.

Museum of Science and History, *1025 Gulf Life Drive* Recently overhauled and expanded, this museum now offers a broad range of displays and hands-on exhibits illustrating local and natural history, physical sciences and a planetarium. The ground floor **Living Room** is inhabited by rescued birds and a slithery collection of native and exotic reptiles such as a vast Burmese python. **Ribbon of Life** focuses on the St Johns River area. In the hands-on section, voice sifters, finger tinglers and fitness testing machinery are popular diversions. **Asteroid Biosphere** introduces space colonists of the future to a new environment. Arrowheads galore decorate the Indian history exhibit – **Peoples of the Mound** – based on findings at the 2,640-year-old Dent Mound outside Jacksonville. Artefacts recovered from the Civil War steamboat **Mapleleaf,** sunk in 1864, illustrate military life of that period. There are daily displays in the **Alexander Brest Planetarium** (seating passes from the front desk), and special musical laser shows (for information, tel: (904) 396 7062 Ext 3).
Open: Monday to Friday 10.00–17.00hrs, Saturday 10.00–18.00hrs, Sunday 13.00–18.00hrs.

On the south bank of the St Johns River where it flows into the Atlantic, Mayport is one of the nation's oldest fishing communities. Famous for its seafood restaurants, the shrimp dock is dwarfed by neighbouring Mayport Naval Station, the fourth largest naval base in the US. A popular outing with children, the base offers free tours of Navy vessels, which can include home-based aircraft carrier USS *Saratoga* (Saturday 10.00–16.30hrs, Sunday 13.00–16.30hrs).

Children enjoy Jacksonville Zoo's miniature train

■ **Follow this coastal route for exciting glimpses into history, for beautiful architecture, for excellent food and for stunning scenery. Northeast of Jacksonville, Route A1A follows a scenic trail up the coast to historic Fernandina Beach. It makes a great day trip, starting with a short ferry ride from Mayport as far as Fort George Island. (Ferries operate every 30 minutes daily, from 06.00 to 22.15hrs.) .....■**

First stop is the **Kingsley Plantation State Historic Site,** the oldest plantation house in the state, owned by eccentric slave trader Zephaniah Kingsley from 1813 to 1839. Kingsley grew cotton, sugar cane, sweet potatoes and citrus fruits; his 200 slaves lived in tabby cabins, visible across the old yard. (*open*: grounds, daily 09.00–17.00hrs; house tours, 09.30, 11.00, 13.30 and 15.00hrs).

Follow A1A north, along the **Buccaneer Trail,** by Little Talbot Island State Park, where five miles of wide sand beach, salt marshes and coastal hammock harbour bobcats, otters, marsh rabbits, water fowl and superb fishing opportunities.

A causeway crosses the Nassau Sound to **Amelia Island,** named by the British after George II's beautiful daughter in 1735. Host to legions of Spanish, French, British, and even Mexican invaders, the island is now a quiet resort area offering bed and breakfast accommodation, small hotels and a handful of deluxe resorts.

The historic town centre of **Fernandina Beach** lies on the west side of the island, with a wealth of fine Queen Anne stick-style and Victorian buildings, antique and craft shops, boutiques, galleries, restaurants and the state's oldest continuously operated hostelry, **The Palace Saloon,** 117 Center Street. This is a good place to sample the local shrimps which are delivered to the docks daily. **Trolley Bus Tours** depart frequently for a 40-minute circuit around the 50-block historic district, but the best way to explore is on foot. The **Amelia Island Museum of History** offers walking tours and strolls (for information, tel: (904) 261 7378; or pick up a map from the Chamber of Commerce, 102 Center Street).

East of the town centre, **Fort Clinch State Park** lies on the south bank of Cumberland Sound, the border with Georgia. Dating from 1847, the brick fortress has worn well, and park rangers, dressed in Union uniforms, cook, clean and take turns to stand guard. There are also picnic grounds, a nature trail, a beautiful beach area, a fishing pier and a campsite. (*Open*: daily 09.00–17.00hrs. For camping information, tel: (904) 261 4212.)

The bright lights of Jacksonville

The St Johns River

■ **To find Florida as it used to be, you need to step back from the coastal strip and explore an area of the state which flourished in the pre-railroad era, but has been largely overlooked for almost a century** .....■

184

The St Johns River has been an important landmark and highway for a very long time - there is evidence of a human presence along its banks as early as 5000BC. Archaeological research has pieced together a picture of these early Floridians. They were tall, dark-skinned people who ate a lot of clams and oysters (mounds of shells bear vivid testimony to that). The shells themselves were used to make tools and to hollow out wooden canoes.

Florida's largest and most important natural watercourse, the St Johns River is also one of the few rivers in the US to flow north. It rises in St Johns Marsh, eight miles north of Fort Pierce, and flows parallel to the Atlantic coast for 250 miles or so before curving east through Jacksonville to reach the ocean.

By the time the first Europeans tried to settle Florida's east coast in the mid-16th century, Timucuan Indians occupied the northeast corner of Florida. They helped French settlers to build a fort near the mouth of the St Johns River (which the French called the River of May), and provided them with native corn.

A strategic gateway To control the lower St Johns River was to control the interior of Florida (and the backdoor to St Augustine), but until the 19th century, pioneer settlers generally restricted their incursions to the immediate coast. During the 1820s, however, Jacksonville was founded, and trading posts were established upriver. Timber, sugar cane and citrus, which flourished along the fertile river banks, were shipped north, and the Steamboat era brought luxurious passenger steamers south.

A popular stop was the fashionable spa at **Green Cove Springs**. Its natural spring attracted the patronage of President Grover Cleveland, and of chain-store magnate J C Penney.

The river is over a mile wide as it describes an S-bend about **Palatka**. The town was named for the Indian word *pilaklikaha*, meaning 'crossing over'. Confederate troops trounced a Unionist outpost here in 1864, but this old

There are various ways of enjoying the river

Steamboat on the St Johns River

lumber town is better known as the modestly titled 'Bass Fishing Capital of the World'. South of Palatka, the river runs through Lake George, with the vast 366,000-acre wilderness of **Ocala National Forest** spreading off to the west. Then it squeezes past the citrus centre, **De Land** (see panel).

Manatees and shell mounds French marine biologist Jacques Cousteau was lured to the St Johns River to film its endangered manatee population. One of the best places to watch these hefty, vegetarian sea cows is Blue Spring.
Blue Spring State Park at 2100 W French Avenue, two miles west of Orange City, is a popular winter resort with manatees, which escape the cooler main river to bask in the 72°F spring from November to March. For human visitors, there are swimming, fishing and canoeing opportunities here, as well as picnic areas, boat tours of the river, and ferries to **Hontoon Island State Park**. This 1,650-acre island has been a boatyard, cattle ranch and pioneer settlement since the Timucuan Indians built the shell mounds visible from the nature trail.

Sanford, 200 miles south of the St Johns' rivermouth at Mayport, is the last navigable stretch of the river. When steamboats ceased to ply the river, Sanford settled for celery and became that vegetable's 'Capital of the World'. Things are changing today, with a revival of interest in St Johns River cruises. This is the place to hop aboard a riverboat for a short sightseeing trip, or do it the old-fashioned way with a two- or four-day cruise downriver to Palatka and Jacksonville. For details contact: **Grand Romance**, 433 N Palmetto Avenue, Sanford (tel: (407) 321 5091).
The St Johns continues upstream from Sanford, through Lake Harney, to gather its headwaters in **St Johns Marsh**. West of Cocoa and Melbourne, there are river camps and recreation areas such as **Lone Cabbage Fish Camp** (SR520), and **Camp Holly** (US192), which provide fishing and boating facilities, airboat rides and campgrounds.

As early tourists made their way upriver on the steamboats, they passed Harriet Beecher Stowe's house on the bank at Mandarin. A famous authoress since the publication of *Uncle Tom's Cabin* in 1852, she was paid by the riverboat companies to sit out on the lawn and wave to their passengers.

De Land was founded by a baking powder manufacturer, but is more notable as the scene of Chinese citrus culturist Lue Gim Gong's experiments with cold weather grapefruit and cherry-sized currants in the 1880s and 1890s. He succeeded in both cases.

The old world arts and crafts area of St Augustine

▶▶▷ **St Augustine**

The oldest continuously occupied settlement in the United States, St Augustine is very definitely 'Historyville, USA'. It was named in 1565, after the feast day of St Augustine (28 August) by Pedro Menéndez de Avilés, the Spanish governor of Florida. The settlement predates the British colony at Jamestown by 42 years, and the Pilgrims by 55 years. None of the earliest buildings remain; they were victims of Sir Francis Drake and of a later British siege in 1702, but the 17th-century **Castillo de San Marcos** and a few early 18th-century dwellings have survived in the old Spanish Quarter. These housed Spanish soldiers garrisoned at the fort, and then of the British during their brief occupation of Florida from 1763 to 1783.

When the Spanish returned, they planted citrus trees, built courtyards off the narrow streets, and added balconies to the simple whitewashed houses. The **Cathedral of St Augustine**, in the town centre, contains the oldest written records in the US, dating from 1594.

St Augustine was a scruffy little garrison town when the Americans finally purchased Florida in 1821. Yellow fever epidemics and the outbreak of the Seminole Wars discouraged early speculators. After the Civil War, tourists began to venture further south, and a significant visitor in the early 1880s was Standard Oil millionaire Henry Flagler. He chose the town to launch a 'Southern Newport', a semi-tropical resort where the wealthy and fashionable could escape the privations of northern winters. A railroad link with Jacksonville was opened in 1883, and Flagler's luxurious **Ponce de Leon Hotel** followed in 1888.

Although the grand resorts have had their day – the famous hotel is now a college – tourism is still the city's prime industry. The best way to explore the old town centre is on foot, but sightseeing trams depart frequently from a stop by the **Old City Gate** to trundle around other main sights. Across the **Bridge of Lions**, on A1A, St Augustine's beach annexe provides an additional choice of restaurants and accommodation, near the landmark black and white striped 1874 **Lighthouse**.

Castillo de San Marcos, *1 Castillo Drive East* St Augustine's most significant historic site, this star-shaped fortress stands on the foundations of nine previous wooden structures, the earliest dating back to 1565. The foundation stone of the present fort was laid in 1672, and during the 25 years it took to complete, supplies of coquina mined on Anastasia Island were reserved exclusively for it. A soft seashell 'rock', coquina proved a remarkably efficient defensive building material. Assailant's cannon balls simply buried themselves in the walls, so they could be dug out and used again.

The walls were covered with a thick layer of white plaster, and the *garitas*, domed sentry boxes on each corner of the star, were plastered in red, making up the colours of the old Spanish flag and therefore a means of identifying ownership of the fort by ships at sea.

Linked by curtain walls, diamond-shaped bastions allowed cannons to set up a deadly crossfire. The entire

fortress is surrounded by a moat with a single point of entry (the sallyport), backed up by a portcullis. Around the gun decks, long-barrelled cannons and short-nosed mortars were supported by musket fire, and the central courtyard, where soldiers drilled, is enclosed by guard-rooms, stores and the all-important powder magazine.
Open: daily; summer 08.45–20.00hrs, winter 08.45–16.45hrs.

Flagler College and Lightner Museum, *King Street*
Henry M Flagler visited St Augustine during the winter of 1883–4, and liked what he saw. He returned a year later to found the Ponce de Leon Hotel, a monumental Spanish/Moorish Revival affair which now houses Flagler College. It was the first major US building to be constructed using poured concrete. The interior was decorated with imported marble, carved oak and Tiffany stained glass. An elegant courtyard leads to the foyer (open to the public), beyond which the Rotunda has been transformed into a grand college dining room.

Across the street, Flagler added the Hotel Cordova to his collection (now St Johns County Courthouse), then built the Alcazar Hotel in 1888. The Alcazar displays the **Lightner Museum**'s collection of decorative arts, a gift of Chicago newspaper baron Otto C Lightner, and opened in 1948. This is a real treasure trove, best visited from top to bottom. The highlight of the collection is the glass on the second floor, featuring the largest gathering of American cut glass, superb Tiffany lamps and other decorative pieces, delicate Venetian glass, scalloped, frilled, satin, coloured and copperised glass.
Open: Flagler College, daily 10.00–15.00hrs; Lightner Museum, daily 09.00–17.00hrs.

Once a hotel – the Lightner Museum

St Augustine loves a festival, and finds any excuse to dress up in period costume and let off a volley of muskets. Spanish Night Watch (third Saturday in June) is a good example: an evening torchlit procession through the old Spanish Quarter with 'troops' dressed in 18th-century costume, re-enacting colonial customs such as locking up the town for the night. September's Founders Day commemorates the 1565 Spanish landing in the grounds of the Mission of Nombre de Dios; and the Grand Christmas Illumination (first Saturday of December) marks the British occupation of St Augustine with a rally at Government House.

Fountain of Youth, *155 Magnolia Avenue* For Fountain of Youth read 'Tourist Trap'. It is a matter of record that Ponce de León discovered neither legendary Bimini, nor the source of eternal youthfulness. But he did discover a spring: there is one in this park. Archaeological digs have revealed the existence of early Timucuan Indians here, and evidence of Christian Indian burial grounds. There are also traces of a 16th-century Spanish presence, and their history is recalled in a film show. A planetarium reconstructs the position of the heavens as seen by Ponce de León.
Open: daily 09.00–17.00hrs.

Oldest House, *14 St Francis Street* Also known as the Gonzalez-Alvarez house, after two former occupants – Tomas Gonzalez, an early 18th-century artilleryman, and Geronimo Alvarez, who bought the house in 1790 – this is one of the best researched and documented houses in the US. It has a fascinating story, told with great gusto and plenty of incidental detail on the frequent guided tours.

There are traces of a crude palm-thatched wooden habitation here dating from the early 1600s. Later, sometime after the great fire of 1702, that was overlaid with a single-storey coquina structure. The coquina blocks, made of compacted shells found on Anastasia Island, were shipped to the site and cemented with 'tabby', a mixture of lime, shells and sand.

A wooden second storey was added in the mid-18th century by the wife of an English soldier, Maria Peavett. She operated a successful tavern and boarding house, and her extraordinary life is the basis for the novel *Maria* by Eugenia Price (on sale in the gift shop). All sorts of excrescences were added to the building during the Flagler period, but most have been removed by the St Augustine Historical Society, which owns the building, and which has furnished each room in a period relevant to the house's history. The gardens are beautiful with deliciously cool arcades and a small **Museum of Florida's Army** with good costumes.
Open: daily 09.00–17.00hrs.

The arrival of explorer Ponce de León at the Fountain of Youth – fanciful reconstruction in St Augustine

Potter's Wax Museum, *17 King Street* One of the oldest wax museums in the US, it has over 170 figures of the good and the great, with characters from biblical times through to the modern era. Henry VIII appears surrounded by his six wives; Jenny Lind, the 19th-century 'Swedish Nightingale' slips in between Brahms and Verdi; greybeards of government, roving explorers and literary types abound. A novel interpretation of he life of Louis Pasteur, discoverer of pasturisation, adds rabbits to the equation.
Open: daily; summer 09.00–20.00hrs, winter 09.00–17.00hrs.

Some of the curiosities in Ripley's 'Believe it or Not!' Museum in St Augustine

Ripley's 'Believe it or Not!' Museum, *19 San Marco Avenue* Robert L Ripley was born in California in 1893, and his story is no less peculiar than most of the strange-but-true exhibits in his museum (one of 17 around the world). He started his working career as a cartoonist in New York, where he created a series of drawings entitled *Champs and Chumps*, featuring unusual athletic achievements. Later the title was changed to *Believe it or Not!*, and as Ripley began to travel, his column expanded to include weird and wacky features from all over the world.

He first visited Europe in 1920, and dropped in on some 198 countries during his lifetime, travelling the equivalent of 18 complete circuits of the world. At the height of its popularity, the column was syndicated to 300 newspapers worldwide and translated into 17 languages. His travelling 'Odditorium' collection at the Chicago World's Fair in 1933 attracted 2 million visitors.

So what sort of things can you find here? Examples of exhibits are: a 24-foot model of the Eiffel Tower made from 110,000 toothpicks, the Lord's Prayer engraved on a pin head, and Van Gogh masterpieces recreated in jellybeans - get the idea?
Open: daily; June to Labor Day 09.00–21.00hrs, rest of year 09.00–18.00hrs.

St Augustine Alligator Farm, *A1A (two miles south of Bridge of Lions)* Founded in 1893, the 'World's Original Alligator Farm' has added a few interesting extras to its menagerie. There are still plenty of crowd-pulling alligators in all shapes and sizes, but visitors will also see monkeys and tropical birds from South America, wallabies from Australia, giant Galapagos tortoises, and snakes from the four corners of the earth. There is a boardwalk nature trail through the swamps, alligator and reptile shows throughout the day, and a petting zoo. *Open*: daily 09.00–17.00hrs.

Spanish Quarter Living History Museum (San Agustin Antiguo), *Triay House, St George Street* Tucked away towards the Orange Street end of St George Street, this is a great little museum. A collection of eight historic buildings dating from the 18th century has been restored and sparsely furnished to recreate colonial life in St Augustine around the 1740s. Triay House starts the visit off with a small display of historic artefacts and information panels, then visitors are transported back in time as they explore the grassy plot and nose around the old houses. In the store, twists of tobacco, candle wax, rope and storage containers illustrate the simple provisions available.

Staff in period costume are on hand to answer any questions, and also perform demonstrations. There is a blacksmith in the smithy, sweating over ancient bellows as he fashions cooking utensils and tools. The spinning demonstration includes an explanation of wool dyeing from locally available materials such as onion skin and bark. Tours happen frequently and are worth waiting for. Included in the admission price is a visit to the **Spanish Military Hospital**, 3 Aviles Street (off the Plaza), which depicts the fate of a soldier-patient in the 18th century. *Open*: daily 09.00–17.00hrs.

In 18th-century colonial St Augustine, food cooked on outdoor fires was provided by hunting, fishing and kitchen gardens, such as those in the Spanish Quarter Living History Museum, planted with chillies, beans aubergines, onions and pumpkins, and even the odd citrus tree, which the Spanish originally imported to counter the risk of scurvy.

Street music in the Spanish Quarter

Walk Jack Island State Preserve

Slow down and keep a sharp lookout for the well-concealed entrance to this wilderness refuge on A1A, north of Fort Pierce Inlet. It is on the Indian River side of A1A.
The 630-acre island is accessible by footbridge from the parking lot, and offers a network of trails called the **Marsh Rabbit Run**, after a local resident. Marsh rabbits are smaller than their cottontail cousins, with shorter ears and hind legs, and darker fur. Spot them in the river as well as the coastal hammock area.

A boardwalk crosses patches of black, red and white mangroves to a 30-foot observation tower overlooking Indian River, which is an excellent vantage point for birdwatching.
Osprey, brown pelicans, great blue herons and ibis are among the many waterbirds to feed here.

Walk Washington Oaks State Gardens

Sandwiched between the Matanzas River and the ocean, on both sides of A1A 20 miles south of St Augustine, these gardens (*open: daily 08.00hrs–dusk*) are a hidden treasure with three distinctly individual walking habitats, and it is easy to take in all three within a couple of hours.

Starting in the west, the nature trail makes a loop along the river through lush coastal hammock woods and tidal marshes inhabited by a host of waterbirds.
Woodpeckers and red cardinals flit among the trees, and there is a good chance of spotting racoons and opossums. (A word of warning: this is prime mosquito territory.) To the north, part of the hammock has been transformed into a marvellous formal garden around a rather whiffy spring. Shaded by towering mature live oaks and palms, soft sawdust paths and luxuriant ferns encircle beds of azaleas, camellias, hydrangeas and a headily scented rose garden. On the beach side, a boardwalk traverses a swathe of coastal scrub alive with butterflies and the flash of brilliantly coloured scrub jays. At low tide, its yellow-orange sand is coarse with crushed seashells, and strewn with seams of coquina which form well-stocked rock pools. Look out for starfish, tiny crabs and sea anenomes. Beware of hidden rocks when swimming.

See also **Contrasting Canaveral**, *pages 194–5.*

Marshlands at dusk

Kennedy Space Center: getting together with an astronaut...

...and close encounters with the Space Shuttle

▶ ▶ ▶   **Space Coast**

Sandwiched between the 'First Coast' to the north and the 'Treasure Coast' in the south, what else could this be but the 'Space Coast', home of the **Kennedy Space Center**? In addition to NASA's high-tech marvels, the area is fast developing into a family-orientated holiday centre offering every possible Florida tourist attraction . Accommodation is plentiful and comfortable but not flash; spring and autumn reductions are excellent value; and Disney World is just an hour's drive away.

The four principal communities, **Cocoa**, **Melbourne**, **Rockledge** and **Titusville**, all lie on the west bank of Indian River, linked to the coastal peninsula by bridges. Established in 1837, Rockledge is the oldest winter resort on Florida's Atlantic coast, with lovely old homes to prove it; Cocoa and Titusville also have historic districts. **Cocoa Beach** is 'Surf City' (do not miss world-famous **Ron Jon Surf Shop**, 4151 N Atlantic Avenue). To the north, **Port Canaveral** is a cruise line terminus. Nature lovers will be amazed by the natural splendours of **Merritt Island National Wildlife Refuge**, which shares a boundary with Kennedy Space Center, as does undeveloped **Playalinda Beach** on the Canaveral National Seashore. The best dive spots are in the south of the region, around **Sebastian Inlet**; keen fishermen (or fisherwomen) should head for the **Lone Cabbage Fish Camp**, 8199 SR520 (west of Cocoa), where there are also airboat rides and boat rentals. Things cultural have not been overlooked either with Melbourne's fine modern **Maxwell C King Center for the Performing Arts** hosting concerts, dance and theatre productions (tel: (407) 242 2219); and the acclaimed **Florida Space Coast Philharmonic**.

Cocoa Village On the west bank of Indian River, just south of SR520, the historic Cocoa Village district has been attractively restored, with cobbled streets, brick sidewalks and neat Victorian shopfronts. There is plenty of browsing to do among the 50 art and antiques galleries, craft shops and boutiques, plus sidewalk cafés to relax in. Elegant **Porcher House**, built in 1916 by citrus grove owner Edward Postell Porcher, is on the National Register of Historic Places and open to visitors, as is the 1924 **Cocoa Village Playhouse**.

Guided tours of the area are offered by the **Brevard Museum of History and Natural Science**, 2201 Michigan Avenue. The museum itself is worth a look. Exhibitions and artefacts trace local history from the original Indian inhabitants through 16th-century Spanish incursions to the Cracker pioneers. A fully-equipped turn-of-the-century kitchen is part of the display. There is also a hands-on Discovery Room for children, and 22 acres with nature trails laid out around the museum grounds.

Kennedy Space Center SPACEPORT USA and Cape Canaveral Air Force Station, *NASA Parkway (SR405)* Just to get it straight: SPACEPORT USA is the visitor centre for the Kennedy Space Center, and launch pad for bus tours of the third most popular visitor destination in the state. Rightly so, for this is a fascinating journey through the history of America's space programme from

Rocketry on display

Cruised Miami Beach? Dived the Keys? Eaten alligator and done Disney? Here is a chance to sample one more Florida speciality, a space shuttle launch from the Kennedy Space Center. Advance information about schedules can be obtained from the NASA Public Affairs Office, Kennedy Space Center, FL 32899 (tel: (407) 867 4636). The limited number of launch passes allowing viewing from inside the security gates is usually booked up well in advance, but there are excellent vantage points along US1 at Titusville and from Cape Canaveral City (A1A). Titusville permits roadside parking from 24 hours before launch time.

the 1950s up until the present day, with a hint of what is to come. Arrive early for a good look around the free exhibits, and to book tickets for the bus tours and IMAX films before the queues start to stretch around the block.

A good place to start is the **Rocket Garden** with its towering bunch of original manned and unmanned craft. The **Gallery of Spaceflight** is packed with space hardware, models, space suits, specially prepared foodstuffs and videos. Space art and the IMAX cinemas are located in the **Galaxy Center** at the north end of the complex. Do not miss a chance to see the stunning 35-minute **The Dream is Alive** presentation with seat-shuddering footage of a shuttle launch, astronauts working in space, and shots of earth translated on to a screen five-and-a-half storeys high and 70 feet across.

Tours Two bus tours depart from SPACEPORT USA; both last two hours, and tickets must be purchased from the Ticket Pavilion near the Gallery of Spaceflight. The **Red Tour** ventures to the heart of the Kennedy Space Center facility to **Launch Complex 39**. The first launch from the base was *Apollo 8* in 1968. *Apollo 11* – carrying Neil Armstrong, Edwin Aldrin Jr, and Michael Collins to the moon – blasted off from here in July 1969. Along the

(Continued on page 196.)

Contrasting Canaveral

■ **A distinctive peninsula which juts out from the Florida coastline into the Atlantic, Cape Canaveral was named by Spanish sailors after the hollow reeds which grow abundantly in the region. Contrary to popular misconception this region is by no means all given over to the space business, in fact, most of it is devoted to wilderness and wildlife .....■**

194

Merritt Island is suspended between the cape and the mainland, marooned to east and west by Banana River and Indian River, and bordered to the north by Mosquito Lagoon and the narrow strand of the **Canaveral National Seashore**. The southern portion of this island houses one of the most technologically advanced facilities in the world, the **Kennedy Space Center**.

A huge area of 220 square miles in the north is given over to the **Merritt Island National Wildlife Refuge**, off SR402. The Visitor Center is open Monday to Friday 08.00–16.30hrs, Saturday and Sunday 09.00–19.00hrs; it is closed on Sundays from April to October.

Since it emerged from the ocean around 1 million years ago, this 25-mile long barrier island has been battered and sculpted by wind and waves, has protected the coastline and has developed a wide variety of habitats with about 300 species of birds, 25 mammals, 117 types of fish, and 65 amphibians and reptiles. A sad statistic is that 22 of these species are endangered, more than in any other wildlife refuge in the whole of the US.

Merritt Island's diverse habitats range from pocket-sized freshwater lagoons to vast saltwater estuaries; brackish marshes give way to hardwood hammocks and to areas of pine flatwoods. Flourishing within the shallow marshlands, a nutritious smorgasbord of worms, snails, crabs, clams and fish attracts crocodiles and shore and wading waterbirds. During winter, a further 23 species of migratory waterfowl take advantage of open-water feeding grounds, while pelicans, cormorants, great blue herons, egrets and wood storks are here year-round.

The well-watered hardwood hammocks provide an ideal enviroment for a lush backcloth of exotic bromeliads (air plants), and tropical and subtropical plants. Pileated woodpeckers, squirrels, armadillos, and migratory warblers are common here.

<< Venture away from the Cape, and downtown Melbourne seems an odd place to go manatee-watching, but the **Crane Creek Promenade** boardwalk along Melbourne Avenue (west of Front Street Park) is a prime site to spot these gentle vegetarian giants. At the Audubon Society's **Turkey Creek Sanctuary** in Palm Bay, a 4,000-foot boardwalk traverses three distinct Florida plant communities which attract a wealth of native wildlife. There is another chance to go turtle-watching with the **Sea Turtle Preservation Society** (tel: (407) 676 1701), which organises nesting season walks along the coast between Satellite Beach and Spessard Holland Park. >>

Walks and trails For a closer look at hammock environments, there are two walking trails off SR402, east of the visitor centre. **Oak Hammock Trail** is a half-mile stroll through subtropical forest, with interpretive signboards along the route. The **Palm Hammock Trail** is a more interesting two-mile hike which includes hardwood forest, cabbage palm hammocks and boardwalk sections over open marshland. Early morning and late afternoon are the best times to undertake the **Black Point Wildlife Drive**, a seven-mile one-way circuit off SR406. There is a series of parking areas for observing the mudflats and lagoon areas, which fairly bustle with bird activity during the height of the winter migration (January/February). A five-mile marsh hike, the **Cruickshank Trail**, begins at Stop 8, and there is an observation tower a five-minute walk along the trail from the parking lot. The optimum time to visit the park is October to April; bring mosquito repellent year-round.

Canaveral National Seashore This extends north for 24 miles from Merritt Island towards Daytona. It is one of Florida's few remaining areas of undeveloped coastal dunes, and

Manatees feed off Cape Canaveral

the 57,000-acre preserve also contains **Mosquito Lagoon**, a shallow saltmarsh estuary with a particularly interesting variety of wildlife, reflecting its location at the point where the American temperate and tropical climates meet. Animals and birds typical to both habitats co-exist around the marsh and areas of coastal forest, which are thick with oaks, cedars and wild orange trees. White-tailed deer, bobcats, racoons and rattlesnakes hide out in the woodlands, while dolphins, manatees, osprey and rare roseate spoonbills enjoy the rich lagoon feeding grounds.

From May to August, the warm sandy beaches are an ideal nesting ground for female green and leatherback sea turtles. Starting in September, the original 'snowbirds' – bald eagles, warblers, even Arctic peregrine falcons – journey up to 6,000 miles to winter here. In early spring, migratory right whales calve off shore. There is parking and access to the seashore from **Playalinda Beach** (SR402). During summer, guided **turtle walks** are led by Merritt Island rangers (for information, tel: (407) 867 0667).

(Continued from page 193.)

way, the tour passes the vast **VAB (Vehicle Assembl[y] Building)**, one of the largest volume structures in th[e] world (129,438,000 cubic feet), where space shuttle[s] are assembled before rolling by monster Crawle[r] Transporters to the launch pad. The **Blue Tour** visit[s] **Cape Canaveral Air Force Station**. When the Nationa[l] Aeronautics and Space Administration (NASA) wa[s] established in 1958, existing rockets and launch pads a[t] the Cape Canaveral facility were modified for the histori[c] Mercury and Gemini programmes. This tour explores th[e] site of the early space projects, stops off at the fascina[t]ing **Air Force Space Museum**, and visits state-of-the-a[rt] launch pads. For information, tel: (407) 452 2121.
Open: daily 09.00hrs–dusk.

Valiant Air Command Museum, *Space Cente[r] Executive Airport (off SR405/US1)* More than 35 vintage World War II and post-war military planes ar[e] housed here. Each March the collection comes alive fo[r] the **Valiant Air Command Warbird Airshow**, whe[re] fans can see the planes put through their paces. Fo[r] schedules, tel: (407) 268 1941.

US Astronaut Hall of Fame, *NASA Parkway (SR40[5)]* This is the story of the Mercury Seven, America's orig[i]nal team of astronauts, including Alan B Shepard, th[e] first American in space in 1961. Rare video footage[,] personal mementoes and artefacts follow the men'[s] careers in a series of fascinating potted histories whic[h] benefit from the personal touch. In addition to the grand fathers of space travel, the Hall of Fame complex i[s] home to **United States Space Camp** which provide[s] hands-on space training for junior astronauts aged seve[n] upwards. For information on the live-in five-day cam[p] programmes, contact US Space Camp, Titusville, F[L] 32780 (tel: (407) 269 6100).

The deep water Port Canaveral

Golf for the ecologically-sound? At the Space Coast's latest championship golf course, The Habitat (tel: (407) 952 4588), wildlife is a welcome distraction as course designers aim to preserve the natural environment. Other public courses in the area include: Royal Oak Resort & Club (tel: (407) 269 4500), winter home of the Canadian PGA; the Sam Snead Executive Golf Course (tel: (407) 632 2890); and Spessard Holland Golf Course (tel: (407) 952 4530).

Drive Along the East Coast

An easy day's excursion from the Space Coast, this drive follows A1A from Cocoa Beach down to the 'Treasure Coast' around Fort Pierce.

Cocoa Beach is a bastion of surfie culture, fluorescent beachwear and hot dogs – both in and out of the water. Just south of Cocoa Beach, the huge **Patrick Air Force Base** borders A1A to the west for the next five miles. There is a display of military rocketry outside the Technical Headquarters.

A seamless run of beach communities continues to spill down the coast: Satellite Beach, Indian Harbour, Indialantic, and Melbourne Beach, where A1A does a little signposted jig slightly inland before the road narrows. It is 14 miles from the southern Melbourne Beach city limit to the entrance for Sebastian Inlet State Recreation Area.
This is a great place to stop off for a couple of hours. The premier saltwater fishing location on the east coast boasts two Atlantic jetties and catwalk, giving access to waters teeming with bluefish, redfish, snook and Spanish mackerel. Surfers flock to a reserved beach area, and there is plenty of opportunity for snorkelling and excellent swimming off white sand beaches.

To visit the McLarty Museum, continue on A1A, then follow signs.
On the site of an old Spanish salvage camp, the **McLarty Museum** is the place to bone up on a history of Spanish shipwrecks off this portion of the coast. There are several more beach access points carved through the thick coastal barrier of palms, oaks, sea grapes and pines.

Rejoin A1A, and continue for 14 miles to Vero Beach, which is signposted.
Vero Beach is an up-market resort town off A1A. The main street is **Ocean Drive** with its exclusive shopping district, and the eccentric **Driftwood Inn (see panel page 178)**. .

Continue for 20 miles to Fort Pierce.
There is more fishing, snorkelling and swimming at **Fort Pierce Inlet State Recreation Area. Fort Pierce** itself has several attractions (see page 177). These include the **Elliott Museum**, right on A1A before Stuart, and **Gilbert's Bar House of Refuge**, at the southern tip of Hutchinson Island.

A1A rejoins US1 at Stuart.

F4-4 Fighter Race Corsair on show at Valiant Air Command Museum

WEST COAST

Lapped by the warm, translucent waters of the Gulf of Mexico, Florida's West Coast is an alluring mix of white sand beaches and watersports, world-class museums and wildlife. Once the butt of retirement jokes, it has developed into a cosmopolitan holiday destination offering a broad range of accommodation and diversions, including areas of exceptional natural beauty.

The early Spanish explorers – Juan Ponce de León, Pánfilo Narváez and Hernando de Soto – all called here, but were discouraged by warring Indians and steaming, insect-infested mangrove belts. Coastal navigation was fraught with danger from reefs and shoals. This was to the distinct advantage of legendary 18th-century pirate, Gasparilla, who was able to operate unhindered.

The US Army arrived in the 1820s, and a handful of fishing settlements began to grow along the coast. **Tampa**, the West Coast's largest city, was put on the map by Henry Plant's railroad in the 1880s. Vincente Martinez Ybor and his cigar industry added the city's Cuban connection, which remains strong even today. Across the bay, **Pinellas County,** with its 28 miles of barrier island beaches, St Petersburg, Clearwater and Largo, is Tampa's Gulf shore playground. To the north, Dunedin and **Tarpon Springs** provide a further touch of cultural diversity – Scottish and Greek respectively – and the Manatee Coast continues up to Cedar Key.

South of Tampa, **Sarasota** is the region's cultural capital, where circus king John Ringling built a fabulous estate and an Italian Renaissance-style museum to house his art collection. Sarasota's two performing arts centres feature nationally acclaimed programmes. The 'City of Palms', **Fort Myers** is renowned for Edison and for islands. The South Seas paradise of the Lee Island Coast is a renowned shelling spot; and inventor Thomas A Edison earned the city its nickname by planting the first royal palms along McGregor Boulevard, outside his winter home. At the southern extent of the coastal strip, elegantly manicured **Naples** luxuriates in society overtones and exclusive shopping malls worthy of Palm Beach. But the golf is much better here; and it is also an ideal launch pad for excursions into the Everglades.

Fun and games on the coast: Naples Beach

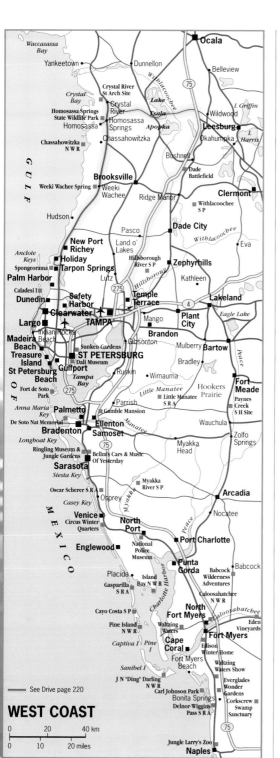

WEST COAST

Waccasassa Bay
Yankeetown
Dunnellon
Ocala
Belleview
Crystal Bay
Crystal River St Arch Site
Crystal River
Lake Tsala
L Griffin
Homosassa Springs State Wildlife Park
Homosassa Springs
Homosassa
Apopka
Wildwood
Leesburg
L Harris
Okahumpka
Chassahowitzka NWR
Chassahowitzka
Bushnell
G U L F
Dade Battlefield
Brooksville
Clermont
Weeki Wachee Spring
Weeki Wachee
Ridge Manor
Withlacoochee SP
Hudson
Pasco
Dade City
Withlacoochee
Eva
New Port Richey
Land o' Lakes
Anclote Keys
Spongeorama
Holiday
Hillsborough River SP
Zephyrhills
Tarpon Springs
Lutz
Kathleen
Palm Harbor
Hillsborough
Caladesi I
Safety Harbor
Temple Terrace
Lakeland
Dunedin
Eagle Lake
Clearwater
Plant City
Mango
Largo
TAMPA
Indian Rocks
Brandon
Madeira Beach
Sunken Gardens
Gibsonton
Mulberry
Bartow
Treasure Island
ST PETERSBURG
Dali Museum
Bradley
Peace
St Petersburg Beach
Gulfport
Tampa Bay
Ruskin
Wimauma
Hookers Prairie
Fort Meade
Fort de Soto Park
Little Manatee
Little Manatee SRA
Paynes Creek SH Site
Anna Maria Key
De Soto Nat Memorial
Palmetto
Parrish
Manatee
Wauchula
Bradenton
Ellenton
Samoset
Longboat Key
Ringling Museum & Jungle Gardens
Bellm's Cars & Music Of Yesterday
Myakka Head
Zolfo Springs
Sarasota
Siesta Key
Myakka River SP
Oscar Scherer SRA
Osprey
Arcadia
M E X I C O
Casey Key
Nocatee
Venice
Circus Winter Quarters
North Port
Peace
Port Charlotte
Englewood
National Police Museum
Punta Gorda
Babcock
Placida
Island Bay NWR
Babcock Wilderness Adventures
Gasparilla SRA
Caloosahatchee NWR
Caloosahatchee
Cayo Costa SP
North Fort Myers
Eden Vineyards
Pine Island NWR
Waltzing Waters
Captiva I
Pine I
Cape Coral
Fort Myers
Edison Winter Home
Sanibel I
Fort Myers Beach
Waltzing Waters Show
J N "Ding" Darling NWR
Everglades Wonder Gardens
Carl Johnson Park
Bonita Springs
Corkscrew Swamp Sanctuary
Delnor-Wiggins Pass SRA
Jungle Larry's Zoo
Naples

See Drive page 220

WEST COAST

0   20   40 km
0 10   20 miles

Mangroves are the only trees in the world that can extract fresh water from salt water. They excrete the rejected salt through the underside of their leaves. The mangroves form a vital part of the coastal ecosystem by stabilising the shoreline, and by creating a unique coastal nursery and feeding ground among their roots for all manner of micro-organisms, crustaceans and fish.

▶▶▷ **Bonita Springs**

Sandwiched between the ever-encroaching cities of Naples and Fort Myers, Bonita occupies a rare pocket of the southwest Gulf shore where large-scale development has been kept to a minimum. The little town is growing fast, inland from the coast, and Bonita Beach has a smattering of hotels. The virgin coastline of **Carl Johnson State Park**, off Hickory Boulevard, is one of the few remaining stretches of natural shell beach, and Bonita's back bay estuary area is teeming with birdlife; there are also manatees here and the fishing is great. Resort facilities are minimal; for after-dark entertainment the **Naples-Fort Myers Kennel Club**, 1601 Bonita Beach Road (tel: (813) 992 3411) lures in the punters for greyhound racing.

Corkscrew Swamp, *CR846 (20 miles east of US41)* Corkscrew was once the northern tip of southwest Florida's immense Big Cypress Swamp. The 11,000-acre sanctuary preserves America's largest remaining unspoiled stand of bald cypress trees, and a unique natural wildlife habitat. The National Audubon Society recognised the area's importance in 1912, when poachers roamed the swamp slaughtering wood storks and egrets for their feathers - much in demand as fashion accessories.Today, it is one of their greatest treasures. (See walks on page 215.)
Open: daily 09.00–17.00hrs.

Estero Bay Boat Tours, *Weeks Fish Camp, Coconut Road* Knowledgeable commentaries and sheer entertainment give value on Charlie Weeks' one-man boat show.

Bonita Beach

There is not a nesting spot, manatee playground or fishing hole on the back bay he does not know about. Daily afternoon cruises and sundown voyages on the Gulf of Mexico are given (for schedules and reservations, tel: (813) 992 2200). To get there, take US41 for nearly five miles north of Bonita Beach Road, then turn west on Coconut.

Everglades Wonder Gardens, *Old US41* Reeking strongly of sulphur from Bonita's springs, this is one of the original Florida attractions. Founded in 1936, it needs a coat of paint, but the selection of Everglades wonders you can see here is hard to fault, and the tour guides provide well-informed and entertaining commentaries. Meet Joe the 14-foot crocodile, eagles, otters, wildcats and more.
Open: daily 09.30–17.00hrs.

▶▷▷ Bradenton
Bradenton lies on the southern bank of the Manatee River, and is bisected by US41. Home to the**South Florida Museum** (see below), it is a good jumping off point for West Florida's only true antebellum building, the **Gamble Mansion** at Ellenton (see page 204). Bradenton's beach lies out to the west, on **Anna Maria Key**, a real old-fashioned narrow beachfront lined with clapboard houses, fast food and ice-cream stands, plus a few posing surfies who do their best to ride the relatively tame Gulf waves. A detour via the beach makes a pleasant change from the highway to or from Sarasota.

De Soto National Memorial, *75th Street* This memorial park commemorates Spanish explorer Hernando de Soto, who is supposed to have landed at this very spot back in May 1539. His 600-man expedition also included 350 horses, bloodhounds and greyhounds for hunting, pigs, weapons and tons of supplies. Park rangers dress up in period costume (December to April) and re-enact life in an early settlement. There is also a good nature trail (see walk on page 215).
Open: daily 08.00—17.30hrs.

South Florida Museum and Bishop Planetarium, *201 W 10th Street* The museum's main crowd-puller is Snooty the Manatee, an eight-foot-long, 700lb male, who has lived here since 1949. Born in captivity at the Miami Seaquarium in 1948, Snooty is fed four times a day: that is about 50lb of food daily - some 24 heads of lettuce, 16 carrots, 16 apples, two vitamin pills, and pineapple as a special treat. He is about to move into a new tank, and there is talk of providing a 'friend' in line with Federal regulations. The museum itself provides good dioramas of Indian life displayed together with archaeological finds, a reconstruction of a midden (shell mound) and a burial mound. Upstairs, set-piece rooms run the gamut from 16th-century Spain to the Victorian era, complete with traditional crafts, costumes and collectables. For information on the planetarium, tel: (813) 746 STAR.
Open: Tuesday to Saturday 10.00–17.00hrs, Sunday 12.00-17.00hrs.

▶ ▶ ▷ Clearwater

One of Pinellas County's eight resort communities, Clearwater is divided between the mainland and its beach sector across the Memorial Causeway.

Beaches Pinellas County boasts 28 miles of coastline, most of it maintained under the public parks system. In fact, it is so well cared for that beach scientists from the University of Maryland have placed two local beaches in their top twenty for the whole of the US: Sand Key is 16th, and St Petersburg's Fort DeSoto Park comes in at 19th.

North of Clearwater, **Honeymoon Island** and **Caladesi Island** are two of the last natural barrier islands on the coast with beautiful white sand beaches. **Clearwater Beach** is reached from the mainland via the Memorial Causeway; then head south for **Sand Key**; smart **Belleair Beach**, home of Henry Plant's Belleview Biltmore hotel; **Indian Rocks Beach** with its 41-foot fishing pier, the longest in the state; **Redington Shores Beach**, where the famed Suncoast Seabird Sanctuary houses around 500 rescued birds; and **Madeira Beach**, which fronts funky John's Pass Village, a shopping and dining enclave with a scenic waterfront stroll along the boardwalk. Treasure hunters be warned: **Treasure Island** was just a name dreamed up as a promotional wheeze in the Land Boom era, and hopes should not be raised too high..

Next stop along the shores is **St Petersburg Beach**, the busiest of them all, dominated by the vast pink outline of the 1928 Don Cesar Hotel. This Land Boom folly of staggering proportions was a playground for the rich and famous from F Scott Fitzgerald to Babe Ruth. Last, but not least, top-rated **Fort DeSoto Park** encompasses the tip of the peninsula.

Not much more than a caber's throw from Greek Tarpon Springs is a corner of Florida with strong Scottish roots. Dunedin's Hibernian links were forged in the 1860s, when Scottish merchants founded the first settlement here and gave it the Gaelic name meaning 'peaceful rest'. Each spring, the town pulls in the crowds for Highland Games complete with bagpipes, a military tattoo and much swaggering around in kilts.

202

Boatyard Village, *16100 Fairchild Drive (at 49th Street, off Roosevelt)* On a corner of the bay, tucked behind the airport, this out of the way area of Clearwater is full of surprises. Beside the access road, a field crammed with old fighter planes, transport aircraft and a US Coast Guard helicopter marks the extent of the **Florida Military Aviation Museum** (*open*: Tuesday, Thursday, Saturday 10.00–1600hrs, Sunday 13.00–17.00hrs). Next door, the wonderfully wacky **94th Aero Squadron Restaurant** has a garden full of army junk and a sandbagged entrance lobby. Opposite the restaurant, **Boatyard Village** is a re-created 1890s fishermen's shanty town of wooden shacks, rusty corrugated iron and raised boardwalks. The weather-beaten old buildings now house craft shops and boutiques, antiques sellers, cafés and snack stops. Gifts and souvenirs come big and small, from pelicans carved with a chainsaw out of tree trunks, to assemble-your-own wooden animals, beads and other goodies from **Junior E Shipp's Mecah.**

Caladesi Island It is just a short ferry hop to this natural barrier island where the only inhabitants are birds, armadillos and the odd alligator. There are swimming beaches linked by boardwalks to picnic and changing facilities, as well as diving and shelling opportunities, and a three-mile nature trail. There is boat access from Dunedin, Clearwater and Honeymoon Island. *Open:* daily 08.00hrs–sunset.

Marine Science Center, *249 Windward Passage* Between the mainland and Clearwater Beach, this center is also a rehabilitation unit for sea creatures, and focuses its displays on local marine life. Outstanding is the new Mangrove/Seagrass Marsh Tank, with a 55-foot long 'Window to the Sea'; irresistible are Sunset Sam, the rescued bottlenose dolphin and his mate Sybil. There are also aquariums of loggerhead turtles, rays and other exotic species. *Open:* Monday to Friday 09.00–17.00hrs, Saturday 09.00–16.00hrs, Sunday 11.00–16.00hrs.

Boatyard Village

203

The Clearwater City Marina is the place to catch scenic cruises on the *Show Queen* (daily, except Monday from September to January, tel: (813) 461 3113). Or sample the menu (and the sunset) aboard the *Admiral Dinner Boat*, Clearwater Beach Marina (Tuesday to Saturday at 19.00hrs, for reservations, tel: (813) 462 2628), which also offers lunch and sightseeing cruises.

Many plantation houses were surrounded by immense bare earth 'yards'. There were three practical reasons for these: fewer bugs, little danger from fire and no cover for hostile Indians. The yards were swept daily by the female house servants.

Stormclouds over the Crystal River

▶▷▷ Crystal River
North of Tampa on US 19

Crystal River is best known for its warm springs. More than 100 of them rise around Kings Bay, and attract wild manatees, especially during the winter months. These vegetarian gentle giants can weigh up to 3,000lb, and are quite safe to swim with. For information about swimming with the manatees, boat trips and canoe rental check with the Crystal River Chamber of Commerce, at 28 US19 (tel: (904) 795 3149).

Just north of the town, the **Crystal River State Archeological Site**, 3400 Museum Point North) is open daily, and is one of the oldest and longest continuously inhabited Indian sites in Florida. The six-mound complex was an important ceremonial centre from around 200bc to ad1400, and it is estimated that up to 7,500 Indians visited the complex every year. Archaeologists have uncovered more than 400 graves revealing prehistoric artefacts, from everyday tools and weapons to a sophisticated astronomical calendar.

▶▶▷ Ellenton's Gamble Mansion
3708 Patten Avenue (SR301 N), Ellenton

One of southwest Florida's first settlers, Major Robert Gamble was granted the original 160-acre plot of land here in 1844. The estate grew to 3,500 acres along the Manatee River. Sugar cane was refined in the plantation's own mill; citrus, wild grapes and olives were shipped to New Orleans. Gamble built himself a classic two-storey antebellum mansion from 'tabby' (limestone and shell blocks cemented with molasses) and brick, its broad verandas supported on 18 columns. To keep the house cool it is only one room wide, and the two-foot-thick whitewashed walls are lined with loose-shuttered windows aligned to catch the breeze. Great care has been taken to maintain the authentic period interior, and the house is also a memorial to Confederate secretary of state Judah P Benjamin, who took refuge here in 1865 as he made his escape to England.

Open: tours on the hour from Thursday to Monday 08.00–17.00hrs.

▶▶▷ Fort Myers

Thomas Edison, the town's most famous winter resident, had it about right when he predicted, way back in 1914, that 'there is only one Fort Myers, and 90 million people are going to find it out'. Airport gateway to the southwest coast, Fort Myers was the fastest growing metropolitan area in the US during the 1970s, but although the city has grown dramatically, life on the off-shore islands and keys is still largely a *mañana* affair of palm-fringed beaches, fabulous shelling, scenic boat trips and deep-sea fishing charters. Sports fishermen from across the world travel to Boca Grande for a chance to play a mighty tarpon; while the 'Sanibel stoop' is an affliction of shell gatherers harvesting the treasures washed up on that island's white sand beaches.

Downtown orientation is made easy by an old-time trolley bus (for information, tel: (813) 275 8726), which tours the historic district and supplies a constant stream of lively anecdote about the town's early residents. There is also a new water shuttle service on the Caloosahatchee Ricer..

Babcock Wilderness Adventures, *US31 N (9.5miles north of SR78)* This is a one-off experience which combines the excitement of a swamp buggy ride with a look around the vast 90,000-acre Babcock Crescent B ranch. Logging baron E V Babcock bought the property in 1914, and logged the cypress swamp during the 1930s. However, he recognised the importance of the trees in the swamp filtration process, and now the clear, brown, tannin-rich waters of 10,000-acre Telegraph Swamp – so named because the telegraph wires had to be routed around it – reflect an amazing display of curious 'cypress knees' uncluttered by weed or grass. Birdlife and alligators thrive, and a boardwalk leads to the cougar enclosure where native American panthers roam and breed in a natural habitat.

The 32-seat swamp buggies, carved from old trucks, make a 90-minute circuit of the property, which includes sightings of the ranch's bison herd, unusual crossbreed Senepol cattle and quarter horses, plus unscheduled appearances by wild hogs, turkey, deer, snakes and the odd Cracker cowman. The original 70-year-old ranch commissary, once occupied by the manager and company stores, is a fine example of Old Florida architecture. A gift wagon sells Babcock honey, and there are picnic facilities, but no food or drink is sold. *Open*: daily January to May, closed Monday June to December. Reservations only, tel: (813) 489 3911.

205

Fort Myers beach and pier

ECHO 17430, *Durrance Road (off SR78, east of Interstate-75* Under its full title, Educational Concerns for Hunger Organization, ECHO does not sound like much of a tourist attraction, but gardeners will find it fascinating. ECHO's brief is to develop a seed bank of unusual food plants for use in the Third World, and at present it exports to 106 countries throughout Africa, Asia and Latin America. Take the moringa tree, for instance: its leaves make highly nutritional baby food; the pods are used as a vegetable; the root makes a horseradish substitute; and the seeds can purify water overnight. There are ideas for space-saving gardens using plastic guttering; lightweight rooftop gardens made of cola cans and grass clippings which can grow ginger and chillis, or (without cans) radishes, lettuces and much more. Flourishing in the gardens are edible landscape plants such as coffee, citrus, carabola (starfruit), pepper and cashew trees.

Open: tours Tuesday, Friday and Saturday 10.00hrs, more frequent in winter (tel: (813) 543 3246).

Eden Vineyards, owned by Earl Kiser (above) is the US' southernmost winery

Eden Vineyards Winery and Park, *19850 SR80, Alva (10 miles east of Interstate-75)* In this southernmost winery in North America, the vines are specially cultivated hybrids designed to combat diseases usually taken care of by frost in more northerly climes. The seven estate wines will probably never win any major prizes, but it is a pleasant trip to the winery, out in the green farmlands east of Fort Myers. A quick tour of the winery area is followed by a more leisurely tasting session, including the latest experimental flavour, carabola wine, made from starfruit. It is suprisingly tasty when served well chilled over ice, and there is a new passionfruit vintage in the pipeline. Other diversions include the Cypress Cathedral nature trail – there are picnic tables under the trees with an on-site deli which serves cold drinks and excellent home-made sandwiches. Harvesting is in June to July, and the winery celebrates with a fun festival of grape-pressing, blue grass music, food and crafts stalls.

Open: daily 10.00–18.00hrs.

Edison Winter Home, *2350 McGregor Boulevard* Inventor of the automatic telegraph, phonograph and incandescent lamp, Thomas Alva Edison can also be credited with 'discovering' Fort Myers. Holidaying in Florida on doctor's orders in 1884–5, he ventured down to this small, semi-tropical fishing village on the Caloosahatchee River and bought a 14-acre plot of land. The winter home he built on the riverbank was an innovation too: its prefabricated sections were constructed in Fairfield, Maine, transported south on four schooners and erected in 1886. Edison and his second wife, Mina Miller Edison, their children and friends spent every winter here until his death in 1931.

The modest house retains its original furnishings, and the surrounding gardens reveal that the wizard inventor was also an expert horticulturist. Friends and colleagues were constantly producing gifts of exotic plants to add to his collection (such as Henry Firestone's monstrous banyan tree), and several varieties of rubber plant and

golden rod are testament to Edison's search for a domestic source of natural rubber. Across McGregor Boulevard, lined with majestic royal palms planted by Edison, is the fully-equipped laboratory. It is still lit by the original carbon filament light bulbs which have shone for 12 hours a day ever since. In the museum here, hundreds of Edison inventions, from talking dolls to miner's lamps, illustrate a handful of the 1,097 patent designs he achieved during his 84 years.
Open: guided tours Monday to Saturday 09.00–16.00hrs, Sunday 12.30–16.00hrs.

Ford Winter Home, *2350 McGregor Boulevard* The Fords visited the Edisons in 1915, and a year later bought the adjacent property, which they named 'Mangoes'. In total contrast to the palatial Ford mansion in Deering, Michigan, the homely interior of their winter cottage has been carefully re-created with the help of photographs using period furnishings, and the gardens have been replanted with citrus trees just as Ford intended. After Edison died, the Fords never returned to Fort Myers, and the house and contents were sold at auction in 1945. The only original item is a recently acquired clock. An example of the cornerstone of the Ford fortunes, a 1914 Model-T Ford, sits in the garage. It was the world's first mass-produced vehicle. A Ford museum is planned to open soon, covering the Ford family and Henry Senior's work up to 1932, when the V8 engine was unveiled, much of it having been designed on the back porch at 'Mangoes'.
Open: guided tours Monday to Saturday 09.00–16.00hrs, Sunday 12.30–16.00hrs.

207

Thomas Edison's laboratory, fit memorial to a great scientist

Fort Myers Historical Museum, *2300 Peck Street* This museum gives the history of southwest Florida in a nutshell. The story begins with Calusa Indian artefacts, and continues through the founding of the fort, the Seminole Wars and events of the 20th century. Housed in an old train depot, it has a refurbished 1930s railroad car, as well as the Cooper collection of Depression and Carnival glassware, plus excellent scale models and a gift shop.
Open: Monday to Friday 09.00–16.30hrs, Sunday 13.00–17.00hrs.

Island hopping Marooned amid the clear blue waters of the Gulf of Mexico, many of the highlights of the Lee Island Coast are only accessible by boat. A generous sprinkling of sun-drenched islands and keys, encircled by secluded beaches and mangroves, offers the promise of a day away from it all. Island hoppers can explore over 100 offshore retreats with ample opportunities for shelling, fishing, birdwatching, or just lazing around.
Across Pine Island Sound, home to one of the most abundant populations of the playful bottlenose dolphin, **Cayo Costa State Island Preserve** is the largest barrier island in the region. Acres of pine forest, oak palm hammock and gum limbo are fringed with deserted sand beaches which offer excellent shelling, particularly during the winter months. There is spectacular birdlife, and sea turtles lay their eggs here.
Calusa Indians left their mark on **Cabbage Key** with a huge shell mound. Today's visitors are more likely to leave an autographed dollar bill pinned to the walls of the island's historic inn – built on top of the mound in 1938 by mystery writer Mary Roberts Rinehart. Day trippers can build an appetite climbing the wooden water tower for a terrific view of the Sound, or follow a nature trail before repairing to the restaurant to recover.

The simple house owned by Henry Ford in Fort Myers

Cruise under sail on the tall ship Eagle

Naturalists should not miss an organised nature tour of **Pine Island**. The tours depart three mornings a week and take a detailed look at the region's aquatic birdlife, Calusa Indian mounds, mangrove areas and active nesting grounds. (For reservations, tel: (813) 283 0888.)

To get there, experienced sailors will find plenty of boat rental outfits offering everything from dinghies to motor boats. Local boat tour operators include: **Fuery's Shelling Charters**, Captiva (tel: (813) 472 3459); **Island Water Tours** (tel: (813) 463 6181 ext 246); and **South Seas Plantation**, Captiva (tel: (813) 472 7549). Full-day luxury cruises on the 38-foot sloop *Marsha Anne* (tel: (813) 466 3600), and the tall ship *Eagle* (tel: (813) 466 SEAS) depart from the Getaway Marina, Fort Myers Beach; while **J C Cruises**, Fort Myers Yacht Basin (tel: (813) 334 7474), ply the Gulf and take tours up the Caloosahatchee River.

Nature Center of Lee County, *Ortiz Avenue (north of Colonial)* Founded in 1970, on a 105-acre plot, the Nature Center was specifically designed with children in mind. In the reception area there is a chance to get acquainted with a collection of local snakes, many of them poisonous; aquariums of snapper and soft-shelled turtles; bees busying themselves in a perspex-enclosed section of honeycomb; and a selection of touch exhibits including sea shells. A popular favourite is an Indonesian musical instrument made out of hollowed cane. Indian history is covered here, and there is a collection of native *chickee* huts outside. The Audubon Society houses a number of its injured birds, particularly raptors (birds of prey), in the Center's aviary. There are two boardwalk trails in the swamp, cypress and pine woods, and a more taxing 2.5-mile Wildlands Trail without the benefit of a boardwalk. The planetarium operates a busy programme of events (for information, tel: (813) 275 3616).

Open: Monday to Saturday 09.00–16.00hrs, Sunday 11.00–16.30hrs.

Here are some tips for shell seekers: Bowman's Beach on Sanibel Island is the acknowledged top spot and Captiva Beach has piles of easily accessible washed up shells. But both of these are very popular, so why not try secluded beaches such as Upper Captiva, Cayo Costa, and neighbouring Johnson Shoals? Only accessible by boat, they are great shelling spots. For expert advice, take a shell safari with Captain Mike Fuery, Tween Waters Marina, Captiva (tel: (813) 472 3459). *Remember, the law limits the collection of live shells to two per species.*

WEST COAST

The horse conch (*Pleuroploca gigantea*), also known as the giant band shell, is Florida's official state shell symbol. It can grow up to a size of around 24 inches, and feeds off clams in waters from a depth of one to 80 feet. Floridians have no qualms about eating their state symbol: conch is the staple filler in local chowders, and appears in various guises on menus from the Panhandle to Key West.

Sanibel and Captiva Islands Linked to the mainland by a mile-long scenic causeway, picturesque Sanibel and Captiva could be hundreds of miles from the busy coastal highways and condominiums. In fact, this is Florida's 'Tahiti', a lush island paradise where pirate José Gaspar is said to have held his female captives among the purple trumpets of morning glory and brilliant hibiscus. Life is easy on the miles of sandy beaches, and in the quirky cafés, friendly restaurants and arty-crafty boutiques.

There is history with the 1884 lighthouse and a brace of turn-of-the-century stilt houses on the eastern tip of Sanibel; and the road north to Captiva passes the **J N 'Ding' Darling National Wildlife Refuge**, a 5,030-acre preserve with a 5-mile scenic drive (good birdlife in the mornings), narrated tram tour, nature trails and canoe rentals. Along the way, **Bowman's Beach** is one of the best, and there is another popular sand strip at **Blind Pass** where the islands meet. **Turner Beach** is considered a prime shelling spot, and an excellent vantage point for the spectacular Gulf sunsets. The Chamber of Commerce, just over the Sanibel Causeway, stocks plenty of helpful brochures and shell guides.

Shell Factory, *US41 (north of Fort Myers)* Worth a mention, this shell supermarket boasts the world's largest collection of shells and coral from inexpensive sand dollars and mixed bags to pricey exotica. There are loads of trashy gift novelties, cheap and cheerful beachwear, jewellery and leather goods.
Open: daily 09.30–18.00hrs.

Examining the wares in the Shell Factory

■ **It starts off with one little whelk and before you know it, you have collected a small mountain of striped, speckled, spotted, striated and smooth sea shells – all begging to be taken home. Shelling is not a hobby in Florida, it is a fixation. Confirmed conchologists are known to hit the beach before dawn, shuffling along with the distinctive 'Sanibel stoop', armed with torches and bags stuffed with treasures .....■**

Several species of cockles, cones, moons and glossy olives are common and easy to collect. Cleaned up, the Atlantic moon bears an eerie resemblance to its nickname, shark's eye. Whelks, with their rounded living quarters and elegant tapered tails, are also a familiar sight on Floridian beaches. Mature whelks can range from three or four inches to 16 inches long depending on the variety, and look out for females of the species which lay leathery chains of eggs or shell-bearing capsules.

Conches Conches come in all shapes and sizes, from the delicate hues of the pink conch to the mottled hawkwing, and strangely named three-inch-long Florida fighting conch. Sheltered bays and saltwater mangrove areas harbour the crown conch, easily identified by its single or several spiky 'crowns'.

Sand dollars Shuffle along a sand bar, and there will be a fortune in sand dollars. Unfortunately, they have not attained currency status, but

they still make a good souvenir. To get that shop-clean look, soak the coarse green discs in a weak bleach solution and then dry in the sun.

La crème de la crème After a storm, the conchologists will be out in force, and a prize find is the junonia, a long whitish shell, decorated with evenly spaced dark brown spots. The lion's paw scallop is another beauty – an exotic cousin of the common scallop with raised 'knuckles' which give it the appearance of a paw. For something softer, look out for delicate janthina shells, home of the violet sea snail.

Only collect dead, empty shells – it's illegal to collect shells with living occupants for the very good reason that the species might be threatened. Only buy shells from reputable sources.

Queen conch (Strombus gigas)

▶▶▷ **Homosassa Springs State Wildlife Park**
9225 W Fishbowl Drive, Homosassa Springs (off US41)
Homosassa Springs has been a tourist attraction since the early 1900s, when trains travelling along what is now Fishbowl Drive used to stop by the spring so that passengers could stretch their legs. The 150-acre wildlife park was developed in the 1960s, and 1964 saw a 157-ton underwater observatory launched into the spring down a ramp 'greased' with edible bananas so as not to distress the fish. It is still the top attraction here, providing an unrivalled view of the 45-foot deep **Spring of 10,000 Fish**. The natural spring pumps 6 million gallons of water to the surface every hour at a constant 72°F, and attracts as many as 34 different species of fish, both freshwater and saltwater varieties, and, of course, manatees. Explore the rest of the park on pontoon boat trips and self-guided nature trails. Look out for river otters, turtles and marvellous birdlife; native wildlife kept in enclosures includes black bears, bobcats and deer.
Open: daily 09.00–17.30hrs.

Feeding the manatees in Homosassa Springs State Wildlife Park

▶▷▷ **Largo: Heritage Park**
11909 N 125th Street (between Washington and Ulmerton)
Surrounded by 21 acres of palms and palmettos, the Pinellas County Historical Society has rescued and reconstructed 14 historic buildings, including seven houses, a school, a church, a train depot, and a Victorian bandstand. All the buildings come from the county, except the depot which was imported from Hillsborough - but then Pinellas was part of Hillsborough until 1912. The setting neatly separates one building from the next with winding brick paths through the park.
Take time for a 20-minute tour of **Seven Gables House**, or the **Plant Sumner Home** - all the other exhibits are open all day long. Built in 1907 for a well-to-do Clearwater family, Seven Gables House gives a fascinating insight into prosperous Victorian life on the bay. The entire interior is panelled with red heart pine, and is beautifully decorated with period furnishings and antiques. The Plant Railroad System's local foreman lived in the more modest Plant Sumner abode. Simpler still is a 14-foot-square honeymoon cottage, and the cosy log cabin festooned with flowers and creepers is a typical Cracker dwelling built by the early pioneers.
Open: Tuesday to Saturday 10.00–16.00hrs, Sunday 13.00–16.00hrs.

▶▶▶ **Naples**
Fast developing into a major tourist destination, Naples is a great après-theme-park escape for the discerning visitor. Unofficial 'Golf Capital of the World', with 40 easily accessible courses, its sweeping Gulf beaches are just a stone's throw from the Everglades. There is a brand-new $18 million arts centre, superb shopping, up-market accommodation and fine dining.

Collier Automotive Museum, *2500 S Horseshoe Drive*
The finest sports car collection in the US, this is an absolute must for motor racing enthusiasts. The sleek mod-

lute must for motor racing enthusiasts. The sleek modern building is just an indication of the treasures within, which include a fabulous 1914 Simplex, MGs (the Collier brothers were America's first MG agents), Bentleys, Cadillacs, Cunninghams, Porsches and more. Fascinating potted histories and knowledgeable volunteer guides are on hand for questions.

Open: Tuesday to Saturday 10.00–17.00hrs, Sunday 13.00–17.00hrs.

Frannie's Teddy Bear Museum, *2511 Pine Ridge Road (east off Airport-Pulling)* A 'beary' nice place to be, Frannie's is cute. Naples philanthropist Frances Pew Hayes opened the $2 million teddy bear preserve with her own collection in 1990, and the 1,800-teddy roll call is growing all the time. Donated bears, both antique and brand new, have swelled the ranks; bear dioramas, a bear theatre and sculpted marble bears are all housed in a little house in the woods.

Open: Wednesday to Saturday 10.00–17.00hrs, Sunday 13.00–17.00hrs.

Jungle Larry's Zoo Park, *1590 Goodlette Road* Top marks go to this excellent zoo garden in a state which is well supplied with the genre. Get a feel for the place with a commentated tram ride, then wander off for a closer look at the 150 animals - from anteaters to wallabies. Thoughtfully designed habitats have contributed to the animals' longevity and several successful captive breeding programmes. Star turns are the big cats – cougars, lions, leopards and tigers – some of which take part in the truly amazing twice-daily show-times with their trusted trainer. Pet an alligator or stroke a snake at the Wildlife Encounter, take a Safari Island cruise, and then buy up the gift shop.

Open: daily 09.30–17.30hrs.

Offshore, south of Naples, is Marco Island, where development has not quite ousted nature or obliterated the memory of the island's early inhabitants, the Calusi Indians. Ancient shell mounds can still be seen, and bald eagles are encourged to breed in artificial nests among the hotels and apartments.

213

NAPLES CITY DOCK

Walk Trails in Cayo Costa State Park

Access is by boat or ferry from Sanibel, Captiva and Pine Islands. Directly south of Boca Grande, and 12 miles west of Cape Coral on the mainland, this park occupies 2,132 acres on the tip of Cayo Costa Island. A barrier island, Cayo Costa shelters Charlotte Harbor and Pine Island Sound from the worst ravages of the Gulf storms, and is a major shelling destination. Between the beaches and dunes of the island's Gulf shore and the bayside mangrove belt, there is a network of attractive short trails that explore the subtropical interior, comprising a mixture of pine flat woods, oak palm hammocks and grassy regions dotted with clumps of palms.

The Quarantine Trail leaves from the Bayside Dock, and works its way north to a picnic area on Pelican Bay. A tram from the dockside crosses the island to the Gulf coast and a Gulf Trail. Cemetery Trail runs north-south, passing the site of an old pioneer graveyard; while the Pinewoods Trail and Scrub Trail run east–west, and the Scrub Trail links with the Quarantine Trail en route to the picnic site.

Walk Collier-Seminole State Park

Tamiami Trail (US41), 17 miles southeast of Naples.

On the northwestern edge of the Everglades, this superb 6,423-acre park is frequently overlooked. Named after 1940s entrepreneur and developer Barron Collier, who first envisaged the park, and after the Seminole Indians who made the area their home, the park offers an introduction to the Everglades, plus fishing, canoeing and boating access to the Ten Thousand Islands in the Gulf of Mexico.

The 6.5-mile hiking trail leaves from the boat basin and winds its way through pine flatwoods and cypress swamp.
A special feature of the park is an unusual tropical hammock (an area slightly raised above the surrounding swamp) which flourishes with trees more commonly found in West Indian coastal forests and in Yucatan. In the woodlands, native Florida black bears and panthers keep to themselves, but wood storks, cockaded woodpeckers and mangrove fox squirrels are frequently spotted. A separate boardwalk system and observation platform overlook the saltmarsh region, where bald eagles circle overhead. A word of warning: biting insects can be a problem. Check park conditions before a visit (tel: (813) 394 3397).

Louisiana heron

Walk Trail in Corkscrew Swamp

CR846, Bonita Springs (20 miles east off Highway 41).

This boardwalk trail covers a minute section of the 11,000-acre sanctuary, but offers an unbeatable opportunity to explore three contrasting native habitats.

Just beyond the park headquarters, a woodland area of slash pines, palmetto and the odd wax myrtle is a great place to spot woodpeckers and tiny grey flycatchers. Then a broad swathe of wet prairie reveals alligator trails and a mass of brilliant wild flowers flourishing among a sea of grasses. In the shade of the thin, silver-grey pond cypresses, look out for masses of little white apple snail eggs, the only food of the rare Everglades kite. Corkscrew's bald cypress stand is the largest in America. These impressive trees, draped in Spanish moss, are hundreds of years old. At their feet, ferns grow in adundance and bromeliads (air plants) nestle against the trunks, gathering nutrition from rainwater. Visit the central marsh in July, and it is aflame with red hibiscus; in autumn it is a sea of primrose willow.

215

Walk Trail in De Soto National Memorial

75th Street, Bradenton.

A short half-mile trail, the great charm of this walk is its breezy waterside location.

Take in the Visitor Center first.
There is a 20-minute video and display of Spanish explorer artefacts, including armour, weaponry and a model shallow-draft caravel.

Set out along the beach.
You can imagine how it must have seemed to the early pioneers, attacking the mangrove thickets. Along the beach, the leaves of the sea grape trees were used by the explorers as stationery. In the undergrowth, broken blocks of 'tabby' (the settlers' solution to concrete – made from sand, limestone and shells) mark William Shaw's 1840s pioneer cottage. This area was known as Shaw Point for many years. The bayside cove is a good place to see pelicans, gulls, terns, ospreys and cormorants.

Sentinel heron

▶▶▷ St Petersburg

On the western shores of Tampa Bay, St Pete (as it is generally known) is the cultural centre of the eight resort communities which make up Pinellas County. The name was taken from the Spanish *punta pinal* (meaning 'point of pines'), and the Pinellas Suncoast is Florida's most popular Gulf resort area, boasting 128 miles of shoreline, 28 miles of superb beaches, golf, tennis, watersports, nature parks and family attractions galore – all just a 90-minute drive from Orlando.

In 1885, one Doctor van Bibber proposed that a 'Health City' should be founded in Pinellas. Now visitors flock here to enjoy its average 361 sunny days per annum; the Guinness Book of Records credits St Pete with the most consecutive days of sunshine on record – some 768 during 1967–9.

Dali Museum, *1000 S Third Street* Opened in March 1982, the museum is the permanent home of the world's largest and most comprehensive collection of Spanish surrealist Salvador Dali's art. The collection was amassed by Cleveland industrialist A Reynolds Morse and his wife, Eleanor Reese, who first encountered Dali's work at a travelling exhibition in 1942. A year later they purchased their first canvas, *Daddy Longlegs of the Evening...Hope!*, the foundation stone of a collection which now numbers some 93 oil paintings, over 100 watercolours and drawings, 1,300 graphics, plus posters, sculpture and decorative pieces. A 2,500-volume library is devoted to Dali and Surrealism.

From 1971–80, the collection was exhibited in the public wing of Morse's and Reese's Ohio office premises –

Sunshine is almost guaranteed on St Pete's beaches

Dali himself attended the opening. However, the collection had outgrown its Ohio home, and Morse and Reese began a nationwide search for a new permanent location. They settled on St Petersburg in 1980, confident that the tourist-orientated nature of the city would ensure maximum exposure of the works. A waterfront warehouse was renovated, and the museum opened two years later.

The exhibits are displayed chronologically, starting in 1914, when the Impressionist influence was a strong feature in the young Dali's work, though the theatrical 1921 *Self Portrait* shows a hint of things to come. Images from the transitional period dally with Cubism, and then reveal a distinct Surrealist flavour from around 1925. The full-blown emergence of his style is seen in *Oeufs sur le Plat sans le Plat* from 1932. The twin obsessions of Dali's classical period – religion and science – are consummately illustrated in *The Discovery of America by Christopher Columbus* (1958), and *Nature Morte Vivante* (1956) respectively. Dali's ability to express himself in various mediums is amply proven by the diversity of sculpture, glassware and even a hologram.

Excellent guided tours are offered throughout the day; and the gift shop provides an exhaustive range of Daliphernalia from books, posters and cards to jewellery, videos and $3,000 carpets.

Open: Tuesday to Saturday 10.00–17.00hrs, Sunday 12.00–17.00hrs.

Fort de Soto Park, *via Pinellas Bayway (toll)* A welcome respite from the high-rise hotels lining the Gulf shore, this 900-acre park is actually made up of five islands extending off the northern tip of Tampa Bay. Its strategic importance led to a fort being constructed on the biggest island, Mullet Key, in 1898, but the hefty 12-inch mortars have never fired a shot in anger. The park boasts three excellent beaches, a couple of popular fishing piers, boat ramps, and picnic and camping facilities. Wear shoes on to the beach to avoid the spiky sand spurs which anchor the sand at the top of the beach.

Open: daily dawn to dusk.

Great Explorations, *1120 Fourth Street* There is hands-on fun for all the family at this splendid state-of-the-art museum. Start your visit by creating instant images in the Phenomenal Arts section using kinetic touch or audio-activated image makers. The 90-foot Touch Tunnel, approached on hands and knees in the dark, is not advised for the claustrophobic, but provides a satisfyingly peculiar experience. In the Body Shop, active testing stations check reactions and muscle tone, and research how lifestyle relates to 'actual age' – are you older than you feel? Meanwhile, the Exchange Pavilion features new exhibits quarterly, such as that old giggle-inducer, the Hall of Mirrors, or displays of illusion and technical trickery which transport visitors to a chilling House of Horrors. There are also great books, games and toys in the gift shop.

Open: Monday to Saturday 10.00–17.00hrs, Sunday 12.00–17.00hrs.

Fish menus are very much the order of the day on the West Coast, and it is not unusual to see dolphin on the list. But do not worry, this is also the term for dorado or mahi-mahi, a delicious fish, not that much-loved mammal, the bottlenose dolphin. Other popular menu features include snapper, grouper, snook, Spanish mackerel, swordfish steaks and mullet.

217

The Dali Museum is one of St Pete's main attractions

WEST COAST

The latest addition to St Pete Beach is the 10,000-square-foot Shipwreck and Treasure Museum opened by the Tampa-based treasure recovery operators Seahawk Deep Ocean Technology. A 65-foot replica of a 17th-century galleon resides in the courtyard, and the museum's façade recalls the pirate city of Port Royal, Jamaica, which slid into the sea during the great 1692 earthquake. Artefacts from Port Royal, sunken treasure and dioramas of life aboard a Spanish galleon make for an entertaining outing.

Museum of Fine Arts, *255 Beach Drive* Housed in an attractive Mediterranean-style villa near The Pier, the museum has several notable collections. The Impressionists are well represented; there is sculpture and paintings from the 17th- and 18th-century European schools; and American art from the 19th and 20th centuries includes some excellent Georgia O'Keefe flower studies. As well as the galleries, there are charming set-piece rooms each carefully decorated in period style. Another treat is the photography collection. Guided tours are available, and the museum frequently hosts special exhibitions from other collections.
Open: Tuesday to Saturday 10.00–17.00hrs, Sunday 13.00–17.00hrs.

The Pier, *800 NE Second Avenue* Projecting into the bay like the superstructure of a vast turquoise and pink aircraft carrier, The Pier combines shopping, dining and sightseeing opportunities all in one. Its lower deck mall houses a variety of boutiques, toy and gift stores, a tourist information point and snack stops. One floor up is the Aquarium (*open*: Monday, Wednesday to Saturday 10.00–20.00hrs, Sunday 12.00–18.00hrs), with its coloured corals and darting exotic fish. Moving on up, Ybor City's famous **Columbia Restaurant** has an outpost here, serving fine Spanish-Cuban cuisine (lunch and dinner); and the top-deck observation platform offers a disco-bar and panoramic view of downtown St Pete and the bay. There is plenty of parking, linked by a free tram service; fishing along the causeway; trike, aquacycle, windsurfer, kayak and Hobie-Cat hire; plus a sunny after-deck with bench seating which provides an excellent spot for outdoor snacking.
Open: Monday to Saturday 10.00–21.00hrs (Friday until 22.00hrs), Sunday 11.00–18.00hrs.

The upside-down pyramid of St Petersburg's pier

Suncoast Seabird Sanctuary, *18328 Gulf Boulevard, Indian Shores* A fascinating excursion across the peninsula from downtown St Pete, the Sanctuary is the largest bird hospital in the US. It all started with a chance encounter between Ralph Heath and an injured cormorant in 1971. Heath had the bird's wing set and nursed it back to health, though Maynard, as the bird was named, would never fly again. Soon word of the 'bird doctor' spread, and injured birds were brought in from far and wide. The aim is to release birds back into the wild unless their injuries are permanent and would affect their ability to survive. Each year some 500 pelicans turn up at the Sanctuary, most of them injured by fish hooks and nylon line. Over 180 chicks have been hatched from breeding couples, and the offspring then rejoin their fellows in the wild. Other successful Sanctuary breeders have been great blue herons and great egrets, and patients have included owls, gannets, petrels, an Arctic loon and peregrine falcons.
Open: daily 09.00–dusk.

Sunken Gardens, *1825 N Fourth Street* Laid out in a former natural sink hole, which was drained in the 1930s, this colourful profusion of exotic plantlife flourishes in the rich layer of fertile soil residue. There are lush tropical corners, brilliant curtains of bougainvillaea and carefully landscaped contours of formal gardens, replenished with around 50,000 plants each year. Keen gardeners will appreciate the hundreds of rare and exotic blooms in the Orchid Arbour, while children are kept amused by parrot shows, walk-through aviaries, and little muntjac deer and monkeys.
Weary visitors will find refreshment in the café-restaurant, there is a biblical wax exhibit, and there is a vast, if rather tacky, souvenir shop which has to be tackled *en route* to the entrance.
Open: daily 09.00–17.30hrs.

Feeding time at Suncoast Seabird Sanctuary

Luxuriant growth in the exotic Sunken Gardens

$\mathscr{Drive}$ **From sugar factories to mermaids**

See map on page 199.

US19 runs south from Tallahassee to Tampa, paralleling the Gulf of Mexico, and the stretch of northern shore known as the Manatee Coast. It can be slow going, however, so if you want to make a day trip from Tampa, follow the directions given below.

Head 70 miles north on fast Interstate-75, then head west on SR44 at Wildwood to Crystal River. The latter section is a pleasant drive past woods, lakes and ranches. Crystal River is famous for its springs. Over 100 of them pump warm water into Kings Bay, attracting manatees. North of town, the **Crystal River State**

Anhinga, or snakebird

Archeological Site was an important Indian cultural centre (see page 204).

From Crystal River, drive south on US19 for almost five miles. Turn right off the main road following signs for Homosassa Springs State Wildlife Park which is on Fishbowl Drive.
Another popular spot with manatees, the park's underwater observatory in the Spring of 10,000 Fish permits a unique fish-eye view of life below the surface. There are also river trips, walking trails and native animal exhibits (see page 212).

Continue for one mile south on Fishbowl Drive.
A State Historic Site, the **Yulee Sugar Mill** was founded in 1849 by one of Florida's first senators, David Levy Yulee. Born in the Caribbean, Yulee operated his mill with 1,000 slaves, and these ruins are the last remains of an antebellum mill structure in the US. The old steam engine is still in place, as are the shallow cooking kettles in which cane juice was heated to make a soft brown sugar.

Return to US19 for a 20-mile run south to Weeki Wachee.
Weeki Wachee Spring is like no other. Instead of manatees, it features human 'mermaids' performing fantastic underwater ballets. Strange, but true (see page 233).

Between Weeki Wachee and Tampa, US19 can be slow and far from picturesque; 25 miles south of Weeki Wachee, take ALT19 for Tarpon Springs.
Another Florida anomaly, Tarpon Springs is a Greek sponge fishing village, complete with bouzouki music. It is definitely touristy, but the food is great and the atmosphere friendly, so it is a fun place to end the day (see page 233).

The skyline of culture city, Sarasota

▶ ▶ ▶   Sarasota

Known as 'the town the circus built', Sarasota was first settled by American pioneers in the 1840s. A Scotsman, John Gillespie, built a 'fine hotel' here in the 1880s, and later introduced golf with a course on the site of the present-day Courthouse. The town prospered, attracting socialites from the north, among them John Ringling.

One of the great joys of Sarasota for the visitor is the compact nature of the city. From a beach hotel on Longboat or Lido Keys, it is only a five-minute drive to Downtown, and the attractive antiques district on **Palm Avenue**. Restored shopfronts lure the collector to browse in over 30 stores, and the **Marie Selby Gardens** are at the bottom of the street. There is waterfront dining and more shopping at the sleek new **Sarasota Center**. Performing arts are big news in Sarasota, with the **Asolo State Theater** blazing a trail as one of the nation's leading regional theatres, and tradition sees the circus back in town to première a new season of shows from its winter headquarters in Venice every December.

Bellm's Cars & Music of Yesterday, *550 N Tamiami Trail (US41)* Conveniently located almost opposite the Ringling Museum, Bellm's presentation is as yesteryear as its artefacts, but there is no doubt that they have some pretty extraordinary items here: over 2,000 different musical pieces from massive fairground organs (calliopes) and horse-drawn hurdy-gurdies to elegant musical boxes and Edison's Home Phonographs, as well as Lloyd Webber on steel discs for modern-day addicts of the music box sound. The old metal discs used to be hand-punched - 500 to 1,000 pinholes for each tune, six tunes to a disc. Some of the rarest specimens are the Vogue Co's lurid 'picture discs' from 1945–9. The car collection is also eccentric: a 1959 Chrysler sits next to Ringling's 1923 Pierce Arrow, while a racy primrose Auburn Special squeezes bumper to bumper with a 1971 Buick.

In 1959, the Ringling Brothers and Barnum & Bailey Combined Circus established their winter headquarters at 1401 S Ringling Drive in Venice (20 miles south of Sarasota). This normally quiet seaside town comes alive as elephants and horses, lion tamers and trapeze artists begin work on the new season shows, premièred here from late December through January. This is also the home of the prestigious Ringling Clown College. Each year several thousand applicants vie for the course's 60 places and a chance to learn the tricks of the trade, from make-up and tumbling to juggling and unicycle riding.

Part of the Ringling art collection

Not content with building a palatial bayfront residence for himself and his wife Mable, Ringling fou nded a magnificent Italian-style palazzo to house his art collection, set up a winter headquarters for his circus, and flung himself whole-heartedly into the Land Boom. To develop Long Key, he built causeways across the bay, and his elegant shopping and dining district, St Armand's Circle, remains a focal point of Sarasota social life today.

John and Mable Ringling Museum of Art, *5401 Bayshore Road* Sarasota's cultural epicentre, the Ringling bayfront estate should not be missed. On trips to Europe between 1924 and 1931, Ringling amassed an extraordinary collection of art works – over 600 paintings, plus tapestries, *objets d'art,* and several tons of statuary. The recently restored galleries of his *palazzo* now display one of the largest and finest collections of European paintings in the US. Ringling's passion was the Italian Baroque period, but he also bought several notable examples of medieval and Renaissance art. Surrounded by three wings of the museum, 20th-century copies of classical statuary adorn formal gardens.

Down on the water's edge is Ca'd'Zan (Venetian dialect for 'House of John'), the Ringlings' winter residence. It was inspired by Mable's two favourite buildings, the Doge's Palace in Venice and the tower of P T Barnum's Old Madison Square Gardens in New York. Around the main hall, 30 luxurious rooms and 14 bathrooms edge the two-and-a-half-storey atrium. The fittings were brought from far and wide: Louis XV furniture from the Astor and Gould estates, a $50,000 Aeolian organ, Flemish tapestries, antique roof tiles from Barcelona and hand-made Venetian glass. The former garages have been transformed into a **Circus Museum,** where posters and memorablilia rub shoulders with sequinned finery, calliopes and cannons for human projectiles.

Open: daily 10.00–17.30hrs, Thursdays October to June 10.00–22.00hrs.

Marie Selby Botanical Gardens, *811 S Palm Avenue* There is no difficulty spotting the exuberant borders lining the sidewalk outside the gardens, but what will amaze many horticulturists is that the botanical gardens are no more than 20 years old. The modest house in the middle of the property was built in 1921 as a temporary residence for Marie Selby and her Ohio oil baron husband, William, until a more palatial home could be constructed. They never bothered, and the 11-acre bayfront estate was donated to the County in 1971 with

a bequest and proviso that it should be laid out as a garden. Some 20,000 plants have now been introduced and 15 distinct garden areas created. Most famous is the orchid collection, but bromeliads, hibiscus and cacti grow in profusion, and there is an interesting tropical food walk.

A small Museum of Botany and Arts is housed in the neighbouring **Payne House** a gracious 1935 mansion which combines all the best features of southern architecture.

Open: daily 10.00–17.00hrs.

Mote Marine Aquarium, *1600 Thompson Parkway* On City Island, the aquarium's main attraction is its 135,000-gallon outdoor shark tank which houses a floating – or rather circling – population which might include lemon and nurse sharks, the hefty mottled jew fish, shoals of sardines and the odd tarpon. The plate-glass windows make for interesting viewing, but there is nothing quite like watching one of those predatory dorsal fins slicing through the water up top. Twenty-two smaller aquariums are inhabited by seahorses, clearnose skates, octopuses and more. Excellent displays and colour photographs explain Mote's research and rescue operations. There is also a great touch tank, a video show and the inevitable gift shop.

Open: daily 10.00–17.00hrs.

John Ringling would have been delighted with Asolo Theater, a dazzling little rococo gem added to his estate in the 1950s. Originally built for the Palazzo Asolo in Italy, it seats 300 in a horseshoe arrangement of rising tiers of boxes, ornately decorated in pastels and gilt with friezes, and lit by small lamps. It is used for concerts, lectures and art film showings.

223

Elegant shopping at Sarasota Quay

■ **John Nicholas Ringling was born on 30 May 1866, in MacGregor, Iowa, the sixth of seven sons raised by immigrant parents. His father, a German-born leather craftsman, and his mother, the daughter of a prosperous French weaver and vineyard owner, moved frequently around the Mid West until they finally settled in Baraboo, Wisconsin in 1875. Though fortunes fluctuated, the boys were given a strict Lutheran upbringing in which the qualities of honesty, dignity and pride in a job well done were rigorously emphasised. These beliefs were to characterise the Ringling brothers' business deals in years to come .....■**

The travelling circus During the 1870s, the newly built railroads opened up the whole country, enabling travelling entertainment acts to reach a vast new audience. Circuses were among the first to take advantage of this new way to reach the people. Entrepreneur Phineas T Barnum also recognised the potential of railroads, and purchased a fleet of railroad cars in 1872, turning his successful freak show into the 'Great Travelling Museum, Menagerie, Caravan and Hippodrome'. Albert, Otto, Alfred and Charles Ringling launched a variety act inspired by Dan Rice's Circus in the same year. It was called the Classic and Comic Concert Company. Their brother John joined them in 1882, and two years later the Ringling Brothers Circus was formed in Baraboo.

The Ringling mansion Ca'd'Zan has more than a touch of the Doge's Palace in Venice

On the up The brothers August and Henry were soon added to the payroll, and responsibilities were divided. John's brains and extraordinary memory earned him the position of transport manager. In his spare time, he invested in oil, real estate, railroads and a variety of smaller concerns. On business trips to Europe, sightseeing visits to the great European museums and palaces fuelled his interest in art. While his brothers wintered in Baraboo, John busied himself in New York and Chicago among cultivated friends drawn from the ranks of artists, celebrities and politicians. By the time he first visited Sarasota in 1911, John Ringling was already a celebrity in his own right, a wealthy businessman and an imposing figure described by a contemporary as '...tall, with the chest of a sea elephant, the chin of a prize fighter and sensitive, artistic hands'.

The move to Sarasota John married Mable Burton, a noted Ohio beauty, in 1905. After he bought a winter property on the Sarasota bayfront in 1912, he and Mable made annual visits, often entertaining the family. Brother Charles built a marble mansion on an adjacent lot, now the University of South Florida's College Hall. In 1917, John began to invest in Sarasota real estate. Circus elephants occasionally helped out with the heavy work as causeways were built to link his barrier island properties to the mainland, and New York landscape architect John Watson was chosen to design the elegant St Armands Circle shopping district: 'Now Mable won't have to go to Palm Beach to shop,' Ringling explained. However, other projects did not fare so well, and work on a luxurious Ritz Carlton hotel on Longboat Key were halted by the collapse of the 1920s Land Boom.

Mable's 'House of John' Meanwhile, Mable had been fully occupied supervising the construction of Ca'd'Zan, a Venetian Gothic-style residence of grandiose proportions truly fit for a circus king. She personally visited the kilns where the terracotta decorations for the the interior and exterior of the house were glazed, accommodated shiploads of columns, doorways, balustrades and Venetian glass windows, and approved the exuberant designs by Ziegfield Follies set artist, Will Pogany, for the ballroom and playroom ceilings. An 8,000-square-foot marble terrace extended west from the house, and an elegant dock was constructed for Mable's Venetian gondola. Christmas 1926 was celebrated in the newly completed house, and in the New Year work began on a museum to house additional treasures.

End of the era After the death of his brothers, John managed the circus alone, and in 1927 moved its winter quarters to Sarasota in an effort to boost the flagging local economy. The Ringlings had purchased Barnum & Bailey's Circus in 1906, and their last major rival, the five circuses of the American Circus Corp, were brought under Ringling control in 1929. It was also the year that Mable died, after just three winters in her dream home. John Ringling opened his museum in 1930, but the last few years of his life were plagued by unhappiness and business disappointments. He had just $350 in his bank account when he died in 1936, but bequested his entire estate to the State of Florida, which finally accepted the $14 million legacy in 1946.

A copy of Michelangelo's David surveys the Ringling Museum of Art

Not a mosque, but the Henry B Plant Museum in Tampa

▶▶▷ **Tampa**

The safe anchorage of Tampa Bay made it one of the first spots marked on early explorers' maps. In 1824, Fort Brooke was established here as a pioneer military outpost for monitoring the Seminole Indians, and during the Civil War a steamship service was opened between Tampa and Cuba. Henry Plant's railway system rolled into the port in 1884. Two years later, Vincente Martinez Ybor moved his cigar industry from isolated Key West to the growing megalopolis of late 19th-century Tampa. In just six years, the bayside fishing village was transformed into a boom town with over 5,000 inhabitants. Plant lured wealthy northerners to winter in his fabulous **Tampa Bay Hotel**, and even used his considerable connections in Washington to make Tampa a troop embarkation point during the 1898 Spanish-American War.

Downtown Tampa in the 1990s is a glistening array of towering skyscrapers, and excellent shopping and dining. But its history is never far away. Plant's dream hotel has survived as a university building; and a mile down the Crosstown Expressway, the Victorian façades and red-brick cigar factories of **Ybor City** are developing into a popular tourist attraction.

Adventure Island, *4500 Bougainvillea Avenue* A one-day pass entitles visitors to try out all the facilities at this 19-acre outdoor water park. The Rambling Bayou offers a leisurely passage via a giant inner-tube through a man-made rain forest complete with weather effects from mist to torrential monsoon. For more exciting watersport, check out the Tampa Typhoon, a 76-foot free-fall body slide, or the Gulf Stream – all 210 feet of it – where sliders reach speeds of up to 25mph. A hot favourite is the recently opened Caribbean Corkscrew, a four-storey translucent tube. Small children are catered for in the scaled down Fountain of Youth pool; there are also beaches, picnic areas and cafés.

Open: mid-March to mid-October. For schedules, tel: (813) 987 5171).

There's fun for waterbabies of all ages at Tampa's Adventure Island

Busch Gardens: The Dark Continent, *3000 E Busch Boulevard (at 40th Street)* Entrance does not come cheap here, but it is great value for an entire day's worth of entertainment and souvenir shopping – and two free 'sample' beers are thrown in for visitors over 21. The beer, and the rest of the fun, comes courtesy of Anheuser-Busch, the giant brewing company, who started this monster 300-acre attraction – the state's second most popular sightseeing stop after Disney World – almost by accident. A few flamingos and parrots were laid on to amuse vistors to the company's Hospitality House after a brewery tour. Then a restaurant was added, a few more animals and, hey presto, the **Serengeti Plain** moved in. Now the 160-acre plain is home to some 500 species of animal from hippos and lions to herds of graceful gazelles, zebras and giraffes.

For getting around the complex, transport is provided by cable car, monorail or a jaunty little red-and-yellow train. In the **Nairobi** district, by the train station, an Animal Nursery cossets all kinds of cute baby animals and birds which have either been injured or rejected by their parents. North of here, **Timbuktu** hosts a glittering ice show in the Dolphin Theater, plus fun-fair rides. There are dodgems and tigers in the **Congo**, Tanzanian crafts-men in **Stanleyville**, a souk in **Morocco**, and the stom-ach-churning Questor time machine simulator in **Crown Colony**. North of the **Bird Gardens**, the brewery is open to tours, and children have the run of **Dwarf Village**.
Open: daily 09.30–18.00hrs (extended in summer). For schedules, tel: (813) 987 5082.

A Bengal tiger cools off in the water at Busch Gardens

Downtown Tampa If you are staying in Tampa, then you will probably want to explore the downtown area, which can comfortably be done on foot.

You will not find any priceless architectural gems or quaint back streets, but you will find a busy, successful district which pays attention to its looks and has invested in quantities of public sculpture. Start your exploration at Tampa City Center Esplanade, where there are restaurants and cafés and a version of one of the city's best-known sculptures, C Paul Jennewein's *Over the Waves*, with its dolphin boy. On Tampa, at the corner of Kennedy, is a stainless steel sculpture called *Solstice*, made by Charles Parry in 1985. Beyond it is George Sugerman's *Untitled* of 1988. If you want more art, then head for the Tampa Museum of Art on Ashley (see page 231). Two of Tampa's best buildings are the art deco Woolworth's building and the ornate Tampa Theater, both on Franklin. You will find more art on Franklin in the shape of the *Franklin Street 1925* mural, and Geoffrey Naylor's 1973 aluminium sculpture, *The Family of Man.* A low wall by the bus stops on Marion (at Kennedy) features Katherine Sokolnikoff's *Cycle of Waves*.

Festivals in Tampa The annual **Gasparilla Festival**, in early February, is Tampa's big day out. It celebrates the bloodthirsty antics of legendary 18th-century pirate José Gaspar, who terrorised Gulf coast shipping between 1785 and 1822. The timetable begins mid-morning when the world's only fully-rigged pirate ship sets sail from Ballast Point Pier, and docks downtown with a full complement of colourful 'pirates', all armed to the teeth. A victory parade sets off down Bayshore Boulevard, culminating in a vast street party.

There is only about a week's breathing space before festival fever breaks out again, and Tampa's ethnic communities take to the streets of Ybor City for **Fiesta Day**. Sideshows and arts, crafts and food stalls line Seventh Avenue, and in the evening the Knights of Sant'Yago (Saint James) set the streets ablaze with dozens of illuminated floats.

Henry Plant Museum, *University of Tampa, 401 Kennedy Boulevard* There is no difficulty in locating Henry B Plant's palatial Tampa Bay Hotel building, now part of the city's university campus. Visitors to the Downtown district will have caught intriguing glimpses of its silver onion-domed minarets. Built in 1891, to

Piratical goings-on in Tampa's Gasparilla Festival

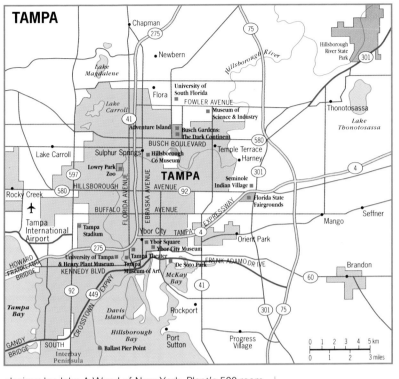

designs by John A Wood of New York, Plant's 500-room hotel cost a staggering $3 million then. A triumph of Moorish revival architecture from its crescent-tipped spires to its acres of red-brick and ornamental fretwork, it is surrounded by broad verandas wide enough to accommodate rickshaws for the guests' convenience, and was furnished with huge numbers of antiques and art treasures collected from Europe and the Orient. All the latest gadgets - electric lighting, hot and cold water piped to private bathrooms, telephones in every room - made the hotel a novelty in itself, and 4,000 wealthy and inquisitive guests made the pilgrimage south to stay during the first season. But the dream died with Plant in 1899; the city paid a mere $125,000 for the property in 1905, and the University moved in in 1933.

The museum only occupies a corner of one wing, but its suite of rooms, decorated with original furnishings, re-creates some of the former splendour of this extraordinary building.

Open: Tuesday to Saturday 10.00–16.00hrs.

Hillsborough River State Park,*SR301* One of Florida's earliest state parks, opened to the public in 1938, Hillsborough is 12 miles north of Tampa. The 2,990-acre preserve, bordering the scenic Hillsborough River, contains **Fort Foster State Historic Site**, a carefully reconstructed 1837 frontier post built during the Second Seminole War. There are weekend tours of the fort, nature trails, swimming, fishing and picnic areas.

Open: daily 08.00hrs–dusk.

Shoppers will have a great time in Tampa's malls. Harbour Island is the latest addition, conveniently linked to Downtown by the People Mover. Old Hyde Park Village, 712 S Oregon Avenue, offers up-market stores in an attractively restored setting. For antique collectables and boutiques, the city's famous cigars and craft shops, do not miss Ybor Square, 8th and 13th Street, in a former Ybor City cigar factory.

Lowry Park Zoo Gardens, *7530 North Boulevard* A multi-million dollar rejuvenation project launched here in the 1980s revolutionised the old city zoo, which was founded in 1937. Pride of place goes to the new **Pepsi Manatee and Aquatic Center** with its three 25,000-gallon manatee treatment tanks and emergency rescue clinic. Natural habitats have been provided for other native Floridian aquatic and wetland creatures, including alligators, snapping turtles and river otters. A 45-foot-high **Aviary** houses 200 birds; there is also an Aviary Nursery with viewing windows. Orang-utans, chimps and lemurs hang out in **Primate World**; tigers, barking deer, tapirs and rhinos reside in the **Asian Domain**. Children will be enchanted by the small-scale inhabitants of **Children's Village**, such as pygmy goats, Vietnamese pot-bellied piglets.
Open: daily 09.30–17.00hrs (until 18.00hrs in summer).

Museum of Science and Industry, *4801 E Fowler Avenue* Florida's largest science centre occupies an unusual inside-out building festooned with exposed pipes with breezeways linking the various exhibition galleries. Energy-saving systems have been incorporated, and there is a strong line in ecological consciousness.
Now for the fun part: 200 hands-on exhibits, including those in **Electricity Plaza**, where a jolly singing lightning bug stars in a demystifying information video and visitors can experience a hair-raising encounter with a van de Graaff generator (capable of producing very high voltages), or pedal power into a lightbulb. Or try the **Weather** exhibit which features a hurricane chamber, simulating winds up to 75mph. Investigate the **Communications Gallery** and its ham radio club.The latest addition to the museum is a series of ' backwoods trails' in the grounds, dotted with stationery compasses and wilderness activities.
Open: daily 09.00–16.30hrs, Friday and Saturday 09.00–21.00hrs.

Tampa's Museum of Science and Industry lets it all hang out with its multicoloured exposed pipes

Sacred Heart Catholic Church, *509 Florida Avenue* For a taste of old Tampa buried among the Downtown high-rises, dive off the beaten track for just a moment to this quiet oasis. Completed in 1905, the Romanesque-style edifice has fine stained glass including scenes from the Life of Christ .
Open: daily.

Tampa Museum of Art, *601 Doyle Carlton Drive (at Ashley and Twiggs)* There are two main, and totally diverse, strands to this museum's collections: 20th-century American art, and a significant holding of Greek and Roman antiquities. The latter collection is on semi-permanent display, and ranges from two grotesque and remarkably contemporary looking heads from the 2nd or 1st century bc, to elegant statuettes and beautifully decorated pottery. The 20th-century collection is too extensive for the six galleries available at present, so is constantly rotated, or even moved out to house travelling exhibitions. American neo-Classical sculptor C Paul Jennewein (1890–1978) is well represented here: his dolphin-boy piece, *Over the Waves*, is a permanent fixture, with a great view of the University of Tampa's Plant Building in the background.
Open: Tuesday to Saturday 10.00–17.00 (Wednesday until 21.00hrs), Sunday 13.00–17.00hrs.

Tampa Theater, *711 Franklin Street Mall* Modestly hailed as 'The Pride of the South', this 1926 rococo-style cinema is a weird and wonderful addition to the Downtown district. Its historic façade is decorated with elegant classical reliefs, while the interior has been transformed into a low-lit grotto-cum-Aladdin's-Cave with roughly finished walls, ornate painted ceilings, and coloured floor tiles. Pillars and arches are topped with gargoyles and statuary, and there is a grand old theatre organ. As well as all of that, the cinema is still operating.
Open: tours by appointment, tel:(813) 223 8286.)

231

Tampa Museum of Art has displays of both ancient and modern art

Ybor City The name Tampa means 'sticks of fire', and its old cigar-making Latin Quarter, Ybor (pronounced E-bor) City, is undergoing a renaissance. Recently designated one of Florida's three National Historic Landmark Districts (along with St Augustine and Pensacola), this century-old Spanish-style district is being polished up with replica turn-of-the-century street lamps, restored wrought-iron balconies, cobbled streets, and an influx of artisans, boutiques and entertainment venues designed to recapture the gaiety of its heyday.

Don Vincente Martinez Ybor moved his cigar-making operation from Key West to Tampa in 1886. Cuban workers were joined by a mixture of Italian, Spanish and German immigrants who brought their own customs, traditions and ethnic clubs to the area, creating a vibrant, bustling community, which entertained Cuban freedom fighter José Marti, Teddy Roosevelt's Rough Riders and every goodtime gal in town.

The heart of the district is La Setima (Seventh Avenue). Just off Seventh, Ybor's original red-brick cigar factory, with its three-storey oak and heart pine interior, has been restored and converted into an attractive shopping and restaurant complex, **Ybor Square** (1901 13th Street). When the factory was operational, hundreds of workers (mostly men) spent long hours at the serried ranks of benches, rolling cigars by hand while a lector (reader) read novels and daily newspapers to relieve the tedium. Cigars are still rolled by hand in a store on the upper level, and photographs show the factory as it used to look. A combination of mechanisation, the rising popularity of cigarettes and the Depression of the 1930s closed many factories, but a major survivor was **Villazon and Company** (3104 Armenia Avenue), which now offers tours of its automated factory. Some 500 million cigars are still produced in Tampa every year.

For a look at life as it used to be lived here, a former

If it's souvenirs you're after, cigars are the obvious buy in Ybor City, but non-smokers can enjoy one of Arnold Martinez's unusual paintings or prints. These local scenes, created with the help of coffee, tea and tobacco colourings, are on sale in his gallery at 2025 E Seventh Avenue. Admirers of the Columbia Restaurant's gorgeous ceramic tiles can track down the artist and his wares a short step away at San Do Designs, 2104 E Seventh Avenue.

Spanish is the style in Ybor City

bakery houses the compact **Ybor City State Museum**, 1818 E Ninth Avenue. Do not miss the furnished worker's 'shotgun' cottage a few doors down. Though the bakery no longer bakes bread, there are plenty of opportunities to sample Cuban cuisine on Seventh Avenue. Feast on a Cuban sandwich or sample traditional fare in one of the family restaurants - an historic favourite is the 1905 **Columbia Restaurant**, at 21st Street, which is decorated with wonderfully photogenic hand-painted tiles (see panel page 232).

▶▶▶ Tarpon Springs

And now for something completely different: a Greek sponge fishing town on the shores of the Gulf of Mexico. A stroll down Dodecanese Boulevard to the sponge docks here is like taking a Mediterranean holiday. The aroma of freshly baked Greek pastries scents the air (there is a more pungent whiff of drying sponges when the fleet is in), and *bouzouki* music accompanies coffee and ouzo in small cafés off the main street.

The Greek community arrived in the early 1900s to harvest the Gulf sponge beds. They imported their customs and culture too, such as **St Nicholas' Greek Orthodox Church**, founded on N Pinellas Avenue (ALT19) in 1907. The present neo-Byzantine building, dating from 1943, contains marble from the Greek pavilion display at the 1939 New York World's Fair. Its broad nave is lined with striking stained glass, and there is a miraculous weeping statue of St Nicholas.

Back on Dodecanese Boulevard, take a 30-minute boat trip around the docks with the **St Nicholas Boat Line**. Frequent daily sailings include a narrated history and demonstration of diving techniques. While in Tarpon Springs, you should certainly sample traditional Greek delicacies such as nut and honey *baklava*, savoury *spanakopita* (spinach) or *tiropita* (cheese) triangles wrapped in flaky filo pastry and sold in bakeries. The old **Sponge Exchange** has been converted into a shopping mall, and there is a little gift shop and café enclave housed in wooden cottages at **Spongeorama**. Souvenirs galore spill out of the shops, and there are sponges of every description hanging from awnings and piled in wire baskets. There are several opportunities to witness Greek dancing and national costume during the year: the most spectacular is the Feast of Epiphany on 6 January.

▶▷▷ Weeki Wachee Spring

US19 (at SR50)

While the rest of the state is getting back to nature, this is one of the original Floridian fantasies, a watery wonderland of make-believe, where human 'mermaids' perform Hans Christian Andersen water ballets 16 feet under water, and the rain forest is nurtured by a sprinkler system. Created in 1947 by an ex-Navy frogman, the mermaid shows (11.30, 14.30 and 17.00hrs) are now part of an entertainment package which includes a Birds of Prey Show, petting zoo (no mermaids), river cruises, and nearby **Buccaneer Bay** (combination tickets available), a spring waterpark. *Open*: daily 09.30–17.30hrs.

The Old Bakery in Ybor City, Tampa

The old cigar factory, the heart of Ybor City, is now a shopping and restaurant complex

The sponge industry

■ The first Florida sponges were discovered off the shores of Key West in the mid-18th century. In 1890, real estate developer John K Cheyney, looking for ways to promote Tarpon Springs, discovered a wealth of sponges growing off the central Gulf coast and began his own small-scale 'hooking' operation. These 'hookers', or early spongers, set off in small rowing boats from a mother ship, armed with a glass-bottomed bucket to survey the sea-bed and long poles with hooks on the end which they used to gather the sponges. Hooking required considerable dexterity, and the spongers were limited to shallow waters no more than 15–20 feet deep .....■

234

Arrival of the Greeks During the Spanish-American War, spongers from Key West joined the Gulf fleet, and their haul was sold at the Tarpon Springs Sponge Exchange. John Cocoris, a Greek sponge buyer from New York, travelled south to deal with Cheyney in 1905. He stayed on and soon sent for his brothers from Greece. Together they worked for Cheyney, while surreptitiously surveying the extent of the sponge beds until they were confident enough to send back to Greece for a diving team. The Greeks had already pioneered the use of diving suits and air pipes in the Mediterranean, and Cocoris' divers revolutionised the Gulf sponge industry. By 1936, Tarpon Springs was recognised as the sponge capital of the world, and its 200-vessel fleet set sail in the traditional Phoenician-style boats built by local Greek craftsmen. They stayed out for six months at a time, curing and cleaning their catch on board as they plied the Gulf from the Keys to the Panhandle.

The sponge boat quay at Tarpon Springs

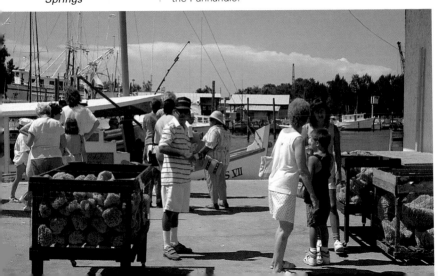

The sponge industry

235

What happens to the sponges? Each sponge is protected by a membrane which solidifies if it dries out. To prevent this when the sponges are harvested, they are graded into types, piled on deck, and covered with canvas. The membrane dies and decomposes over two to three days, leaving the sponge skeleton which is then cleaned with high-pressure hoses. Beaten, washed and turned constantly to remove all the dead matter, the sponges are then placed in big string bags and hung on the rigging until they are prepared for market. At auction, the sponger displays his catch in strings of 50 sponges varying in size, but all of the same type. Wool sponges are the highest grade, followed by yellow, grass and wire varieties. A successful bid sees the sponges removed to a wholesaler's packing house where they are bleached from grubby brown to a soft yellow colour, cut, clipped into shape with shears, and then sold for one of the 1,400 commercial uses.

Disaster and recovery In the 1940s a bacterial blight ripped through the Gulf sponge beds. Nothing grew for almost 20 years, until most divers had moved away, grown too old, or turned to shrimping and fishing. The recovery rate was slow, and only four or five sponge boats operated during the 1970s. They had to work up to 100 miles offshore, collecting just 200 to 300 pieces per day. In 1985, Hurricane Elena swept up the Gulf coast and spent a couple of days churning up the seabed in the crook of the Panhandle. A year later, a boat belonging to one George Billiris was hove to in the face of a storm, about 5 miles offshore. One of the divers went down to look at the old sponge beds and discovered... wall-to-wall sponge. The hurricane had redistributed the larvae and they were flourishing. In four or five days Billiris collected 4,000 pieces of sponge, and the $3 million Gulf sponge industry was back on its feet.

Spongeorama in Tarpon Springs, source of spongy souvenirs

Sponge is a living multi-celled organism, one step up the evolutionary ladder from an ameoba. Sponges are hermaphrodites: they produce both male and female cells and reproduce themselves. The main requirement is firm anchorage for the larvae – rocks are ideal, but not sand. The sponge grows at a rate of about half an inch in diameter each month for four to five years, then the growth rate slows, but does not stop. They can grow up to 10 feet across. Fragments left behind when a sponge is picked will grow again, and state law prohibits the harvesting of any sponge less than five inches in diameter.

THE PANHADLE

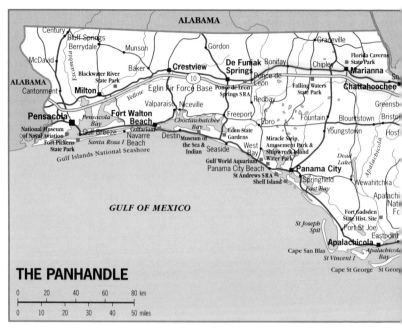

THE PANHANDLE

```
0    20    40    60    80 km
|----|----|----|----|
0  10   20   30   40   50 miles
```

A year-round Florida resident, the common mockingbird (*Minus polyglottus*) was chosen as the state bird in 1927. About 10 inches in length, with a 15-inch wingspan, greyish upper body, white underside and patches on the wings and tail, mockingbirds are great songsters, singing well into the night on balmy moonlit spring evenings.

Sandwiched between the Gulf of Mexico, Georgia and Alabama, Florida's Panhandle extends west from the peninsula in a dark green ribbon of pine forest edged by pristine white quartz beaches. This is 'Florida with a Southern accent', where *Gone with the Wind* antebellum mansions grace historic plantations, oak-canopied roads draped with Spanish moss tunnel into the countryside, and Deep South hospitality serves up grits and throws 'all comers welcome' mullet fries.

In its early days, the region was bandied between foreign invaders like a shuttlecock. French, British, and two terms of Spanish rule left a handful of fortresses,

Oyster boats off Apalachicola

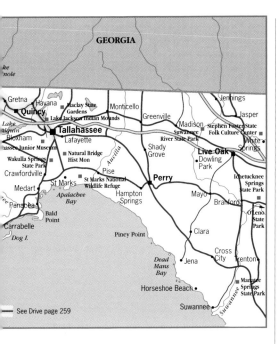

— See Drive page 259

foreign place names and a clutch of shipwrecks. Historic **Pensacola** was the main settlement until the 1820s when, mid-point between Pensacola and St Augustine, **Tallahassee** was chosen as the site of the new state capital. Despite several latter-day attempts to move the government power centre south, Tallahassee is where it remains, an attractive small city, a stone's throw from the Georgia border.

Largely bypassed by northern tourists fleeing south on the interstate highway, and international visitors pouring into Orlando and Miami, the Panhandle is a well-kept secret. Its fabulous beaches and unbelievably low accommodation rates have been enjoyed almost exclusively by holiday-makers from Alabama, Georgia and Mississippi, earning it the nickname the 'Redneck Riviera'. In the back country, tight-knit, bible-thumping Cracker communities maintain a singular isolation from mainstream 20th-century life. Hidden in the pine forests, bottomless freshwater springs feed narrow creeks; the subterranean beauty of the **Florida Caverns** is a popular outing; and major rivers, like the Apalachicola, which once transported cotton, sugar, lumber and turpentine, are now favoured playgrounds of canoeing enthusiasts.

The rich coastal estuaries these rivers create are a haven for fish and birdlife – Apalachicola's oyster beds are renowned. To the west, the **Gulf Islands National Seashore** preserves tracts of spectacular undeveloped shoreline. On the Emerald Coast, named for its glassy, green waters, the seaside towns of **Fort Walton, Destin** and **Panama City** offer excellent deep-sea fishing and diving opportunities, alongside family-orientated entertainments and accommodation with an emphasis on the cheap and cheerful.

▷▷▷ Apalachicola

If miles of uncrowded beach, superb fishing and wildlife, historic houses, low-price accommodation and buckets of fresh oysters daily sounds like heaven, it could be named Apalachicola. This modest fishing village, 60 miles southwest of Tallahassee, is a real find for a quiet break. Founded as a rivermouth customs post back in 1823, the town's history and prosperity has long been tied to the Apalachicola River, Florida's largest natural waterway. As settlers further north developed plantations, so river transportation increased, and thanks to 'King Cotton', Apalachicola's customs post grew to be the third largest port on the Gulf of Mexico. In 1836, 43 three-storey brick warehouses and brokerage operations lined the waterfront, turning over some 55,000 bales of cotton per annum; a $6.8 million business by 1840. But a Civil War blockade, and the arrival of the railroads threatened to relegate the port to a trade backwater.

Turning to the sea, fishing, oystering and sponge diving became the order of the day, and a Sponge Exchange was established on the wharf. Mullet, pompano, mackerel, bluefish and trout were staples, while oyster canning factories replaced the cotton warehouses along the quayside. The 20th-century lumber boom had Apalachicola humming to the sound of sawmills until the supply of cypress was exhausted in the 1930s. Again the town turned to the sea. Apalachicola's oystermen still harvest their catch by hand, prying oysters from the beds with long-handled tongs worked like scissors from small boats bobbing on the surface of the bay.

Apalachicola's boom periods in the mid-19th and early 20th centuries were translated into some wonderful buildings. The dock area has crumbled almost beyond

(Continued on page 240)

Apalachicola, source of the Florida oyster

Oyster Stew

1 pint shucked oysters
quarter cup butter
1 quart milk
salt, pepper, paprika

Drain oysters; reserve juice. Remove any shell particles. Add oysters and juice to butter; cook for three minutes, or until edges of oysters start to curl. Add milk, salt and pepper. Heat thoroughly, but do not boil. Sprinkle with paprika and serve at once.

The Barrier Islands

■ **The four barrier islands off the Franklin County coast protect St George Sound, one of the most productive fishing regions on the Gulf of Mexico. Largely undeveloped – two of them are uninhabited – they are superb natural preserves .....■**

Dog Island Set five miles across the Sound from Carrabelle, Dog Island has the highest sand dunes in the state. Its tiny population is linked to the mainland by a daily ferry service; most of the island is a wildlife preserve of coastal dunes, with marsh and mangrove enclaves on the protected bayside.

St George Island and Little St George The biggest of the islands (25 miles long), and the most developed, St George is reached by a four-mile causeway from the east bank of the Apalachicola River. The central and western part of the island boasts a shop, the characterful St George Inn, several café-bars and a clutch of weatherboard homes (on stilts), many of them available for rent.

Nine miles of undeveloped Gulf and bay beaches on the eastern end are protected by a State Park. Here, the wind has sculpted the fine sand into miniature mountains, their ridges and hummocks crested with sea oats and scrub grasses. Waves and currents move 180,000 cubic yards of sand west along the island coast annually. Pine trees have been buried up to their crowns by these drifts, and the boardwalk trail completely disappears in places. On the Gulf shore, ghost crabs and the little wading birds called sanderlings scuttle around the seashells in the surf; the back bay woodlands are full of birds, and ospreys and bald eagles ride the thermals above the fishing grounds.

Once part of the main island, uninhabited **Little St George Island** is now separated by a channel, and can only be reached by boat.

St Vincent Island Nine miles off shore, and part of the National Wildlife Refuge System, 2,358-acre St Vincent is the least accessible of the barrier islands, and therefore the most enticing for naturalists. Its remarkably diverse habitats, including dunes, tidal marshes, freshwater lakes, oak ridges, pine flatwoods, magnolia and cabbage palm hammocks attract an equally diverse cross-section of wildlife. Captive breeding programmes for endangered native species, such as the red wolf, exist alongside such exotic surprises as sambar deer (originally from India), introduced by hunters in the 1920s. There is a visitor centre in Apalachicola (for information, tel: (904) 653 8808).

Fishing off the islands

THE PANHANDLE

Destin marina, where there are sea-fishing boats for rent

A young physician from Charleston, South Carolina, John Gorrie moved to the mosquito-infested estuary port of Apalachicola in 1833. During the next 22 years, until his death in 1855, he served as the town's mayor, postmaster, treasurer, councillor, bank director and church founder, and still found time to practise medicine. Ignorant of the mosquito's role in spreading yellow fever, gorrie and others believed that humid marsh air was to blame, and he set about devising a method of cooling and purifying the air in the sickroom. *En route* he invented an ice-making machine, and the concept of refrigeration and air conditioning was born.

(Continued from page 238)

the point of repair, but many gracious houses lining **Chestnut Avenue** (Avenue E), and the streets to either side, are evocative of the prosperous Victorian lifestyle enjoyed by the town's more successful merchants. The **Raney House**, 128 Market Street, is a fine example, which now houses the Chamber of Commerce. Built by prominent local businessman David G Raney in 1838, its fashionable Greek Revival portico was added in the 1850s. Another beauty is the lovely privately-owned Steamboat-style **Myers-Macy-Brash** House on the corner of Avenue C and Fifth. Carpenters and joiners are busy all over town refurbishing other historic gems. With time to spare, the best way to see Apalachicola is on foot. There are around 200 houses dating from 1840–1880, and the Chamber of Commerce provides an exhaustive walk tour map of town. It covers all sorts of interesting spots from the pre-1830s **Chestnut Street Cemetery**, with its memorials to the town's early settlers, yellow fever victims and Confederate soldiers, to the Water Street riverfront and the *Sea Dream*, a plucky little craft which rescued survivors of a German U-boat attack in 1942. Sixth Street crosses Chestnut Street and leads down to **Battery Pier**, where the shrimp boats dock, close to the 1877 schooner *Governor Stone*. Half-way down the street, the town's history and its most celebrated resident are commemorated in the **John Gorrie State Museum**. (*Open:* Thursday to Monday 09.00–12.00, 13.00–17.00hrs.) A reproduction of Gorrie's original ice-making machine is the centre-piece of the interesting little one-room museum. Gorrie's tomb is found across the street at the **Trinity Episcopal Church** which was assembled from sections shipped from New York in 1837.

St George Island is a short drive from downtown Apalachicola, across a 4-mile causeway from the fishing community of Eastpoint. Facilities are basic, but there is a comfortable inn and several miles of magnificent white sand beach in the State Park (see page 239). The half-a-million acre **Apalachicola National Forest** contains Fort Gadsden **State Historic Site** (off SR65) where the British once recruited Indians and escaped slaves to fight the Americans. Further east, the extensive **St Marks National Wildlife Refuge** is a winter destination for thousands of migratory birds, and has some great hiking trails ((see page 253).

▶ ▷ ▷ **Destin**

Set on what is effectively an island, Destin is separated from mainland Florida by Choctawhatchee Bay. It is an important fishing centre.

Destin Fishing Museum, *Moreno Plaza (US98, one mile east of Destin Bridge)* 'Curiouser and curiouser,' said Alice, and this little museum, planted in a row of boutiques, is just that. Lighting and sound effects transport visitors straight to the bottom of the Gulf of Mexico as they walk along a sandy 'seabed' littered with bits of coral, sponges and sea fans, while inspecting walls lined with aquariums. A video and display of artefacts show

the importance of the local fishing industry.
Open: Tuesday to Saturday 11.00–16.00hrs, Sunday 13.00–16.00hrs.

Eden State Gardens and Mansion *21 miles east of Destin via US98, nearly 2 miles north on SR395* Tucked away off a back road, this lovely two-storey Southern mansion was built by mill-owner William H Wesley in 1897. Timber logged in the nearby woods was floated down the Choctawhatchee River to this site until the mill was burned down and the family sold out. Later, the house was bought by New York journalist Lois Maxton, who restored the antebellum structure, filled the rooms with family heirlooms and antiques, created the gardens and eventually left the whole estate to the State of Florida, in memory of her parents. Towering, moss-draped live oaks dot the lawns and shade picnic tables down by the river. This is where the barges would load up from pontoons by the mill, and ferry the lumber to Pensacola. Camellias and azeleas bloom from late October to May; peak flowering time is mid-March.
Open: gardens, daily 08.00hrs–dusk; *house*, guided tours 09.00–16.00hrs, daily May to September, Thursday to Monday, October to April.

Museum of the Sea and Indian, *Beach Highway (eight miles east of Destin)* Local marine life and some weird imported species occupy the space here. The roll call sounds like a circus act – drunken fish ('one of the sea's strange specimens'), dog fish ('looks as if he could bite'), and huge mola-mola ('all head, no brains'). In addition to the piscine line-up, there are: Indian artefacts from both North and South American tribes; a Fun Spook House; and a Live Zoo with alligators, peacocks and monkeys.
Open: daily, summer 08.00–19.00hrs; winter 09.00–16.00hrs.

Fishing – when to go for 'the big one'.
Amberjack (1-65lb): all year.
Barracuda (3-60lb): April–November.
Black/Red Grouper (1-60lb): all year.
Blue Marlin (45-700lb): May–November.
Jack Crevalle (2-40lb): May–October.
Red Snapper (1-40lb): all year.
Sailfish (5-100lb): April–November.
Tarpon (3-90lb): April–November.
Wahoo (8-100lb): April–October.
White Marlin (20-150lb): May–December.
But note: you need a licence for sea fishing off Florida.

You'll see what you might expect in the Museum of the Sea and Indian, near Destin

*Showtime at Fort
Walton's Gulfarium*

242

Several of the caves in
Florida Caverns State Park
have special names,
suggested by the formations,
such as the Wedding
Cavern, with its glittering
white 'wedding cake'.
Several weddings have
actually taken place here in
the cool 61–6° constant
temperatures.

▶ ▷ ▷　Fort Walton

Its setting beside the sea and the sheltered waters of
the Choctawhatchee Bay, plus miles of white sand
beaches, make Fort Walton a popular holiday
destination.

**Air Force Armament Museum and Eglin Air Force
Base**, *14 Eglin Parkway (north of Fort Walton Beach)*
The largest US Air Force base in the world, Eglin covers
some 720 square miles of the mainland, and rules the
skies over a further 86,500 square miles of test area in
the Gulf of Mexico. The base's Armaments Museum
displays an array of lethal weaponry, from a 1903
Springfield rifle to the 6,000-rounds-per-minute GAU8,
plus the 180-piece Sikes Antique Pistol Collection. The
latter includes flintlock duelling pistols, six-shooters and
firearms dating back to the Civil War. A comprehensive
aircraft collection is arranged inside and around the building. There is a very limited number of tickets for tours of
the base, which operate between January and March
(details can be obtained from the museum, or tel: (904)
651 5253).
Open: daily 09.30–16.30hrs.

Gulfarium, *1010 Miracle Strip Parkway (east US98)*　A
short distance east of Fort Walton Beach, Gulfarium was
one of the area's pioneering seaside attractions,
founded in 1955. Showtime includes aquabatic entertainment from performing porpoises and sea lions. The
Living Sea exhibit has a varied collection of sharks,
stingrays, sea turtles, sinuous eels and performing
scuba divers. The tropical penguin colony is a must; so
are the otters. Other bird colonies include the Duck and
Pelican Roost, and the Geese and Swan Sanctuary.
Open: daily, May to September 10.00–18.00hrs; October
to April 10.00–16.00hrs.

▶ ▶ ▷　Marianna

Florida Caverns State Park, *SR167 (north of Marianna)*
The Florida peninsula is a vast limestone plateau honey-
combed with underground caverns, rivers and sinkholes.
Most of the caverns are permanently flooded because
they are below the water table level, but at Marianna the
Chipola River has cut deep into the limestone, reducing
water levels, and revealing a superb network of caves.
The upper level caverns are permanently dry; the lower
levels, around 65 feet below ground, fill with water during the flood season. Within the caverns, stalactites, stalagmites, rimstones, flowstones and ribbon formations
continue to develop all the time – very slowly. It takes
roughly 100 years to grow a single cubic inch of solid
calcite. The formations are caused by precipitation: rainwater collects carbon dioxide from the air to create a
weak carbonic solution which filters through the limestone to the dry cave. There, it evaporates into a con-
centrated limestone solution, and speleotherms (cave
formations) gradually develop. At Marianna, the formations come in two different colours: brilliant white,
formed by calcium carbonate; and an orange-yellow tint,
from iron oxide in the soil.
Above ground, the 1,280-acre park offers two good

nature trails, picnicking areas, canoeing, fishing and a swimming hole.
Open: daily 08.00hrs–dusk, frequent cave tours 09.00–16.00hrs.

▷▷▷ **Monticello**

Named after Thomas Jefferson's Virginia mansion, Monticello was founded in 1827, at one of the highest points in the state – some 235 feet above sea-level. Today, it is an important agricultural centre with a pre-ponderance of hardware stores, and roots which can be traced back to the cotton plantations established in the area before the town itself. In the early days, the citizens of Monticello were both prosperous, reactionary and influential. Noted politicians, judges, and the state's first elected governor, William D Moseley, came from the district, and local lobbyists were at the forefront of Florida's 1861 secession from the Union.

During the mid-19th century, Monticello acquired a wealth of elegant Greek and Classical Revival mansions, pretty stick-style homes with gingerbread detail, and needle-spired churches. Several pre-Civil War buildings have survived, and there are over 40 registered buildings in the Historic District. A walk tour map is available from the Chamber of Commerce, 420 Washington Street (US90) – tel: (904) 997 5552.

At the centre of town, traffic is routed around the 1909 **Jefferson County Courthouse**, and on the southwest corner of Washington Street is the red-brick 1890 **Perkins Opera House**. It is the focus of a lively arts scene, featuring local and visiting theatre groups, and lecture and cinema societies. The ornate Operatic Chamber's excellent acoustics are an ideal showcase for musical and dramatic performances, while the ground floor space hosts exhibitions (for information, tel: (904) 997 4242.)

Jefferson County celebrates its status as the 'Watermelon Capital of the State' with an annual festival held during the last week of June. Activities include a beauty pageant, a canoe race, a parade, a golf tournament and a mess of good 'ole country cookin'. The highlight has got to be the Watermelon Seed Spittin' Contest. Make a few practice runs, then prepare to pucker up and fire.

243

The Courthouse in Monticello

■ **There is no better way to explore the quiet backwaters of Florida than paddling one's own canoe, and the state has 36 designated canoe trails totalling 950 miles of scenic waterways. The Panhandle region offers plenty of waterborne opportunities, from a gentle novice meander to more challenging water courses for experienced canoeists .....■**

Canoe Capital of Florida Milton, north of Pensacola, is the self-styled 'Canoe Capital of Florida', and is a good base for the tannin-stained **Blackwater River** as it winds its way through the dense woodlands of the Blackwater River State Forest. Local canoe rental operations provide equipment hire and shuttle services for visitors to the Blackwater, considered one of the purest sand-bottomed rivers in the world, and to **Coldwater Creek**. For real back-to-nature adventurers, there is camping in the state park.

Further east Holmes Creek, which rises in Georgia and eventually empties into Choctawhatchee Bay, makes for a lazy day's paddling. There is good fishing along its sandy banks and lush swamplands. The 52-mile **Chipola River Trail** starts in the Florida Caverns State Park, north of Marianna. There the river flows through high limestone bluffs, caves

Canoeing camp

and round a series of small rapids and shoals. The going is rougher on the top section of narrow, twisting **Ecofina Creek**, but this 22-mile trail also offers beautiful springs and gentler waters along its lower reaches.

State Park facilities Four state parks and canoeing facilities abut the **Suwannee River**, and its tributary, the Sante Fe. At the **Suwannee River State Park**, 20 miles east of Madison, where the much-sung-about Suwannee is joined by the Withlacoochee River, there is great canoeing country, with otters, beavers and gopher tortoises bustling about the river swamp and hardwood hammock habitats. **Ichetucknee Springs State Park**, one of the most beautiful riverfront parks in Florida, is good for tubing (ie, floating in an inner-tube) as well as canoeing, and **O'Leno State Park** marks the point where the Santa Fe resurfaces after a three-mile journey underground. Both are close to US441, south of Lake City. At **Manatee Springs State Park**, 23 miles short of the Gulf of Mexico, there is canoeing, fishing and scuba diving.

<< Officially designated canoe trails are managed as part of the Florida Recreational Trail System. For further details, contact the Florida Department of Natural Resources, Office of Communications, 3900 Commonwealth Boulevard, Tallahassee FL32399 (tel: (904) 487 2018). >>

Gulf Islands National Seashore

■ The offshore barrier islands and keys of the Gulf Islands National Seashore stretch for a total of 150 miles across the top of the Gulf of Mexico, from Florida's Santa Rosa Island in the east to West Ship Island off the coast of Mississippi. Abundant plant and animal communities flourish in this magnificent natural preserve, and the three main habitats – dunes, marsh and woodlands – are all represented within the six areas of the Florida district: Santa Rosa, Okaloosa, Naval Live Oaks, Fort Pickens, Pensacola Forts and Perdido Key .....■

Naval Live Oaks Just across the bay from Pensacola, Naval Live Oaks, at Gulf Breeze (SR98), is the park headquarters and visitor centre. Natural history and historical exhibits, together with an audio-visual presentation, give an overview of the park, and there is plenty of helpful information.

Santa Rosa The park's beach preserve, Santa Rosa lies east of Pensacola Beach along CR399. There are miles of incredibly white sand, with not a condominium in sight.
To protect the fragile dunes, it is strictly boardwalk access only to the shore from designated parking areas. Once on the beach, there is a Day Use Facility at the Navarre Beach end, with picnic shelters, toilets and a concession stand.

What else is there? The other park areas offer several pleasant nature trails, such as the marsh, forest and sandhill trail at **Johnson Beach** on Perdido Key. **Fort Pickens** (see page 249) offers two short and markedly diverse trails: a quarter-mile dune walk, and the half-mile Blackbird Marsh circuit in the maritime forest. On the mainland, the **Fort Barrancas** trail explores woodlands near the Naval Air Station.

The 1,378-acre woodland park which surrounds Naval Live Oaks is dominated by majestic live oaks. It is so called because in 1828 the US government reserved great tracts of southern oak forest to be managed exclusively for shipbuilding. The heaviest of all the oaks, weighing up to 75lb per cubic foot, live oaks are also remarkably resistant to disease and decay. There are several nature trails through the forest, which is a haven for foxes, bobcats and racoons, as well as reptiles from skinks to coral snakes.

The Panhandle's barrier islands are on the move. Littoral currents erode the fine quartz sand from the eastern tip of the islands and deposit it at the western end. Constant winds and storms rearrange the dunes ceaselessly, and their only protection is the hardy stems and elaborate root systems of the salt-spray-loving sea oats. Sea oats are a protected species along the coast: disturbing them or picking them is against the law.

▶▶▷ **Panama City Beach**

The fun-loving annexe of blue-collar Panama City, Panama City Beach is typified by its 'Miracle Strip' of neon, concrete and candyfloss, which extends for almost 27 miles along the gleaming white Gulf beaches. Love it or loathe it, there is no disputing its distinctive flavour and broad-ranging family appeal. With 16,000 hotel rooms offering everything from secluded luxury resort accommodation, to beachside motels and RV (recreational vehicle) parks, there is plenty of opportunity to join in or flop out. Watersports are top of the activities list with snorkelling, diving, jet-skiing, windsurfing, sailing and para-sailing on the doorstep. Fishermen can go for 'the big one' on single or party charter boats, or just take it easy and hang a line off one of the numerous piers and jetties. Golf is increasingly popular: there are over 20 excellent courses within a 40-mile radius. Several clubs have added top-class hard surface and clay tennis court facilities.

Meanwhile, back on 'The Strip', miniature golf is all the rage: half a dozen ingenious courses littered with ship-wrecks, moated castles and gaping monsters are open from early to floodlit late, late night. Restaurants, bars, boutiques and video arcades abound, and as the sun goes down the neon snaps into action, and the serious fun begins. Entertainment crosses the board from comedy to Broadway-style music shows, screaming fair-ground thrills to beachclub discothèques.

Although Panama City Beach is turning into a year-round destination, the main season runs from April through September. Hotel rates are bargains during the winter months, but many attractions are closed off-season.

Panama City Beach with its Miracle Strip Amusement Park

Gulf World Aquarium, *15412 W US98-A* Boardwalks shaded by palms and edged by colourful hibiscus wind past the various attractions at this compact marine

showcase in the main beach area. Take in the Parrot Show, an informative Underwater Show and Scuba Demonstration, and the Stingray Petting Pool, where visitors are encouraged to feed the rays with slivers of fish held between their fingers. They have had their barbs removed and are, therefore, 'safe'; visitors may have their own views about the moral issues raised. Dolphins can be stroked, sharks fed, and there is lots of splashing around in the Sea Lion and Dolphin Show.
Open: summer 09.00–19.00hrs, winter 09.00–15.00hrs.

Junior Museum of Bay County, *1731 N Jenks Avenue, Panama City* Designed with younger visitors in mind, there is a wide range of diversions for the whole family here, and the emphasis is on getting involved. The museum's displays of Indian tools and other historic artefacts are accompanied by a chance for kids to get interested at tee-pee level in the lifesize Indian tent, and to join in traditional games in the Children's Room. Natural history exhibits are backed up with a nature trail which explores typical Panhandle environments such as hardwood swamps and hammocks, and a pine island. A re-created pioneer village has a farm homestead and barn, complete with chickens and ducks. Science and art also have their place, and the museum hosts a full programme of special events and travelling exhibitions.
Open: Monday to Saturday 09.00–17.00hrs, Sunday 12.00–17.00hrs.

Miracle Strip Amusement Park, *12000 W Front Beach Road* Right opposite the beachside Visitor Information Center, this is northwest Florida's biggest crowd-puller, and one of the top ten attractions in the state, with nine acres of brash, loud, gaudy fun, swings, roundabouts, contests and games.
Undisputed king of the park is the 2,000-foot roller coaster, rated one of the world's foremost rides by coaster *aficionados*. Another 59 stomach-churning rides include the 40-foot high Sea Dragon Viking Ship, which rocks passengers up to 70 feet in the air, the Ferris Wheel, the Log Flume, and the Abominable Snowman-Scrambler. There is live entertainment in summer, and a battalion of snack concessions and fast food joints serve up everything from pizzas and hot dogs to home-made fudge.
Open: June to Labor Day, Monday to Friday 17.00–23.30hrs, Saturday 13.00–23.30hrs, Sunday 15.00–23.30hrs; March to May, restricted weekend opening (for information, tel: (904) 234 5810).

Museum of Man in the Sea, *17314 Back Beach Road* Sponsored by the Institute of Diving, this unusual, small museum traces the definitive history of diving, from the earliest records through to miracles of modern science, such as the landmark orange Sealab I deep-diving capsule anchored in the car park. Dioramas, models and a mass of equipment illustrate marine salvage and construction activities, oil drilling and archaeology, scuba, saturation diving, and even astronauts training for weightlessness.
Open: daily 09.00–17.00hrs.

The Gulf of Mexico's crystal-clear waters offer great diving opportunities. Wrecks here include the tanker Empire Mica, the Grey Ghost and the 220-foot Chippawa. There are several natural coral reefs, and they all teem with fish, lobsters and shellfish. Snorkellers and divers can explore the St Andrews State Park Jetties, which range in depth from just one foot to 50 feet. For details of dive and snorkelling trips, contact Hydrospace (tel: (904) 234 9463, or (1 800) 874 3483).

Try out the rides in Shipwreck Island Water Park, then recover in the sun

St Andrews State Recreation Area, *Thomas Drive* On the eastern tip of Panama City Beach, this 1,063-acre park is one of the most popular in the state. Nature trails explore the woodlands and dunes, offering plenty of opportunities for spotting wild deer, racoons, alligators and seabirds. Bayside fishing piers give access to speckled trout, red fish and flounder, while bonita, pompano, Spanish and king mackerel can be caught on the Gulf side. There are picnic areas and boat rental; and the park is also excellent for young children as man-made reefs around the jetties form a shallow play area. *Open*: daily 07.30hrs–dusk.

Shell Island, *Access by boat* Scheduled to become a state park in the near future, this sheller's paradise lies just off Panama City Beach. Also known as Hurricane Island, its seven miles of untouched shoreline are shaded by a smattering of pines. Three-hour shell safaris leave from **Captain Anderson Davies Marina**, 5500 North Lagoon Drive (tel: (904) 234 3435), and **Treasure Island Marina**, 3605 Thomas Drive (tel: (904) 234 6533) from April to early October. There are also glass-bottomed boat trips and dolphin-feeding excursions.

Shipwreck Island Water Park, *12000 W Front Beach* Back to back with the night-time Miracle Strip Amusement Park complex, Shipwreck Island is the answer to what you can do during the day. There are six exotically landscaped acres of watery fun park, fully equipped with life-guards, restaurant facilities, snack bars, sundecks, shopping opportunities and free parking. Meander down the 1,600-foot Lazy River on an inner tube; check out the Gulf recreation, Ocean Motion; shoot the 370-foot White Water Tube Ride, or 35mph Speed Slide; dare the Rapid River run; and then settle down under a sun umbrella while tiddlers splash about in the thoughtfully miniaturised Tadpole Hole. *Open*: June to August, daily 10.30–18.00hrs; very limited hours in April, May and September (for information, tel: (904) 234 2282).

▶▶▷ Pensacola

Pensacola is proud of its history, and has three fine historical districts to prove it: the **Seville District**, where the first stockade was erected in 1752; **Palafox Street**, leading down to the waterfront; and 19th-century **North Hill**, with its elegant houses built by wealthy timber merchants. Sightseeing also includes sophisticated state-of-the-art technology on display at the **National Museum of Aviation**.

Across the bay, Pensacola's beaches are responsible for turning the city into a major resort – 40 miles of 99 per cent pure quartz sand. **Pensacola Beach**, on Santa Rosa Island, is lined with hotels, boutiques and cafés, and is popular for watersports. **Perdido Key**, in the west, has free showers and changing facilities in the Johnson Beach area; or head east along SR399 for the fabulous undeveloped dunes of the **Gulf Islands National Seashore** and **Navarre Beach**.

Fort Pickens, *W Santa Rosa Island* Strategically sited at the entrance to Pensacola Bay, Fort Pickens was the largest of four defensive fortresses constructed to protect the harbour in the early 1800s. More than 21 million locally made bricks were transported out to the island on barges to reinforce the massive five-sided earthworks.

Originally, the fortress was surrounded by a 10-foot-deep moat, but this has since been filled. Bastions with a broad range of firepower anchor the corners, and heavy cannon once lined the walls. To the left of the sallyport (entrance), the officers' quarters were used to house the captured Apache chief Geronimo, whose enforced stay (1886–8) generated the beginnings of Pensacola's tourist industry, as curious folk came to ogle at his downfall. In the central parade ground, Battery Pensacola is a more recent gun emplacement, added in 1898.

Open: daily 08.00hrs–dusk.

In 1559, 500 Spanish soldiers and 1,000 colonists sailed into Pensacola Bay and established a settlement. It lasted just two years. But the Europeans were back to stay in the late 17th century, and in less than 100 years the area was controlled by Spanish, French and British interests. The Confederate forces of the 19th century, and post-Civil War America add up to Pensacola's nickname, the 'City of Five Flags'.

Inside Pensacola's Fort Pickens

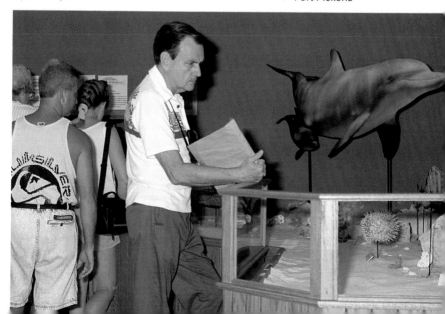

Historic Pensacola Village, *Zaragoza and Tarragona Streets* Also known as the **Seville Historic District**, this is one of three exceptional preservation districts found in Pensacola. The original street plans were laid out by the British in the mid-18th century, and were later retained by the Spanish, although the names were changed.

Today, the area looks much as it would have appeared in the late 1880s, and a good place to begin a visit is the **Museum of Commerce**, Zaragoza and Tarragona Streets. Here, a short video presentation covers Pensacola's history, and a re-created late 19th-century shopping street features a print shop and a pharmacy, hardware, music and toy stores, and a deliciously leather-scented saddlery. Across the street, two old warehouses have been knocked together to house the **Museum of Industry**. Exhibits illustrate Pensacola's two founding strengths, the maritime and lumber trades, by way of a reconstructed ship's chandlery and the massive Piney Woods sawmill. Tours of the village's historic houses leave from here daily (for information, tel: (904) 444 8905).

Opposite the museum are two prime examples of early architecture. The plain wooden house, **Julee Cottage**, was built in 1805, and owned by renowned Pensacolian Julee Panton, a 'free woman of color'. Its companion, the **Lavalle House** (pronounced La-va-lay), is an eye-catching affair dating from the same year. It was built by one Charles Lavalle with the specific intention of attracting French Creole lodgers, who he reckoned would prefer the bright colour scheme, smooth plastering on the front porch, bevelled planks and rounded handrails.

Florida's oldest Protestant church, **Old Christ Church**, faces Seville Square, and across the street, the **Dorr House** is a beautifully restored 1870 Greek Revival building. Even the wallpaper is copied from original patterns found in historic Georgia mansions. Last of the village's official properties, **Quina House** is a cosmopolitan mixture of Spanish-cum-French Creole architecture constructed in 1821.

There is plenty more to see with the help of the self-guided *Historical Guide to Pensacola* leaflet. Many of the houses have been converted into folksy law offices, and local boutique and restaurant owners are usually delighted to regale visitors with tales of their historic surroundings.

Two more local museums worth checking out are the **Pensacola Historical Museum**, housed in Old Christ Church, and the **TT Wentworth Florida State Museum**, on Jefferson beween Government and Zaragoza streets. The first recalls the five different flag nationalities which have had a hand in developing the area; the latter contains the eclectic collections of Mr Wentworth, from fossils and pottery fragments to election buttons and Coca-Cola memorabilia from the Hygeia Bottling Works.

National Museum of Naval Aviation, *NAS Pensacola, Navy Boulevard (via US98)* 'Top Gun fun' shrieks the slogan, and this is indeed an amazing free attraction.

Doubled in size since 1990, the complex is now one of the largest air and space museums in the world. For sheer scale, check out the full-size reconstruction of

Affectionately known as 'The Cradle of Naval Aviation', the US Naval Air Station in Pensacola was founded way back in 1915. It trains both Navy and Marine Corps pilots, unleashing around 750 flight operations every day. The big thrill is a performance by the base's Blue Angels flight demonstration team, established in 1946. As well as the National Museum of Aviation, enthusiasts can also visit the Air Station's Land Survival Exhibit, where trainee pilots are taught survival skills (open: Tuesday 09.00–15.00hrs, Wednesday and Friday 08.00–15.00hrs, Thursday 13.00–15.00hrs, Saturday and Sunday 12.00–16.00hrs).

World War II aircraft carrier, USS *Cabot* in the West Wing. The model displays Corsair, Avenger and Hellcat fighters on its wooden decking, while examples of Wildcat, Dauntless and Kingfisher aircraft are locked in stationary flight poise overhead.

The collection features aircraft from the earliest wood and canvas pioneer prototypes to sophisticated space gadgetry such as the Skylab command module. Unwieldy flying boats, supersonic jets, moon buggies and naval aviation memorabilia all earn a place in the Hall of Fame. Video presentations deliver the excitement of flight second-hand; for a closer call, the F-4 and A-7 jet cockpit simulators are a major hit with the young; or there is a chance to take the controls of a TH-57 helicopter trainer. A visit to the Hanger Bay restoration facility provides an intriguing opportunity to watch museum volunteers refurbish historic aircraft.

Open: daily 09.00–17.00hrs.

Inside the National Museum of Naval Aviation

One of America's best-loved musical storytellers, Stephen C Foster never saw the Suwannee, or even visited Florida. Looking for a good ole Southern name for one of his compositions, he had no compunction about tailoring the Suwannee to 'S'wanee' in order to fit the two-syllable cadence he needed. A prolific author, Foster has about 200 songs to his credit, including sing-along favourite *Oh Susannah*, and the lilting *Jeanie with the Light-brown Hair*.

Pensacola Zoo, *5701 Gulf Breeze Parkway (12 miles east of Gulf Breeze, on US98)* The Panhandle's only zoo, this has more than 600 animals, botanical gardens, a children's petting corner and a safari train which rides around 'natural habitat' enclosures. Two miles west, the **Wildlife Rescue and Sanctuary Park** (*open*: Tuesday to Sunday 10.00–16.00hrs) rehabilitates and houses injured birds and animals.
Open: daily, summer 09.00-17.00hrs; rest of the year 09.00–16.00hrs.

▶▶▷ Ponce de Leon Springs SRA
Ponce de Leon (off US90, north of Interstate-10)
Driving across the Panhandle on a baking hot day, this is a great place to stop off for a picnic and cooling swim. The park's main spring produces more than 14 million gallons of crystal-clear water daily, and its constant 68°F temperature is a lot more refreshing than the lukewarm waters of the Gulf. There are picnic benches and barbecue grills (bring charcoal) in the shade of pine and cypress trees. Canoe rental and fishing are available in the park; two self-guided nature trails explore the sandy pinewoods; and park rangers conduct seasonal guided walks.
Open: daily 08.00hrs–dusk.

▶▶▷ Suwannee River
White Springs (US41)
In 1851, composer Stephen C Foster immortalised the state's second largest river in his popular melody *Old Folks at Home*, better known as *Way down upon the Swanee River*. It was adopted as Florida's official state song in 1935. A former spa resort, 10 miles northwest of Lake City, White Springs has cashed in on the free promotion with the annual **Florida Folk Festival** held here each May. Near by, the **Stephen Foster State Folk Culture Center** contains the remnants of the original Victorian spa; a collection of rare musical instruments; and a 93-bell carillon which runs through a medley of Foster compositions. There are also trips on a paddlewheel boat, *Belle of Suwannee* (summer season only).

On the Suwannee River, Florida's most famous waterway

Panhandle Trails

■ Over three-quarters of the Panhandle's 27 state parks offer short nature walks within their preserves, but for something a little more exacting there are several longer distance designated trails. In 1979, the Florida Recreational Trails Act authorised the establishment of a network of scenic and historic trails, and there are plans to create a series of hiking routes from Pensacola across to Lake Okeechobee, and from Big Cypress Swamp in southwest Florida up to the Gulf Islands National Seashore .....■

Rails to trails One way to create routes is to convert abandoned railway tracks into multi-use trails, and the first of these rails-to-trails routes to open was the **Tallahassee-St Marks Historic Railroad State Trail** in the eastern Panhandle. Once a transport corridor for cotton and other goods, the trail starts just south of Tallahassee (off SR363), and is now open to hikers, cyclists and horseback riders.

St Marks National Wildlife Refuge Within St Mark's National Wildlife Refuge on Apalachee Bay, there is a great choice of trails from the half-day Ridge Trail (4.5 miles) and Stoney Bayou Trail (6 miles), to the longer Otter Lake Trail (8 miles) and Deep Creek Trail (12 miles). The 45-mile St Marks Trail winds deep into some of the more remote areas of this vast coastal marsh and swampland preserve. It ends just east of Sopchoppy, where the Apalachicola Trail begins its 22-mile hike across four rivers into the wilderness regions of the Apalachicola National Forest.

Other trails For a shorter introduction to the forest, take the circular Camel Lake Trail (4 miles) from the Camel Lake Recreation Area off CR12 north of Wilma. West of Apalachicola, St Joseph Peninsula State Park is the start of the 18-mile St Joseph Peninsula Trail which loops through the wilderness preserve via the beach, pine woods

and marshlands. It is an excellent birdwatching area with over 209 recorded species to spot. In the western Panhandle region, hikers can venture across the Blackwater State Forest on the Jackson Red Ground Trail (21 miles), or sample the Sweetwater Hiking Trail, a short 4.5-mile walk from the Krul Recreation Area in the middle of the forest near Munson.

A grey squirrel in the Apalachicola Forest

THE PANHANDLE

The name Tallahassee comes from the Apalachee Indian for 'land of the old fields' or 'abandoned villages'. Archaeological surveys of the Lake Jackson area, north of the city, have revealed evidence of a Mississippi Indian ceremonial centre dating back over eight centuries. spanish explorer Hernando de Soto celebrated the first Christmas Mass on the continent here in 1539.

The Fourth of July parade in Tallahassee

 ▶▶▶   **Tallahassee**

By the 1820s the hunt was on for a government seat where Florida's newly elected state legislature could meet, somewhere between the two historic centres of St Augustine and Pensacola. A scout was sent out from each city, and they met on the hill called Tallahassee. Suggestions that the Capitol should shift to the growing urban and business centres in the southeast have met with rebuff, and present-day Tallahassians guard their position and history jealously.

Surrounded by gently rolling hills, forests and lakes, old plantations and the accents of America's Deep South, Tallahassee seems a world away from the crowded southern tourist trails. Quiet, tree-lined streets draped with Spanish moss and scented by fragrant magnolias exude old-fashioned charm minutes from the bustling **Capitol Complex** at the centre of downtown.

Two major universities are based here: Florida State (FSU), with its mighty Seminoles football team; and Florida Agricultural and Mechanical (FAMU), founded in 1887. Florida's 'Sunshine Act' made it one of the first states to insist that legislative sessions be open to the public, so a visit to the State Capitol during the January to March sessions is a popular excursion. The nearby elegant **Governor's Mansion**, 700 N Adams Street, modelled on General Andrew Jackson's Tennessee plantation home, is open to view at the same time.

A good way to get around is on the **Old Town Trolley**, which provides its services for free and makes frequent stops at 15 downtown locations. Shopping in Tallahassee means the malls along Apalachee Parkway; **Governor's Square** offers the best range of boutiques and department stores, with the bonus of an unrivalled view of the Old and New Capitol buildings at the top of the Parkway heading back into town. Springtime visitors will find Tallahassee in a festive mood with a four-week (March to April) jamboree of arts, crafts, entertainment and parades.

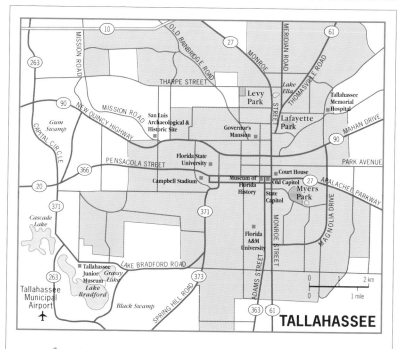

Walk Downtown Tallahassee

Start from the Old Capitol on Monroe Street at Apalachee Parkway.
Across the street, the twin granite slabs of the **Vietnam Veteran's Memorial** commemorate the 1,942 known Floridian casualties of the conflict. The **Union Bank Building**, facing Apalachee Parkway, is Florida's oldest surviving bank. This restored 1841 Federal-style edifice now houses a small exhibition devoted to the history of banking in the state.

Walk back up to Monroe; turn right.
The **Exchange Building**, 201 Monroe, is a fine example of art deco office architecture, built in 1927 and decorated with reliefs and stone griffins.

Take a left on College; then left again on to Adams.
This attractive restored area is known as the **Adams Street Commons**.

Turn right on Jefferson for two blocks to Bronough.
The **Museum of Florida History**, 500 S Bronough, is situated just across the intersection (see page 257).

Continue along Bronough to Madison, and turn left.
On the corner of Madison and Monroe, the **Jackson Square Marker** indicates the original site of downtown Tallahassee circa 1824, a village of wooden cottages and stores which stretched from Call Street to the south wing of the Old Capitol.

THE PANHANDLE

A B Maclay State Gardens, *3540 Thomasville Road*
Just north of Interstate-10, this is one of the loveliest gardens in Florida, founded by New York financier Alfred B Maclay in 1923. Maclay's creative landscaping combined native pines and oaks with a diverse selection of exotic imported species, all incorporated into a network of walks, paths, pools and lawns surrounding his house and stretching down to Lake Hall. The camellias (around 100 varieties) commence their flowering season in December, and the gardens are at the height of their beauty from January to April, when the furnished house is also open to the public. Big Pine Nature Trail winds through the woodlands around the lake, and picnicking, swimming, boating and freshwater fishing are provided for. Alligators and turtles have been spotted in the lake, and over 150 species of birds and animals inhabit the woodlands.
Open: daily 08.00hrs–dusk.

Capitol Complex, *S Monroe (at Apalachee Parkway)*
The towering 22-storey State Capitol building may dominate Tallahassee's modest skyline, but the **Old Capitol** remains curator of Florida's early legislative history. Haste was of the essence when the original Capitol was constructed on this site in 1845. A half-century later it had to be completely remodelled by architect Frank P Milburn. His classical designs incorporated triangular tympana above the columned porticoes of the east and west entrances, which are embossed with pressed metal reliefs of details from the state seal. Crowning the creation is a 136-foot dome with colourful stained-glass decoration. The distinctive candy-striped awnings also date from Milburn's day. The building was further enlarged in 1923, housing the Senate Chamber at one end, and the House of Representatives at the other, with the Supreme Court downstairs. The restored chambers have been furnished with authentic reproductions of the original wicker-seated armchairs, arranged in wide semi-circles. In between, former offices house an excellent permanent history exhibit illustrated with memorabilia, photographs and fascinating tales of early legislators and their times.
The State Legislature in the modern Capitol is in session from January to March, and visitors can watch the proceedings in both chambers from viewing galleries on the fifth floor. The 22nd-floor Observatory affords a panoramic view of the city (hemmed in by woodlands which extend to the horizon), plus an exhibition gallery for Floridian artists.
Open: Old Capitol, Monday to Friday 09.00–16.30hrs, Saturday 10.00–16.30hrs, Sunday 12.00–16.30hrs; State Capitol, Monday to Friday 08.00–17.00hrs, Saturday and Sunday 11.00–16.00hrs.

Museum of Florida History, *500 S Bronough Street*
Interesting and informative, this user-friendly jaunt through Floridian history starts with geological relics and the skeleton of a giant mastodon, then runs through sunken treasures salvaged from Spanish galleons and Civil War battle flags right through to the Roaring Twenties. You can go 'all aboard' for a 19th-century

The Capitol Complex in Tallahassee

riverside view, or, in contrast, campers might like to see how their predecessors set up 'tin can' holiday campgrounds in the first great tourist boom of the 1920s.
Open: Monday to Friday 09.00–16.30hrs, Saturday 10.00–16.30hrs, Sunday 12.00–16.30hrs.

Park Avenue and Calhoun Street Historic District
These gracious tree-shaded streets are lined with the homes and churches of Tallahassee's prominent 19th-century citizens. Built in 1830, the Greek Revival-style **Columns,** 100 N Duval (at Park), is the city's oldest surviving structure. **Knott House Museum**, 301 Park, is also known as 'The House that Rhymes' after 1920s occupant Luella Knott, who decorated the antique furnishings with examples of her poetry, tied on with ribbons. Quiet Calhoun Street offers a good mixture of architectural styles. The visitors' centre has a *Downtown Tallahassee Historic Trail* walk tour map. For guided tours, tel: (904) 488 3901.

San Luis Archaeological and Historic Site, *2020 Mission Road (at Ocala Road)* Located on a hillside west of the downtown district, this site, with its dual history as a Spanish mission site and Apalachee Indian village, has revealed a wealth of archaeological relics, and work is still in progress. Recovered artefacts include pottery, weapons and jewellery. The Spanish settlement was in existence in 1656, and contained a religious complex and houses built alongside a large Indian council house. The entire village was burned to the ground in 1704 to prevent it falling into British hands.
Open: Monday to Friday 09.00–16.30hrs, Saturday 10.00–16.30hrs, Sunday 12.00–16.30hrs.

A short drive east of Tallahassee, Lafayette Vineyards and Winery (one mile west of Interstate 10 at Exit 31-A) is one of just five Florida wineries, and has won more than 100 national and international awards for its home-grown vintages.. Tours are free, and culminate in a tasting session of red, white and sparkling wines (tours Monday to Saturday 10.00–18.00hrs, Sunday 12.00–18.00hrs).

257

The Old Town Trolley

Tallahassee Junior Museum, *3945 Museum Drive (off Lake Bradford Road)* This excellent outdoor museum has a wide range of exhibits, from an 1880s-style Big Bend Farm to bobcats and brown bears. In a shady glade, the main farmhouse is surrounded by outbuildings including a smithy, smokehouse and barn. Other historic buildings include an 1890s schoolroom, the 1850 Bellevue Plantation house, and the Bethlehem Missionary Baptist Church, built in 1937 by one of Florida's first Black Baptist congregations, founded in the 1850s.

Pigs, geese, sheep and goats are tended by staff dressed in period beards and braces. Cotton and cane grow in the garden, and mules munch away in the stables. A boardwalk trail spans a cypress swamp area on Lake Bradford, and then continues around natural habitat enclosures for basking alligators, Florida panthers, red foxes, skunks and white-tailed deer. The walk-through aviary provides interesting bird-spotting. Finally, look out for the white squirrels, a genetic mutation introduced from the Apalachicola River area in the 1960s. There are picnic and play areas, and a gift shop.

Open: Monday to Saturday 09.00–17.00hrs, Sunday 12.30–17.00hrs.

Wakulla Springs State Park, *15 miles south of Tallahassee via US319, SR61 and CR267* The centre-piece of this 2,860-acre park is a pool above the main spring, which native American Indians called 'mysteries of strange water'. Some 600,000 gallons of water per minute flow from an underground river into the 4.5 -acre pool, so astonishingly clear that even the deepest point (185 feet) is visible, as is the entrance to a subterranean cavern where mastodon bones have been discovered. A glass-bottomed boat makes regular sorties around the pool. Another boat ferries passengers down the scenic Wakulla River, and deer, turtles, alligators and the abundant birdlife along the river banks are pointed out. Nine species of herons and egrets, plus vultures, anhinga, kites and osprey nest and feed here year round, the population swelling dramatically during the northern winter migration. There is a swimming hole, shady picnic tables and barbecue grills, as well as accommodation and a restaurant (for information, tel: (904) 222 7279).

Open: daily 08.00hrs–dusk.

One of 72 buildings across the US constructed under the Works Project Administration during the 1930s Depression years, the foyer of the Old US Courthouse, 110 W Park Avenue, is well worth a quick stop for its humorous murals. Laced with amusing detail, a series of gentle, tongue-in-cheek scenes illustrate the development of the state from aboriginal Indians through the muskets and flags of the Spanish explorers and Civil War to the emancipated lady golfers and sunseekers of the 1920s and 1930s.

Farming 1890s style at the Tallahassee Junior Museum

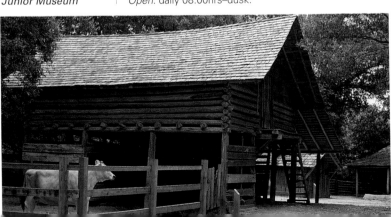

Drive **Into the Panhandle**

See map on page 236.

This drive west into the central Panhandle from Tallahassee makes an equally good day trip or an off-interstate route half-way to Pensacola. Along the way there are opportunities for antiques shopping, discovering beautifully preserved antebellum houses, some underground exploration, picnicking and a cooling swim.

Leave Tallahassee on N Monroe Street (US27), and cross Interstate-10. In Havana (11 miles), continue one block from the junction with SR12, and park on Seventh Avenue.
Havana's tiny, but attractive antiques district is a popular spot for browsers. **Old Timey Things**, Main Street, offers easily portable mementoes, such as old-time posters, advertising cards and vintage *Time Life* magazines.

Retrace your route to SR12 at Ninth Avenue; turn right (west). At the first traffic light in Quincy (11 miles), turn left on Madison. The red brick Chamber of Commerce is on the corner.
Explore **Quincy**'s elegant antebellum heritage on foot with the Chamber's excellent brochure *A Tour of Historic Quincy*. Founded in 1828, Quincy's fortunes were built on tobacco and on the Quincy State Bank's far-sighted investment in the fledgling Coca-Cola Company.

By the Courthouse, turn right on US90 (west) for 20 miles.
The next landmark is **Chattahoochee**, with a panoramic view of the central region's pine and oakwood forests. The **Apalachicola River** marks the change to Central US Time (watches back one hour). On **Victory Bridge**, look north for a view of the 6,130-foot Jim Woodruff Hydroelectric Dam, built in the late 1950s. It is a great fishing spot and a watersports centre. For a closer look, there is an observation point off to the right (two miles from Chattahoochee).

In Marianna (25 miles from Chattahoochee), follow signs for the Florida Caverns via a right turn on to Jefferson Street.
Florida Caverns State Park reveals the very foundations of the state in a series of magnificent limestone caves cut into the plateau.

Back at US90, day-trippers can head back to Tallahassee via the fast Interstate-10 (turn left on US90, and follow signs for the interstate). For Pensacola, turn right on US90.
One last stop *en route* to Pensacola is a refreshing swim at **Ponce de Leon Springs State Recreation Area** (47 miles). (See page 252.)

Interstate-10 is just one mile from Ponce de Leon.

On the Apalachicola River

TRAVEL FACTS

Arriving

Air routes Most North American airlines operate regular scheduled services to Florida from numerous destinations within the US and Canada.

The only direct scheduled flights from the UK are London to Miami and Orlando, though several airlines and tour operators offer direct charter flights and one-stop services from regional airports such as Luton, Manchester and Glasgow. From Eire, there are one-stop flights ex-Dublin. One-stop flights are also available from New Zealand (ex–Auckland); two-stop flights ex-Sydney, Melbourne and Brisbane from Australia.

Entry requirements UK and New Zealand residents with return or onward tickets on a business or holiday trip lasting less than 90 days no longer require a visa. Holders of full valid passports can fill out a visa waiver form issued by travel agents or at check-in to be handed to US immigration control on arrival. Residents of Eire and Australia still need a non-immigrant visitor's visa. Forms are available from travel agents to be completed and sent to the nearest US embassy or consulate together with a full passport. Leave plenty of time for the documentation to be completed before departure.

Customs declarations must be filled in by all travellers arriving from outside the US. Fresh foods, agricultural products, items from Cuba, Kampuchea, North Korea and Vietnam, obscene materials, lottery tickets (even though Florida has a lottery), chocolate liqueurs and pre-Columbian art will be confiscated on arrival. Illegal drug smuggling is treated with severity, and penalties are harsh. There is no limit on currency brought into the US, but amounts exceeding US$5,000 (or their foreign equivalent) must be declared.

Duty-free customs allowances on arrival permit persons of 18 and over to import 200 cigarettes and 100 cigars (*not* Cuban); at 21 or over add one litre of drinking alcohol for personal use.

Ground transport Some hotels provide airport transfers, while car rental companies operate shuttle services to their parking lots. Otherwise there are local bus services, and a plentiful supply of taxis. Taxis are often worth the added expense for speed and convenience, and fares to downtown areas are usually reasonable. (For fuller details of transport into Miami, see page 84).

Major Florida Airports

Fort Lauderdale (tel: (305) 357 6100)
Jacksonville (tel: (904) 741 2000)
Key West (tel: (305) 296 5439)
Miami (tel: (305) 871 7090)
Orlando (tel: (407) 826 2001)
Palm Beach (tel: (407) 471 7400)
*St Petersburg/
Clearwater* (tel: (813) 531 1451)
Tampa (tel: (813) 276 3400)

Camping

Camping is popular in Florida. There are privately run campgrounds, plus resort, national and state parks offering camping opportunities throughout the state. Facilities range from elaborate 'pull thru's' designed for RVs (recreational vehicles) to rustic backwoods campsites for hikers. Many campgrounds offer on-site trailer and tent hire, but it is advisable to make reservations in advance, particularly during the winter months.

The *Florida Camping Directory* lists some 200 member sites around the state together with information about their RV and camping facilities, plus listings covering on-site amenities such as pools, shopping and children's playgrounds. For a copy of the directory, contact the **Florida Campground Association**, 1638 N Plaza Drive, Tallahassee, FL 32308–5364 (tel: (904) 656 8878). For information about camping in the state's parks, contact the **Florida Department of Natural Resources**, Bureau of Operational Services, Mail Station 535, 3900 Commonwealth Boulevard, Tallahassee, FL 32399 (tel: (904) 488 9872).

A popular option is to hire an RV from a local rental company. **Cruise America**, 5959 Blue Lagoon Drive,

TRAVEL FACTS

Suite 250, Miami, FL 33126 (tel: (305) 262 9611/(800) 327 7778) provide local and one-way motorhome and van rentals from several gateway destinations within Florida. Services include airport transfers.

Children

Florida's informal lifestyle is a gift for families on the move. Many resorts and facilities make a special point of catering to the family market. Children are welcome in restaurants, and many family-style eateries lay on special portions and amusements. Hotels in every price bracket frequently offer free lodging for children up to 18 staying with their parents, so look out for bargains. Babies' and children's items such as baby foods and high factor sunblock are readily available at any grocery store or pharmacy. Larger theme parks provide a range of child services from changing rooms with all the requisite toiletries to strollers (pushchairs). While on the subject of theme parks, do take advantage of the child name tags often available at park information offices. Lost children can be speedily reunited with their family if the authorities know who to contact.

Perhaps the greatest danger to young children is the sun. Its rays can burn tender skin within a few minutes. If children are going to be exposed to the sunlight for any length of time, and that means sightseeing not just the beach, cover

them liberally with sunscreen. Hats are essential for small children, while older, fashion-conscious young can generally be induced to cover up with a baseball cap.

Climate

Florida winters, especially in the southern part of the state, are mild. Except in the northern regions, winter temperatures seldom drop below freezing; snow is a rare event anywhere in Florida. The shoulder seasons of spring and autumn generally provide the best weather of all, ideal for sightseeing and sports. Summer days can be real scorchers. The early part of the summer is typically hot and dry. As summer progresses, high humidity and a pattern of almost daily afternoon thunderstorms sets in.

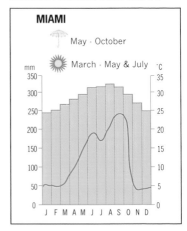

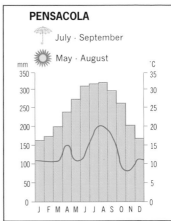

Crime

For the most part, Florida is as safe as anywhere in the world. Its notorious reputation is largely based on a handful of trouble spots such as the Overtown and Liberty City districts of Miami. These are definitely to be avoided. As in many cities, there are certain other areas which may be unsuitable for lone travellers, particularly women, and especially at night. Rather than take a chance, ask at hotel or motel desks if there are parts of the city which should not be visited for safety reasons, and follow this advice. When in doubt about an area do not explore alone; take a cab instead of walking.

Car travellers should take a few simple precautions which should prevent most problems.

- keep the doors locked when driving through unfamiliar areas.
- Ignore any attempts by civilians (including hitchhikers) to flag the car down.
- Lock all the doors and the trunk when parking the car, and ensure packages, cameras and other valuables are out of sight.

In the event of an accident, find a well-lit telephone – gas stations, stores or diners are recommended – and dial 911. This call is free, even at pay telephones, and will connect with law enforcement agencies within seconds.

Disabled Travellers

Facilities for the disabled are widespread in the US, and Florida is no exception. Public buildings are required to have some form of access for the wheelchair-bound, and many public buses are now supplied with wheelchair lifts. Local telephone directories list disabled support groups such as deaf service centres which can provide 'interpreters' who 'speak' American Sign Language, and information on TDDs (Telecommunication Devices for the Deaf) – telephones whereby deaf travellers can send and receive messages. The visually impaired, travelling with guide dogs, will find it relatively easy to take their dogs into attractions.

Most attractions accept disabled visitors, though viewing may be somewhat restricted and access to certain rides impossible or forbidden for safety reasons. Generally, efforts are made to provide tips, assistance and wheelchairs for disabled visitors. Walt Disney World offers a useful *Guidebook for Disabled Visitors*, and transport services with motorised platforms between its hotels and the parks.

Specially equipped hotel rooms are also available and should be booked well in advance. Avis, Hertz and National car rentals have a limited number of hand-controlled cars available. Again, early reservations are a must.

Useful addresses

Information about individual and group tours for disabled travellers is available from The Society for the Advancement of Travel for the Handicapped, 26 Court Street (Penthouse), Brooklyn NY 11242 (tel: (718) 858 5483). For a brochure and further details about services for disabled visitors to Florida, contact the Bureau of Domestic Tourism, Collins Building (Room 526), 107 Gains Street, Tallahassee, FL 32399–2000.

Immigration laws covering the entry qualifications for mentally handicapped travellers to the US should be checked out in advance with a travel agent or directly with the US Embassy before departure.

Hollywood Boulevard, WDW

TRAVEL FACTS

Drinking

The sale and consumption of alcohol in bars, restaurants, stores and other public places is restricted to adults aged 21 and over. It is also illegal to drink have an opened can or bottle of an alcoholic beverage in a car.

Driving

Renting a car Car rental in Florida is cheaper than anywhere else in the US. Car rental companies are located throughout the state, with concessions at major airports and some hotels. Car rental companies operating in Florida include:

Alamo, tel: (305) 522 0000/(800) 327 9633
Avis, tel: (305) 635 7777/(800) 331 1212
Budget, tel: (407) 423 4141/(800) 525 0700
Dollar, tel: (813) 289 4912/(800) 421 6868
Hertz tel: (407) 275 6430/(800) 654 3131
National, tel: (305) 638 5900/(800) 328 4567
Thrifty, tel: (305) 871 2277/(800) 376 2277
Value, tel: (305) 429 8300/(800) 327 2501

The minimum age limit for a driver's licence in Florida is 16; the minimum car rental limit is 21, though many companies impose the limit at 25. Arranging car rental in advance can

Sunshine Skyway, Tampa

prevent the latter restriction from ruining a holiday. Additions to the basic rental charge include CDW (Collision Damage Waiver), which covers damage to the vehicle, and a small state tax; both of these are charged on a daily basis. full insurance is also available. Credit cards are the preferred method of payment, otherwise a large cash deposit will be required. Major airlines and tour companies offer a wide range of good value fly-drive packages which conveniently tie up all these details in advance.

In general, foreign nationals can drive and hire a car in the US for a period of up to one year with a valid full driver's licence from their country of origin, provided they have held it for one year.

Before setting off in an unfamiliar rented car, check all the systems. Power steering is common even in the lowest range cars; be aware of central locking; and beware of automatic seat-belts which pinion unsuspecting drivers and front seat passengers to their seats as the doors shut.

Fuel Gas (petrol) is cheap. It is sold by the US gallon (3.8 litres), and rental cars generally run on unleaded gas available in three grades. At many self-service gas stations it is necessary to pay first (or leave a credit card with the cashier) to release the pump.

Rules and regulations

- Driving is on the right
- Speed limits on interstate roads and highways are set at 55mph, with some exceptions where the limit is raised to 65mph. In built-up areas limits vary between 20 and 40mph.
- In Florida it is legal to turn right on a red light unless posted otherwise. The car must come to a complete halt before turning. In built-up areas avoid the right-hand lane unless intending to turn right.
- Parking can be a problem. Look for designated metered parking places or find a car park. Illegally parked vehicles are ticketed and/or towed away with remarkable alacrity.

Electricity

The electrical current in the US is 110 volts AC; most sockets are designed for two-pronged plugs. Most European visitors will need an adaptor for their electrical appliances; these can be purchased from some electrical goods stores, or ask at the front desk of large tourist hotels.

Emergencies

Dial: 911

Emergency help is easily summoned in the US by the use of this single number. An operator or despatcher will connect calls to the appropriate emergency service including the police and fire departments, ambulance and medical services. To ensure the emergency services arrive as quickly as possible give accurate directions including the street name and nearest cross-section together with any further details to assist them.

On interstate highways, call boxes have been installed every quarter to half mile. These boxes allow callers to alert police, ambulance and mechanical services without dialling 911.

Etiquette

In general Floridians are so laid back and welcoming it is difficult to imagine how to offend them. Certainly the dress code for restaurants and social gatherings is informal to a degree, but this does not apply on the beach. Topless sun-bathing for women is actually illegal, though allowances are made for bare-breasted visitors on certain sections of the beach in more risqué resort areas such as Miami. Do not try this around the hotel swimming pool, or on a family beach in the Panhandle. Check out local reaction with a discreet enquiry at the hotel. Smokers in Florida will find the atmosphere a lot more friendly than in health-crazed California. Some restaurants, particularly of the family variety, will provide both smoking areas for addicts of the weed and non-smoking areas. Movie theatres, public transport, elevators and many public buildings are smoke-free zones.

Health

There is no national health system to provide medical cover for foreign citizens visiting the US, and private health care is exorbitantly expensive. Therefore, it is vital for foreign travellers to arrange health insurance before they leave home. Travel agents and tour companies can provide information and arrange a policy. Keep all insurance documents in a safe place.

For minor ailments, pharmacies (drug stores) are plentiful and usually open between 09.00hrs and 21.00hrs; most larger towns and cities have walk-in medical and dental clinics listed in the telephone directory. Sunburn is a common complaint, and a chronic case of it is agony. So do not under-estimate the sun's power reflected off sand and sea.

- Use plenty of sunscreen.
- Wear a hat.
- Restrict the time you spend in the sun, at least on the first few days.
- Drink plenty (not alcohol, which is dehydrating).

265

Hitch-hiking

The best advice is not to do it, and do not pick up hitch-hikers either. In legal terms, hitch-hiking is forbidden on toll roads and interstates, and throughout the Florida Keys.

Lost Property

For lost property in hotels, check with the front desk or hotel security. Cab companies and public transport telephone numbers are listed in local telephone directories. Lost or stolen travellers' cheques and credit cards should be reported to the issuing company immediately (keep a list of the numbers) and to the police. The police should also be informed of lost travel documents, and it is advisable to obtain a police report about valuable items for insurance.

Maps

Car rental companies are a good source of basic maps, but for extensive touring it is a good idea to pick up large scale Rand McNally motoring maps from a bookstore. (If lost in a city, a helpful rule of thumb is to remember **avenues** run north–south, and **streets** east–west.)

CONVERSION CHARTS

FROM	TO	MULTIPLY BY
Inches	Centimetres	2.54
Centimetres	Inches	0.3937
Feet	Metres	0.3048
Metres	Feet	3.2810
Yards	Metres	0.9144
Metres	Yards	1.0940
Miles	Kilometres	1.6090
Kilometres	Miles	0.6214
Acres	Hectares	0.4047
Hectares	Acres	2.4710
Gallons	Litres	4.5460
Litres	Gallons	0.2200
Ounces	Grams	28.35
Grams	Ounces	0.0353
Pounds	Grams	453.6
Grams	Pounds	0.0022
Pounds	Kilograms	0.4536
Kilograms	Pounds	2.205
Tons	Tonnes	1.0160
Tonnes	Tons	0.9842

MEN'S SUITS

UK	36	38	40	42	44	46	48
Rest of Europe	46	48	50	52	54	56	58
US	36	38	40	42	44	46	48

DRESS SIZES

UK	8	10	12	14	16	18
France	36	38	40	42	44	46
Italy	38	40	42	44	46	48
Rest of Europe	34	36	38	40	42	44
US	6	8	10	12	14	16

MEN'S SHIRTS

UK	14	14.5	15	15.5	16	16.5	17
Rest of Europe	36	37	38	39/40	41	42	43
US	14	14.5	15	15.5	16	16.5	17

MEN'S SHOES

UK	7	7.5	8.5	9.5	10.5	11
Rest of Europe	41	42	43	44	45	46
US	8	8.5	9.5	10.5	11.5	12

WOMEN'S SHOES

UK	4.5	5	5.5	6	6.5	7
Rest of Europe	38	38	39	39	40	41
US	6	6.5	7	7.5	8	8.5

Chambers of Commerce produce local maps, details of walking tours, bicycle routes and other points of interest; while state and national parks issue maps of scenic drives, hiking and interpretive trails on admission. The **Florida Division of Tourism** will provide state maps on application to the Department of Commerce, Division of Tourism, 107 W Gaines Street, Tallahassee, FL 32399–2000 (tel: (904) 487 1462), or at their offices abroad.

Media

Newspapers Most Florida communities produce weekly bulletins, while the main cities all have their own daily newspapers such as the *Miami Herald*, *Orlando Sentinel*, *Tampa Tribune* and Jacksonville's *Florida Times-Union*. The national daily *USA Today* is widely available from self-service news bins in every town; the *New York Times* and *Wall Street Journal* can be found at newsstands. A small selection of foreign newspapers may be available in tourist areas.

Television and radio There is hardly a motel or hotel room in the state without a television, though chi-chi bed and breakfasts tend not to permit them among the Victoriana. The least sophisticated offer no less than six to eight channels; if a hotel shells out for cable stations such as HBO or Cinemax, the choice increases dramatically. Among the main stations are CNN for continuous news reports, and ESPN for sports.

Radio stations abound with a wide range of formats such as hard or soft rock, easy listening and country-and-western, broken up by news, weather bulletins and commercials.

Money Matters

Foreign visitors should invest in US dollar travellers' cheques. Foreign currency is extremely difficult to exchange throughout the US. US travellers' cheques and major credit cards (American Express, Carte Blanche, Diners Club, Mastercard Visa) can be used for most transactions from buying gas to paying restaurant bills.

For non-US visitors here is a rundown on the currency. The dollar is divided into 100 cents. Dollar bills are all green ($1, 5, 10, 20, 50, 100) so look carefully before spending; coins are half a dollar (50 cents), a quarter (25 cents), a dime (10 cents), a nickel (5 cents), and one cent. Local taxes, which vary throughout the state, are levied on a range of items including clothes, books, sightseeing attractions, restaurant meals and accommodation. The tax may not appear on the price tag.

National Holiday
New Year's Day 1 January
Martin Luther King's Birthday 15 January
President's Day February (third Monday)
Good Friday
Memorial Day May (last Monday)
Independence Day 4 July
Labor Day September (first Monday)
Columbus Day October (second Monday)
Veterans' Day 11 November
Thanksgiving November (fourth Thursday)
Christmas Day 25 December

Opening Hours
Banks: Monday to Thursday 09.00–15.00hrs, Friday 09.00–17.00hrs.
Drugstores: daily 09.00–21.00hrs, some are open 24 hours.
Offices: Monday to Friday 08.00 or 09.00–17.00hrs or 18.00hrs.
Shops: Supermarkets, Monday to Saturday 08.00–21.00hrs, Sunday 08.00–19.00hrs; some are open 24 hours; downtown, Monday to Friday 10.00–18.00hrs, Saturday 10.00–13.00hrs or 18.00hrs; malls, Monday to Saturday 10.00–21.00hrs, Sunday 10.00–18.00hrs.

Organised Tours
With Florida's many miles of coastline and proximity to offshore islands, the most obvious opportunity for touring is taking a cruise. These range from two-hour cruises to week-long (or longer) trips to Bermuda, the Bahamas, and beyond.
Many of these longer trips depart

Street bar, Miami

from Miami, but shorter excursions – one-day, half-day, or evening cruises – depart from many places in the state. A few of the shorter trips offer casino gambling on board. For information about local cruises, contact the Visitors and Convention Bureau where you are staying.

Places of Worship
Most communities have churches of several denominations. Contact the local Chamber of Commerce.

Police
Law enforcement in the US is divided into three main jurisdictions: **City Police** within the urban areas; the **Sheriff** outside the city limits; and the **Highway Patrol**, who handle traffic accidents and offences beyond the city limits. Other agencies also deal with specific areas of law enforcement such as drugs and major criminal investigations.
In an emergency dial **911** for all services. Non-emergency police numbers are listed in local telephone directories.

Post Offices
Post office hours vary, but in most places are 09.00 to 16.30 or 17.00hrs on weekdays. Some are open on Saturday mornings. Postage stamps may be purchased at hotels and drugstores as well as post offices. Keep small change for stamp machines.
US Mail boxes are blue bins on legs on the sidewalk.

Interstate bus

Public Transport

The most popular method of transport on the ground is, without doubt, the car (see **Driving**). For more economical, though less convenient travel options, check out **Greyhound/Trailways**'s extensive bus network which connects some 148 Florida destinations. Skeleton **Amtrak** rail services call at Miami, Jacksonville, Orlando, Tallahassee, Tampa and 19 other stops. Amtrak, 60 NE Massachusetts Avenue, Washington, DC 20002 (tel: (202) 906 2002/(800) USA RAIL).Lines Inc, PO Box 660362, Dallas, TX 75266-0362 (tel: (214) 419 3905/(800) 531 5332.

Taxi cabs can be picked up at airports, bus and rail stations or from major hotels. They tend not to cruise the streets looking for fares.

Senior Citizens

Many hotels, resorts, restaurants and attractions offer seniors discounts or special rates. Be sure to ask, if no information is on display.

Sports and Recreation

Regional visitors' information bureaux can provide a wealth of information about sporting and recreational opportunities in their areas. For the statewide picture, contact:

Diving: Department of Commerce, Division of Tourism, Office of Sports Promotion, Collins Building (Suite 510E), Tallahassee, FL 32399–2000

(tel: (904) 488 8347).

Fishing and hunting: Game and Freshwater Commission, 620 S Meridian Street, Tallahassee, FL 32399–1600 (tel: (904) 488 1960).

Golf: Florida State Golf Association, PO Box 21177, Sarasota, FL 33585 (tel: (813) 921 5695).

Polo: Palm Beach Polo and Country Club, 13198 Forest Hill Boulevard, West Palm Beach, FL 33414 (tel: (407) 798 7000).

State Parks: Department of Natural Resources, Office of Communications, 3900 Commonwealth Boulevard, Tallahassee, FL 32399–3000 (tel: (904) 488 9872).

Tennis: Florida Tennis Association, 801 NE 167th Street (Suite 301), North Miami Beach, FL 33162 (tel: (305) 652 2866).

Student and Youth Travel

There are ten youth hostels in Florida, one each in Miami Beach, Daytona Beach, St Augustine and Panama City, and two each in Fort Lauderdale, Orlando and St Petersburg. For complete information on these facilities and their requirements, contact the **Florida American Youth Hostel**, PO Box 533097, Orlando, FL, 32853–3097 (tel: (407) 649 8761).

Telephones

Florida's telephone system is divided between half a dozen companies. Overseas visitors should note that some of these do not route overseas calls: AT&T and ITT do. The simplest solution is to call overseas collect via the operator (dial 0), who can also place telephone credit card calls (overseas credit cards are valid). To dial direct from a coin box (dial 011 + country code + area code + telephone number) bring at least $6-worth of quarters, dimes and nickels. This is an appalling juggling operation. Calling from a hotel room will cost more, but it can be worth the time and energy saved.

Codes Florida is divided into four area codes: north Florida, 904; west central, 813; east central, 407; extreme south, 305. To call within the area code dial 1+ telephone number; to call outside the area code dial 1 + area code + number. All 800 (toll free) numbers must be prefixed with 1, ie 1 + 800 + telephone number. To call home from anywhere in Florida, you will need first to dial 011 to get the international operator. Then dial the access code for the country: 44 for the UK, 353 for Eire, 61 for Australia, 64 for New Zealand.

Time
Florida has two time zones. Most of the state operates on Eastern Standard Time (GMT −5), while the Panhandle region west of the Apalachicola River keeps Central Standard Time (GMT−6). All clocks go forward one hour for Daylight Saving between the first Sunday in April and the last in October.

Tipping
The standard tip for a restaurant bill or taxi ride is 15 per cent; 10–20 per cent for barbers and hairdressers; 50 cents per bag for the bellman.

Tourist Information
Most towns throughout Florida boast at least a Chamber of Commerce, while cities offer full-blown Convention and Visitors Bureauxwith visitors' enquiries. For information in advance of travelling, contact the Florida Division of Tourism, USTTA (US Travel & Tourism Administration) or any of the main regional offices listed here:
Florida Division of Tourism, (US) 107 W Gaines Street, 566 Collins Building, Tallahassee, FL 32399–2000 (tel: (904) 488 7598); (Canada) 150 W Bloor Street, Suite 310, Toronto, Ontario, M5S 2X9 (tel: (416) 928 3111); (UK/Europe) 18–24 Westbourne Grove, London W2 5RH(tel: (071) 727 1661).
USTTA, (Australia) Suite 6101, MLC Centre, King and Castlereagh Streets, Sydney, NSW 2000 (tel: (612) 233 4666).
Cocoa Beach Area Chamber of Commerce (Space Coast), 400 Fortenberry Road, Merritt Island, FL 32952 (tel: (407) 459 2200).
Destination Daytona, 126 E Orange Avenue, PO Box 910, Daytona, FL 32115 (tel: (904) 255 0415).

Greater Fort Lauderdale Convention and Visitors Bureau, 200 E Las Olas Boulevard, Suite 1500, Fort Lauderdale, FL 33301 (tel: (305) 765 4466).
Greater Miami Convention and Visitors Bureau, 701 Brickell Avenue, Suite 2700, Miami, FL 33131 (tel: (305) 539 3000).
Jacksonville and its Beaches Convention and Visitors Bureau, 6 E Bay Street, Suite 200, Jacksonville, FL 32202 (tel: (904) 353 9736).
Florida Keys and Key West, PO Box 114–7, Key West, FL 33041 (tel: (305) 296 3811).
Lee County Convention and Visitors Bureau, PO Box 2445, Fort Myers, FL 33902 (tel: (813) 335 2631).
Naples Area Chamber of Commerce, 3620 N Tamiami Trail, Naples, FL 33942 (tel: (813) 261 6141).
Orlando/Orange County Convention and Visitors Bureau, 7208 Sand Lake Road, Suite 300, Orlando, FL 32819 (tel: (407) 363 5800).
Palm Beach County Convention and Visitors Bureau, 1555 Palm Beach Lakes Boulevard, Suite 204, West Palm Beach, FL 33401(tel: (407) 471 3995).
Panama City Beach Convention and Visitors Bureau, PO Box 9473, 12015 Front Beach Road, Panama City Beach, FL 32417 (tel: (904) 233 6503).
Pensacola Convention and Visitors Information Center, 1401 E Gregory Street, Pensacola, FL 32501 (tel: (904) 434 1234).
Pinellas Suncoast Tourist Development Council, Florida Suncoast Dome, Suite A, St Petersburg, FL 33705 (tel: (813) 892 7892).
St Augustine and St Johns County Chamber of Commerce, 1 Riberia Street, St Augustine, FL 32084 (tel: (904) 829 5681).
Sarasota Convention and Visitors Bureau, 655 N Tamiami Trail, Sarasota, FL 34236 (tel: (813) 957 1877).
Tampa/Hillsborough Convention and Visitors Association, 111 Madison Street, Suite 1010, Tampa, FL 33602 (tel: (813) 826 8358)).

DIRECTORY

Accommodation

Budget motel or deluxe resort? Cosy B&B or self-catering apartment? The choice of accommodation in Florida is enormous, varied and extraordinarily good value.

You can save money by visiting Florida out of season (April to December) when accommodation prices plummet by as much as half. The exception is the Panhandle and northern East Coast, the only bit of Florida to feel the cold in winter, where prices are lower in October to May. Here, for visitors from abroad, is a run-down on some of the accommodation options and facilities on offer.

Florida accommodations are generally spacious with room for up to four people in some double rooms. There is often no charge for children under 18 sharing with their parents.

Another popular option is self-catering accommodation. Rooms supplied with cooking facilities are known as 'efficiencies' and can be found in most budget or moderate hotels and motels. Self-catering apartments (condominiums or 'condos') are an excellent solution for families, though most have a minimum stay of three to seven days. Families should also look out for hotel resorts. A 'resort' in local terms does not mean a town. Instead it refers to the facilities provided by a hotel, motel or condo property, such as a range of different accommodations, sports facilities, games rooms, health club and a choice of dining. Many resorts now offer special children's programmes as well.

Restaurants

Florida's cuisine, like its culture, is diverse. The basic ingredients – seafood, prime steak and ribs, fresh vegetables and exotic fruits – are all produced locally, but cooking styles can be worlds apart. Bahamian and Creole cooking flourishes in the Keys; Cuban cuisine, based in Miami and Tampa, has outposts throughout the state; while European cuisines from French to Greek all find a niche in Florida's numerous eateries. There is *nouvelle cuisine* New American-style, spicy Cajun food, and down home country cooking with a distinctive Southern flavour. The good news is that it will not cost a fortune to try out any of them.

Dining out in Florida is a casual affair. Even top restaurants which prefer gentlemen in jackets do not expect ties. Families are welcome just about everywhere, with special children's portions a regular feature on most menus, and money-saving 'early bird' specials (usually served between 17.00 and 19.00hrs) especially popular.

MIAMI

Accommodation

Expensive

Cavalier, 1320 Ocean Drive, Miami Beach (tel: (305) 534 2135/(800) 338 9076). Art Deco district gem (see also **Art Deco Hotels** under **Moderate**).

Doral Ocean Beach Resort, 4833 Collins Avenue, Miami Beach (tel: (305) 532 3600/(800) FOR-ATAN). 420-room beachfront spread with watersports, fitness centre, restaurants and free transport to sister resorts **Doral Saturnia International Spa** and: **Doral Resort and Country Club**, 4400 NW 87th Avenue (tel: (305) 592 2000). Superb complex with 550 rooms and suites, golf, tennis, Olympic pool, restaurants, nightclub, child care.

Fontainebleau Hilton Resort and Spa, 4441 Collins Avenue, Miami Beach (tel: (305) 538 2000/(800) 548 8886).

Monster jewel in Miami's crown. 1,226 rooms and suites on 20 acres of oceanfront; tennis, watersports, 6 restaurants, nightclubs.

Mayfair House, 3000 Florida Avenue, Coconut Grove (tel: (305) 441 0000/(800) 341 0809). 48 individual suites with private balconies around an exclusive shopping mall; rooftop pool, bar, restaurant and nightclub.

Sheraton River House (Miami Airport), 3900 NW 21st Street (tel: (305) 871 3800/(800) 325 3535). 408 rooms/suites; wide range of facilities from restaurant and nightclub to tennis, pool, and saunas.

Sonesta Beach Hotel, 350 Ocean Drive, Key Biscayne (tel: (305) 361 2021/(800) 343 7170). 278 rooms and suites in luxurious beachfront resort; tennis, watersports, free children's entertainment programme.

Moderate

Airport Regency, 1000 NW LeJeune Road (tel: (305) 441 1600/(800) 432 1192). 175 rooms; tropical décor; facilities include pool, restaurant, nightclub.

Art Deco Hotels: Cardozo, Carlyle, Leslie, 1320 Ocean Drive, Miami Beach (tel: (305) 534 2135/(800) 338 9076). Three archetypal Deco hotels, restored and furnished in period style. Ocean views, complimentary breakfast, terrace café.
(See also **Cavalier** under **Expensive**.)

Bay Harbor Inn, 9660 E Bay Harbor Drive, Bay Harbor Islands/Miami Beach (tel: (305) 868 4141). 36 attractive rooms/suites in waterfront location; pool, good restaurants, breakfast.

Best Western Miami Airport, 1550 NW LeJeune Road (tel: (305) 871 2345/(800) 528 1234). 207 rooms/suites. Good facilities include pool, child care nursery, restaurant.

Deauville Hotel and Tennis Club, 6701 Collins Avenue, Miami Beach (tel: (305) 865

DIRECTORY

DIRECTORY

8511/(800) 327 6656). 560 rooms/suites in recently renovated oceanfront complex; pool, tennis, watersports, restaurants nightclub, child care nursery.

Hampton Inn, 2500 Brickell Avenue (tel: (305) 854 2070/(800) HAMPTON). 69 rooms by entrance to Key Biscayne; pool, breakfast, child care. Good location for sightseeing.

Hotel Place St Michel, 162 Alcazar Avenue, Coral Gables (tel: (305) 444 1666/(800) 247 8526). Charming 30-room hotel on the expensive side of moderate. Ceiling fans, antiques, award-winning restaurant.

Palms on the Ocean Resort, 9449 Collins Avenue, Miami Beach (tel: (305) 865 3551/(800) 327 6644). 170 rooms/suites on ocean near Bal Harbor; pool, fitness, restaurant.

Park Central, 640 Ocean Drive, Miami Beach (tel: (305) 538 1611). 76 rooms in Art Deco classic; restaurant, complimentary breakfast, child care.

Budget

Budgetel Inn, 3501 NW LeJeune Road (tel: (305) 871 1777/(800) 528 1234). Modern motel near airport; 150 rooms and suites with efficiencies; pool, breakfast, airport transport.

Days Inn - Miami Airport, 3401 LeJeune Road (tel: (305) 871 4221/(800) 325 2525). 155 rooms; pool, restaurant, airport transport.

Golden Sands Hotel, 6901 Collins Avenue, Miami Beach (tel: (305) 866 8734/(800) 932 0333). 102 rooms/efficiencies on ocean; pool, restaurant; close to shopping, dining.

Howard Johnson Port of Miami, 1100 Biscayne Boulevard (tel: (305) 358 3080). 115 rooms in central Downtown location; pool, restaurant.

Inn on the Bay, 1819 79th Street Causeway (tel: (305) 865 7100/(800) 351 2131). 120 rooms in friendly, family B&B hotel with

marina between Miami Beach and mainland; pool.

Miami Beach Youth Hostel, 1438 Washington Avenue, Miami Beach (tel: (305) 534 2988). Beach bargain, 80 rooms in the Art Deco district.

Seabrook Resort Hotel and Apartments, 9401 Collins Avenue, Miami Beach (tel: (305) 866 5446). 90 rooms/efficiencies by beach; pool, restaurant, close to shops.

Restaurants
Expensive

Chef Allen's, 19088 NE 29th Avenue, North Miami Beach (tel: (305) 935 2900). New American 'spa cuisine' at its titillating best; elegant Decoesque furnishings.

Dominique's, Alexander Hotel, 5225 Collins Avenue, Miami Beach (tel: (305) 865 6500). Sumptuous surroundings, dramatic presentation, classic/exotic menu, outdoor area.

Grand Café, Grand Bay Hotel, 2669 S Bayshore Drive, Coconut Grove (tel: (305) 858 9600). Elegant dining room, award-winning international cuisine, seafood specialities, al fresco.

Le Pavillon, Hotel Inter-Continental, 100 Chopin Plaza, Miami (tel: (305) 577 1000). Distinguished continental cuisine, innovative specials, harpist for musical accompaniment.

Mark's Place, 2286 NE 123rd Street, North Miami (tel: (305) 893 6888). Pretty setting with plenty of greenery; inspired New American menu, fresh fish, warm salads.

Mayfair Grill, Mayfair House Hotel, 3000 Florida Avenue, Coconut Grove (tel: (305) 441 0000).

Intimate, low lit dining room; well-constructed, appealing New American cuisine.

St Michel, Hotel Place St Michel, 162 Alcazar Avenue, Coral Gables (tel: (305) 444 1666). Enchanting Old World dining room; deliciously tempting French/American cuisine.

Moderate

Casa Juancho, 2436 SW 8th Street, Little Havana (tel: (305) 642 2542). Authentic Spanish cuisine in rustic surroundings; entertainment nightly.

Chart House, 51 Chart House Drive, Coconut Grove (tel: (305) 856 9741). Nautical décor, waterfront location; seafood, steaks and salad bar.

Crawdaddy's, 1 Washington Avenue, Miami Beach (tel: (305) 673 1708). Fun spot stuffed with Victoriana; bay views; large and eclectic menu.

Firehouse Four, 1000 S Miami Avenue, Miami (tel: (305) 379 1923). Renovated 1923 fire station; broad menu, entertainment, outdoor seating area.

Giovanni's, 801 S Bayshore Drive, Miami (tel: (305) 374 8066). Italian specialities and warm welcome in smart downtown location.

Joe's Stone Crab, 227 Biscayne Street, Miami Beach (tel: (305) 673 0365). Seafood institution; informal atmosphere; expect queues. (Closed June to early October.)

Las Tapas, Bayside Marketplace, 401 Biscayne Boulevard, Miami (tel: (305) 372 2737). Spanish décor, paella a speciality, outdoor seating area.

Monty's Bayshore, 2550 S Bayshore Drive, Coconut Grove (tel: (305) 858 1431). Steaks, seafood, snacks; raw bar, restaurant and entertainment.

Rusty Pelican, 3201 Rickenbacker Causeway, Key Biscayne (tel: (305) 361 3818). Panoramic views from the rustic bayside dining room; fresh seafood specialities, steaks.

Señor Frog's, 3008 Grand Avenue, Coconut Grove (tel: (305) 448 0999). Copious Mexican food; mariachi band.

Stefano's, 24 Crandon Boulevard, Key Biscayne (tel: (305) 361 7007). Fresh pasta, seafood and northern Italian specialities; dancing in nightclub.

Trattoria Pampered Chef, 3145 Commodore Plaza, Coconut Grove (tel: (305) 567 0104). Convivial candle-lit spot serving creative pasta dishes.

Two Dragons, Sonesta Beach Resort, 350 Ocean Drive, Key Biscayne (tel: (305) 361 2021). Cantonese, Mandarin and Szechuan cuisine in pretty Oriental surroundings.

Victor's Café, 2340 SW 32nd Avenue, Coral Gables (tel: (305) 445 1313). Traditional Cuban cuisine served in elegant, Old Havana colonial style.

Zanzibar Café, 3468 Main Highway, Coconut Grove (tel: (305) 444 0244). Trendy sidewalk café on the main drag; soups, salads, fresh fish.

Budget:
Benihana, 1665 NE 79th Street, North Bay Billage (tel: (305) 866 2786). Sushi and American favourites with a specialJapanese twist.

Big Fish, 55 SW Miami Avenue, Miami (tel: (305) 372 3725). Small menu, fresh fish; outdoors and informal.

Bijan's Fort Dallas Restaurant & Raw Bar, 64 SE 4th Street, Miami (tel: (305) 381 7778). Seafood by the Miami River; weekend entertainment.

Café Tu Tu Tango, CocoWalk, 3015 Grand Avenue, Coconut Grove (tel: (305) 448 6942). Pizza, chicken wings, steak; outdoor seating, early bird specials.

Chichuahua Charlie's, 1580 Washington Avenue, Miami Beach (tel: (305) 531 9082). Friendly Mexican joint; award-winning *fajitas*.

Granny Feelgood's, 190 SE First Avenue, Miami (tel: (305) 358 6233). Terrific vegetarian menu with some chicken dishes.

La Carreta, 3632 SW 8th Street, Little Havana (tel: (305) 446 4915). Cuban specials served in casual, family atmosphere.

News Café, 800–804 Ocean Drive, Miami Beach (tel: (305) 538 6397). Hip café-society hang-out on the Beach; great brunches.

Waldorf Café, Waldorf Towers Hotel, 860 Ocean Drive, Miami Beach (tel: (305) 531 4612). People-watching a speciality; hamburgers, pizza, pasta and salads in the Art Deco district.

Wolfie's, 2038 Collins Avenue, Miami Beach (tel: (305) 538 6626). Landmark Jewish deli-restaurant with mile-high bagels.

KEYS AND EVERGLADES

Accommodation
Expensive
Banyan Resort, 3444 N Roosevelt Boulevard, Key West (tel: (305) 296 7593/(800) 624 2401). 38 suites/efficiencies in 8 buildings, including 4 Victorian houses; downtown location; gorgeous gardens, pools, bar, breakfast.

Cheeca Lodge, MM 82.5, Islamorada (tel: (305) 664 4651/(800) 327 2888). 203 units in famous resort complex with golf, tennis, fishing, watersports, fine dining, and children's activities.

Curry Mansion Inn, 512 Caroline Street, Key West (tel: (305) 294 5349). 15 enchanting rooms in historic house and modern annexe off Duval. Home-cooked breakfasts; tiny pool, but use of facilities at:

Pier House, 1 Duval Street, Key West (tel: (305) 294 9541/(800) 432 3414). Rambling, relaxing 101-room hotel; beach area, pool, convivial bars, five restaurants and terrace café.

Sheraton Key Largo Resort, MM 97, Key Largo (tel: (305) 852 5553/(800) 826 1006). 200 attractive rooms and suites on private bayside beach. Boat trips, fishing, watersports, pools, tennis, three restaurants, children's activities.

Moderate
Chesapeake Motel, MM 83.5, Islamorada (tel: (305) 664 4662/(800) 338 3395). 65 rooms/efficiencies; beach, freshwater pool, tropical gardens and boat dock.

Flamingo Lodge, Everglades National Park (tel: (305) 253 2241). 102 modern rooms and cottages; facilities include pool, camper's store, marina, restaurant.

Kingsail Resort Motel, MM 50.5, Marathon (tel: (305) 743 5246/(800) 423 7474). 43 rooms/efficiencies; pool, boat ramp, dive/fishing charters.

Largo Lodge Motel, MM 101.5, Key Largo (tel: (305) 451 0424/(800) IN THE SUN).Six efficiencies set in a tropical garden; airconditioning, screened porches.

Marina del Mar Resort and Marina, MM100, Key Largo (tel: (305) 451 0424/(800) 253 3483). 130 well-equipped rooms, suites and villas in bayside resort and oceanside marina. Dive packages, dining and dancing.

Ragged Edge Resort, MM 86.5, Treasure Harbor Drive, Islamorada (tel: (305) 852 5389). 10 rooms/efficiencies with tropical décor on ocean; pool, marina, fishing pier.

South Beach Oceanfront Motel, 508 South Street,

DIRECTORY

Key West (tel: (305) 296 5611/(800) 354 4455). 49 pleasant rooms at the southern end of Duval. Pier, small public beach, use of facilities at:

Southernmost Motel, 1319 Duval Street, Key West (tel: (305) 296 6577/(800)354 4455). 127 rooms in tropical setting. Daytime snacks and drinks from poolside tiki bar; close to restaurants and nightlife.

Sugarloaf Lodge, MM 17, Sugarloaf Key (tel: (305) 745 3211). 55 rooms in 120-acre island complex; pool, mini-golf, tennis, pet dolphin show.

Budget
Econo Lodge Resort, MM 3 Key West (tel: (305) 294 5511/(800) KEY WEST). 43-room motel; off-season bargains (but expensive in the season); pool, tennis, family restaurant.

Gilbert's Resort, MM 107.9, Key Largo (tel: (305) 451 1133). 36 units by marina; pool, restaurant.

Grandma Newton's Bed & Breakfast, 40 NW 5th Avenue, Florida City (tel: (305) 247 4413). Five comfortable rooms; enormous breakfasts. Close to Everglades National Park.

Harbor Lights Motel, MM 85, Islamorada (tel: (305) 664 3611/(800) 327 7070). Budget corner of **Holiday Isle Resort**, 33 rooms/efficiencies on ocean; good facilities.

Island Bay Resort, MM92.5, Tavernier (tel: (305) 852 4087). eight small guesthouse/efficiencies in friendly complex; dive boat and dock.

Key West Hostel, 718 South Street, Key West (tel: (305) 296 5719). International youth hostel; central.

Restaurants
Expensive
Atlantic's Edge, Cheeca Lodge Resort, MM 82.5, Islamorada (tel: (305) 664 4651). Elegant semi-circular dining room on the ocean with award-wining cuisine and fine wines.

Louie's Backyard, 700 Waddell Avenue, Key West (tel: (305) 294 1061). Intriguing and innovative menu with local specialities featuring a Spanish-Caribbean twist; eclectic art works on the walls; chic diners.

Marker 88, MM 88, Plantation Key (tel: (305) 852 9315). Spectacular sunset views accompany adventurous seafood dishes, steaks (including alligator) and wonderful salads.

Pier House, 1 Duval Street, Key West (tel: (305) 296 4600). Bayside setting for gourmet New American cuisine. Local seafood with fruits and baby vegetables or plain grilled; non-fish choices; perfect Key lime pie.

Snook's Bayside, MM 100, Key Largo (tel: (305) 451 3070). Fine dining on Florida Bay; this local favourite offers a chance to dress up a bit. Mainly seafood.

Moderate
Bagatelle, 115 Duval Street, Key West (tel: (305) 296 6609). Historic 'conch' architecture and interesting Caribbean specials on the main drag.

Buttery, 1208 Simonton Street, Key West (tel: (305) 294 0717). Innovative New American cuisine in a collection of attractively quirky dining rooms.

Coconuts Lounge, Marina del Mar Resort, MM 100, Key Largo (tel: (305) 451 4107). Steaks, seafood and dancing nightly on the waterfront.

Fish House Restaurant & Seafood Market, MM 102.4, Key Largo (tel: (305) 451 HOOK). Home-made conch specialities and a singing waiter.

Flamingo Lodge, Everglades National Park, Flamingo (tel: (305) 253 2241). Closed May–October. Steak, ribs, seafood; overlooks Florida Bay.

Green Turtle Inn, MM 81.5, Islamorada (tel: (305) 664 9031). Local favourite since 1947. Great home-baking (Key lime pie) and chowders. Often busy.

Kelsey's, MM 48.5, Faro Blanco Bayside, Marathon (tel: (305) 743 9018). Dockside views of the Gulf; superb fresh, locally caught seafood.

Pepe's, 806 Caroline Street, Key West (tel: (305) 294 7192). Little pine-clad diner with garden. Big breakfasts, daily specials, barbecues.

Rod & Gun Club, 200 Riverside Drive, Everglades City (tel: (813) 695 2101). Old hunting and fishing lodge by the water. Dine on veranda from small but well-prepared menu.

Whale Harbor Inn, MM 84, Islamorada (tel: (305) 664 4959). Staggering all-you-can-eat buffet, raw bar, grill, nightly entertainment.

Budget
A&B Lobster House, 700 Front Street, Key West (tel: (305) 294 2535). Local seafood institution overlooking the harbour marinas.

Baiamonte's, 1223 White Street, Key West (tel: (305) 296 2200). Popular budget spot; seafood and Italian specials, submarine sandwiches.

Coral Grill, MM 83.5, Islamorada (tel: (305) 664 4803). Restaurant dining downstairs and generous buffet upstairs; good for families.

Ganim's Country Kitchen, MM 99.6, Key Largo (tel: (305) 451 2895). Home-cooking, monster subs, lunchtime specials.

Half Shell Raw Bar, Land's End Village, Key West (tel: (305) 294 7496). Oysters, fish sandwiches and specials; overlooking the docks.

Herbie's, MM 50.5, Marathon (tel: (305) 743

6373). Informal, friendly budget find; great spicy chowder.

Mac's Bar-B-Q, MM 101.5, Key Largo (tel: (305) 451 9954). Hickory-smoked chicken and ribs, steaks, fresh seafood and Key lime pie.

Mrs Mac's Kitchen, MM 99.8, Key Largo (tel: (305) 451 3722). International beer-obilia galore; home-cooked specials such as meatloaf and chilli.

Shuckers Raw Bar & Grill, 1415 15th Street, Marathon (tel: (305) 743 8686). Nautical décor to match fishy menu; great value fish baskets.

Turtle Kraals, Land's End Village, Key West (tel: (305) 294 2640). Noisy, popular dockside bar-restaurant; turtles for viewing only.

Woody's Italian Gardens Pizza, MM 82, Key Largo (tel: (305) 664 4335). Pizza, pasta and subs for filling up the family.

CENTRAL

Accommodation
Expensive
Buena Vista, Palace, Lake Buena Vista (tel: (407) 827 2727). 1,028 deluxe rooms; pool, fitness, golf, tennis, restaurants, transport to WDW.

Grand Cypress, 60 Grand Cypress Boulevard, Orlando (tel: (407) 239 4600). 750-room resort with tennis, golf, equestrian and fitness centres, nature reserve.

The Peabody, 9801 International Drive, Orlando (tel: (407) 352 4000). 891 luxurious rooms; fine restaurants, pool, tennis, fitness.

WDW Disney Inn, **Grand Floridian Beach Resort**, **Polynesian Resort** (Magic Kingdom), **Dolphin**, **Caribbean Beach Resort**, **Swan**, **Yacht** and **Beach Club Resorts** (Epcot), Central Reservations, Box 10100, Lake Buena Vista, FL 32830 (tel: (407) 934 7639/(800) 647 7900). Spacious family rooms, excellent facilities , transport to parks.

Moderate
Cabot Lodge Bed and Breakfast, 3726 SW 40th Boulevard, Gainesville (tel: (904) 375 2400/(800) 331 8215). 208 comfortable modern rooms off Interstate 75; pool, complimentary breakfast.

Chalet Suzanne, off US27, Lake Wales (tel: (813) 676 6011). 30 rooms in cute and quirky country inn on lake. Good restaurant.

Homewood Suites, 3100 Parkway Boulevard, Kissimmee (tel: (407) 396 2229). 112 attractive suites (sleep 4) with efficiencies close to WDW; pool, fitness centre, shop, breakfast.

Radisson Inn Maingate, 7501 W Irlo Bronson Highway, Kissimmee (tel: (407) 396 1400). 580 pleasant rooms 1 mile from WDW; pool, tennis, health club, family restaurant.

Ramada Resort Maingate East at the Parkway, 2900 Parkway, Kissimmee (tel: (407) 396 7000/(800) 225 3939). 716 spacious rooms; pool, spa, tennis, deli, restaurant.

Residence Inn by Marriott, 4001 SW 13th Street, Gainesville (tel: (904) 371 2101/(800) 331 3131). 80 suites with efficiencies and complimentary breakfast; central location; swimming pool.

Residence Inn by Marriott - on Lake Cecile, 4786 W Irlo Bronson Memorial Highway, Kissimmee (tel: (407) 396 2056/(800) 648 7408). 160 roomy efficiency suites on lakeside close to WDW; watersports, tennis, breakfast, grocery service.

Seven Sisters, 820 SE Fort King Street, Ocala (tel: (904) 867 1170). B & B in lovely Queen Anne house; five antique-filled rooms.

WDW Caribbean Beach Resort, Port Orleans, Dixie Landings, Central Reservations, Box 10100, Lake Buena Vista, FL 32830 (tel: (407) 934 7639). Caribbean/Deep South themed resort hotels; great Disney facilities at moderate prices.

Budget
Comfort Inn, Lake Buena Vista (tel: (407) 239 7300). 604 rooms close to WDW; pool, restaurant.

Condo Care Vacation Rentals Inc, 250 N Orange Avenue/Suite 820, Orlando, FL 32801 (tel: (407) 633 9474). 2–3-bedroom fully-equipped villas (sleep 6–8) close to Orlando area sights.

CRS - Orlando Budget Hotels Reservation Service, 300 Wilshire Boulevard/Suite 225, Orlando, FL 32730 (tel: (800) 548 3311).

Econo Lodge Maingate Hawaiian Resort, 4311 W Irlo Bronson Memorial Highway, Kissimmee (tel: (407) 396 7100/(800) 826 0778). 173 rooms with tropical theme; close to WDW; pool.

Howard Johnson Downtown, 304 W Colonial Drive, Orlando (tel: (407) 843 8700/(800) 826 1365). 273 rooms in chain motel with personal touch; swimming pool, good family restaurant.

Langford Resort Hotel, 300 E New England Avenue, Winter Park (tel: (407) 644 3400). 214 very pleasant rooms just north of Orlando; pool, golf, health club, restaurant. Bargain.

Larson's Lodge, 2009 W Vine Street, Kissimmee (tel: (407) 846 2713/(800) 624 5905). 212 pretty rooms/suites 10 minutes from WDW; pools, tennis, family restaurant, playground; also 128-room **Larson's Lodge - Maingate**, 6075 W Irlo Bronson, Memorial Highway, Kissimmee (tel: (407) 396 6100/(800) 327 9074). with similar facilities.

DIRECTORY

Orlando International Youth Hostel, 227 N Eola Drive, Orlando (tel: (407) 843 8888). Shared/single rooms in downtown location; kitchen, pool.

WDW Fort Wilderness Resort and Campground, Central Reservations/Box 10100, Lake Buena Vista, FL 32830 (tel: (407) 934 7639). 407 fully-equipped trailers (sleep 4–6). Woodland setting; great facilities.

Restaurants

Expensive
Chalet Suzanne, off US 27, Lake Wales (tel: (813) 676 6011). Charming, eccentric country inn with tempting small menu of chef's specials.

Chefs de France, Epcot Center, Walt Disney World (tel: (407) 824 4000). Classic French menu devised by three of France's top chefs: Verge, Bocuse and Lenôtre. Elegant surroundings in the French pavilion; a real treat.

Dux, Peabody Hotel, 9801 International Drive, Orlando (tel: (407) 352 4000). Sumptuous gourmet restaurant with innovative menu; fine cellar.

Empress Room, Empress Lilly, Walt Disney World Village, Buena Vista (tel: (407) 828 3900). Plush Victorian dining room on permanently moored riverboat; very popular (make reservations well in advance).

Maison et Jardin, 430 S Wymore Road, Altamonte Springs (tel: (407) 862 4410). Romantic French restaurant in lovely surroundings; revered by Orlando's gourmet connoisseurs.

Moderate
Bubble Room, 1351 S Orlando Avenue, Maitland (tel: (407) 628 3331). Kitsch treasure trove with emphasis on fun and monumental portion control.

Cheyenne Saloon, Church Street Station, 129 W Church Street, Orlando (tel: (407) 422 2434). Generous barbecue platters in Wild West setting.

Clewiston Inn, 108 Royal Palm Avenue, Clewiston (tel: (813) 983 8151). Fine old Southern-style dining room in historic inn; local specials.

Gary's Duck Inn, 3974 S Orange Blossom Trail, Orlando (tel: (407) 843 0270). Nautical décor and seafood menu, which includes fresh snapper and crab.

Fiddler's, University Center Hotel, 1535 SW Archer Road, Gainesville (tel: (904) 371 3333). Fine continental cuisine, great rooftop views.

Fort Liberty, 5260 US 192 East, Kissimmee (tel: (407) 351 5151). Themed four-course dinner with Wild West show and trading post.

Ming Court, 9188 International Drive, Orlando (tel: (407) 351 9988). Chinese food in attractive Oriental surroundings; dancing.

Mitsukoshi, Epcot Center, Walt Disney World (tel: (407) 824 4000). Watch the preparations and sample traditional Japanese cuisine.

Outback, Buena Vista Palace Hotel, 1900 Buena Vista Drive, Buena Vista (tel: (407) 827 3430). Luxuriant greenery, waiters in nifty bush suits; grilled steaks and seafood.

Royal Orleans, 8445 International Drive, Orlando (tel: (407) 352 8200). Superb Cajun cuisine; Louisiana blue crabs and crawfish flown in daily.

Yearling Cross Creek, CR 325, Cross Creek (tel: (904) 466 3033). Cracker cooking as recorded by literary type Marjorie Kinnan Rawlings.

Budget
Cattle Ranch, 6129 Old Winter Garden Road, Orlando (tel: (407) 298 7334). Vast steaks sizzled over orange wood in cowboy-style tourist-free zone.

Commander Ragtime's Midway Grill, Church Street Station, 129 W Church Street, Orlando (tel: (407) 422 2434). Hamburgers, fast food snacks and video games; popular with the young.

Garden Café, Bok Tower Gardens, Lake Wales (tel: (813) 676 1408). Soups, sandwiches and snacks from terrace-café set in ravishing gardens.

Hard Rock Café, Universal Studios, 5401 Kirkman Road, Orlando (tel: (407) 363 ROLL). Hamburgers, barbecue and salads in guitar-shaped diner.

Johnny's Pizza Palace, 4909 Lake Underhill Road, Orlando (tel: (407) 277 3452). Pizzas of every description, pasta and sandwiches.

Numero Uno, 2499 S Orange Avenue, Orlando (tel: (407) 841 3840). Hearty Cuban specialities such as pork and beans in busy, friendly dining room.

Ponderosa Steak House, 7598 W Irlo Bronson Memorial Highway, Kissimmee (tel: (407) 396 7721). Family restaurant, breakfast buffet, salad bar.

TGI Friday's, 6426 Carrier Drive, Orlando (tel: (407) 345 8822). Popular and lively; big menu; happy hour.

Wheeler's Goody Café, 13 S Monroe Avenue, Arcadia (tel: (813) 494 3909). Cracker country cooking; steaks, pies, cold drinks and sandwiches.

GOLD COAST

Accommodation

Expensive
Boca Raton Resort & Club, 501 E Camino Real, Boca Raton (tel: (407) 395 3000). 963 deluxe rooms in superb Mizner/modern creation;

golf, pools, tennis, restaurants,

Breakers, 1 S County Road, Palm Beach (tel: (407) 655 6611). Fabulous 528-room historic landmark on the ocean; golf, tennis, fine dining.

Colony Hotel, 155 Hammon Avenue, Palm Beach (tel: (407) 655 5430). 94 classy rooms between beach and Worth Avenue; pool, fitness, restaurant.

Marriott's Harbor Beach Resort, 3030 Holiday Drive, Ft Lauderdale (tel: (305) 525 4000). 660 chic rooms on the beach; attractive setting and excellent facilities.

Palm Beach Polo and Country Club, 13198 Forest Hill Boulevard, West Palm Beach (tel: (407) 798 7000). Golf and tennis packages with villa accommodation; superb facilities set in 2,200-acre estate; fine dining.

Moderate
Best Western Sea Spray Inn, 123 Ocean Avenue, West Palm Beach (tel: (407) 844 0233). 50 rooms/efficiencies on beach; pool, tennis, restaurants, etc.

Hollywood Beach Resort Hotel, 101 N Ocean Drive, Hollywood (tel: (305) 921 0990/(800) 331 6103). 360 rooms/studios with Deco touches; pool, tennis, fitness, restaurants, shopping, child care.

Howard Johnson Oceanside, 930 US1, Juno Beach (tel: (407) 626 1531). 108 rooms/suites (some efficiencies) near beach; pool, restaurant.

Inn at Boca Teeca, 5800 NW Second Avenue, Boca Raton (tel: (407) 994 0400). 47 rooms (1 mile from beach); pool, tennis, golf, fitness.

Largo Mar Resort & Club, 1700 S Ocean Lane, Ft Lauderdale (tel: (305) 523 6511/(800) 366 5246). 180 rooms/suites in attractive beachfront complex; pools, tennis, mini-golf, restaurant and entertainment.

Palm Beach Hawaiian Ocean Inn, 3550 S Ocean Boulevard, South Palm Beach (tel: (407) 582 5631).

58 rooms/suites on beach; attractive South Seas décor, pool, raw bar, restaurant.

Pelican Beach Resort, 2000 N Atlantic Boulevard, Ft Lauderdale (tel: (305) 568 9431). 48 good value rooms/efficiencies on beach.

Riverside Hotel, 620 E Las Olas Boulevard, Ft Lauderdale (tel: (305) 467 0671). 117 spacious rooms in attractive old hotel; central location; pool, restaurant.

Sailfish Marina, 98 Lake Drive, Palm Beach Shores (tel: (407) 844 1724). 14 rooms two blocks from beach; pool, sportfishing charters, shuttle.

Sun Castle Resort, 1380 S Ocean Boulevard, Pompano Beach (tel: (305) 941 7700). 105 rooms/efficiencies in landscaped grounds; pool, tennis, golf, dining. Families welcome.

Budget
Admiral's Court Apartment Motel and Marina, 21 Hendricks Isle, Ft Lauderdale (tel: (305) 462 5072/(800) 248 6669). 37 rooms/efficiencies in villa by canal; private dock, gardens, close beaches/Las Olas.

Bayshore Waterfront Apartments, 341 N Birch Road, Ft Lauderdale (tel: (305) 463 2821). 38 units on waterway (1 mile to beach); efficiencies; quiet.

Howard Johnson Oceans Edge Resort, 700 N Atlantic Boulevard, Ft Lauderdale (tel: (305) 563 2451). 144 rooms; pool, restaurant, beach frontage.

Island Queen Motel, 2634 West Way, Singer Island (tel: (407) 848 4448). 80

rooms by ocean, lake or pool; tennis, shuttle to town/airport.

Ocean Lodge, 570 Ocean Drive, Juno Beach (tel: (407) 626 1528). 32 rooms on beach; pool.

Riviera Palms Motel, 3960 N Ocean Boulevard, Delray Beach (tel: (407) 276 3032). 17 rooms/efficiencies 100ft from beach; pool.

Sea Chateau Motel, 555 N Birch Road, Ft Lauderdale (tel: (305) 566 8331). 16 pretty rooms/efficiencies 200 yards from beach; pool, coffee and pastries.

Villas-by-the-Sea, 4456 El Mar Drive, Lauderdale-by-the-Sea (tel: (305) 772 3550/(800) 247 8963). 148 smart rooms/efficiencies in landscaped grounds by beach; pool, tennis, barbecue grills, airport shuttle.

Restaurants
Expensive
Brazilian Court Dining Room, 301 Australian Avenue, Palm Beach (tel: (407) 655 7740). Gorgeous 1920s dining room opening on to fountain court; superlative light, elegant cuisine.

Burt & Jack's, Berth 23, Port Everglades, Ft Lauderdale (tel: (305) 522 2878). Elegant Spanish villa on the waterfront with impressive American menu. (Co-owned by *the* local actor.)

Café L'Europe, 150 Worth Avenue, Palm Beach (tel: (407) 655 4020). Stylish European dining room serving superb French dishes with finesse.

Café Max, 2601 E Atlantic Boulevard, Pompano Beach (tel: (305) 782 0606). American cooking meets the classics to delicious effect; fresh seafood specialities; Art Deco styling.

Casa Vecchia, 209 N Birch Road, Ft Lauderdale (tel: (305) 463 7575). Lovely 1930s villa on the water; Mediterranean cuisine from France, Spain, Turkey and North Africa.

Down Under, 3000 E Oakland Park Boulevard, Ft

DIRECTORY

Lauderdale (tel: (305) 563 4123). Elegant waterfront bistro; jazz piano accompanies diverse American-French menu.

Moderate

15th Street Fisheries, 1900 SE 15th Street, Ft Lauderdale (tel: (305) 763 2777). Award-winning seafood specialities with waterfront views.

By Word of Mouth, 3200 NE 12th Avenue, Ft Lauderdale (tel: (305) 564 3663). Ingenious New American cuisine in cosy, small restaurant.

Chuck & Harold's, 207 Royal Poinciana Way, Palm Beach (tel: (407) 659 1440). Tropical décor, tiles and beams frame varied Californian menu.

Harpoon Louie's, 1065 A1A (at US1), Jupiter (tel: (407) 744 1300). Casual waterfront eatery; innovative menu with surf and turf combinations.

Il Giardino, 609 E Las Olas Boulevard, Ft Lauderdale (tel: (305) 763 3733). Northern Italian specialities; chic modern décor and garden.

Paesano, 1301 E Las Olas Boulevard, Ft Lauderdale (tel: (305) 467 3266). Elegant presentation; specialities include charcoal grilled seafood.

Riverview, 1741 E Riverview Road, Deerfield Beach (tel: (305) 428 3463). Old Florida seafood house on the Intracoastal Waterway; prime beef too.

Taboo, 221 Worth Avenue, Palm Beach (tel: (407) 835 3500). Diverse and tempting menu; generous starters make a light meal; busy bar.

This Is It Pub, 424 24th Street, West Palm Beach (tel: (407) 833 4997). Rack of lamb or seafood, pasta or bouillabaisse in pubby ambience.

Budget

Banana Boat, 739 E Ocean Avenue, Boynton Beach (tel: (407) 732 9400). Casual waterfront spot; mostly seafood; dockside bar, entertainment.

Bimini Boatyard, 1555 SE 17th Street, Ft Lauderdale (tel: (305) 525 7400). Informal waterfront café with diverse California-style menu.

Café L'Express, 150 Worth Avenue, Palm Beach (tel: (407) 833 2117). Pasta, seafood and take-out deli delights on balcony of Esplanade.

Cielito Lindo, 4480 N Federal Highway, Pompano Beach (tel: (305) 941 8226). Tex-Mex cuisine in South of the Border setting; margaritas.

Docksiders, 908 N Ocean Drive, Hollywood (tel: (305) 922 2265). Family dining on the Intracoastal Waterway; open air terrace.

Hortz Bar-B-Q Shanty, 4261 Griffin Road, Ft Lauderdale (tel: (305) 581 9085). Great barbecue and Cajun home-cooking in friendly atmosphere.

John G's, 10 S Ocean Boulevard, Lake Worth (tel: (407) 585 9860). Busy, informal and on the beach; burgers, omelettes, pasta and sandwiches.

Lester's Diner, 250 SR 84, Ft Lauderdale (tel: (305) 525 5641). Local institution with 24-hour breakfast service (lunch/dinner).

Tom's Place, 1198 N Dixie Highway, Boca Raton (tel: (407) 368 3502). Lip-smackin' barbecued ribs and chicken; home-cooking favoured by NFL giants.

Tony Roma's, 2215 Palm Beach Lakes Boulevard, West Palm Beach (tel: (407) 689 1703). Family-dining chain; burgers, ribs and other fillers.

EAST COAST

Accommodation

Expensive

Amelia Island Plantation, 3000 First Coast Highway, Amelia Island (tel: (904) 261 6161/(800) 874 6878). Superb resort set in 1,000-acre nature preserve; beach, pools, tennis, golf, fishing, riding, fine dining.

Cocoa Beach Hilton, 1550 N Atlantic Avenue, Cocoa

Beach (tel: (407) 799 0003). 300 rooms by the ocean; swimming pool, tennis, restaurants, nightclub, children's activities, babysitting.

Daytona Beach Marriott, 100 N Atlantic Avenue, Daytona (tel: (904) 254 8200). 405 rooms on oceanfront; prime location; pools, fitness, children's facilities, restaurants.

Omni Hotel, 245 Water Street, Jacksonville (tel: (904) 355 6664/(800) THE OMNI). 354 classy rooms/suites around luxuriant atrium; pool, health club, excellent restaurant.

Moderate

Anastasia Inn, A1A at Pope Road, Anastasia Island (tel: (904) 471 2575). 142 rooms in St Augustine's beach annexe; pool, restaurant.

Conch House Marina Resort, 57 Comares Avenue, Anastasia Island (tel: (904) 829 8646). 21 rooms/efficiencies with tropical flavour; pool, bayside beach, restaurant.

Crossway Inn, 3901 N Atlantic Avenue, Cocoa Beach (tel: (407) 783 2221). 144 rooms/50 suites (some efficiencies) in beachfront resort; pool, playground, restaurant.

Days Inn, 1920 Seaway Drive, Ft Pierce (tel: (407) 461 8737/(800) 447 4732). 40 rooms/efficiencies near beach; pool, fishing.

1890 Inn, 83 Cedar Street, St Augustine (tel: (904) 826 0287). Friendly B&B; 3 chintzy rooms in town centre.

House on Cherry Street, 1844 Cherry Street, Jacksonville (tel: (904) 384 1999). 4-room B&B in beautiful old house down leafy Riverside lane.

Hutchinson Inn Seaside Resort, 9750 S Ocean Drive, Jensen Beach, Ft Pierce (tel: (407) 229 2000). 21 units on ocean; pool, tennis, friendly free barbecue for guests Saturday nights.

Perry's Ocean Edge, 2209 S Atlantic Avenue, Daytona (tel: (904) 255 0581). 204 rooms/efficiencies on beach; family orientated; pool, breakfast.

Sea Turtle Inn, 1 Ocean Boulevard, Jacksonville Beach (tel: (904) 249 7402). 200 rooms by the ocean; pool, restaurant, lounge, airport shuttle.

Seaside Inn, 1998 S Fletcher Avenue, Fernandina Beach (tel: (904) 261 0954). 10 rooms in delightful restored inn by the beach; restaurant.

Sun Viking Lodge, 2411 S Atlantic Avenue, Daytona Beach Shores (tel: (904) 252 6252/(800) 874 4469). 91 rooms and efficiencies in friendly family resort; activity programme, beachfront, pools, waterslide, spa, café.

Budget

Bayfront Inn, 138 Avenida Menendez, St Augustine (tel: (904) 824 1681). 39 Spanish-style units around pool; convenient for historic quarter.

Best Western Aku Tiki, 2225 S Atlantic Avenue, Daytona (tel: (904) 252 9631). 132 rooms/efficiencies on oceanfront; pool, restaurant.

Days Inn Oceanfront, 5600 N Atlantic Avenue, Cocoa Beach (tel: (407) 783 7621). 120 rooms in family-style motel; pool, 24-hour restaurant.

Eastwinds Motel, 1505 S First Street, Jacksonville Beach (tel: (904) 249 3858). 25 cheerful rooms/efficiencies; pool.

Harbour Light Inn, 1160 Seaway Drive, Ft Pierce (tel: (407) 468 3555/(800) 433 0004). 34 units with balconies on inlet; pool, barbecue, fishing.

Mainsail Motel, 281 S Atlantic Avenue, Ormond Beach (tel: (904) 677 2131/(800) 843 5142). 50

nautical-style rooms on beach (north of Daytona); pools, restaurant, family resort.

Marine Terrace Apartments, 306 S Ocean Drive, Ft Pierce (tel: (407) 461 8909). Spick-and-span efficiencies on beach; family owned; fishing.

Villas de Marin, 142 Avenida Menendez, St Augustine (tel: (904) 829 1725). 16 tasteful efficiencies with views in restored bayfront building.

Restaurants
Expensive
Mango Tree, 118 N Atlantic Avenue, Cocoa Beach (tel: (407) 799 0513). Elegant tropical décor, garden aviary; delicious light, fresh American cuisine.

Raintree, 102 San Marco Avenue, St Augustine (tel: (904) 824 7211). Beautifully restored old house; seasonal menu with plenty of seafood, marvellous puddings.

Sterling's Flamingo Café, 3351 St Johns Avenue, Jacksonville (tel: (904) 387 0700). Romantic and elegant small restaurant serving gourmet ;New American cuisine in Riverside area.

Moderate
Columbia, 98 St George Street, St Augustine (tel: (904) 824 3341). Paella and other Spanish specialities in the historic district.

Crustaceans, 2321 Beach Boulevard, Jacksonville Beach (tel: (904) 241 8238). Seafood menu and live music on summer weekends.

Gatsby's, 520 W Cocoa Beach Causeway, Cocoa Beach (tel: (407) 783 2389). Dining and entertainment complex with choice of eateries.

Grenamyer's, 4000 St Johns Avenue, Jacksonville (tel: (904) 387 3880). Fun, popular jazz café with eclectic menu in Riverside district.

Jad's, Palmetto Walk Village, Fernandina Beach (tel: (904) 277 2350). Pretty,

relaxing setting; tempting seasonal menu with local seafood.

Kay's Coach House, 734 Main Street, Daytona Beach (tel: (904) 253 1944). Long menu of ribs, steaks and seafood. Families welcome; cocktails.

Mangrove Matties, 1640 Seaway Drive, Ft Pierce (tel: (407) 466 1044). Great waterfront views, broad menu and sumptuous Sunday brunch.

Ocean Grill, 1050 Sexton Plaza (Beachland Boulevard), Vero Beach (tel: (407) 231 5409). Candlelit local favourite; fish, steaks, ocean view.

Ragtime, 207 Atlantic Boulevard, Atlantic Beach (tel: (904) 241 7877). Young, fun and New Orleans jazzy; Creole and Cajun specialities.

Sliders, Seaside Inn, 1998 S Fletcher Street, Fernandina Beach (tel: (904) 261 0954). Rustic beach hang-out which offers mainly seafood menu.

Topaz Café, 1224 S A1A, Flagler Beach (tel: (904) 439 3275). A real find serving fresh, home-cooked and inventive New American cuisine.

Budget
Checker's Café, Broadway & A1A, Daytona Beach (tel: (904) 252 3626). Burgers, sandwiches and dinner specials in family-friendly café.

Chimes, 12 Avenida Menendez, St Augustine (tel: (904) 829 8141). Good value home-cooking in the centre of town.

Crawdaddy's, 1643 Prudential Drive, Jacksonville (tel: (904) 396 3546). Casual riverfront seafood and Cajun spot; dancing.

DIRECTORY

Homestead, 1712 Beach Boulevard, Jacksonville Beach (tel: (904) 249 5240). Generous country cooking and homey atmosphere.
Kountry Kitchen, 1115 N Courtenay Parkway, Merritt Island (tel: (407) 459 3457). Generous home-cooked spread; near Kennedy Space Center.
Norris's Famous Place for Ribs, 3080 N US1, Ft Pierce (tel: (407) 464 4000). Local family-style favourite; groaning platters of barbecue goodies.
Ocean Pier, A1A at Main Street, Daytona Beach (tel: (904) 238 1212). Fast food with a view right in the heart of things.
Panama Hattie's, A1A (opposite the Pier), St Augustine Beach (tel: (904) 471 2255). Lively youth favourite; broad snacky menu; open-air bar.
Santa Maria, 135 Avenida Menendez, St Augustine (tel: (904) 829 6578). Seafood, steaks and chicken in family-run landmark by the marina.
TC's Top Dog, 425 N Atlantic Avenue, Daytona Beach (tel: (904) 257 7766). Hot dog heaven; also chilli, cheese or coleslaw on a bun. Kids' choice.

WEST COAST

Accommodation
Expensive
Don Cesar, 3400 Gulf Boulevard, St Petersburg Beach (tel: (813) 360 1881). 226 rooms/51 suites in fabulous pink palace on beach; pool, watersports, children's programme.
Edgewater Beach Hotel, 1901 Gulf Shore Boulevard, Naples (tel: (813) 262 6511/(800) 282 3766). 124 attractive suites with kitchenette and balcony;

friendly atmosphere; beach, pool, fitness, chic dining room.
Innisbrook Resort, US19, Tarpon Springs (tel: (813) 937 3124/(800) 456 2000). 1,200 rooms/suites in 1,000-acre woodland setting; golf and tennis packages, children's programme, fine dining, nightclub.
Saddlebrook Golf & Tennis Resort, 100 Saddlebrook Way, Wesley Chapel (tel: (813) 973 1111/(800) 222 2222). 700 rooms/suites in countryside 15 miles north of Tampa; Palmer-designed golf course, tennis, fitness, award-winning dining. Good value packages.
South Seas Plantation, Captiva Island (tel: (813) 472 5111/(800) 282 3402). 656 deluxe rooms/suites in family/sporting resort; beach, pools, golf, tennis, watersports, boat trips, dining choice.
Wyndham Harbour Island Hotel, 725 S Harbour Island Boulevard, Tampa (tel: (813) 229 5000/(800) 822 4200). 300 spacious rooms/suites with views in central Downtown location; pool, health club, restaurants, shopping.

Moderate
Beach Castle, 5310 Gulf of Mexico Drive, Longboat Key, Sarasota (tel: (813) 383 2639). 19 lovely apartments with gulf/bay views (1-week minimum stay); gardens, swimming pool, dock, canoes.
Breckenridge Resort Hotel, 5700 Gulf Boulevard, St Petersburg Beach (tel: (813) 360 1833). 200 fine rooms/efficiencies on beach; pool, tennis, watersports, restaurant.
Days Inn Marina Beach Resort, 6800 S 34th Street, St Petersburg (tel: (813) 867 1151). 212 rooms/efficiencies on bay; pools, tennis, sailing school, fishing, restaurant.
Half Moon Beach Club, 2050 Ben Franklin Drive, Lido Key, Sarasota (tel: (813) 388 3694/(800) 358 3245). 85 spacious rooms/efficiencies around pool and courtyard;

beach frontage, restaurant, easy drive from sights.
Hilton, 17120 Gulf Boulevard, North Redington Beach (tel: (813) 391 4000). 124 airy rooms on ocean; pool, watersports, fishing, restaurant.
Holiday Inn Busch Gardens, 2701 E Fowler Avenue, Tampa (tel: (813) 971 4710). 399 rooms; pool, fitness centre, restaurant.
Outrigger Beach Resort, 6200 Estero Boulevard, Ft Myers Beach (tel: (813) 463 3131/(800) 226 3131). 144 rooms/efficiences on Gulf; pool, tiki bar, coffee shop.
Pink Shell Beach and Bay Resort, 275 Estero Boulevard, Ft Myers Beach (tel: (813) 463 6181/(800) 237 5786). 180 rooms/condos/cottages in landscaped surrounds; family style, with pool, tennis, watersports, fishing.
Radisson Bay Harbor Inn, 7700 Courtney Campbell Causeway, Tampa (tel: (813) 281 8900/(800) 333 3333). 257 rooms on beach; pool, fitness centre, restaurant, child care.
Safari Resort Inn, 4139 E Busch Boulevard, Tampa (tel: (813) 988 9191). 100 rooms in Serengeti trim close to Busch Gardens; pool, restaurant, entertainment lounge.
Sailport Resort, 2506 Rocky Point Drive, Tampa (tel: (813) 281 9599/(800) 255 9599). 237 fully-equipped efficiencies with waterfront balconies; pool, breakfast. Value for families.
Tradewinds, 5500 Gulf Boulevard, St Petersburg Beach (tel: (813) 367 6461). 395 (moderate to expensive) rooms/efficiencies in excellent resort; pools, tennis, sailing, children's activities.
Vanderbilt Beach Motel, 9225 N Gulf Shore Drive, Naples (tel: (813) 597 3144). 66 rooms/efficiencies on shore; pool, tennis, fishing pier.

Budget
Bay Winds Resort Motel, 7345 Bay Street, St

Petersburg Beach (tel: (813) 267 2721). 24 rooms/suites on oceanfront; pool, windsurfer rental, boat charters, restaurant.

Beach House, 4960 Estero Boulevard, Ft Myers Beach (tel: (813) 992 2644). 14 rooms/apartments in delightful house amid condos.

Beach View Cottages, 3306 W Gulf Drive, Sanibel Island (tel: (813) 472 1202). Efficiencies in relaxed family-style complex right on beach.

Best Western Golden Host, 4675 N Tamiami Trail, Sarasota (tel: (813) 355 5741). 80 rooms in landscaped grounds; pool, close to restaurant.

Buccaneer Resort Motel, 10800 Gulf Boulevard, Treasure Island (tel: (813) 367 1908/(800) 826 2120). 62 rooms/efficiencies on beach; pool.

Comfort Inn, 9800 Bonita Beach Road, Bonita Springs (tel: (813) 992 5001/(800) 221 2222). 69 pleasant modern rooms/efficiencies around pool.

Days Inn, 2520 N 50th Street, Tampa (tel: (813) 247 3300/(800) 433 8033). 200 rooms in central location; pool, restaurant.

Diplomat Resort, 3155 Gulf of Mexico Drive, Longboat Key, Sarasota (tel: (813) 383 3791). 50 spacious units in beachfront apartment complex (2-day minimum stay); pool.

Expressway Inns, 3688 and 3693 Gandy Boulevard (US92), Tampa (tel: (813) 837 1921/(813) 837 1971). Pleasant motels with pool.

Fairways Motel, 103 Palm River Boulevard, Naples (tel: (813) 597 8181). 32 fine rooms around pool courtyard; quiet and close to golf.

Restaurants
Expensive
Bern's Steak House, 1208 S Howard Avenue, Tampa (tel: (813) 251 2421). Clubby décor, exemplary service, aged prime steaks accompanied by taste-sensation organic

vegetables.

Black Swan, 13707 N 58th Street, Clearwater (tel: (813) 535 SWAN). Perfect for romantic evening; varied and innovative cuisine with classic base, stunning desserts.

Café L'Europe, 431 St Armand's Circle, Sarasota (tel: (813) 388 4415). Fashionably elegant, arty setting; delicate French *nouvelle cuisine* seafood, veal and beef dishes.

Chef's Garden, 1300 Third Street, Naples (tel: (813) 262 5500). Culinary landmark in delightful surroundings; creative seasonal cuisine; also moderately-priced bistro, **Truffles**.

Moderate
Bubble Room, Captiva Road, Captiva (tel: (813) 472 5353). Wacky 1940s kitsch décor; monster platters of home-cooking and killer desserts.

Columbia, 21st Street at Broadway, Ybor City (tel: (813) 248 4961). Landmark Spanish restaurant; rustic décor and traditional menu.

Joe Di's, 3260 W Hillsborough Avenue, Tampa (tel: (813) 876 6666). Smart, romantic and renowned for creative pasta and fresh seafood.

Kapok Tree, 923 McMullen-Booth Road, Clearwater (tel: (813) 726 0504). Take a camera to this al fresco mirage; luxuriant greenery, simple food.

Lobster Pot, 17814 Gulf Boulevard, Redington Shores (tel: (813) 391 8592). Local favourite renowned for its seafood; also prime steaks.

Louis Pappas' Riverside, 10 W Dodecanese Boulevard, Tarpon Springs (tel: (813) 937 5101). Busy tourist spot; great Greek food.

McCully's Rooftop, Hickory Boulevard, Bonita Springs (tel: (813) 463 7010). Lovely waterfront views; steaks, seafood and entertainment.

Prawnbroker, 6535 McGregor Boulevard, Fort Myers (tel: (813) 489 2226). Long-time local favourite; mainly fish menu, steak and poultry.

Ristorante Bellini's, 1549 Main Street, Sarasota (tel: (813) 365 7380). Robust Italian cuisine and extensive wine list.

Riverwalk Fish & Ale House, 1200 S Fifth Avenue, Naples (tel: (813) 263 2734). Informal dockside dining in the Old Marine Marketplace.

Rosario's Italian, 1930 E 7th Avenue, Ybor City (tel: (813) 247 6764). Old World Italian cuisine; pasta, chicken, seafood and steaks.

Sunset Café, 537 Douglas Avenue, Dunedin (tel: (813) 736 3973). Small, welcoming café with terrific pasta and seasonal specialities.

Veranda, 2122 Second Street, Fort Myers (tel: (813) 332 2065). Historic buildings with garden court; innovative regional Southern menu.

Wine Cellar, 17307 N Gulf Boulevard, Redington Beach (tel: (813) 393 3491). Warm atmosphere, plus award-winning American and Mittel–European menu.

Budget
Algiers Seafood Market, 1473 Periwinkle Way, Sanibel. Tremendous range of seafood cooked to order; home-baking, ice creams.

Big Apple Bistro, 4000 Central Avenue, St Petersburg (tel: (813) 327 5784). All American cuisine from Detroit B-B-Q to Creole shrimp.

Cactus Club, 1601 Snow Avenue, Tampa (tel: (813) 251 4089). Lively and fun; Southwestern cuisine, huge desserts.

Captain's Table, Dock Street, Cedar Key (tel: (904) 543 5441). Great dockside position; seafood specialities.

DIRECTORY

Doe-Al's Southern Cookin', 85 Corey Avenue, St Petersburg Beach (tel: (813) 360 8026). Family-style home cooking (XXX–large portion control).

Frascati's Italian, 1258 N Airport Road, Naples (tel: (813) 262 6511). Convenient restaurant-deli for museums; good sandwiches.

Roger's Real Pit Bar–B–Que, 12150 Seminole Boulevard, Largo (tel: (813) 586 2629). Baby back ribs, franks and beans plus wonderful salad bar.

Silver Ring Café, 1831 E 7th Avenue, Ybor City (tel: (813) 248 2549). Cuban sandwich emporium since 1947.

Walt's Fish Market, 560 N Washington Boulevard, Sarasota (tel: (813) 365 1735). Terrific choice of fish dinners, plus Raw Oyster Bar.

Wildflower, 5218 Ocean Boulevard, Siesta Key, Sarasota (tel: (813) 349 1758). Exotic vegetarian and fish dishes in friendly café.

PANHANDLE

Accommodation
Expensive
Edgewater Beach Resort, 11212 Front Beach Road, Panama City Beach (tel: (904) 235 4044/(800) 874 8686). 464 deluxe units/villas by beach or golf course in good central location; pools, tennis, watersports.

Governor's Inn, 209 S Adams Street, Tallahassee (tel: (904) 681 6855/(800) 342 7717). 40 luxurious rooms/suites in central historic district; VIP treatment, elegant dining room, breakfast, airport shuttle.

Marriott's Bay Point Resort, 100 Delwood Beach Road, Panama City Beach (tel: (904) 234 3307/(800) 874 7105). 400 elegant rooms/suites/villas; beach, woods, golf, tennis, watersports, children's activities.

New World Inn, 600 S Palafox Street, Pensacola

(tel: (904) 432 4111). 16 deluxe rooms/suites each reflecting a famous historic US personality and featuring antique furnishings; excellent restaurant; airport shuttle.

Sandestin, 5500 US98, Destin (tel: (904) 277 0800). 500 rooms/efficiencies in complex spanning barrier island from bay to seashore; pools, golf, tennis, fitness, fine dining.

Moderate
Cabot Lodge West, 2735 N Monroe Street, Tallahassee (tel: (904) 386 8880/(800) 223 1964). 160 comfortable B&B rooms; pool, restaurant near by.

Carousel Beach Resort, 571 Santa Rosa Boulevard, Ft Walton Beach (tel: (904) 243 7658/(800) 523 0208). 105 rooms/efficiencies on Gulf; pool, fishing, bar, close to shops.

Conquistador, 874 Venus Court, Ft Walton Beach (tel: (904) 244 6155/(800) 824 7112). 87 apartments/efficiencies on dunes; pool, close to shopping.

Dunes, 333 Ft Pickens Road, Pensacola Beach (tel: (904) 932 3536). 140 rooms in friendly, family-orientated complex beside beach; pool.

Gibson Inn, Market Street, Apalachicola (tel: (904) 653 2191). 30 rooms in fine restored building; dining.

Holiday Inn, 165 Ft Pickens Road, Pensacola Beach (tel: (904) 932 5361/(800) 465 4329). 150 rooms on Gulf; pool, tennis, watersports, dining, airport shuttle, child care.

Killearn Country Club & Inn, 100 Tyron Circle, Tallahassee (tel: (904) 893 2186/(800) 476 4101). 40 units in relaxing woodland setting; pool, city's finest golf course, tennis, fitness, fine dining.

Mark II Beach Resort, 15285 Front Beach Road (US98), Panama City Beach (tel: (904) 234 8845/(800) 874 7170). 202 spacious rooms/efficiencies on beach; pools, watersports,

tennis, restaurant, close to attractions.

Rendezvous Inn Resort, 17281 Front Beach Road (US98), Panama City Beach (tel: (904) 234 8841/(800) 874 6617). 72 efficiencies in lively beachside complex; pool, tennis, restaurant.

St George Inn, St George Island, Apalachicola (tel: (904) 670 2903). 8 rooms in lovely wood-frame house close to beach, nature reserve.

Wakulla Springs Lodge, 1 Springs Drive (SR26), Wakulla Springs (15 miles south of Tallahassee). 27 rooms in Spanish-style inn in State Park; home-cooked meals in large dining room, dusk and dawn animal-spotting.

Budget
Days Inn, 710 N Palafox Street, Pensacola (tel: (904) 438 4922/(800) 325 2525). 157 rooms/efficiencies near historic district; pool, coffee shop, airport shuttle.

Driftwood Beach Club, 683 Nautilus Court, Ft Walton Beach (tel: (904) 243 1716/(800) 336 3630). 28 rooms/efficiencies on beach; pool; close to shopping, restaurants, watersports.

Flamingo Motel, 15525 Front Beach Road (US98), Panama City Beach (tel: (904) 234 2232/(800) 828 0400). 67 pleasant efficiencies around tropical garden on beach; family atmosphere; pool.

Georgian Terrace, 14415 Front Beach Road (US98), Panama City Beach (tel: (904) 234 3322). 30 wood-panelled, cosy efficiencies on beach; pool.

Holiday Inn Parkway, 1302 Apalachee Parkway, Tallahassee (tel: (904) 877 3141/(800) HOLIDAY). 167 units around pool; fitness, family restaurant.

Hospitality Inn, 6900 Pensacola Boulevard, Pensacola (tel: (904) 477 2333/(800) 821 2073). 126 efficiencies; swimming pool, breakfast.

Leeside Inn & Marina, 1350 US98 Ft Walton Beach (tel:

(904) 243 7359/(800) 824 2747). 109 rooms/efficiencies adjoining National Seashore; pool, watersports, fishing, restaurant.

Sandpiper Inn, 23 Via de Luna, Pensacola Beach (tel: (904) 932 2516). 32 compact, attractive units close to beach; pool.

Sportman's Lodge, SR65 (north of US98), Eastpoint, Apalachicola (tel: (904) 670 8423). 22 rooms/efficiencies by secluded bayside marina; fishing.

Tallahassee Motor Lodge, 1630 N Monroe Street, Tallahassee (tel: (904) 224 6183). 92 spacious rooms close to Downtown and shopping; pool.

Tomahawk Landing, SR 87 12 miles north of Milton (tel: (904) 623 6197). Fully equipped woodland cabins for visitors to Blackwater River.

Restaurant

Expensive

Andrew's Second Act, 102 W Jefferson Street, Tallahassee (tel: (904) 222 2759). Political district favourite serving small, elegant New American menu in a Frenchified setting.

Fiddler's Green, Marriott's Bay Point Resort, 100 Delwood Road, Panama City Beach (tel: (904) 234 0220). Refined gourmet dining in deluxe resort overlooking lagoon.

Jamie's, 424 E Zaragoza Street, Pensacola (tel: (904) 434 2911). Lovely historic home transformed into gourmet candlelit restaurant; delicate, classic cuisine.

Moderate

Boar's Head, 17290 Front Beach Road, Panama City Beach (tel: (904) 234 6628). Woodsy interior; generous prime rib and seafood platters.

Chez Pierre, 115 N Adams Street, Tallahassee (tel: (904) 222 0936). Attractive French café with broad menu, light lunches, pàtisseries.

Flamingo Café, 414 E US98, Destin (tel: (904) 837 0961). Chic black, white and pink décor, harbour views; veal and fish specialities.

Gibson Inn, Market Street, Apalachicola (tel: (904) 653 2191). Historic inn serving varied menu of classic dishes; semi–formal.

Harbour House, 3001-A W 10th Street, Panama City (tel: (904) 785 9053).Waterfront family dining; great value lunch buffet.

Melting Pot, 1832 N Monroe Street, Tallahassee (tel: (904) 386 7440). Cheese, meat seafood and dessert fondues for a cosy evening.

Michael's, 600 S Palafox Street, Pensacola (tel: (904) 434 7736). Pretty dining rooms in downtown historic district; fresh, innovative cuisine.

Oaks Restaurant, US98, Panacea 20 miles south of Tallahassee (tel: (904) 984 5370). Popular out-of-town dining spot; seafood Southern style.

Perri's, 300 Elgin Parkway, Fort Walton (tel: (904) 862 4421). Popular Italian restaurant with broad menu and plenty of pasta favourites.

Scotto's, 300 S Alcaniz Street, Pensacola (tel: (904) 434 1932). Friendly family-run Italian restaurant in fine old house.

The Wharf, 4141 Apalachee Parkway, Tallahassee (tel: (904) 656 2332). The state capital's top seafood spot.

Budget

Andrew's Café, 228 S Adams Street, Tallahassee

(tel: (904) 222 3444). New York-style deli and grill with outdoor seating in restored district.

Barnacle Bill's, 1830 N Monroe Street, Tallahassee (tel: (904) 385 8734). Pasta and poultry in addition to seafood; kids eat free on Sundays.

Billy's Oyster Bar I, 3000 Thomas Drive, Panama City Beach (tel: (904) 235 2349). Oysters every which way, lobster, crawfish, crab and shrimp.

Cajun Inn, 477 Beckrich Drive, Panama City Beach (tel: (904) 235 9987). Generous platters of Southern specials such as spicy jambalaya.

Captain Dave's, 3796 Old Highway 98, Destin (tel: (904) 837 2627). Family-style seafood spot overlooking the Gulf; dancing and entertainment.

Cap'n Jim's, 905 E Gregory Street, Tallahassee (tel: (904) 433 3526). Family-run fish restaurant on the bay; house specialities recommended.

Food Glorious Food, 106 E College Avenue, Tallahassee (tel: (904) 222 5232). Modern American open-air café, great pastries.

The Hut, US98, Apalachicola (tel: (904) 653 9410). Rustic seafood and steak joint; popular bar.

Liollio's, 14 Miracle Strip Parkway, Ft Walton Beach (tel: (904) 243 5011). Greek seafood, steaks and huge salads; families welcome.

McGuire's Irish Pub, 600 E Gregory Street, Pensacola (tel: (904) 433 6789). Ribs, burgers, sandwiches, seafood and rollicking good times.

Mr P's Sandwich Shop, 221 E Zaragoza Street, Tallahassee (tel: (904) 433 0294). Homey historic district soup, salad, sandwich and cool drink stop.

Spring Creek Restaurant, US365, Spring Creek (tel: (904) 926 3751). Unpretentious seasonal seafood dishes in bayside fishing village.

283

Index

INDEX

287

INDEX/ACKNOWLEDGEMENTS

Acknowledgements

The Automobile Association would like to thank the following photographers, libraries and associations for their assistance in the preparation of this book. PETE BENNETT (© AA Photo Library) took most of the pictures, with the exception of: ALACHUA COUNTRY VISITORS & CONVENTION BUREAU 26 Florida Fields Gainsville, 27 Gatornationaus ALLSPORT UK LTD 173 Daytona race action (Jim Gund), 174 NASCAR pit crew (Jim Gund) BABCOCK WILDERNESS ADVENTURES 20, 32 Babcock BUSCH GARDENS 24/5 Mystic Sheiks of Morocco, 226 Adventure Island Tampa, 227 Bengal Tiger HENRY FLAGLER MUSEUM 160 Henry Flagler FLORIDA DEPT OF COMMERCE 8 Daytona Beach, 23 Rodeo, 41 Seminoles, 48 Miami Crandon Park, 49 International Drive, Orlando, 64 Miami Seaquarium, Metro Tiger, 82 Horse-racing, 83 Skin diving, Orange Bowl, 154 Cave diving, 164 Baseball, 165 Polo, Tennis, 175 Daytona Beach, 183 Jacksonville at night, 184 Fisherman, 188 Sunset, 190 St Augustine, 191 Sea Oats, 225 Ringling Museum, 244 Canoeing, 245 Sunset, 246 Panama City, 248 Shipwreck Isle, 251 Naval Air Museum, 255 Tallahassee GEIGER & ASSOCIATES 15 Turkey Creek Sanctuary, 18/9 American Bald Eagle, 195 Manatee, Florida Space Coast, 196 Port Canaveral, 197 F4-4 Fighter – Race Corsair, 214 Water fowl 253 Beach scene GRAND ROMANCE 185 Riverrship Grand Romance KISSIMEE FUN 'N' WHEELS 116 Fun 'n' Wheels KISSIMEE ST CLOUD CONVENTION & VISITORS BUREAU 184 L Tohopekaliga LEE COUNTY VISITORS & CONVENTION BUREAU 200 Bonita Beach, Captiva Beach, 205 Fort Myers Beach Pier, 206 Earl Kiser, 209 Tall Ship *Eagle* MARY EVANS PICTURE LIBRARY 37 Philip II of Spain, 39 Pirates NATURE PHOTOGRAPHERS LTD 95 Fire coral, 155 The reef (D A Smith), 157 Osprey (P R Sterry), 159 Royal tern (W S Paton), 211 Queen conch (P R Sterry) HENRY PLANT MUSEUM 226 Henry Plant Museum POLK COUNTY TOURIST DEVELOPMENT COUNCIL 135 Lake Wales POPPERFOTO 42 Union guns at Fort Brady ROYAL GEOGRAPHIC SOCIETY 32 Map ST AUGUSTINE/ST JOHNS COUNTY CHAMBER OF COMMERCE 26 Tennis 43 St Augustine – The Castillo SARASOTA CONVENTION & VISITORS BUREAU 222 Selby Gardens, Ringling Museum, 223 Sarasota Quay, 224 Circus galleries, Ringling Museum, Ca'd'Zan SEAWORLD 118 Penguins EMMA STANFORD 34/113 Ocala Appleton Museum TAMPA/HILLSBOROUGH CONVENTION & VISITORS BUREAU 228 Gasparilla Festival THE MANSELL COLLECTION 36/7 Don Juan Ponce de Leon UNIVERSAL STUDIOS FLORIDA 109 King Kong WALT DISNEY CO (COPYRIGHT) 28 *Honey I shrunk the Kids* set, 29 Main Street Magic Kingdom, 119 Wild West stunt show, 120 Chinese Theater – Roger Rabbit, 121 Spectromagic, 122 Earffel Tower, Star Tours, 125 Epcot Center, 126 Dumbo ride, Pleasure Island Manaquin, 127 Monorail, 128 Main Street USA Magic Kingdom, 129 Cinderella's Castle, 130 Epcot Center, 133 Pirates of the Caribbean, 263 Hollywood Boulevard MGM ZEFA PICTURE LIBRARY (UK) LTD (LANNY PROVO) Cover Bahia Honda, 2 Inn sign, Miami skyline, 14 Middle Keys, 16 Flower, 17 Native palms, 19 Lake Okeechobee, 21 Blue Hole, 22 Fort Lauderdale, 33 Fairchild Gardens, Cranes Point, 38 Shipwreck Museum, Key Largo, Fisherman's Museum, Key West, 44 Gold Coast Museum, 45 Key West Steamer, 47 J Penne Kamp State Park, 48 Miami Bayside, 50/1 Bayside at night, 52 Ocean Drive Miami, 53 Coconut Grove Miami, 54 Coral Gables Miami, 58 Baccardi Art Gallery, 61 Fairchild Gardens, 62 HMS *Bounty*, 65 Sailing Bay Miami, 70 Key West conch, 78 Band, 79 Opera, 80 M B Hotel, 81 Carbozo Hotel, 81 Colony Hotel, 97 Cypress airboat, 88 Everglades Big Cypress, 91 Mangrove, 92 Glades, 93 Everglades, 97 Shipwreck Museum, Key Largo, 98 Audubon House, 100 Wreckers Museum, Key West, 104 Palms, 105 Bahia Honda, 106 Blue Hole, 107 7 Mile Bridge, 138 Boca Raton Red Reef Park, 139 Boca Hotel, 140 Boca Children's Museum, 141 Market, Boca National Park, 142 Fort Lauderdale, 144 Mangrove swamp, 148/9 Fort Lauderdale, 150 H Taylor Birch Park, 152/3 Fort Lauderdale Ocean World, 156 Strannaham House, 160 Flagler Railroad, 161 Palm Beach, 162 Flagler House, 163 Hibel Museum, 166 West Palm Beach, 167 Breher Zoo, 168 Norton Gallery, 169 Polo, 170 Worth Avenue Palm Beach, 171 Fort Lauderale Las Olas, 194 Keys, 244 Fort Taylor State Park, 245 J Pennekamp State Park, 250 Westwear Grove, 261 Old Flagler Bridge ZEFA PICTURE LIBRARY (UK) LTD 3 Key Islamorada Marina, 213 Naples City Dock, 218 St Petersburg Pier, 220 Everglades ZIMMERMAN AGENCY 257 Tallahassee Old Town Trolley, 259 Tallahassee Junior Museum